ANTITRUST, INNOVATION, AND COMPETITIVENESS

ANTITRUST, INNOVATION, AND COMPETITIVENESS

Edited by
THOMAS M. JORDE
DAVID J. TEECE

New York   Oxford
OXFORD UNIVERSITY PRESS
1992

Oxford University Press

Oxford   New York   Toronto
Delhi   Bombay   Calcutta   Madras   Karachi
Petaling Jaya   Singapore   Hong Kong   Tokyo
Nairobi   Dar es Salaam   Cape Town
Melbourne   Auckland

and associated companies in
Berlin   Ibadan

Copyright © 1992 by Oxford University Press, Inc.

Published by Oxford University Press, Inc.,
200 Madison Avenue, New York, New York 10016

Oxford is a registered trademark of Oxford University Press

Library of Congress Cataloging-in-Publication Data
Antitrust, innovation, and competitiveness /
Thomas M. Jorde, David J. Teece, editors.
p. cm.   Includes bibliographical references and index.
ISBN 0-19-506769-X
1. Antitrust law—Economic aspects—United States.
2. Competition—United States.   3. Competition, International.
4. Technological innovations—Economic aspects.
I. Jorde, Thomas M.
II. Teece, David J.
KF1652.A495   1992   343.73′0721—dc20   91-16148

9 8 7 6 5 4 3 2

Printed in the United States of America
on acid-free paper

To Leigh and Mary Anne
whose love and perseverance
sustained this joint enterprise
and fueled others.

Preface

This book had its origins in a conference that we organized in Berkeley in November 1988.[1] We saw the centennial year of the Sherman Act looming before us. We also saw an active debate on U.S. competitiveness, spurred by lackluster U.S. productivity growth (Table P-1). But the connections between competition policy and concern over U.S. competitiveness were rarely investigated. Here was an opportunity to bring together leading figures in the field and to discuss how competition policy might be linked to U.S. competitiveness.

We did this against a backdrop of recent profound changes in U.S. antitrust law and policy. Efficiencies were being recognized; some progress was being made toward taking global competition into account; and courts were showing greater sophistication concerning market power and its measurement. Most antitrust scholars and lawyers seemed satisfied with these changes.

Yet, we had a sense of unease because antitrust law was not connected to trade policy or to innovation policy. Despite its focus on competition, antitrust did not seem to have much to say about "competitiveness." Americans were confronted by a paradox: their country was long on competition and short on competitiveness. Our concerns were shared by the President's Commission on Industrial Competitiveness, which specifically appealed for new "antitrust law to reflect the new global markets within which American firms operate."[2]

What was striking to us was that antitrust, despite the revolution that it had just come through, did not really have the conceptual apparatus—or even the vocabulary—to deal with many of the new questions emerging in the global economy. In particular, U.S. antitrust policy did not seem to recognize how seminal innovation was to competition and to the U.S. standard of living.

The explanation for this state of affairs appeared to us to be relatively clear. The economic theory that the Chicago School had used to modify antitrust analysis effectively was almost bereft of reference to innovation. It seemed to us that the static microanalysis embedded in antitrust economics, as it had emerged by the late 1980s, did not provide an adequate framework for analyzing the contemporary business environment. Judicial and policy errors could therefore be expected to continue—both in terms of being too permissive in some circumstances and not sufficiently restrictive in others—despite the important progress that had been made.

We saw the Sherman Act centennial as an opportunity to needle our colleagues about these matters. Most took our challenge in the right spirit. Others did not. Some antitrust scholars, having just been forced to revamp their intellectual tool kits to deal with Chicago, did not seem at all enthusiastic about revamp-

Table P-1 Average Annual Productivity Growth by Sectors, 1960–1987

	Agriculture	Manufacturing	Service	Total Economy
United Sates	3.1%	2.8%	0.9%	1.2%
Canada	3.3	2.7	1.5	1.8
Japan	3.9	7.8	3.9	5.4
Germany	5.0	3.4	2.3	3.1
European Community	5.2	4.0	1.9	3.1

Source: Organization for Economic Cooperation and Development, *Historical Statistics, 1960–1987* (Paris, 1989).

ing once again to take account of innovation and what has been called dynamic competition. Many thought the existing frameworks dealt with such matters satisfactorily. Others seemed to think these matters were not particularly important or central to U.S. competitiveness. The following chapters embody those diverse views. (A synopsis of each chapter is provided in the last section of our Introduction.) We believe that in the following pages a strong suggestion emerges that U.S. antitrust policy needs additional adjustment before it connects soundly with the reality of global competition driven by technological and organizational innovation.

Berkeley   T.M.J.
April 1991   D.J.T.

NOTES

1. We are extremely grateful for financial support from the Alfred P. Sloan Foundation which made the conference and the book possible. Staff support has also been critical to this endeavor. In particular, Denise Kidder made the necessary conference arrangements, Lou Maull facilitated the finances, and Patricia Murphy tirelessly and enthusiastically prepared conference materials and the papers for this book. The editors are very grateful for their dedicated help, for their tenacity, for their good humor, and for their consummate skill.
2. President's Commission on Industrial Competitiveness, *Global Competition: The New Reality,* vol. 1 (Washington, D.C.: Superintendent of Documents, 1985), p. 42.

Contents

Contributors

PHILLIP AREEDA
Harvard University

WILLIAM J. BAUMOL
*Princeton University/New York
University*

FRANK H. EASTERBROOK
*United States Court of Appeals,
Seventh Circuit*

ANN I. JONES
*Law Offices of Blecher and Collins,
Los Angeles, CA*

THOMAS M. JORDE
University of California/Berkeley

ROBERT P. MERGES
Boston University

RICHARD R. NELSON
Columbia University

JANUSZ A. ORDOVER
New York University

RICHARD SCHMALENSEE
*Massachusetts Institute of
Technology*

LAWRENCE A. SULLIVAN
University of California/Berkeley

DAVID M. TEECE
University of California/Berkeley

OLIVER E. WILLIAMSON
University of California/Berkeley

ANTITRUST,
INNOVATION, AND
COMPETITIVENESS

1

Introduction

THOMAS M. JORDE
AND DAVID J. TEECE

A centennial is a time for stock taking—to reflect on past accomplishments and to survey future challenges. In the area of economic and industrial policy, it ought not to be a time for complacency since economic progress in the United States is slower than it has been historically, and less than that to which the nation seems to aspire. Moreover, the President's Commission on Industrial Competitiveness has recommended that the United States change its antitrust laws "to reflect the new global markets within which American firms operate," and has noted that "the uncertainty as to what constitutes antitrust violations has deterred actions that could have desirable competitive effects."[1] This volume selectively explores ways in which the U.S. antitrust laws affect the innovation process. We believe this is an important focus and concur with Baxter (1985) that "if our antitrust laws were to impede technological development to any substantial degree, the net effect of those laws on our well-being would surely be negative."

U.S. antitrust law has undergone significant changes since the passage of the Sherman Act in 1890. We do not intend in this Introduction to recount the major developments in antitrust law over the past century. Nor do we intend to survey comprehensively the many changes that have occurred in our economic systems and in the global economy. Rather, we will describe in general terms certain ways in which U.S. antitrust thinking and antitrust laws may be at odds with technological progress and economic welfare.

We do not by any means wish to assume that all the authors of the various chapters follow our point of view. Indeed, we are confident that several of them do not share it. However, by inviting them to write a chapter to celebrate the Sherman Act's centennial year, they have, either implicitly or explicitly, stated their views on what they believe is the current condition of the law. Most agree that the antitrust laws are in good shape, and, at most, only minor modifications to the law and its enforcement appear to be in order. We are less sanguine.

The organization of this chapter is as follows. In the next section we discuss the goals of antitrust. In the section "The Nature and Importance of Competition," we consider the nature of competition and its importance to a properly functioning market economy. We explain how competition driven by innovation generally stimulates rivalry and promotes economic welfare far more effectively than does competition that focuses on price reductions. Yet innovation-driven competition is not what U.S. antitrust laws emphasize. We discuss the implications of this for interfirm agreements, for product market definition, and for certain other aspects of antitrust law in the section "Competition Through Innovation." In the section "Antitrust Law as Industrial Policy," we briefly explore the relationship between antitrust policy and industrial policy. In the last section we summarize each of the individually authored chapters.

THE GOALS OF ANTITRUST

About a decade ago Robert Bork (1978) wrote that "the overriding need of antitrust today is a general theory of its possibilities and limitations as a tool of national social policy. Yet there exists a surprising lack of agreement concerning the most basic questions. The disagreement, though variously phrased, is finally about two issues: (1) the goals or values the law may legitimately and profitably implement; and (2) the validity of the law's vision of economic reality" (p. 7). While much has been accomplished on both counts over the last decade, there is still considerable dissonance in the literature with respect to both issues. In this volume, we have attempted to inject into the debate and scholarly discussion an explicit consideration of the innovation process, and how the antitrust laws may propel and impede it. While not every contributor has been willing to become a fellow traveler on this mission, several have, at least with respect to the second issue. We begin with a brief discussion on the first issue—the goals of antitrust. The next section will consider the reality of competition and juxtapose it against its textbook rendition.

Professional economists are in almost universal agreement that economic welfare ought to be the goal of antitrust policy. We agree. However, even when the economic welfare goal is accepted, it is sometimes not correctly implemented. One reason is that so much of the economic theory that is used to help guide courts and policy makers is extraordinarily static—that is, it tends to look at the impact on consumer welfare today, and not in the future. This thinking is because much of the apparatus of applied microeconomics that underpins contemporary antitrust economics is single period in its focus. The focus on static analysis may also be the result of greater data and measurement difficulties associated with longer-run analysis. Unfortunately—and importantly—in static analysis there is almost no reference to innovation and its importance to competition and to economic welfare.[2]

We take it as axiomatic that innovation and its rapid and profitable commercialization are the key factors driving productivity improvement and economic welfare. Consumer welfare is enhanced through the generation and application of new technology and new organizational forms. Efforts to link antitrust to consumer welfare may fall wide of the mark whenever the focus is on present consumer welfare, which is the common focus of microeconomic theory. Accordingly, if consumer welfare is to be the goal of antitrust, it needs to be couched in a forward-looking context. Otherwise, antitrust policy may hinder technological progress and the creation of national wealth. At minimum, we would propose that when the promotion of static consumer welfare and innovation are in conflict, the courts should favor the future impact. This may well make analysis less tractable, but at least it will be focusing on the correct issues.

THE NATURE AND IMPORTANCE OF COMPETITION

Americans have a long-standing and well-founded belief in competition. This tradition is rooted in part on political beliefs. Competitive systems that are open to newcomers provide important checks and balances on monopoly power; monopoly power is often seen as being correlated with political influence. Open and competitive systems are thus often seen as a corollary of democracy. Indeed, in part, it was concern about the political power of the trusts that motivated the passage of the Sherman Act in the first place.

While professional economists were outspokenly unconcerned about the trust problem and resisted the antitrust movement, the economics profession, particularly in the postwar period, has subsequently spilled a great deal of economic content into the various antitrust laws which Congress enacted. Antitrust law and policy have generally benefited.

However, the dominant image of competition that is embedded in mainstream antitrust thinking is still that of perfect competition. In the world of neoclassical perfect competition, firms compete on price,[3] and typically employ identical technologies. The profit motive ensures marginal revenue equal to marginal cost at all times, and perfect competition ensures zero profits, and prices equal to marginal cost. In this world, monopolists create unfortunate welfare losses by restricting output and charging prices above competitive levels. The model of perfect competition supposedly provides useful insights into how the world ought to look, at least with respect to prices and output.

Although this highly stylized view of economic reality can sometimes be helpful, we are concerned that it overlooks important aspects of the competitive process and distorts others. Indeed, as Schumpeter (1942) suggested half a century ago, the kind of competition embedded in standard microeconomic analysis may not be the kind of competition that really matters if enhancing economic welfare is the goal of antitrust. Rather, it is dynamic competition propelled by the introduction of new products and new processes that really counts. If the antitrust laws were more concerned with promoting dynamic rather than static competition, which we believe they should, we expect that they would look somewhat different from the laws we have today.

There are at least two types of regimes that are associated with innovation. Incremental innovation occurs when new products are introduced in rapid succession, each one such an improvement on the prior product that the new drives out the old. In regimes characterized by incremental innovation, the population of firms in an industry is likely to be relatively stable. However, established firms will fall into relative decline if they do not keep up with changing technology.

Good contemporary examples of industrial regimes characterized by incremental innovation are the aircraft, chemical, and VCR industries.

The other regime is one where radical innovation is predominant. Few industries are characterized by this form for long periods of time. However, when the transistor arrived it clearly did more to invigorate competition and provide economic benefits than did any level of rivalrous behavior among the manufacturers of vacuum tubes. Likewise, the invention of the compact disk engendered competition in the recording business of a kind that firms competing with vinyl records could not supply. And the arrival of the steamship sharpened competition in ocean freight in ways that intense competition among sailing ships could never have done.

Conceding the importance of dynamic competition flowing from both of these regimes of innovation would not constitute any tension with existing antitrust law if the world of perfect competition envisaged in the textbook was the ideal structure for supporting innovation, be it incremental or radical. However, there is no evidence that the world of perfect competition to which antitrust doctrine seems to aspire is in fact ideal for promoting innovation. Nor is there evidence that the world of monopoly is ideal.

In fact, the weight of the evidence would appear to suggest that the structure of markets — whether competitive or monopolized — has little impact on innovation (Cohen and Levin, 1989). The evidence does suggest that monopoly is rarely a barrier; most truly radical innovations emerge from outside an established industry, and access to the infrastructure provided by incumbent firms is rarely important for ultimate success. Incremental innovation is not much affected by market structure either.

What, then, does innovation require? The evidence is sketchy. However, we can identify several classes of factors that are important: availability of a labor force with the requisite technical skills; decentralized economic structures that permit considerable autonomy and entrepreneurship; economic systems that permit and encourage a variety of approaches to technological and market opportunities; access to "venture" capital, either from a firm's existing cash flow or from an external venture capital community; good relationships between the scientific community, especially the universities,[4] and the technological community, and between users and developers of technology; adequate protection of intellectual property, or at least the availability of strategies and structures to enable innovating firms to capture a return from their investment (unless social returns are equal to the private returns, firms will underinvest in the development of new technology); in fragmented industries, the ability to quickly build or access co-specialized assets inside or outside the industry.[5]

Few of these relate to competition (antitrust) policy. But while competition policy may not be central to the innovation process, it would be wrong to assume that it is unimportant. The ability of innovating firms to cooperate by striking necessary vertical and horizontal agreements, or entering into alliances, often raises issues in antitrust as do other elements of business strategy. For instance, if innovating firms engage in exclusionary behavior to exclude "me-too"-type imitators, they can sometimes entangle themselves in a web of costly litigation, the result of which will turn on the proper assessment of durable market power.

In short, we contend that (1) dynamic, not static, competition is what the antitrust laws should promote to advance the goal of enhancing economic welfare, and (2) the implicit embodiment in antitrust policy of the model of perfect competition — which is inherently short run — can lead to significant policy errors. Accordingly, the editors favor policies and legal standards that promote Schumpeterian competition.[6] We believe Bowman (1973) was right to argue that perfect competition "cannot be a workable standard for judging legality under the antitrust laws" (p. 5). As we enter the decade of 1990, we are concerned by the extent to which the model of perfect competition still holds considerable sway and influence over antitrust economics and legal scholarship.

COMPETITION THROUGH INNOVATION: IMPLICATIONS FOR MARKET DEFINITION AND FOR COOPERATION

Market Definition

There is no area where antitrust policy so clearly displays its focus on static competition than in its treatment of market definition.[7] Market definition is the key pillar to antitrust theory and enforcement policy. In the absence of market power, practically every form of business behavior, other than price fixing and its economic equivalents, is legal. Once market power is proven, business practices will be closely scrutinized to determine whether they are reasonable. In standard treatments, market power itself may be proved by evidence of a firm's ability to restrict output or exclude competition, "dominance," prices above costs, or profits above "competitive levels."

Standard approaches to competition can assign market power incorrectly to an innovating firm. Even though the market power associated with innovation is often quite transitory, standard entry barrier analysis — with its one-to-two-year fuse for entry[8] — will often not undo a finding of market dominance and associated market power for an innovator. Accordingly, innovators may need to constrain severely their business conduct in order to avoid violating the antitrust laws or the threat of private treble damage actions. Ironically, in today's global economy, with low or nonexistent tariffs, one of the few ways to build market share in the United States is through innovative success.

With a Schumpeterian concept of competition in mind, one finds the current methodology for defining product markets troublesome. Applying the Schumpeterian concept, market power can be ephemeral in industries characterized by rapid technological change. As a result, Schumpeterian competition is not readily incorporated into the standard analytical frameworks used to define relevant antitrust markets.

For example, consider how the U.S. Department of Justice (DOJ) approaches market definition.[9] As explained in the *U.S. Department of Justice Merger Guidelines* (1984), the DOJ will include in the product market a group of products such that "a hypothetical firm that was the only present and future seller of these products ('monopolist') could profitably impose a small but significant and nontransitory increase in price — generally five percent lasting one year."

Our focus here is not so much on the 5 percent threshold, but on the fact that the implicit assumption adopted is that products in a market are homogeneous and competitors compete on price. Such is often not the case. As a result, application of the 5 percent test in an industry where competition is Schumpeterian rather than neoclassical is likely to create a downward bias in the definition of the size of the relevant product market, and a corresponding upward bias in the assessment of market power.

Consider the minicomputer industry. In this industry, a variety of systems compete on price and performance while exhibiting price differences of several 100 percent.[10] Too literal an application of the DOJ's 5 percent test would suggest that each manufacturer is in a different market, otherwise, product substitution would occur that would stimulate pressures for price equalization.

Such an interpretation, however, would ignore the realities of competition in the computer industry. A variety of systems with quite different price-performance attributes successfully occupy the same market at a given point in time. As new systems are introduced and the prices of existing systems change, it takes some time for resulting price-performance implications to be digested and understood by the market. One reason is simply that it takes time for users to experience and test the products. Moreover, to the extent that the product is durable and a replacement for existing equipment, purchase decisions are complicated by the need to retire existing equipment. In addition, new computer systems usually require new support systems, including applications software, so that even computer systems that are consensually superior on price and performance dimensions will take time to diffuse and be adapted. In such situations, 5 percent or even 25 percent price increases may be met with no substitution until the performance of the products can be assessed and existing equipment can be economically replaced. Even a 25 percent price increase may seem insignificant if accompanied by a performance enhancement. In such circumstances where competition is performance based, the DOJ's one-year-5 percent rule is not likely to identify markets that are in any way meaningful.[11] We outline a brief version of our approach to this problem, which is more fully developed in Hartman, Teece, Mitchell, and Jorde (1990).

When competition proceeds primarily on the basis of features and performance, the pertinent question to ask is whether a change in the performance attributes of one commodity would induce substitution to or from another. If the answer is affirmative, then the differentiated products, even if based on alternative technologies, should be included in the relevant product market. Furthermore, when assessing such performance-induced substitutability, a one-year or two-year period is simply too short because enhancement of performance attributes involves a longer time to accomplish than price changes. While it is difficult to state precisely (and generally) what the length of time should be, it is clear that the time frame should be determined by technological concerns. As a result, it may be necessary to apply different time frames to different products and technologies.

When assessing performance-based competition among existing producers, the product changes to be included as a metric should involve the re-engineering of existing products using technologies currently known to existing competitors.

Product changes, which depend on anticipated technologies and are not currently commercial, should be excluded. Thus if firm A, by modifying its product X using its existing proprietary product and process technology and public knowledge, could draw sales away from product Y of firm B, such that B would need to improve its products to avoid losing market share to A, then X and Y are in the same relevant market. If such changes are likely to occur yet would take longer than one year, the one-year rule should be modified.

When assessing potential competition and entry barriers, the two-year-5 percent rule must also be modified to include variations in performance attributes of existing and potentially new technologies. In high-technology innovative industries, it is this potential competition that is often most threatening, also the most important from a welfare standpoint,[12] takes the longest time to play out, and is the most difficult to fully anticipate. A more realistic time frame must be determined over which the new products and technologies may be allowed to enter. The precise length of time allowed for the entry of potential competitors must also reflect technological realities. Hence, it too may vary by product and technology.

The need to assess performance competition argues for the use of "hedonic methods." A growing body of hedonic literature has addressed the importance of product attributes in economic behavior. This literature has been both theoretical and empirical and has focused on product demand and production cost (hence supply). The demand literature has addressed the importance of product attributes in determining prices[13] and market share.[14] The cost literature demonstrates and measures the impact of product attributes on production costs.[15]

Thus assume that several firms offer various products with different attributes. Assume that one producer improves the performance of a certain attribute, holding price and other attributes constant. If a decrease in the demand of a similar product results, there exists a performance cross elasticity between the two products. If this cross elasticity is high enough, the products are in the same market. However, if the producer were to improve the performance of a certain attribute, while simultaneously raising the product's price such that no substitution occurs, this does not necessarily mean that the products are in different markets.

This framework allows one to analyze and quantify both price and performance (attribute) competition. Using it, one can retain the 5 percent price rule while extending the DOJ approach to incorporate performance competition. For example, analogous to the 5 percent price rule, one could assess the effects of percentage changes in performance. However, such an extension is far from straightforward. One needs to specify rules of thumb carefully regarding the threshold size of performance competition and the time period over which such competition is allowed to unfold.

In general, performance changes are more difficult to quantify than price changes because performance is multidimensional. As a result, quantification requires measuring both the change in an individual attribute and the relative importance of that attribute. Unlike price changes, which involve altering the value of a common base unit (dollars), performance changes often involve changing the units by which performance is measured. Nonetheless, rough quantification is possible, based on the pooled judgments of competent observers, particularly product users.

In terms of threshold effects, we suggest introducing a 25 percent rule for a change in any key performance attribute. This threshold implies the following. Assume that an existing manufacturer lowers the quality of a key performance attribute of an existing product up to 25 percent, ceteris paribus. If no substitution to other products occurs, then the original product constitutes a distinct antitrust market. If substitution to other products does occur, then those other products share the market with the original product. Conversely, assume that a new product is introduced that is identical to an existing product in all ways except that it offers up to a 25 percent improvement in a key performance attribute. If there is no substitution to the new product, then the products represent distinct markets. If there is substitution from the existing product to the new product, then the two products share the same antitrust market.

The criterion of 25 percent performance improvement for a single key performance attribute is conservative. Not only is a 25 percent improvement small compared with those that commonly occur in industries experiencing rapid technological change, but a 25 percent improvement in a single attribute is likely to imply an overall performance improvement of considerably less than 25 percent. This performance threshold must furthermore be judged in terms of feasibility. While it is always feasible to raise prices, it is not always feasible to increase performance. This problem is most severe in the case of quantum changes, such as the introduction of a specific application for a device. Following introduction, however, most product changes take place along a relatively continuous trajectory of technological improvement. Many product users are familiar with the key development programs of their suppliers and are able to assess the likelihood that a particular product change will emerge in the near future.

An effective measurement procedure, therefore, would be to rely on the informed judgments of users of existing products. This procedure would involve identifying market experts, asking them to list key performance attributes, and then asking them to assess the substitutive effects of changes in the attributes. The sample of product users could be supplemented by a corresponding sample of commercial participants, although care would be required to avoid introducing competitive bias into the judgments.[16] A sample of such participants could be asked whether a 25 percent change in the performance of any one attribute would lead to product substitution.

In addition to threshold rules regarding performance changes, market definition requires an identification of a time frame for the competitive product changes—that is, the definition of the "near future." We argued above that the DOJ one-year and two-year rules are too short for almost any case of serious technical advance. Indeed, because there is significant variation among products, no single number will be appropriate for all cases. Nonetheless, we suggest that a four-year period be established as a default time frame, with the option of adjusting the period if strong evidence suggests that it would be appropriate in an individual case. Like the DOJ's one-year rule or the patent law's seventeen-year grant, a fixed four-year rule will not be optimal in all cases. It could provide too broad a market definition in some cases and too narrow a definition for others;

however, its unambiguous nature has the advantage of being easily understood and not requiring negotiation or litigation to determine an appropriate time frame.

Finally, one needs to address the question of the appropriate Herfindahl-Hirschmann Index thresholds. The *Merger Guidelines* selects critical HHIs at 1000 and 1800. It is difficult to hypothesize and propose alternative HHIs for technologically dynamic markets. However, the inclusion of performance competition and the extension of the time frame of competitive response may mean that it is not necessary to change these critical HHIs. Furthermore, we believe that with technologically dynamic markets, the dynamics of market structure in the past should provide some guidance to assessing market definition and predicting likely changes in market concentration. Key factors are the change in concentration and the trend in the number of competitors.

Failure to recognize that competition is often on the basis of performance attributes and not price will lead courts and the antitrust agencies to underestimate the breadth of product markets in industries characterized by rapid technological change. This process, in turn, will lead courts and agencies to exaggerate antitrust dangers. As a consequence, technological development may be retarded.[17]

Cooperation

There appears to be little room in accepted antitrust creed for cooperation if it involves "competitors," despite the obvious importance of cooperation to economic activity and to the innovation process in particular. The primary reason why economists are skeptical of the benefits of interfirm cooperation is that the coordination function which an economy requires is almost uniformly perceived to be executed with present and forward dispatch by the price mechanism. Indeed, the "Chicago years" have probably strengthened antitrust hostility toward horizontal cooperation.

However, the price mechanism does not achieve coordination well when no market exists for the inputs needed, or if the markets are "small numbers" markets. By small numbers markets we are referring to circumstances where trading is relatively infrequent because user demands are specialized. Such circumstances are ubiquitous, particularly where innovation is involved. Thus the developer of a new instant camera may discover that it requires a new type of instant film. The number of potential developers of the instant film may be quite small ex ante, and even if large ex ante may be small ex post because of what Oliver Williamson (1985) has referred to as the "fundamental transformation." In such circumstances, the ability of a camera developer to contract with a film developer in an arm's length, open market is likely to be quite restricted.

If one recognizes the need for cooperation to spur and commercialize innovation, even among firms that may be competitors, then one is likely to be skeptical, as we are, of the antitrust hostility toward horizontal cooperation. If one is prepared to abandon this hostility, there are at least three ways to go. (1) The more radical approach is to abandon antitrust law altogether.[18] This appears to be the position of Armentano (1986). (2) An alternative approach, and one advanced by Richard Schmalensee in Chapter 5, would be to abandon the per se illegality of price fixing and adopt a rule of reason approach instead. We support such an approach, although it is not our preferred alternative for advancing innovation. (3) A third approach and the one we favor as an interim solution, which is outlined in Chapter 3, would be to permit a "safe harbor" for cooperative agreements among competitors innovating and commercializing innovation, if their combined market share is less than 25 percent of the relevant market. We would favor rule of reason analysis for shares greater than 25 percent. Our rule of reason analysis would pay close attention to the requirements of the innovation process, and the intellectual property protection available to innovators if the cooperative activity is designed to help facilitate the development or the commercialization of new technology. We describe our approach in more detail in Chapter 3.

ANTITRUST AS INDUSTRIAL POLICY

The American antitrust laws are an important element of U.S. industrial policy. Moreover, U.S. antitrust laws are a more central aspect of industrial policy in the United States than in Europe or Japan.

We define a nation's industrial policy as the aggregate of policies that directly and indirectly affect industrial performance through its impact on microeconomic variables. Key elements of industrial policy in the United States are trade policy (including adjustment assistance), certain aspects of tax policy, government procurement policy, regulation, science and technology policy, and competition (antitrust) policy.[19] Antitrust policy, it seems to us, ought to be assessed not just on a stand-alone basis, but also on how it integrates with other aspects of U.S. industrial policy. Without judging whether antitrust or other components of industrial policy are at fault, it seems appropriate to flag certain areas of tension, if not conflict.

Antitrust and trade policy are often at odds. The semiconductor trade agreement with Japan—which required Japanese firms to collude in reducing exports to the United States—was in conflict with antitrust policy, as were the orderly marketing agreements for steel and automobiles negotiated during the 1970s.

Antitrust law and patent law, while they both purport to have enhancing economic welfare as their goal, sometimes conflict, although they need not. Market power obtained from a patent is not illegal, although patents can be misused. Nevertheless, a not uncommon response to a patent suit is an antitrust counterclaim.

U.S. telecommunications regulation, up through the divestiture, required AT&T to provide universal service and to engage in cross-subsidization. But when AT&T moved to cripple new entrants, whose actions systematically served to undo the structure of cross-subsidies regulators had imposed, AT&T had sufficient antitrust exposure to cause it to enter a settlement agreement with the government. Telecommunication policy and antitrust policy have thus been at odds with each other. But antitrust policy prevailed. U.S. telecommunication equipment trade balances were transformed from a $203 million surplus in 1982 to a $1.8 billion deficit by 1989.

These conflicts suggest that antitrust policy is frequently in conflict with other aspects of industrial policy. This tension needs to be addressed and resolved. Furthermore, as markets become increasingly global, antitrust policy needs to become global in scope as the reach of policies and governance systems must match the domain of the activity in question. But U.S. antitrust policy can only impact foreign business behavior through its impact on U.S. commerce, and then only if the behavior in question is not sanctioned by foreign government(s). Thus the most egregious anticompetitive structure of the postwar period—the Organization of Petroleum Exporting Countries (OPEC) cartel—has not been touched by U.S. antitrust law, despite the fact that it has tremendous impact on U.S. consumer welfare. Indeed, by preventing countervailing cooperative strategies by U.S. oil companies, U.S. antitrust has strengthened, not weakened, OPEC's power. Retaliatory cooperative acts by U.S. oil companies that could have served to unpick the cartel are decidedly illegal. Ironically, the most far-reaching exercise of market power in the U.S. marketplace has been completely untouched by U.S. antitrust laws, while these same laws have prevented efforts to exercise countervailing market power by U.S. petroleum companies.

Our point is simply that as foreign commerce continues to become increasingly important, the U.S. antitrust system looks increasingly antiquated as a guardian of American economic welfare.[20] There is no administrative apparatus in place in the United States to enable antitrust policy to be integrated with trade policy or science and technology policy. We need to address this problem. Otherwise, antitrust will likely continue to be associated with unnecessary costs and missed opportunities.[21]

SUMMARIES OF THE INDIVIDUAL CHAPTERS

Chapter 2. Antitrust Law as Industrial Policy: Should Judges and Juries Make It?

In this sweeping review of U.S. antitrust policy, Phil Areeda points out that antitrust is a major component of U.S. industrial policy. Antitrust law has served America well, he claims, and will serve her even better in the future as scholars continue to refine their knowledge about the way the economic system operates. If we can be realistic in identifying competition, particularly foreign competition, where it exists and recognize that productivity, efficiency, and innovation are not achieved automatically by our economic system but must be nurtured, Areeda believes that "the Sherman Act may well be good for another century."

Areeda provides a number of important insights on the antitrust–industrial policy nexus. One is that by having antitrust as a central component of industrial policy, society is using judges and not planners to create and implement industrial policy. He points out that the power of judges to conduct industrial policy in the United States is very considerable. After all, the divestiture of AT&T—the most significant piece of telecommunications policy ever implemented—was made by a few lawyers in the Department of Justice and a single federal district judge. The Federal Communications Commission (FCC), the federal institution with the statutory responsibility for telecommunications, was not significantly involved. Areeda remarks that "there is no other country in the world in which such important national economic decisions are made on such a decentralized, undebated, and largely non-expert basis."

At least four hypotheses could be put forward to explain this unusual reliance. (1) The antitrust laws have become an icon in a society that continues to have greater trust in courts than in administrators. (2) If the courts err, Congress has the power to set matters right. (3) The system works well; at least it is not demonstratably worse than other more administratively managed systems. (4) Antitrust law is a mere charade having little impact on economic welfare.

While all of these have some merit, Areeda suggests that the most powerful is the lack of any strong conviction that administrators generally do a better job than the courts, even though administrators generally have wider discretion than the courts. For instance, Areeda believes that the Department of Transportation (DOT) probably erred in approving several airline mergers during the 1980s; the courts would probably have done better. Indeed, as Areeda points out, there is practically no support in the United States for the government "picking winners"—that is, identifying "sunrise" industries that warrant special support—which is what a full-blown industrial policy might require. This is because even assuming experts could give guidance, citizens fear that the system would become too politicized. But as Areeda points out, although "antitrust law has the virtues of integrity, non-partisanship, and indifference to geographical impact," it fails "either to cushion declines or conceivably to stimulate progress. . . . [E]fficiency and progress, in short, are valued among just about everyone, except some legal scholars and judges. . . . [R]ead antitrust literature and some judicial dicta and you will find efficiency and innovation denigrated as only one of the values that antitrust law should promote."

Areeda provides several historical explanations for the prevailing thinking in the antitrust community that efficiency is unimportant: (1) A mixture of attitudes denigrating concerns about low cost production or rapid innovation stemming from the view that the United States is an affluent society and does not need to worry about wealth creation. (2) Belief in the inevitability of technical progress; it will fall like manna from heaven and will not be impeded by wrong-headed antitrust. (3) A view that the United States is ahead of its foreign rivals in productivity and innovation; a belief which persists in some quarters, although unfortunately it is now largely a myth. (4) A misplaced fear that an efficiency defense would support widespread monopoly. (5) Anti-efficiency assumptions drawn from the antitrust laws themselves. (6) Fear that efficiency defenses are not administratable.

With respect to (6), Areeda sees no reason to believe that such errors will exceed those that result from not taking prospective efficiencies into account. And indeed, he believes that at least the lower courts do protect efficiency, although the courts have not been clear on whether efficiencies are an absolute defense or merely a factor to be weighed in balancing the anti- and procompetitive tendencies of challenged conduct.

Areeda recognizes several impediments to efficiency, growth, and innovation receiving their proper weight in the context of litigation. (1) Many of the facts about anti- and procompetitive effects in any particular case, especially predictions about the future, are obscure. (2) Judges often state the law only at highly general and abstract levels that acquire meaning only from their application. (3) The intent of the parties often receives disproportionate emphasis relative to the analysis of positive and negative market effects. (4) Judges often regard market definition as matters for the jury. (5) Judges too often think that "reasonableness" in antitrust law is like "reasonable care" in tort and leave the final conclusion to the jury on the basis of vague instruction rather than deciding more questions "as a matter of law."

With respect to (1), Areeda doubts that courts have the legal power to sacrifice the interests of today's consumers for future benefits. "If society wishes to make such a trade-off, it cannot rely on antitrust law to do so." Part of the problem is that courts would seldom have a sufficient factual predicate for trading off present benefits for larger future ones. With respect to (2), Areeda points out that antitrust law may discourage desirable activities because it creates uncertain risks of liability—uncertainty that is magnified when juries are allowed to define the type of conduct which the law permits. Areeda suggests that it is better to have judges rather than juries discussing and deciding what criteria to use, how they are to be proved, and the exceptions to be recognized.

Areeda professes optimism that the antitrust laws can serve us better if our antitrust institutions continue to improve understanding of economic and business behavior and formulate tentative presumptions to guide actual discussions. In addition, he suggests, admittedly with some hesitation, that Congress may need to create some kind of power to exempt certain arrangements from antitrust liability. This point is the springboard for the next chapter by the editors.

Chapter 3. Innovation, Cooperation, and Antitrust

The Jorde-Teece chapter places primary focus on the horizontal issues—that is, agreements among firms that are arguably competitors. While the Jorde-Teece treatment is couched in the context of innovation, this chapter's policy conclusions are quite similar in a number of ways to those of Schmalensee, Baumol and Ordover, and Easterbrook. Like Schmalensee (Chapter 5), they argue for a different approach to horizontal restraints. Indeed, much of the chapter is devoted to a description of the innovation process to provide a framework which the courts and Congress can use to sort out desirable constraints from undesirable ones. Like Easterbrook (Chapter 6), they argue for a safe harbor to shield from antitrust liability interfirm agreements involving firms with less than 20 to 25 percent of the relevant market. As with Baumol and Ordover (Chapter 4), they caution that preoccupation with static market power can cause antitrust policies to inhibit innovation. Jorde and Teece are primarily concerned that unless the microeconomics employed to inform antitrust analysis is sensitive to the requirements of the innovation process, there is a good chance that well-meaning efforts to promote competition will have the opposite effect. In short, their chapter is an appeal to the antitrust community to get the efficiency story straight by complementing the analysis of static efficiencies with an analysis of dynamic efficiencies.

Jorde and Teece argue that the innovation process can no longer be adequately characterized as a linear process, where an idea moves from R&D through design production and marketing. Rather, the process involves much greater interdependencies with tight linkages and feedbacks among and between the various activities. In large firms all of this may take place inside the corporation; increasingly, however, the requirements are such that no single firm has the capacity to conduct all of this activity alone, for reasons of cost, competence and timeliness.

The innovation process thus is requiring and propelling an increasing number of interfirm linkages and alliances. So long as these activities take place inside the firm, they are shielded from antitrust scrutiny. Now that an increasing proportion of the necessary linkages and interactions need to occur between firms, they are exposed to antitrust challenge, including challenge from third parties pursuing treble damage actions.

The state of the law in the United States is such, however, that managers face considerable uncertainty as to how these agreements will be treated. While the DOJ has guidelines for cooperation effectuated through merger, there is no such clarity with respect to the treatment of interfirm agreements. Moreover, there is very little case law to provide guidance as to how the courts might interpret interfirm agreements to promote the development and commercialization of new technology. While it is clear that the courts will probably use rule of reason analysis, the rule of reason standards are murky.

In response, the authors develop the criteria that they believe should be the focus of rule of reason analysis. These include the appropriability regime in which firms find themselves, the pace of technological change, the diversity of new sources of knowledge, and the need to access complementary assets and technologies. They also suggest, as outlined earlier in this introductory chapter, the need for the courts to recognize, in assessing the scope of the market, that in high-technology industries competition commonly proceeds on the basis of product attributes, not price.

Jorde and Teece recognize that many of these changes can be accomplished by the courts and they invite the courts to take the necessary steps. However, the authors also see a need for new legislation that would extend the "registration" approach of the National Cooperative Research Act of 1984 to cover cooperative efforts to commercialize innovation, and that would "establish a 'certification' procedure, involving both the Justice and Commerce Departments, which would permit evaluation and possible certification of cooperative arrangements among firms with higher market shares, when dynamic efficiency gains are likely and rivalry is robust." If accomplished, these changes would bring U.S. law with respect to cooperation closer to that currently prevailing in Europe. As the authors report, Congress is moving toward adopting many of these suggestions.

Chapter 4. Antitrust: Source of Dynamic *and* Static Inefficiencies?

William Baumol and Janusz Ordover contend that contestability is the unrecognized ideal of antitrust activity. They suggest that perfect contestability should displace perfect competition as the ideal theoretical model for antitrust and discuss important sources of rent seeking in antitrust litigation. They suggest a list of policy proposals which, if adapted, would enhance the benefit flowing from antitrust law.

The authors begin by pointing out that while monopoly, particularly when coupled with large organizational size, may have negative effects on static efficiency, its effects on intertemporal (dynamic) efficiency are not so one sided. It can help soften free rider problems, provide incentives to invest in R&D, overcome scale economy barriers, and, in the case of complete monopoly, eliminate the risk that a competitor will obtain a blocking patent. Accordingly, if the antitrust laws do reduce the attainment and exercise of monopoly, they may impede dynamic efficiency. Given the schizophrenia implicit in the standard views of monopoly and competition, the authors see an opportunity to suggest that antitrust analysis adopt contestable markets as the ideal structural result. Contestable markets, the authors contend, are "capable (in theory) or performing optimally in static terms, and of doing better than either perfect competition or monopoly in dynamic performance."

The virtue of contestability, the authors contend, is that it permits large firms the benefits that flow from scale and scope, and it brings with it effective competitive pressures without requiring an industry to be populated by midget firms. However, the weakness of contestability, as the authors see it, is that it does nothing to weaken the free rider problems commonly associated with innovation. Indeed, by allowing the complete absence of entry barriers, perfect contestability, like perfect competition, eliminates the reward mechanism — temporary monopoly profits — that elicits the Schumpeterian innovation process. Thus contestability cannot claim to bring dynamic and static efficiency at the same time.

Yet contestability is the implicit ideal of antitrust; witness that whenever the Department of Justice (DOJ) or the Federal Trade Commission (FTC) has contemplated structural relief, the goal was at most to create a modest number of moderately sized companies, never to create atomistic firms. "The antitrust community implicitly chose to forego all use of perfect competition as its guiding ideal." Moreover, the *U.S. Department of Justice Merger Guidelines* state that the Department will not challenge merger proposals where entry is easy. Easy entry is a sufficient defense.

The authors then explore ways in which antitrust is an impediment to static and to intertemporal efficiency. With respect to the former, the authors highlight the rent seeking opportunities provided for plaintiffs in private antitrust suits. Plaintiffs with cases that are ultimately found to lack merit are not assessed a share of defendant litigation costs; unscrupulous attorneys bring litigation in the hope of obtaining a contingency fee from settlement. This leverage comes from the huge potential cost of litigation and business disruption that accompanies antitrust litigation; and with jury trials, the threat of treble damage motivates payoff to the attorneys, creating a kind of antitrust "green mail." In short, the antitrust arena offers the prospect of large rents to attorneys and plaintiffs without the performance of productive activities. Furthermore, antitrust has on occasion been used by inefficient firms to hobble competitors. In these instances, antitrust also creates a detriment to static efficiency. The authors do not contend that these problems cause the antitrust laws on balance to have negative effects in static efficiency, but they do signal the presence of significant problems that need to be remedied.

However, when it comes to dynamic efficiency, Baumol and Ordover suggest that

> the antitrust laws and their execution can well constitute an impediment to growth in productivity and in output per capita. . . . [T]he main source of the problem is the fact that the design of defensible antitrust policy for dynamic industries, meaning industries in which product and process innovation constitute key market strategies, raises significant methodological difficulties. These difficulties arise precisely because, when narrowly perceived, antitrust policies seem too much preoccupied with static market power and competition at the expense of dynamic considerations.

Despite recent efforts by the courts to be more appreciative of innovation, antitrust policies do shape the decisions of innovators on matters such as interface and compatibility standards, pricing decisions, product announcements, and cooperative activity. These decisions are partly offset, in Baumol and Ordover's view, by the positive effect that antitrust has on entrepreneurship. The authors advance the novel view that the entrepreneurs who might be busy running monopolies, except for the antitrust laws, will find themselves steered into productive entrepreneurial endeavors.

The authors' policy recommendations aim to reduce the impediments they identify. These include preventing antitrust (and other regulation) from inhibiting innovation, abandonment of fully distributed cost as a standard for predation, discouragement of antitrust for rent seeking by attorneys and plaintiffs, and various other measures that recognize the importance of dynamic competition and permit responses to market failures.

Chapter 5. Agreements Between Competitors

Richard Schmalensee observes with satisfaction that the per se rule for horizontal restraints is dead.[22] He then outlines a structured rule of reason that provides an acceptable trade-off between predictability and economic rationality.

Schmalensee points out that the per se rule produced unfortunate results in *Sealy* and *Topco*. While both cases involved market division, and *Sealy* involved price fixing, "neither have more than a superficial resemblance to the cartel arrangements that are the real target of section 1" of the Sherman Act. "In both cases it seems likely that overall economic efficiency was enhanced by—and even that consumers benefited from—the arrangements that were declared *per se* illegal by the Court." While two wrong decisions do not make a case for abandoning the per se rule, if the probability of confusing socially desirable arrangements with undesirable ones is nontrivial, and if horizontal restraints are as often not desirable as desirable, then a per se rule is likely to create social mischief. Many of the theoretical reasons for cooperation that have been advanced in the vertical areas are applicable in the horizontal areas as well. Relatedly, "the horizontal/vertical distinction is often not nearly as sharp in practice as it seems in the classroom," a point we stress as well in Chapter 3. The fact that vertical and horizontal are so often blurred is all the more reason to be cautious of a per se rule for "horizontal" restraints. Moreover, cases in which horizontal restraints are likely to be beneficial in practice seem to occur with some frequency. Yet they are not so frequent as to support the per se legality of horizontal restraints.

A sound policy toward horizontal restraints requires a workable procedure for distinguishing desirable restraints from undesirable ones. It must first specify the residual domain of application, if any, of the per se rule, and, second, it must say something about the analysis to be applied in the remaining rule-of-reason cases.

Schmalensee's chapter surveys various approaches to horizontal restraints. One approach, advanced in *Addyston Pipe* and advocated by Robert Bork in *The Antitrust Paradox*, distinguishes between "naked" restraints (such as bid rigging) and "ancillary" restraints, the former serving only to limit competition, the latter serving to make a legitimate "primary" transaction more effective. Bork would retain the per se rule for naked restraints and apply a structural rule of reason to ancillary restraints. The problem, as Schmalensee sees it, is that there is no obvious workable general rule for classifying naked restraints. As with pornography, you know it when you see it. Schmalensee suggests that it is important to look at the total package of horizontal restraints in any particular case and to ask whether that package constitutes a naked restraint of trade. The outcome of any such inquiry within Bork's framework will then turn in at least some cases on the standards for judging the presence of a legitimate primary transaction. Moreover, "the distinction between primary and ancillary provisions of a complex agreement is somewhat blurry and is not particularly useful in distinguishing between harmful and beneficial restraints." And if a contract or other agreement has multiple provisions and multiple effects, there is no rigorous general way to decide what is "primary" and what is "ancillary." It is the package as a whole that matters.

The beginnings of an alternative approach, which Schmalensee favors, can be found in the Department of Justice publication *Antitrust Guidelines for International Operations*. In this approach, the appropriate scope for the per se rule is first defined. This definition is limited to naked restraints that have no significant economic potential other than to restrain price or output. Other restraints are examined under rule of reason where the DOJ asks two questions. (1) Does the restraint reduce competition in a relevant market by creating or facilitating the exercise of market power? A number of market conditions are relevant to this, such as the number of competitors that are not party to the restraint and entry barrier conditions. (2) Would any risk of anticompetitive effect be offset by significant efficiency benefits? If it would, then the restraint would not be lawful. Of course, procompetitive factors like these need not be explored if the conduct in question does not create or facilitate the exercise of monopoly power.

Following the DOJ *Guidelines for International Operations*, Schmalensee sees the most likely examples of naked restraints in price fixing (except price fixing that lowers price) and bid-rigging schemes among competitors, and in territorial and customer restrictions. Again following the DOJ *Guidelines*, Schmalensee would engage rule-of-reason analysis by applying a two-tier procedure involving (1) Explanation of whether the agreement, taken as a whole, facilitates the exercise of market power. If not, it is legal. If yes, proceed to the second tier. (2) Does the agreement produce important economies that could not be readily achieved by an obvious, less restrictive arrangement? If not, the agreement is illegal. If yes, a full balancing of costs and benefits must be conducted.

Note that the DOJ–Schmalensee framework is partially consistent with the Jorde–Teece approach in Chapter 3. Implicitly, Schmalensee has a safe harbor provision. Jorde and Teece would not automatically put territorial and customer restrictions in the per se category; if such restrictions limit free riding by imitators, we are likely to find them attractive in certain cases. In many instances where Schmalensee might cause a court to engage in difficult cost-benefit balancing, we would not, because we employ a safe harbor approach. We would simply approve. Most important, however, the Schmalensee approach does not provide any guidance as to how dynamic efficiencies would be recognized and measured. The Schmalensee approach and the DOJ *Guidelines* are cast in a static framework, when, in the editors' view, the framework ought to explicitly recognize and make room for technological innovation.

Chapter 6. Ignorance and Antitrust

In this lucid essay, Judge Frank Easterbrook reminds us that U.S.-style common law antitrust legislation is high risk, high delay litigation. The period from complaint to trial is far longer than the product life cycle, particularly in industries experiencing rapid technological change. Other nations with legal systems able to deliver quick and binding answers to tough questions will take the baton. "Antitrust must recognize this and adjust, or a system designed to promote consumers' welfare will inflict the wounds of Amfortas." The central aspect of the adjustment Easterbrook favors would involve greater reliance on simple rules, and less on rule-of-reason analysis.

Many readers will recognize the validity of Easterbrook's fundamental claim. Notwithstanding the significant intellectual efforts of the economics profession to push back the boundaries of ignorance, and the increasing proclivity of judges to pay attention to economic analysis, there remain significant barriers to the implementation of good antitrust jurisprudence. For courts and other enforcers to think like economists is easier said than done, because economic analysis is often data hungry, and because economic analysis often requires scientific and statistical thinking alien to those trained in the law. Furthermore, as this book demonstrates, economic thinking is itself in a state of flux. Indeed, Easterbrook claims that economists are still debating the merits of almost every business practice (except cartels), from mergers to monopoly.[23]

Despite these uncertainties and ambiguities, Easterbrook believes that the courts are better off relying on rules rather than letting the court start from scratch and determine whether a novel practice in particular circumstances satisfies the rule of reason. In some areas, however, Easterbrook recognizes that simple rules are not available. Indeed, business practices often come to the courts before they have been analyzed and understood by economists, as in *Aspen Skiing*.

Even when economists do have the chance to study the phenomenon ahead of the courts, case-by-case analysis of complex business practices is hard, as demonstrated in *Jefferson Parish Hospital District No. 2* v. *Hyde*, *NCAA* v. *Board of Regents of the University of Oklahoma*, and *Fishman* v. *Estate of Wirtz*. These three cases illustrate the norm in antitrust: ignorance and uncertainty. This stems not only from what Easterbrook considers the poorly developed understanding of complex business behavior, but because at first blush efficient practices often look like anticompetitive ones. Likewise, cooperation, as in standard-setting, may appear at first glance to be mischievous when in fact it is highly beneficial.

In other areas, political factors confound economic analysis, as in the assessment of potential competition. When entry into airline markets is a function not just of economic factors but also of administrative and legislative factors, which inherently are unpredictable, uncertainty is rife. In such cases, Easterbrook believes that the courts would do better to create simple rules. Per se rules conserve on information and on the costs of litigation. So would greater use of the market power threshold.[24] Likewise, administrative safe harbors, such as those proposed by the editors in Chapter 3, enable administrators to provide certainty and to encourage the kinds of business cooperation that will be needed as the economy moves from one based on nuts and bolts to one based on bits and bytes.

Chapter 7. Antitrust Lenses and the Uses of Transaction Cost Economics Reasoning

Oliver Williamson argues that antitrust analysis can benefit from having available to it several conceptual lenses for understanding complex organizations and complex business practices. Williamson sets out to identify the main features of two such complementary lenses: applied price theory and transaction cost economics. With respect to each, he focuses in particular on the questions asked, the data examined, the conceptualization of the firm, the assessment of organizational boundaries, and the interpretation of hybrid modes of organization.

Regarding questions asked by these two approaches to antitrust analysis, Williamson sees transaction cost economics as more unabashedly interested in interpreting variety and solving puzzles. The applied price theory approach comes close to arguing that prices and quantities are the only relevant data, while transaction cost analysis adopts a comparative contractual approach in which the transaction is the basic unit of analysis, and data on transaction frequency, the specificity of assets needed to support exchange, and uncertainty are reviewed. While applied price theory sees the firm as a production function, transaction cost economics views it as a governance structure. Whereas the former sees the firm boundaries as being technologically determined, Williamson sees them as being determined by the nature of the analyzing transactions that need to be supported. Technology may influence these transactions, but it is rarely determinative.

The two paradigms differ with respect to their ruling orientation. Whereas applied price theory approaches to antitrust, particularly those generated from Harvard, saw monopolistic purposes as the main reason for nonstandard or unfamiliar business practices, transaction cost economics sees economizing as the main case.[25] Vertical integration and conglomerates appear more benign, and generally procompetitive, from this perspective.

Nonstandard forms of contracting are usually interpreted by the applied micro theory school as devices that effectuate price discrimination, such as tie-ins, block booking, reciprocal dealing, or as mechanisms to check free riding, as with vertical market division. In Williamson's view, price discrimination has become a "utility fielder" to explain whatever could not be explained by free riding—itself a good (but limited) argument that has been taken to extremes. Where applied price theory appeals to price discrimination, transaction cost economics places stock on oversearching and credible commitments. And where Chicago appeals to free riding, the transaction cost school is also likely to investigate the transaction cost reasons for free riding, if it is in fact a problem, and also to explore other kinds of externalities.

Finally, with respect to innovation, transaction cost economics also has a bearing. This flows in part from the fact that the transaction cost paradigm focuses on uniqueness and the role of transaction specific assets, including knowledge. The result is that transaction cost economics is more sensitive to the various forms of complex contracts needed to support the innovation process, and the contractual dilemmas posed by weak appropriability. Integration as a response to this problem is certainly viewed as a possibility under the transaction cost paradigm.

In short, as with other aspects of economic organization and business behavior, applied price theory can go only so far in explicating efficiency and monopoly rationales for complex organizations and complex forms of business behavior. Transaction cost economics is a necessary complement.

Chapter 8. Monopoly Conduct, Especially Leveraging Power from One Product or Market to Another

In this chapter, Larry Sullivan and Ann Jones reaffirm the traditional antitrust approaches to monopoly, but do not explicitly address how antitrust should treat competition in high technology industries. Implicitly, this chapter asserts the conventional approaches that focus on static issues and deny the special relevance of dynamic competition to economic performance. The authors observe that monopoly is not unlawful and then identify the forms of conduct that should be forbidden for monopolists; they then examine these general proscriptions with respect to the issue of leverage and essential facilities.

The reasons why monopoly, benignly acquired, ought not be illegal stem from the fact that monopoly may be the most efficient way to organize a market. The chance of establishing a monopoly is sometimes a spur to innovation and efficiency. To attempt to forbid monopoly pricing would require courts to perform a task that they are ill-equipped to do—that is, to regulate prices whenever substantial market power is present. These three second-best reasons constitute what the authors term "the protective rationale" for the lawful monopoly. Summarizing the law, they point out that a monopolist is not, and should not, be free to exploit its rivals, suppliers, or customers by engaging in various forms of conduct that are not essential to encourage efficiency. The kinds of conduct courts found objectionable during the period 1940–1970 included excess capacity, payments to suppliers for cutting off rivals, and the stockpiling of unused resources or technology.

Sullivan and Jones note that revisionist scholars in the 1980s have criticized these conduct tests as being too broad. Some courts have followed. The authors' conviction is that "little, if any, retreat from the traditional conduct test is called for." *Aspen Skiing* appears to reaffirm the traditional approaches.

Sullivan and Jones discuss the application of the conduct test in leverage situations. They believe that when a firm leverages power held in one market into a different one, the inference, at least initially, ought to be that "unreasonably restrictive and exploitative consequences will result. Competition is being restricted in the second market and the monopolist, by increasing its monopoly return, is in all likelihood exploiting consumers and distorting allocative efficiency to a degree that cannot be justified under the protective rationale for monopoly."

The authors then discuss the related concept of the essential facilities doctrine. What if an essential facility has been created by a single firm that then derives monopoly power from that facility? The authors believe that when the facility innovator operates in a vertically related market, the monopolist may have motives to use leverage to distort outcomes in the vertically related market. This can happen if, for instance, the monopolist raises its rivals' costs. The authors believe that the protective rationale ought not save such conduct. In short, the authors find no reason to believe that the conventional conduct test is too severe.

Chapter 9. Market Structure and Technical Advance: The Role of Patent Scope Decisions

In this chapter, unlike the others in the volume, Robert Merges and Richard Nelson do not deal explicitly with antitrust but with innovation and competitiveness, and focus on a critical public policy issue—the appropriate scope of patents. The basic argument is that if creating and fostering an environment for technical advance is the objective, the U.S. Patent Office and the courts ought to be careful not to grant patent claims that are too broad. While there is undoubtedly waste and duplication in a rivalrous system, such a system is likely to stimulate technological change and creativity more assuredly than where one or a few organizations control developments. This reasoning argues against granting patents of unduly wide scope—something the U.S. Patent Office may have done recently in granting Drs. Leder and Stewart a patent for their successful work involving transgenic mice, and to Genentech for the insertion of a gene into a host and the subsequent expression of the protein for which that gene codes. Indeed, in an earlier period, the grant by the patent office of a patent for an automobile (the infamous Seldon patent which claimed a basic internal combustion, engine-powered automobile configuration) and for broadly defined airplane stabilization and steering systems (the Wright patent) may well have closed off important subsequent innovation.

The nature of the innovation process is important to the authors' argument.

Taking considerable editorial license, we summarize key aspects of their argument and how the nature of the technological environment enters the analysis.

The innovation process is rarely discrete, with innovations standing isolated from each other. Rather, innovations tend to cluster, like an archipelago, with access to the frontier dependent on access to neighboring islands, and with the discovery of any one island highly dependent on the discovery, often made by others, of neighboring islands. To the extent that each innovation constitutes a stepping stone, and discovery is a multiactor process, the determination of patent scope requires that the courts take into account the cumulative multiactor dimension of the innovation process.

One view of patent scope, associated in particular with Edmund Kitch, is that patents ought to be broad rather than narrow. According to this view, invention is seen like fishing from a pool of undiscovered knowledge. Each innovator (fisherman) knows that as others innovate (catch fish), there are fewer profits (fish) in the common pool. This can lead to patent races or too much innovative activity (over fishing). Kitch argues that efficiency purposes are served if patents are granted on broad prospects (the entire fishing bank). He contends that once the presence of the broad prospect (fishing bank) is detected and located, the technology pool (fishing bank) could be developed (fished) in an orderly way, without the problems caused by fear of competitor pre-emption.

Clearly, patent scope discussions have an important impact on the environment for subsequent innovation and for competition. There are two broad classes of environments in which technological change takes place that can be identified. The first is circumstances where inventions are discrete and stand separate. Here, when the technology does not point the way to wide-ranging subsequent technical advances (although the basic invention may be amenable to tailoring for different uses or classes of customers), possession by that firm of a proprietary lock on the invention is not a serious hindrance to inventive work by other firms in any broadly defined field. Examples include the King Gillette safety razor and the ballpoint pen. Thus if ownership of a patent merely means control of a particular well-defined product or process, and close substitutes that are made obvious by the invention (and do not differ in essential ways from it), the effect of allowing broad scope is simply to curtail the ability of competitors to invent around the patent by developing these obvious substitutes. This is not only unobjectionable, it is desirable as it would enable the innovator–patent holder to keep control over a new process or product until its competitors invented something that was not a close substitute. In effect, broader patent scope would translate into longer time of control—up to the maximum of seventeen years—over a particular innovation. Under these circumstances, the traditional analysis in terms of incentives to innovate versus the inefficiencies from market power would suffice.

The second class of environments, by far the more common, is where technological development occurs *cumulatively*. In industries like aircraft, semiconductors, automobiles, computers, and video games, today's efforts to advance the technology start from and aim to improve yesterday's. In many cases the technology in question involves a system with many components, subcomponents, peripherals, and complementary technologies. The grant of a broad gauge patent to one party, or the grant of a patent that subsequently becomes used for broad gauge exclusionary purposes, may lead to a situation where no one can or will advance the technology in absence of a license from someone else. This control could enable the holder of the patent to block technological progress.

Thus, allowing patent scope to be overbroad may enable the individual or firm who first came up with a particular practical application, or some other patentable device, to control a broad array of other potential applications or improvements. Compared with the costs of allowing monopolization of a particular discrete invention, the potential costs to society of ceding to one firm control of a sizeable arena of future technological developments ought to be of great concern.

NOTES

1. We accept the definition of competitiveness provided by the President's Commission on Industrial Competitiveness, namely, "Competitiveness is the degree to which a nation can, under free and fair market conditions, produce goods and services that meet the test of international markets while simultaneously maintaining or expanding the real incomes of its citizens" (President's Commission on Industrial Competitiveness, 1985, p. 6). We note, parenthetically, that this is almost identical to the definition supplied to the Commission by one of the editors and his Berkeley colleagues (Cohen, Teece, Tyson, and Zysman, 1985, p. 2).
2. For an excellent exposition of static microeconomics as applied to antitrust analysis, see Posner (1976).
3. This follows in part from the homogeneous goods assumption that underlies perfect competition.
4. This ensures access to technological opportunities due to discoveries in basic science.
5. For a good survey of some of the relevant literature, see Dosi (1988).
6. Baumol and Ordover (Chapter 4) are also critical of a static form of antitrust analysis and favor the adoption of contestable markets as the ideal structural result.
7. This section is based on Jorde and Teece (1988) and Hartman, Teece, Mitchell, and Jorde (1990). Our treatment here is preliminary.
8. See *U.S. Department of Justice Merger Guidelines*, June 14, 1984.
9. While frequently criticized, this approach is widely accepted by scholars and the courts. For a critique, see Harris and Jorde (1983).
10. See Hartman and Teece (1990).
11. In Section 3.411, the *U.S. Department of Justice Merger Guidelines* state that with heterogeneous products "the problems facing a cartel become more complex. Instead of a single price, it may be necessary to establish and enforce a complex schedule of prices corresponding to gradations in actual or perceived quality attributes among competing products. . . . Product variation is arguably relevant in all cases, but *practical considerations dictate a more limited use of the factor*." As a rule of thumb, if the product is completely homogeneous (very heterogeneous), "the Department of Justice is more (less) likely to challenge the merger."
12. As noted earlier, Schumpeter (1942) stressed that potential competition from new products and processes is the most powerful form of competition, stating "in capitalist reality, as distinguished from its textbook picture, it is not that kind [price] of competition that counts but the competition that comes from the new commodity, the new technology, the new source of supply. . . . This kind of competition is as much more

effective than the other as bombardment is in comparison with forcing a door, and so much more important that it becomes a matter of comparative indifference whether competition in the ordinary sense functions more or less promptly."

13. See Brown and Mendelsohn (1984); Brown and Rosen (1982); Epple (1987); Hartman (1987); Hartman and Doane (1987); Hartman and Teece (1990); Ohta and Griliches (1976); and Rosen (1974).

14. See Atkinson and Halvorsen (1984); Hartman (1982); Hausman (1979); and Mannering and Winston (1984).

15. See Epple (1987); Friedlaender et al. (1983); Fuss (1984); Fuss and Waverman (1981); and Spady and Friedlaender (1978).

16. If an employee of a competitor of a firm for which market power was being determined was included in the sample, for instance, that person would have incentives to overestimate the difficulty of performance improvement. The need to inform these economic decisions with technological reality would argue for a closer working relationship between the Antitrust Division of the Justice Department and the National Science Foundation or the Office of Technology Assessment.

17. One example was the Justice Department's challenge to the sale of EMI Inc.'s U.S. operations to General Electric.

18. George Stigler (1985, p. 8) has noted that "if a nation wished to foster competition, it would be at least a tenable position that the common law doctrine of nonenforceability of restrictive agreements was sufficient legal action."

19. We realize that for a brief period in U.S. history—in the late 1970s and early 1980s—industrial policy became an ideologically loaded phrase describing quasi-national planning activities such as "picking the winners" and "weeding out the losers." Few people ever took the notion of heavy-handed interventionist planning apparatus seriously, and the debate died a natural death. We trust we will not be misinterpreted here in our use of the term "industrial policy."

20. Witness the AT&T divestiture. The severing of the vertical supply links between Western Electric—the equipment arm of the Bell system—and the Bell operating companies created tremendous opportunities for foreign telecommunications equipment suppliers. U.S. interests would undoubtedly have benefited if the divestiture could have been used to leverage concessions from trading partners.

21. Phillip Areeda (Chapter 2) explicitly explores the links between antitrust policy and industrial policy in the U.S. context.

22. Relatedly, Professor Areeda (Chapter 2) had indicated that "we should only classify as price fixing that which ought to be condemned per se."

23. The editors believe that this claim downplays the very considerable areas of agreement among economists; yet they are very cognizant of their suggestion in this volume that the microanalysis brought to antitrust in the last several decades is remarkably deficient with respect to its ability to take into account innovation and the requirements of the innovation process.

24. Easterbrook (Chapter 6) notes that "treating the lack of market power as a trap door out of antitrust law not only saves parties and courts the costs of inquiry but also dramatically reduces the likelihood of mistaken condemnation of beneficial practices. . . . Antitrust is a complex body of law requiring exceedingly expensive tools, with great potential to injure the economy by misunderstanding and condemning complex practices."

25. The editors note that the Chicago School approach also sees economizing as the main case, particularly for vertical restraints. Chicago appears less sanguine, however, about horizontal restraints, as we discuss in Chapter 3.

REFERENCES

Atkinson, Scott E., and Roger Halvorsen. (1984). "A New Hedonic Technique for Estimating Attribute Demand: An Application to the Demand for Automobile Fuel Efficiency." *Review of Economics and Statistics* 66:417–426.

Armentano, Dominick T. (1986). *Antitrust Policy: The Case for Repeal.*. Washington, D.C.: Cato Institute.

Baxter, William F. (1985). "Antitrust Law and Technological Innovation." *Issues in Science and Technology* (Winter): 80–91.

Bork, Robert. (1978). *The Antitrust Paradox: A Policy at War with Itself.* New York: Basic Books.

Bowman, Ward S. (1973). *Patent and Antitrust Law.* Chicago: University of Chicago Press.

Brown, Garoner, Jr., and Robert Mendelsohn. (1984). "The Hedonic Travel Cost Method." *Review of Economics and Statistics* 66:427–433.

Brown, James N., and Harvey S. Rosen. (1982). "On the Estimation of Structural Hedonic Price Models." *Econometrica* 50:765–768.

Cohen, Wes M., and Richard C. Levin. (1989). "Empirical Studies of Innovation and Market Structure." In Richard Schmalensee and Robert Willig, eds. *Handbook of Industrial Organization*, vol. 2. Amsterdam: North Holland.

Cohen, Stephen, David J. Teece, Laura Tyson, and John Zysman. (1985). "Competitiveness." *Global Competition: The New Reality*, vol. 3. Washington, D.C.: President's Commission on Industrial Competitiveness.

Dosi, Giovanni. (1988). "Sources, Procedures, and Microeconomic Effects of Innovation." *Journal of Economic Literature* 26 (September):1120–1171.

Epple, Dennis. (1987). "Hedonic Prices and Implicit Markets: Estimating Demand and Supply Functions for Differentiated Products." *Journal of Political Economy* 95: 59–80.

Friedlaender, Ann F., Clifford Winston, and Kung Wang. (1983). "Costs, Technology and Productivity on the U.S. Automobile Industry." *Bell Journal of Economics* 14:1–20.

Fuss, Melvyn A. (1984). "Cost Allocation: How Can the Costs of Postal Services Be Determined?" In Roger Sherman, ed. *Perspectives on Postal Service Issues*. Washington, D.C.: American Enterprises Institute, pp. 30–52.

Fuss, Melvyn A., and Lawrence Waverman. (1981). "Regulation and the Multiproduct Firm: The Case of Telecommunications in Canada." In G. Fromme, ed. *Studies in Public Utility Regulation*. Cambridge: MIT Press.

Harris, Robert G., and Thomas J. Jorde. (1983). "Market Definition in the Merger Guidelines: Implications for Antitrust Enforcement." *California Law Review* 71:464–496.

Hartman, Raymond S. (1982). "A Note on the Use of Aggregate Data in Individual Choice Models: Discrete Consumer Choice Among Alternative Fuels for Residential Appliances." *Journal of Econometrics* 18:313–336.

Hartman, Raymond S. (1987). "Product Quality and Market Efficiency: The Effect of Product Recalls on Resale Prices and Firm Valuation." *Review of Economics and Statistics* 39:367–372.

Hartman, Raymond S., and Michael J. Doane. (1987). "The Use of Hedonic Analysis for Certification and Damage Calculations in Class Action Complaints." *Journal of Law, Economics and Organization* 32:351–372.

Hartman, Raymond S., and David J. Teece. (1990). "Product Emulation Strategies in the

Presence of Reputation Effects and Network Externalities: Some Evidence from the Minicomputer Industry." *Economics of Innovation and New Technology* 1: 157–182.

Hartman, Raymond S., David J. Teece, Will Mitchell, and Thomas M. Jorde. (1990). "Product Market Definition in the Context of Innovation." Unpublished working paper (rev.) (September).

Hausman, Jerry A. (1979). "Individual Discount Rates and the Purchase and Utilization of Energy-Using Durables." *Bell Journal of Economics* 10:33–54.

Jorde, T. M., and D. J. Teece. (1988). "Product Market Definition in the Context of Innovation." University of California at Berkeley: Working Paper No. BPP-29, Center for Research in Management (February).

Mannering, Frederick, and Clifford Winston. (1984). "Consumer Demand for Automobile Safety." *American Economic Review* 74:316–318.

Ohta, Makoto, and Zvi Griliches. (1976). "Automobile Prices Revisited: Extensions of the Hedonic Hypothesis." In Nester E. Terleckyj, ed. *Household Production and Consumption*. Washington, D.C.: National Bureau of Economic Research Conference on Research in Income and Wealth, Studies in Income and Wealth, pp. 325–390.

Posner, Richard. (1976). *Antitrust Law: An Economic Perspective*. Chicago: University of Chicago Press.

President's Commission on Industrial Competitiveness. (1985). *Global Competition: The New Reality*, vol. 1. Washington, D.C.: Superintendent of Documents.

Rosen, Sherwin. (1974). "Hedonic Prices and Implicit Markets: Product Differentiation in Pure Competition." *Journal of Political Economy* 82:34–55.

Schumpeter, Joseph A. (1942). *Capitalism, Socialism and Democracy*. New York: Harper Brothers.

Spady, Richard H., and Ann F. Friedlaender. (1978). "Hedonic Cost Functions for the Regulated Trucking Industry." *Bell Journal of Economics* 9:159–179.

Stigler, George. (1985). "The Origins of the Sherman Act." *Journal of Legal Studies* 14: 1–11.

U.S. Department of Justice, Antitrust Division. (1984). *U.S. Department of Justice Merger Guidelines*, June 14. Washington, D.C.: GPO.

Williamson, Oliver E. (1985). *The Economic Institution of Capitalism: Firms, Markets, Relational Contracting*. New York: Free Press.

2

Antitrust Law as Industrial Policy: Should Judges and Juries Make It?

PHILLIP AREEDA

For 100 years, the Sherman Act has been at the core of America's industrial policy. Whether antitrust law can meet the challenge of that office for the next century depends on (1) its receptivity in principle to efficiency, growth, and innovation; (2) its ability to implement its principles in practice; and (3) the availability of supplementary mechanisms to insulate an occasional arrangement from the usual antitrust tribunals.

Industrial policy, in its most comprehensive sense, is the sum of everything that affects production and innovation, as well as consumption and investment. No longer so confident that our mix of policies enables or encourages American industry to rival foreign efficiency and innovation, I ask whether antitrust law supports or impedes productivity, efficiency, and innovation, discussing briefly disputes about these matters and what courts actually do. I then consider some of the practical impediments in antitrust litigation to giving efficiency and innovation full measure, concluding with a reminder that other institutions can supplement antitrust law where it proves to be deficient.

THE BREADTH AND OBJECTS OF INDUSTRIAL POLICY

Industrial Policy Generally

"Industrial policy" is a term without precise meaning. It embraces the mix of government decisions affecting the demand for and the supply of goods and services, both for further production and for ultimate consumption. Taking other relevant social values into account, industrial policy seeks to maximize goods and services desired by our people as consumers and as citizens. This broad definition reminds us that the composition, cost, progress, and volume of the national product is affected by virtually every public policy — far beyond those in the conventional basket of competition policies.

Indeed, our common law legal system is itself industrial policy. An undisclosed invention is deemed to be "property" that an employee is not allowed to appropriate. The ability to make and enforce promises is indispensable to a market economy. Moreover, every doctrine of contract or tort that reduces the certainty of planning or exposes an actor to liability increases the costs of economic activity and thereby alters the national output. Without suggesting that all uncertainty and liability are unwise, I emphasize that industrial policy is made daily by common law judges — often without conscious awareness of the consequences for society at large — even in everyday suits about the duty of good faith in contracts, the scope of product liability in tort, or the discretion of managers and directors in the law of associations.

Of course, we have social institutions that consciously trade off security or compensation for an apparently injured party with the cost to society in lost efficiency, reduced innovation, or resources consumed by disputes and litigation. Legislators have the mandate and resources, although not always the will, to do so. Legislation in general terms — for example, banning discrimination against the handicapped or unreasonable trade restraints — leaves critical policy decisions to judges who lack any general mandate, training, experience, or resources to make needed investigations and trade-offs.

A different and very powerful form of industrial policy is society's allocation of income between consumption and savings. Related to this is government management of the money supply and its surplus or deficits. I suppose we should be grateful that presidents and Congresses express concern about inflation and unemployment even if they seldom ask whether their policies overstimulate consumption rather than investment.

Yet another type of industrial policy arises from the relative incentives for each type of activity. The resources devoted to tax avoidance or to financial manipulation may be lost to more productive undertakings. Making lawyers more plentiful than engineers or using public funds to pay lawyers but not engineers may induce more litigation than production.

Although these examples emphasize the breadth of industrial policy, my particular concern is that corner of industrial policy where competition is addressed and believed to be too little, too much, or just right.

Competition Policy

Competition is not our universal policy, because some markets cannot support or sustain it. Production at a minimum cost is sometimes possible only on a scale where a few firms or even a single firm satisfies the entire demand. The local distribution of electricity is a clear example. Unrestrained by competing suppliers, the prices and services of such a natural monopolist may be supervised by public regulators, who aspire to choose the right price while encouraging innovation. Regulation also tends to be imperialistic, expanding into areas with adequate competition. For example, one impulse toward the unnecessary regulation of trucking in the 1930s was the demand of regulated railroads for equal regulation of their competitors, who were happy to replace hard competition with protective regulation.[1]

Regulation is not readily abandoned even when it proves to be unnecessary. Sometimes technological change makes competition possible where once it was not. The growth of microwave and satellite long-distance communication is a good example of competition replacing monopoly. Or regulatory limits on entry or price competition may have been mistaken in the first place, as in trucking or airlines. And there are even those who believe that regulation is never necessary because a market can enjoy an infinite number of bidders who would like to be, for example, the sole local distributor of electricity.[2] Awarding a temporary franchise to the firm offering the "best" service at the "lowest" price would reap the benefits of the bidding competition, and the franchise could then be rebid every few years to keep price and service at the competitive level. I do not pause on the length of the franchise or the exit protection and transfer provisions necessary to make such a scheme work.

At the other extreme, competition is believed too severe, in at least two different senses. The first and most "political" sense is that producers simply want, and succeed in getting, greater revenue than competition provides. For example, producers of oranges, raisins, or milk were allowed to limit industry output or sales[3] for little reason beyond their own profit. Similarly, limiting foreign competition usually seeks only to protect producers at the expense of consumers.

Another sense of unduly severe competition is the "market failure" that denies society the usual benefits of competition, which reflects the social interest only when the full social costs are borne by producers and the full social benefits are enjoyed by buyers. In fact, however, some of these costs and benefits are "external" to the sellers and buyers and therefore are not reflected in immediate costs and prices. The usual example is the chemical company discharging pollutants into a river without paying anything to reflect the cost of cleaning the water for downstream users.

The patent system reflects a distinctive response to another externality. Although new technology contributes enormously to our economic welfare, the inventors and developers may not gain enough from successful inventions to cover their costs and compensate their risk if rival firms, who have not borne the costs of development, can rapidly imitate the invention. In this event, "too little" invention might occur in competitive markets. A society might then stimulate invention by granting bounties or honors to successful inventors or, as we do, grant inventors patent monopolies that prevent competition for a period of years. Of course, much innovation occurs even in areas where no patent protection is given—for example, innovative ideas, which are not patentable, or inventions that are kept secret rather than disclosed in a patent. That an invention can be copied, moreover, does not always mean that imitation will occur quickly, overcome the innovator's head start, or bring about perfectly competitive prices depriving innovators of an adequate return.[4]

Although the incremental innovation attributable to patent protection is unknown, the universality of patent protection in industrialized countries testifies to the importance placed on innovation. At least since Schumpeter wrote nearly fifty years ago, innovation has been thought to contribute far more to our well-being than keeping prices closer to costs through competition.[5] Moreover,

Schumpeter argued, monopolists (or near monopolists) are likely to be more innovative because they have the resources and incentives to finance risky research and to develop the results, the stable future that enables them to invest with a view to a long stream of future returns, and the insulation from imitators who would otherwise appropriate some of the gains from innovation.

This is not the place to pursue the connection between market structure and innovation.[6] It is enough for present purposes to see that vigorous antitrust policy does not attempt to bring about atomistic perfect competition but lives with a mixture of large and small firms that have not been supposed to be generally inadequate for an innovative economy.

Thus, patent monopolies and citrus cartels are departures from the mainstream rule that the social interest in most markets is best served by vigorous competition, enforced by the antitrust laws. Broadly speaking, therefore, American industrial policy has been the hundred-year-old Sherman Act, supplemented by the slightly younger Clayton Act and the Federal Trade Commission Act.

Judges Versus Planners

The result might seem curious. With the exception of the few judges administering a very general statute, our welfare is, in great measure, left to private actors pursuing their own interest. At the same time that entrepreneurs are unshackled, courts shape the economy through the manner in which they interpret and apply the antitrust laws. Most of the time, moreover, neither litigants nor judges suppose they are enforcing any political ideology outside the antitrust laws themselves.

The result is an extremely highly decentralized industrial policy, although surprisingly strong on occasion. One need only recall the breakup of the telephone company, eliminating any single institutional responsibility for a national telecommunications network.[7] Whether wise or unwise, the breakup was largely the product of a few lawyers in the Justice Department and one federal district judge. The federal institution with the statutory responsibility for communication, the FCC, was largely, as the politicians say, "out of the loop." There is no other country in the world in which such important national economic decisions are made on such a decentralized, undebated, and largely nonexpert basis.

Why does the country tolerate it? Or to put the same question in a somewhat different way, why would a rational and thoughtful czar ever set up the system we have or keep it for another hundred years? One reason might be that antitrust law has become an icon in our society, which continues to have greater trust in courts than in administrators. Moreover, if the courts err, Congress has the power to set things right. Another reason might be that the system works pretty well, or at least not demonstratively worse than other more administratively managed industrial policy institutions. Finally, perhaps antitrust law is a mere charade that usually operates in the economic backwaters with little impact on GNP. Whether Sharp calculators are handled by one or two retailers in Houston,[8] whether Mr. Ronwin gets in the Arizona bar,[9] whether some tort damages get trebled under the antitrust law, whether local asphalt producers go to jail, whether a skier's multiday ticket includes Aspen Highlands as well as the three other mountains in Aspen[10] — none of this will greatly affect the volume, composition, or distribution of goods and services or national competitiveness.

All of these explanations have force, but perhaps the most powerful is the lack of any strong conviction that administrators generally do a better job than the courts, even though administrators generally have far wider discretion and are more conscious of industrial policy. Consider the many airline mergers approved by the Transportation Department in the few years following deregulation. In the absence of antitrust immunity resulting from agency approval, the courts applying the antitrust laws would wisely have found at least several of these mergers anticompetitive. Of course, believing that the administrators erred hardly shows that judges do not. Nevertheless, there is no groundswell of opposition to the antitrust version of industrial policy and no groundswell of support for allowing administrators to organize or supervise markets generally.

Indeed, little support has appeared for more active governmental involvement in supporting industries or products that "deserve it" or in channeling resources to them via public subsidies. Whether the effectiveness of such programs in other countries is exaggerated or clear, there is little confidence in this country that extensive government involvement in the rise and fall of industries would promote the welfare of consumers and citizens generally. Skeptics doubt that anyone knows the "best" path of invention, growth, or decline. Although markets do not always work well or quickly to serve the public with minimum disruption, markets are splendidly impersonal, unlike the senators who pressure a government agency to continue, contrary to most medical judgments, financing development of an artificial heart in their states.

Still, markets work, at best, in the short run while planners with greater vision might indeed improve our long-run welfare by suppressing or altering market forces. When our country was young, it was often said that imports should be restrained to shelter our "infant industries" from well-established and more efficient foreign producers. Although our citizens would have to pay more in the short run, the burden would allegedly be only temporary — until the infant industries matured to compete on equal terms with foreign firms. At that time, moreover, we would have the industrial and technological base for future advances, becoming more efficient than foreign rivals and growing in productivity — not only giving employment to our people but raising their living standards.

Similar arguments are offered today in support of import restrictions, antitrust immunity, and government-stimulated cooperation, mobilization, and subsidies. Of course, these programs, funds, and energies are not to be used for mature or declining products or industries but only at new technological frontiers where future development, productivity, and national prosperity lie. However, a skeptic foresees support for declining industries to cushion the impact of their decay on workers, owners, and communities. After all, the voters aware of decline far outnumber those who know they will be benefited in the future by a reallocation of resources or by developments at the technological frontier. Even as to the latter possibilities, a skeptic fears that Congress will insist, as it often does, on geographical "equity" in deciding what to support. Cynics assume that allocations will either be corrupt or too late to approach any technological frontier.

Although antitrust law has the virtues of impersonal generality, nonpartisanship, and indifference to geographical impact, it has the alleged vices of failing either to cushion declines or failing consciously to stimulate progress. As to antitrust law's supposed indifference to the future social benefit of limiting competition today, the proponents of more active industrial policy apply the same infant industry arguments used to justify import restrictions or direct subsidies: a temporary suspension or limitation of competition can generate long-run gains far exceeding the immediate detriments. The questions then to be considered are these: Does suspending or limiting competition often generate such a long-run benefit? Does antitrust law now recognize either short- or long-run gains and, if not, can it readily be altered to do so?

Leaving the empirical questions to other speakers, who actually know something about the economy, I want to address what antitrust law and procedure do about efficiency and innovation.

EFFICIENCY AND PROGRESS AS ANTITRUST VALUES

It is widely agreed that efficiency and innovation are of great importance to the well-being of our society—or at least there is such widespread agreement among economists, sociologists and social workers, politicians, financiers, and members of Congress. Efficiency and progress, in short, are valued by just about everyone, except some judges and legal commentators.

It is no wonder that so many economists and businessmen believe that the antitrust laws obstruct efficiency and progress and tie one hand around the back of American business, even in its home market. If you read antitrust literature and some judicial dicta, you will find efficiency and innovation denigrated as but one of the values that antitrust law should promote and no more important than preserving a large number of small high-cost firms.[11]

Why Has Efficiency Been Denigrated?

Why does so much legal uncertainty and scholarly dispute attend the question whether the potential for a substantial resource saving or innovation justifies mergers or cooperative activity that might otherwise seem anticompetitive? The answer, I think, lies in several overlapping assumptions about our economy, about statutory premises, and about administration of the law.

So long as American consumers depended exclusively on domestic producers and so long as economic progress seemed inevitable, it was prudent to err on the side of preserving competition even at the sacrifice of some efficiencies. Until recently, the antitrust community largely assumed that foreign producers offered little protection to American consumers. Often, not only was trade obstructed, but foreign producers were not as advanced as their American rivals; and producers abroad were members of cartels which, even when lacking American members, were hardly dedicated to intense price competition in U.S. markets. If ever true, it is not true now. Some high-tech products are now made only abroad. And foreign firms are ready to exploit any opening provided by eager consumers or sluggish domestic firms. Indeed, because of their ability to expand exports quickly, the foreign firms' present market shares understate the degree to which they limit the actual or potential power of American firms.

In principle, foreign firms are recognized by antitrust law, which purports to deal with economic reality and to recognize those broad, even worldwide, markets indicated by the evidence.[12] Nevertheless, foreign producers are not always given full measure as protectors of American consumers. Foreign competition may be interrupted or limited by exporting or importing governments or by foreign cartels, although the latter are less likely than in the decades before World War II. As a practical matter, moreover, antitrust courts often adopt the market definition for which it has the most reliable data — more often domestic than worldwide. Nor is the connection between actual imports and the elasticity of additional imports well understood.[13] Fortunately, improvement is possible on all these fronts.

Also obsolete is the second historical explanation for thinking efficiency unimportant in antitrust law — a mixture of attitudes denigrating concern about low cost production or rapid innovation. In a supposedly "affluent society," greater output at lower cost might be thought immaterial to consumers who were already satiated with goods and services. Even if the typical American desired or even needed additional goods and services, he would not worry when progress seemed inevitable. Riding the crest of World War II successes and implementing the pent-up technology of the 1930s and the war years, American industry seemed invincible. In that frame of mind, why not err on a side of preserving a larger number of rivals and limiting their collaboration. Even if efficiency or innovation suffered, what did it matter? Productivity was growing inexorably at a significant, compound rate; nothing could be lost to backward, imitative foreign producers.

How quaintly naive such attitudes proved to be. The average citizen is not sated. Productivity gains are not inexorable, but have to be won, especially in a society favoring security over efficiency and progress. Imports have driven the message home: far from invincible, American industry is at risk. It seems clear, therefore, that complacency toward efficiency and innovation is obsolete.

As the final factual assumption, many have feared that bigger is almost always better and, therefore, that an efficiency defense would support widespread monopoly. Were most markets really natural monopolies, such monopolies would presumably have occurred through nonpredatory expansion, for antitrust law does not prevent the unilateral achievement of scale economies. That they have not occurred supports limited empirical evidence indicating that efficiency does not mandate widespread monopoly, at least not in the large national markets of the United States.[14] Moreover, once international competition is taken into account, it would be rare indeed for minimum efficient scale within the United States to generate a monopoly or even a tight oligopoly.

Let me turn now to several antiefficiency assumptions drawn from the antitrust laws themselves. It is often said that the antitrust laws seek the social and political objectives of a larger number of smaller firms even when fewer, larger firms would operate at lower cost and even satisfy consumers at lower prices. Even Learned Hand mused, "Throughout the history of these statutes it has been constantly assumed that one of their purposes was to perpetuate and preserve, for its own sake and in spite of possible cost, an organization of industry in small units which can effectively compete with each other."[15] Of course, one might ask how can inefficient firms "effectively compete" with more efficient firms unless the law prevents real competition. Moreover, such formulae to not tell judges, or others, how to decide the degree to which high-cost producers should be favored over consumers. Nevertheless, efficiency denigrators find support in two other concerns.

The price-reducing force of a cost saving or innovation may be outweighed by the price-raising consequence of any accompanying increase in concentration.[16] This is true, although higher domestic concentration does not lead to noncompetitive pricing when international competition is strong or when demand is highly elastic. Moreover, shifting from competitive to monopoly pricing will still produce lower prices when an accompanying cost saving or innovation is significant. Thus, many cost savings and innovations undoubtedly benefit consumers.

There are at least two situations in which consumers do not benefit directly in the short run or in which they might gain even more in the long run by prohibiting an efficiency–creating arrangement that would increase concentration and that would probably lead to higher prices. *First*, the cost savings may be too small to offset the price-raising force of the challenged activity. Although greater efficiency conserves society's resources whether or not it enriches producers at consumers' expense, we cannot entirely ignore such distributional consequences. For example, we would readily condemn the perfectly discriminating cartel that did not affect output but merely transferred funds from consumers to producers. But even those who would make higher prices decisive would presumably favor a "big" efficiency, especially one that appears far more certain than noncompetitive pricing. *Second*, even a "big" efficiency might not be forever lost but might only be delayed if the law condemned the efficiency-creating arrangement that also increased concentration. The loss to consumers from the delay might then be more than offset by the benefits of continued future rivalry in price, service, and innovation. However, resources would have been wasted in the meantime, and perhaps American industry would have suffered a serious blow were foreign firms to obtain a head start through activities denied their American rivals. In any event, beneficial delay will be hard to identify in practice.

As a related concern based on assumed statutory policy, efficiency skeptics may fear overly broad definitions of "efficiency" and "consumer welfare." Because those who own producing firms are also consumers—and may even be widows and orphans—broadly defined consumer welfare rises whenever the sum of producer and consumer gains rises, even when producers exploit consumers. Similarly, welfare is said to rise when consumers are misled to value a differentiated product more than a physically identical alternative. More puritan commentators see not the virtue of greater perceived value but the vice of misled sheep.[17] One might even decry much innovation as minor product variations that society doesn't "really need." Without pausing to examine the implicit premises of these and related arguments, they are not weighty obstacles to valuing efficiency. If we do not value selected claimed efficiencies, then we can ignore them without throwing the baby out with the bathwater. And if we cannot disentangle undesirable efficiencies, there still is no reason to believe that they predominate. Furthermore, the process of innovation and product differentiation is extremely valuable even though heaven would declare a particular result wasteful.

Since heaven has declined to address the matter, an efficiency defense to otherwise unlawful conduct might seem unadministrable. If allowed, such defenses will be claimed frequently, supposed "experts" will testify to its presence and magnitude, and antitrust tribunals will inevitably err. That is true, but I see no ground to believe that such errors will exceed those that result from not taking prospective efficiencies into account.[18] Instead, uncertainties about efficiencies typify the uncertainties in applying all of antitrust law, as I will address after pausing briefly on what antitrust courts actually hold with respect to efficiency.

What Courts Actually Do

When we turn from judicial and scholarly dicta to what courts actually do, the principles applied are relatively clear, except in the merger area. Several Supreme Court merger cases declared that greater efficiency would not save a merger that was otherwise unlawful under Clayton Act §7.[19] The Court has even counted increased efficiency against a merger.[20] Although one might hesitate to permit a monopoly-creating merger on efficiency grounds, resource saving should never be counted against a merger. Nor should we condemn an efficiency-creating merger that barely offends a prophylactic standard of illegality. In any event, antiefficiency tests are not likely to affect many mergers unless the Justice Department and Federal Trade Commission oppose efficiencies, for most private parties with standing have little incentive to attack mergers on the basis of the future harms satisfying prophylactic §7 standards,[21] and those with the impulse to sue often lack standing or antitrust injury.[22]

As to the fate of efficiencies under other sections of the Clayton Act, the issue has not been much focused under §3, although the Supreme Court has appeared receptive. In an exclusive dealing case involving a twenty-year requirements contract, the Court gave positive weight to the buyer's planning reasons for wanting such a long-term arrangement.[23] And in dealing with tie-ins, the Supreme Court expressly approved a package price lower than the sum of component prices by the amount that packaging reduced costs,[24] included efficiency factors in defining what constitutes two products,[25] and has not ruled out affirmative defenses to tie-ins. Amended Clayton Act §2, the Robinson-Patman Act, might be ignored as outside the main thrust of antitrust law, although the courts have wisely moved the test of primary line injury into that mainstream by more-or-less equating it with the test for predatory pricing under the Sherman Act.[26]

As to Sherman Act §2, Judge L. Hand pointed simultaneously in different directions in his *Alcoa* decision.[27] He noted the view that antitrust law instructs firms to compete and should not turn on those who follow that instruction and achieve monopoly power through "superior skill, foresight, and industry." At the same time, he seemed to absolve only the rare firm whose monopoly was thrust on it. The Supreme Court perpetuated the uncertainty in *American Tobacco* by endorsing Hand's opinion, but then clarified matters in *Grinnell* where it made clear that monopolies resulting from "business acumen" do not offend the Sherman Act.[28] Most recently, the Court reiterated in *Aspen* that a monopolist may lawfully act for "legitimate business purposes" which the Court defined in terms of efficiency.[29]

The lower courts also regularly protect efficiency and innovation against charges of monopolization and attempted monopolization. Vertical integration for legitimate business purposes, including efficiency, has been allowed.[30] Innovation has been approved even though the innovator intended to unsettle competitors.[31] Efficient pricing has generally been regarded as legitimate rather than predatory.[32] Similarly, in appraising collaboration among competitors under Sherman Act §1, the presence of a recognized "redeeming virtue" moves the challenged restraint out of the per se-illegal category and into the rule-of-reason category, in which that virtue counts toward the reasonableness of the restraint.[33]

Thus we see that cost savings and "efficiencies" are generally deemed legitimate, although the courts have not been clear on whether efficiencies are an absolute defense or merely a factor to be weighed in balancing the anti- and procompetitive tendencies of challenged conduct. This issue has not been much focused in the cases or literature, perhaps because the doctrinal context seems to provide an answer.

Collaboration of the kind that can generate efficiencies is put in the rule of reason category, which requires challengers to bear the burden of proving the conduct unreasonable.[34] In that context, efficiency is said to be a factor to be weighed in the balance. However, I hazard the generalization that a clearly proved efficiency of significant magnitude that cannot reasonably be achieved in a substantially less restrictive way will save most restraints.

When the charge is attempted monopolization, the existence of an efficiency, even one that could be achieved in a less restrictive way, usually precludes inferring the requisite "specific intent" to monopolize.[35] When the charge is monopolization, legitimate business purposes seem to validate the conduct.[36] Although conduct that limits competition with a monopolist significantly more than necessary to achieve a claimed efficiency does not seem desirable, the practical problem here, and throughout antitrust law, is how to deal with uncertainty about the facts of the particular case and even uncertainty about the way that markets work generally.

ADMINISTERING ANTITRUST LAW: LIVING WITH UNCERTAINTY

To praise efficiency, growth, and innovation is not enough if they receive inadequate weight in the course of actual litigation. There are several impediments to proper weight. *First*, many of the facts about anti- and procompetitive effects in any particular case, especially predictions about the future, are obscure.[37] *Second*, judges often state the law at highly general and abstract levels that acquire meaning only from their application. They too often think that "reasonableness" in antitrust law is like "reasonable care" in tort and leave the final conclusion to the jury on the basis of vague instruction rather than deciding more questions "as a matter of law."[38] Let me elaborate briefly.

Obscure Facts and Long-Versus Short-run Gains

Antitrust law's greatest difficulty lies not in choosing goals but in knowing the facts and predicting likely consequences. In the particular context of efficiency-innovation claims, we need to know (1) whether the challenged activity saves any relevant costs or makes innovation more likely; (2) whether such benefits are significant; (3) whether such benefits can be obtained as well, or nearly as well, through other means posing fewer dangers to competition; and (4) unless significant benefits not otherwise available are to be an absolute defense, whether the benefits outweigh any evils accompanying the challenged activity. Our ability to answer these questions will vary with the type of activity challenged and the type of benefit claimed. Consider a few examples.

Imagine intense interest in a potential technological breakthrough in computer chips and suppose that all domestic firms, except the industry leader, form a joint venture to develop and manufacture such a superchip. Space prevents me from considering the possibility that centralization may stifle creativity as compared with individual researchers operating independently or the possibility that firms excluded from the joint venture may be unable to match its effort and therefore may fall by the wayside if the venture is successful. The major danger to competition from a joint research venture is that sharing research reduces each firm's hope of getting ahead of its rivals or its fear of being left behind and therefore reduces the incentives for engaging in expensive research at all. This risk does not seem severe in my hypothetical because the joint venture will continue to face the research rivalry of the dominant firm and of foreign firms.

Indeed, if the venturers were unable to do this research individually, their collaboration increases competition in research. Even if they could or would have proceeded separately, they might have "wasted" resources by, speaking loosely, repeating the same experiment rather than doing it once or trying other avenues. Sharing information among researchers both reduces cost and increases the likelihood of success. If the venture were industrywide and required a quantification of such benefits relative to the alternative, an antitrust tribunal or administrator would have great difficulty in deciding what potential for cost savings or innovation offsets reduced incentives for research.

Without trying to restate this question as the tension between long-run and short-run gains for society, let me pose a different claim of efficiency and innovation potential. Suppose a market with significant entry barriers and that all the firms there merge into one, claiming that economies of scale make monopoly inevitable. If monopoly is truly inevitable, the industrywide merger saves resources and minimizes disruption. On the other hand, if monopoly is not inevitable, society would be burdened by an unnecessary monopoly attained via mergers that antitrust law could have blocked. Although a marketplace fight to the finish might be wasteful, it provides an actual test that a natural monopoly exists. Because the social cost of unnecessary monopoly is so high, as is the incentive of the collaborators to believe that a monopoly is justified, both an administrator and a court would surely require powerful proof of the monopoly's inevitability before concluding that economies of scale dictate it. However, the administrator differs from the court in several respects. The administrator is likely to have some experience and more expert help in assessing scale economies and their significance in the market. In this respect the administrator is probably superior to a judge and almost surely superior to a jury, to which many judges delegate such decisions.

Another difference is best focused by altering the example. Imagine the claim that consolidating an industry into a single firm would lead to greater innovation because research would be more efficient—in any of the senses of the joint research venture noted earlier—or because monopoly profits at the expense of consumers today will finance or motivate innovations that will benefit society many times over in future years. A similar argument with a somewhat different twist would be that antitrust law should force a monopolist to hold prices above the short-run competitive level in order to encourage the entry of high-cost rivals who, with experience, would become efficient and innovative and make the market far more competitive in the future.[39]

To uphold such arguments is to engage in double speculation. Although the claimed facts are not impossible or even implausible, both the fact of future benefit and its magnitude relative to society's losses from monopoly are entirely uncertain—perhaps little more than the assertions that come so easily to the tongue of would-be monopolists. I would not expect such claims to be honored either by an antitrust court or by an administrator empowered to approve the transaction.

Let us suppose, however, that foreign progress suggests a development that cannot be equaled or matched without an otherwise illegal domestic arrangement, and that this development, if successful domestically, would contribute importantly to domestic productivity, employment, and the balance of payments. If there are such cases, judicial and administrative dispositions are likely to diverge. An administrator may think himself empowered to buy such future benefits with modest present harm to American consumers. I doubt that a court would sacrifice the interests of today's consumers. Even were a court to possess such power, however, it would indulge a strong presumption against its exercise, knowing that it would seldom have a sufficient factual predicate for doing so. If society wishes to make such a trade-off, it cannot rely on antitrust law to do it.

Judge Versus Jury

Even within its domain, antitrust law may discourage desirable activities because it creates uncertain risks of liability—an uncertainty magnified when juries are allowed to define the type of conduct permitted. Because the facts are obscure and the ultimate balance so difficult, judges often leave both to the jury, often with vaguely worded instructions and excessive weight for a party's intention. In *Aspen*, for example, the Supreme Court allowed a jury to condemn a monopolist's refusal to market its product jointly with a rival because the jury found that the refusal was an "anticompetitive or exclusionary means" or was undertaken "for anticompetitive or exclusionary purposes."[40]

Berkey is a good example of what even an experienced and talented district judge leaves to the jury.[41] Asked to assess Kodak's monopoly power, the jury was told erroneously that it could consider "the degree to which a firm is active in different markets within a given industry" and its "size . . . in absolute terms." The jury was also told, "It is for you to decide whether the evidence indicates that Kodak was able to exclude competition or control prices to a substantial or significant degree." However, the judge did not give the jury any indication of what was substantial or significant, although this is the critical issue in deciding whether a degree of market power amounts to the monopoly power that triggers Sherman Act §2.

With respect to Kodak's behavior, the judge told the jury that it could find that Kodak acted improperly in printing its name on the color photoprint paper it manufactured and sold to independent photofinishers if doing so was "anti-competitive"—which the court did not define. The judge also allowed the jury to hold Kodak an illegal monopolist because it failed to give advance warning of its new products to its competitors. Acknowledging that no such duty was ordinarily imposed, the judge allowed the jury, in effect, to require predisclosure if rivals needed it in order to compete and "in the light of other anticompetitive practices found by the jury." The judge also allowed the jury to find that Kodak monopolized by introducing new products designed to unsettle competitors "rather than to give consumers something genuinely better."

The Second Circuit correctly appraised the conduct itself. New products would only harm rivals if consumers preferred them, and consumer preference determines superiority. Predisclosure to rivals of one's discoveries would obviously reduce the gains from invention and thus the incentives for it and thereby obstruct innovation, which is one of antitrust law's primary objectives.

The Court of Appeals thus had a far better grasp than many judges of the respective role of judge and jury in making industrial policy. Of course, the traditional trial lawyer may think irrelevant the question as to whether juries should be asked to make industrial policy. The litigator would say: so long as the Sherman Act employs standard litigation, then antitrust law must be governed by the usual litigation rules and techniques; after all, Congress is free to provide different mechanisms for industrial policy if it disapproves of traditional litigation methods.

First, although forceful, that objection is not determinative, for judges have always decided which questions of fact (for example, the intended meaning of a written contract) are to be decided by judges rather than juries and *therefore* to be called questions of law. Second, as to matters generally left to juries, judges have always set the bounds beyond which juries may not stray. Third, judges have always recognized their obligation to formulate the law as clearly as they can, and industrial policy is both a question of law and beyond the experience or competence of lay jurors.

Rule Versus Discretion: Disciplining the Rule of Reason

Antitrust law illustrates the tension between clarity and flexibility in implementing the law's task of formulating wise rules that have sufficient clarity to allow citizens to organize their affairs and sufficient flexibility to do justice in the particular case. The essence of antitrust law in practice may consist less in legal doctrine or in the facts of each particular case than in guesses or presumptions about how markets and businesses behave and about what is worth trying to prove in particular cases.

Open-ended legal standards applied by juries under general instructions have the virtue of flexibility, but at the expense of quixotic results. These standards make antitrust litigation too much of a crap shoot. Bright line legal rules avoid that problem, but at the cost of rigidity. They are not fully responsive to the purposes of the law or to the complexities of life that the law is intended to govern.

Carefully formulated presumptions to implement open-ended legal rules can approach the clarity of bright line rules without sacrificing flexible responsiveness to the peculiarities of the particular case. Such presumptions would be based on the purposes of the legal rule and our perceptions about the real world. Such presumptions would, of course, be tentative, subject to revision in the light of experience and rebuttable. These presumptions also would be designed to allow fact finders, whether judges or juries, to decide actual controversies more confidently without a coin flip. By forcing the judge to articulate the presumptions on which he proceeds, commentators and other judges would be in a position to discuss, adopt, reject, or modify such presumptions in the light of empirical studies and analysis of the purposes of the law. This process would move antitrust law toward greater clarity.

The utility of bright line rules is well understood. Their clarity guides conduct, simplifies planning, minimizes conflict, reduces resort to the courts, simplifies the conduct of litigation, allows juries and judges to reach confident and consistent results, and promotes justice in the sense of similar treatment for those similarly situated. Examples are the rules that price fixing agreements among competitors are "per se unlawful"[42] and that a monopolist who prices below marginal cost is engaged in illegal predatory pricing.[43]

Of course, the certainty provided by bright lines is far from complete. For example, no antitrust rule is more firmly established that the "per se" condemnation of price fixing agreements, without regard to their effect or to the defendant's power, purpose, or justifications. But how should one classify an agreement between two or two thousand copyright holders to establish a body to license the performance of their compositions at a price fixed by that body? That too is price fixing, as laymen or Webster would define it. Obviously, however, the judicial power was never lodged with Webster. The only sensible way to classify conduct as price fixing or not is by reference to the rationale for the per se rule against price fixing. We should only classify as price fixing that which ought to be condemned per se.

Students used to laugh when I said this because of the apparent paradox of looking at the power or justification of challenged conduct in order to decide whether to put it in a classification that purports to exclude examination of power or legitimacy. They no longer laugh, or at least not at me, for the Supreme Court has used this very same technique for classification.[44]

When courts apply bright line rules mechanically, the results can approach the bizarre. For years, the antitrust courts regarded tying agreements—I will not sell you my camera unless you buy my film—as a seriously anticompetitive vehicle by which a dominant camera producer could use its camera power to dominate the independent film market and thereby "leverage" monopoly power from one market to the other. This is not the place to explore whether that theory had or has any validity,[45] but when expressed as a per se prohibition of tying arrangements, truly silly results occur.

For example, a fast food franchisor of allegedly delightful chicken licensed franchisees to make and market that product under the Chicken Delight name, in return for the franchisees' promise to buy his paper plates and napkins from the franchisor at prices specified in the franchise agreement.[46] Obviously, these prices exceeded the normal market price for paper plates, because the premium extracted by the franchisor was the price he charged for the use of his name and methods. The court saw a tie-in and applied its per se condemnation, although, I can assure you, there was no danger that Chicken Delight would thereby acquire a monopoly of the paper business; nor was any other antitrust policy implicated by the method that the franchisor chose to measure the value of the franchise to the franchisee. Again, the Supreme Court has relaxed the apparent per se rule against tying arrangements in ways that reduce the likelihood of such absurd results.[47]

As the tying cases illustrate, the advantages achieved through bright line rules bring with them costs. The inevitable trade-off for clarity is over or under inclusiveness in terms of the policy objectives that a rule is designed to serve. Thus, clear rules carry the cost of depriving courts of the discretion to incorporate elements excluded by the rule but serving its policy.

One final characteristic of clear rules is that judges find it difficult, although not impossible, to adopt them. Categorical rules have a certain arbitrary quality that judges working in the common law tradition regard as nonjudicial. They would cheerfully enforce a legislative command that mergers involving firms with an aggregate market share of 13.5 percent should be condemned and that anything less should be allowed, but few judges would feel comfortable in adopting so arbitrary a cut-off in implementing a statutory or common law standard allowing "reasonable" mergers. Furthermore, where history or the legislature has spoken in general terms, judges may hesitate to sacrifice a party's claim of legal right or justice to "their own convenience" in efficient judicial administration.

By contrast with clear rules, general standards are very appealing to judicial lawmakers: general standards give judges the comfort of apparently addressing all relevant factors and balancing them. Multipart balancing tests appear comprehensively responsive to each policy that has been identified as relevant to the case at hand. Given then the illusion of justice tailored to the particular case, the general standard thus sacrifices clarity for, it is often said, justice for the particular litigants. Indeed, given the immediacy of the plight of the parties before the court, modern courts have a strong inclination toward general but vague rules.

The obvious costs of such general standards are uncertainty, which in turn breeds more extensive and costly planning, more litigation, which in turn is lengthier and more expensive because the parties are less clear on what they have to prove or rebut. Injustice may result, because juries or even judges don't know how to apply multipart balancing tests or even single-part inquiries, vaguely phrased. In that sense, general standards have the potential for injustice.

As I have indicated, these disadvantages of general standards are obviously exacerbated when the very generality of the standard leads the judge to leave its application largely to the unfettered and little-informed discretion of the jury.

Uniquely in America do we leave the federal courts to decide which mergers will be permitted, which chip makers may jointly research a superchip, what kinds of trade associations may be formed, whether computer companies may agree on a common operating system, and many similar questions, as well as what kinds of unilateral behavior are permitted the individual firm. Most of these questions are decided under some variant of a "rule of reason," which is a vague catalogue of generalities that do not lead one to a conclusion except by the addition of numerous assumptions of fact about the way the world works. Unfortunately, the world is not much illuminated by the particular case.

Although not often put this way, concern about vagueness, uncertainty, and the judge-jury role is often implicit in many rules about the kinds of decisions allocated to juries in, for example, the law of contracts. But here, I'll take an antitrust illustration. When one firm reduces its price, its rivals may be unhappy and may even suppose that they are the victims of predatory pricing. For many years the courts simply submitted such claims to the jury with extremely vague advice that the jury was to decide whether the defendant's intent was "predatory" (undefined) or the effect was "anticompetitive" (also undefined). In response to scholarly commentary, the courts have defined predation more precisely and have made its proof depend largely on a showing that prices were below certain measures of cost.

To be sure, a price can be predatory even though it exceeds any measure of cost. The circuits have adjusted to this fact in three different ways. Some courts say that it is better to have an easily administered although imperfect test than more complex litigation and quixotic results.[48] Another circuit now says that the specified price-cost test is presumptively determinative.[49] The price below that threshold is presumptively unlawful unless the defendant proves a stated non-X; a price above that threshold is lawful unless the plaintiff proves X; in some circumstances, the proof must be by clear and convincing evidence.[50] Although the X was not clearly defined, it ultimately will be. Yet other circuits come close to the formulation just stated although less clearly. Those courts say that a specified price-cost test is very helpful although not determinative, but then reject evidence pointing in a different direction unless that evidence is very strong.[51]

My point is not that any particular test of predation is right or wrong, but that it is far better to have courts discussing and deciding which test to use, how they are to be proved, and what kinds of exceptions should be recognized. This is far preferable to dumping the question in the black box called a jury after vague and largely meaningless instruction.

That is all very well, but where do such workable presumptions come from? The sources are the judges themselves, the litigants, and the legal scholars—but that is another lecture.

THE FUTURE

Although not America's only source of industrial policy, antitrust law has become an icon and a very useful one. It sets a powerful presumption that vigorous competition, for all its pain, promotes our interests as consumers and as citizens. I am optimistic that it will serve us even better in the future, as our antitrust institutions, including academic commentators, continue to refine our guesses about the way the world works and to formulate tentative presumptions to guide actual antitrust decisions. If we can be realistic in identifying competition, especially foreign competition, where it exists, and in recognizing that productivity, efficiency, and innovation are not inexorable but have to be worked at, then the Sherman Act may well be around for another century.

Of course, only the most romantic trustbuster would suppose that existing antitrust institutions always suffice. Maybe some other power will work better or existing antitrust tribunals will fail to see or weigh an important public service that could result from an otherwise illegal arrangement. Congress, with all the other demands on its attention, can not be relied on to respond to the needs of a particular market. We may therefore need to create some kind of power to exempt an arrangement from antitrust liability. I say that with some hesitation, for agencies with such power have generally seemed, in my view, too generous in exercising it, and even an antitrust agency can be overruled by its masters. Still, I believe we need to give more thought to improving the business review procedures of the Department of Justice and the Federal Trade Commission and perhaps empowering them to grant a full exemption in selected circumstances.

Even so, our presumption should continue to favor competition rather than its limitation. After all, that is the strength of the Sherman Act and it has served us well.

NOTES

1. See, generally, S. Breyer, *Regulation and its Reform* (1982).
2. Compare, e.g., H. Demsetz, "Why Regulate Utilities?" *J.L. & Econ.* 11 (1968): 55, with O. Williamson, "Franchise Bidding for Natural Monopolies — In General and with Respect to CATV," *Bell J. Econ.* 7 (1976):73.
3. E.g., respectively, Sunkist Growers v. Winckler & Smith Citrus Prods. Co., 370 U.S. 19 (1962); Parker v. Brown, 317 U.S. 341 (1943); United States v. Borden Co., 308 U.S. 188 (1939).
4. See, e.g., F. Machlup, *An Economic Review of the Patent System*, Study No. 15 of the Subcomm. on Patents, Trademarks, & Copyrights of the Sen. Judiciary Comm., 85 Cong., 2d sess., Committee Print (1958); A. Kahn, "The Role of Patents," in J. P. Miller, ed., *Competition, Cartels and Their Regulation* (1962); R. Nelson, "The Simple Economics of Basic Scientific Research," *J. Pol. Econ.* 67 (1959):297.
5. J. Schumpeter, *Capitalism, Socialism, and Democracy*, (1942), chs. 7–8.
6. A sampling of the literature will be found in F. M. Scherer and D. Ross, *Industrial Market Structure and Economic Performance* (3d ed. 1990), ch. 17. See also P. Areeda & D. Turner, 2 *Antitrust Law* ¶407 (1978).
7. United States v. AT&T, 552 F. Supp. 131 (D.D.C. 1982), aff'd mem. sub nom. Maryland v. United States, 460 U.S. 1001 (1983).
8. Business Electronics Corp. v. Sharp Electronics Corp., 108 S.Ct. 1515 (1988).
9. Hoover v. Ronwin, 466 U.S. 588 (1984).
10. Aspen Skiing Co. v. Aspen Highlands Skiing Corp., 472 U.S. 585 (1985).
11. E.g., Brown Shoe Co. v. United States, 370 U.S. 294 (1962).
12. See P. Areeda & D. Turner, 3 *Antitrust Law* ¶523b6 and ¶523.1–.2 (1978 & Supp. 1991).
13. Ibid.

14. For a review of the literature see Scherer and Ross, *supra* note 6, at 97–141.
15. United States v. Aluminum Co., 148 F.2d 416, 428–429 (2d Cir. 1945).
16. See Areeda & Turner, 4 *Antitrust Law* ¶¶939–940 (1980).
17. See the discussion in P. Areeda, 8 *Antitrust Law* ¶1612 (1989).
18. For suggestions about handling efficiency claims in the merger context, see Areeda & Turner, 4 *Antitrust Law* ch. 9E (1980).
19. E.g., FTC v. Procter & Gamble Co., 386 U.S. 568 (1967).
20. *Brown Shoe, supra* note 11.
21. See Areeda & Turner, 2 *Antitrust Law* ¶335d (1978).
22. Cargill v. Monfort, 107 S.Ct. 484 (1986).
23. Tampa Electric Co. v. Nashville Coal Co., 365 U.S. 320 (1961).
24. United States v. Loew's, 371 U.S. 38 (1962).
25. Jefferson Parish Hospital District No. 2 v. Hyde, 466 U.S. 2 (1984).
26. See P. Areeda & H. Hovenkamp, 8 *Antitrust Law* ¶720′ (1991).
27. See *supra* note 15.
28. American Tobacco Co. v. United States, 328 U.S. 781; United States v. Grinnell Corp., 384 U.S. 563 (1966).
29. See *supra* note 10.
30. See Areeda & Hovenkamp, *supra* note 26, at ¶729.2
31. Berkey Photo v. Eastman Kodak Co., 457 F.Supp 404 (S.D.N.Y. 1978), rev'd in part, 603 F.2d 263 (2d Cir 1979), *cert. denied*, 444 U.S. 1093 (1980).
32. See Areeda & Hovenkamp, *supra* note 26, at ¶711.1c.
33. See P. Areeda, 7 *Antitrust Law* ¶1505 and ¶1510 (1986).
34. See *id*. at ¶1505 and ¶1507.
35. See Areeda & Turner, 3 *Antitrust Law* ¶821–¶824 (1970).
36. See *id*. at ¶626.
37. Rather than analyze such effects, lawyers feel much more comfortable litigating a party's intentions. See Areeda, 7 *Antitrust Law* ¶1506 (1986).
38. Another questionable delegation to juries is the task of choosing the relevant market and determining market power. See, e.g., Areeda & Hovenkamp, *supra* note 26, at 518.3c.
39. See Areeda & Turner, 3 *Antitrust Law* ¶¶715a and 714.1 (1978 and Supp. 1989).
40. See *supra* note 10.
41. See *supra* note 31.
42. United States v. Socony-Vacuum Oil Co., 310 U.S. 150 (1940).
43. See Areeda & Hovenkamp, *supra* note 26, at ¶711.1c.
44. Broadcast Music v. Columbia Broadcasting System, 441 U.S. 1 (1979).
45. See P. Areeda, 9 *Antitrust Law* ¶¶1704–1707 (1991).
46. Siegel v. Chicken Delight, 448 U.S. 43 (9th Cir. 1971), *cert. denied*, 405 U.S. 955 (1972).
47. See United States Steel Corp. v. Fortner Enterprises, 429 U.S. 610 (1977); *Jefferson Parish, supra* note 25.
48. Northeastern Telephone Co. v. AT&T, 651 F.2d 76 (2d Cir. 1981), *cert. denied*, 455 U.S. 943 (1982).
49. William Inglis & Sons Baking Co. v. ITT Continental Baking Co., 668 F.2d 1014 (9th Cir. 1981), *cert. denied*, 459 U.S. 825 (1982).
50. Transamerica Computer Co. v. IBM, 698 F.2d 1377 (9th Cir.), *cert. denied*, 464 U.S. 955 (1983).
51. E.g., Chillocothe Sand & Gravel Co. v. Martin Marietta Corp., 615 F.2d 427 (7th Cir. 1980).

3

Innovation, Cooperation, and Antitrust

THOMAS M. JORDE
AND DAVID J. TEECE

Nobel Laureate Robert Solow and his colleagues on MIT's Industrial Productivity Commission recently noted: "Undeveloped cooperative relationships between individuals and between organizations stand out in our industry studies as obstacles to technological innovation and the improvement of industrial performance" and that "interfirm cooperation in the U.S. has often, though not always, been inhibited by government antitrust regulation" (Dertouzos, Lester, and Solow, 1989, pp. 7, 105). These striking conclusions warrant further exploration.

Unfortunately, industrial organization textbooks still discuss horizontal cooperation and competition almost exclusively in terms of standard cartel theory. (On the other hand, vertical cooperation and contracting is viewed differently; some textbooks provide treatments of supplier–buyer relationships in which cooperation is viewed as enhancing efficiency.) Both in the textbooks and in policy discussion among economists, cooperation among competitors is highly suspect, being perhaps the last bastion of what was once referred to as the "inhospitality tradition" in antitrust. As a result, very little literature addresses how cooperation among competitors may sometimes be essential if innovating firms are to compete in today's increasingly global markets (Imai and Baba, 1989). Such cooperation is already important in Japan and in Europe.[1]

This paper begins by describing the nature of the innovation process. We then explore socially beneficial forms of cooperation that can assist the development and commercialization of new technology, and suggest modifications to current U.S. antitrust law that would remove unnecessary impediments to organizational arrangements that support innovation and stimulate competition in the United States. The modifications we propose would create "safe harbors" for various forms of cooperative activities among competitors in unconcentrated markets and would permit cooperation in more concentrated markets if commercialization and appropriability were thereby facilitated. These modifications would bring U.S. antitrust laws closer to what is already in place in Europe and Japan and would promote competition more assuredly than would existing law.[2]

We have no illusion that our proposed changes, standing alone, would dramatically improve the performance of U.S. industry, although specific industries might be transformed. We recognize that other policies affecting innovation are also important, as well as savings rates, investment in education and technological skills, and appropriate financial and tax incentives. However, the changes we propose in antitrust law are also important and have the attraction that they do not require the expenditure of public funds. In short, we see existing antitrust law as a self-imposed impediment to U.S. economic performance.[3]

THE NATURE OF INNOVATION

Innovation is the search for and the discovery, development, improvement, adoption and commercialization of new processes, products, and organizational structures and procedures.[4] It involves uncertainty, risk taking, probing and re-probing, experimenting, and testing. It is an activity in which "dry holes" and "blind alleys" are the rule, not the exception. Many of these aspects are well-known and have been frequently analyzed in the economics literature.

However, other aspects of innovation, particularly its organizational requirements, have not been sufficiently explored. The traditional serial model that has served as the basis for current antitrust policy is described below. Its inadequacies are then addressed in light of the "simultaneous" nature of the process, which is particularly relevant in certain industries, like microelectronics, experiencing high rates of technological change.[5]

The Traditional Serial Model

Traditional descriptions of the innovation process commonly break it down into a number of stages that proceed sequentially; theoretical treatments of R&D in industrial organization reflect this model. According to this view, the innovation process proceeds in a linear and predictable fashion from research to development, design, production, and then finally to marketing, sales, and service (Grossman and Shapiro, 1986, p. 319; Tirole, 1988, p. 389). In simple models, there is not even any feedback or overlap between and among stages.

If the serial model adequately characterizes innovation today, then it is mainly innovation that occurs in some scale-intensive industries. The initial development of nylon at Dupont perhaps fits this model. The Manhattan Project during World War II might also be illustrative. The serial model does not address the many small but cumulatively important incremental innovations that are at the heart of technological change in many industries, especially well-established industries like semiconductors, computers, and automobiles. The serial model of innovation is an analytic convenience that no longer adequately characterizes the innovation process, except in special circumstances.

The serial model has enabled economists to view innovation as a vertical process. Inasmuch as antitrust policy toward vertical restraints is very permissive, many economists and legal scholars do not understand how U.S. antitrust laws could stand in the way of the various kinds of standard and nonstandard contracting agreements often needed to support the commercialization of innovation. But as we shall see, matters are not so simple.

The Simultaneous Model

The simultaneous model of innovation recognizes the existence of tight linkages and feedback mechanisms that must operate quickly and efficiently, including links between firms, within firms, and sometimes between firms and other organizations like universities. From this perspective, innovation does not necessarily begin with research; nor is the process serial. But it does require rapid feedback, mid-course corrections to designs, and redesign.[6] This conceptualization recognizes aspects of the serial model—such as the flow of activity, in certain cases through design to development, production, and marketing—but also recognizes the constant feedback between and among activities, and the involvement of a wide variety of economic actors and organizations that need not have a simple upstream-downstream relationship to each other.[7] It suggests that R&D personnel must be closely connected to the manufacturing and marketing personnel and to external sources of supply of new components and complementary technologies so that supplier, manufacturer, and customer reactions can be fed back into the design process rapidly. In this way new technology, whether internal or external, becomes embedded into designs that meet customer needs quickly and efficiently.

The simultaneous model visualizes innovation as an incremental and cumulative activity that involves building on what went before, whether it is inside the organization or outside the organization, and whether the knowledge is proprietary or in the public domain. The simultaneous model also stresses the importance of the speed of the design cycle and flexibility. IBM followed this model in developing its first PC, employing alliances with Microsoft and others to launch a successful personal computer system. Sun Microsystems and NeXT Computer also launched themselves in this way and have remained in this mode for subsequent new product development. Microprocessor development at Intel often follows this logic too.

When innovation has this character, the company that is quickest in product design and development will appear to be the pioneer, even if its own contribution to science and technology is minimal, because it can be first to "design in" science and technology already in the public domain. Both small and large organizations operate by this model, reaching out upstream and downstream, horizontally and laterally, to develop and assemble leading edge systems.

In short, much innovation today is likely to require lateral and horizontal linkages as well as vertical ones. As we discuss below, and particularly for small firms, innovation may require accessing complementary assets which lie outside the organization. If innovating firms do not have the necessary capabilities in-house, they may need to engage in various forms of restrictive contracts with providers of inputs and complementary assets. The possibility that antitrust laws could be invoked, particularly by excluded competitors, thus arises. Lying in the weeds to create mischief for unsuspecting firms engaged in socially desirable but poorly understood business practices are plaintiffs' attorneys and their expert economists entreating the courts to view reality through the lens of monopoly theory and modern variants such as raising rivals' costs. These theories have been honed in the context of a hypothetical world of unchanging technology. If new technology does arrive it often falls like manna from heaven; behavior which is anticompetitive in the static context may be procompetitive in a dynamic one. Because the study of innovation is largely outside the mainstream of economic research and antitrust jurisprudence, the possibility of expensive and distracting litigation followed by judicial error is significant.

Paradoxically, the giant integrated enterprises are not most heavily at risk. Instead, most at risk are mid-sized enterprises that have developed and commercialized important innovations. Since these firms are likely to have some market power (under orthodox definitions), they need to engage in complex forms of interfirm cooperation. Because of these risks, managers may moreover choose to forego socially desirable arrangements and investments, and innovation and the competition it engenders will be attenuated.

ORGANIZATIONAL REQUIREMENTS OF INNOVATION

Whether innovation is serial or simultaneous, it requires the coordination of various activities. The serial model suggests a rather simple organizational problem; the simultaneous model a more complex one, often employing various forms of nonstandard contracting. To the extent that economists employ just the serial model, they greatly oversimplify the organizational challenges that innovation provides and underestimate potential antitrust problems. Also, they probably exaggerate the importance of research and downplay the importance of other factors. As discussed below, except in special cases, a firm's R&D capability is for naught if it cannot organize the rest of the innovation process efficiently and effectively, particularly if that innovation is taking place in an already-established industry.

For innovations to be commercialized, the economic system must somehow assemble all the relevant complementary assets and create an interactive and dynamically efficient system of learning and information exchange. The necessary complementary assets can conceivably be assembled by administrative processes or by market processes, as when the innovator simply licenses the technology to firms that already own the relevant assets or are willing to create them. These organizational choices have received scant attention in the context of innovation. Indeed, the serial model relies on an implicit belief that arm's length contracts between unaffiliated firms in the vertical chain from research to customer will suffice to commercialize technology. In particular, there has been little consideration of how complex contractual arrangements among firms can assist commercialization—that is, translating R&D capability into profitable new products and processes. The one partial exception is some literature on joint R&D activity (Grossman and Shapiro, 1986; Ordover and Willig, 1985), but this literature addresses the organization of R&D and not the organization of innovation.[8]

If innovation takes place in a regime of tight appropriability—that is, if the technological leader can secure legal protection, perhaps by obtaining an ironclad patent (Teece, 1986)—and if technology can be transferred at zero cost as is commonly assumed in theoretical models, the organizational challenge that is created by innovation is relatively simple. In these instances, the market for intellectual property is likely to support transactions enabling the developer of the technology to simply sell its intellectual property for cash, or at least license it to downstream firms who can then engage in whatever value-added activities are necessary to extract value from the technology. With a well-functioning market for know-how, markets can provide the structure for the requisite organization to be accomplished.

But in reality, the market for know-how is riddled with imperfections (Arrow, 1962). Simple unilateral contracts, where technology is sold for cash, are unlikely to be efficient (Teece, 1980, 1982). Complex bilateral and multilateral contracts, internal organization, or various hybrid structures are often required to shore up obvious market failures (Williamson, 1985; Teece, 1986). This section will examine various market failures and the institutional arrangements that can ameliorate them.

Technology Transfer Efficiency

The transfer of technology among the various activities that constitute innovation is not costless. This is especially true if the know-how to be transferred cannot be easily bundled and shipped out in one lot—which is clearly the case when the development activity must proceed simultaneously and when the knowledge has a high-tacit component.[9] In these instances, the required transfer of technology cannot be separated from the transfer of personnel, which is typically difficult if the contractual relationship is arm's length and nonexclusive.

Besides the problems of getting technology-driven concepts to market, there is the converse problem of getting user-driven innovations to developers. In some industries, users other than the manufacturers conceive of and design innovative prototypes. The manufacturers' role in the innovation process is somehow to become aware of the user innovation and its value, and then to manufacture a commercial version of the device for sale to other users. User-dominated innovation accounts for more than two-thirds of first-to-market innovations in scientific instruments and in process machinery used in semiconductor and electronic subassembly manufacture (von Hippel, 1988). Clearly, user innovation requires two kinds of technology transfer: first, from user to manufacturer, and then from the manufacturer to the developer-user and other users.

Mirroring the role that users play in stimulating innovation upstream is the role that suppliers play in stimulating downstream innovation. For example, a good deal of the innovation in the automobile industry, including fuel injection, alternators, and power steering, has its origins in upstream component suppliers. Bendix and Bosch developed fuel injection and Motorola the alternator. The challenge to the manufacturer then becomes how to "design in" the new components and how to avoid sole source dependency. As discussed below, deep and enduring relationships need to be established between component developer-manufacturers and suppliers to ensure adoption and diffusion of the technology.[10] These relationships, while functionally vertical, could well turn out to be viewed as horizontal by a court. Unless the courts have an adequate model of innovation and competition presented to them, beneficial contractual arrangements with attendant restraints could well be viewed negatively.

Scale, Scope, and Duplication Issues

Successful new product and process development innovation often requires horizontal and lateral as well as vertical cooperation. It is well understood that horizontal linkages can help overcome scale barriers in research; they can also assist in defining technical standards. But it is common to assert that if firms need to engage in joint research to achieve these economies, the maintenance of competition requires that firms participating in joint research go their own way with respect to related activities such as manufacturing. However, a requirement that firms participating in a joint research arrangement commercialize the technology independently can impose an unnecessary technology transfer burden. As discussed above, the imposition of a market interface between "research" and "commercialization" activities will most assuredly create a technology transfer challenge, a loss of effectiveness and timeliness, and higher costs.

Collaborative research also reduces what William Norris, CEO of Control Data Corporation, refers to as "shameful and needless duplication of effort" (David, 1985). Independent research activities often proceed down identical or near-identical technological paths. This activity is sometimes wasteful and can be minimized if research plans are coordinated. The danger of horizontal cooperation, on the other hand, is that it may reduce diversity. This concern is legitimate and is commonly stressed by economists.[11] Unquestionably, a system of innovation that converges on just one view of the technological possibilities is likely to close off productive avenues of inquiry.

However, a private enterprise economy, without horizontal coordination and communication, offers no guarantee that the desired level of diversity is achieved at the lowest cost. In addition, cooperation need not be the enemy of diversity. If firms can coordinate their research programs to some degree, duplication can be minimized without the industry converging on a single technological approach. Indeed, Bell Labs has been noted for the very considerable internal diversity it has been able to achieve, at least in the predivestiture period.

Rent Dissipation Issues

Innovation has well-known free rider and public good characteristics. Know-how leakage and other spillovers impair incentives to innovate by redistributing benefits to others, particularly competitors and users. To maintain adequate incentives to invest in innovative activity, without providing government subsidies, free riding must be curtailed. This rationale is how economists justify patents, copyrights, trade secrets, and other aspects of intellectual property law.

The organizational form in which innovation takes place, interacting with the protection provided by intellectual property law (Teece, 1986), will affect the degree of rent dissipation which the innovator experiences. If the innovation has value and intellectual property protection is effective, an innovator specializing just in early stage activity is in a good position to capture a portion of the returns from innovation.

But surveys show that intellectual property law has a limited ability to provide protection from imitation,[12] even though there have been recent efforts by the courts to tighten enforcement. For a sample of 48 patented product innovations in the chemical, drug, electronics, and machinery industry, one group of researchers found that within four years of their introduction, 60 percent of the patented successful innovations in the sample were imitated (Mansfield et al., 1982). Not surprisingly, the social returns to innovation are greater than the private returns. So underinvestment in innovative activities is to be expected.

A "research joint venture" may not do enough to overcome appropriability problems, unless many potential competitors are in the joint venture. Thus, a single firm or even a consortia with good intellectual property protection will often need to bolster its market position and its stream of rents by other strategies and mechanisms. These mechanisms include building, acquiring, or renting (on an exclusive bases) complementary assets and exploiting first-mover advantages. We use the term *complementary assets* to refer to those assets and capabilities that need to be employed to package new technology so that it is valuable to the end user.[13] Broad categories of complementary assets include complementary technologies, manufacturing, marketing, distribution, sales, and service.

It is essential to further distinguish between generic and specific complementary assets. Generic assets include general purpose facilities and equipment and nonspecific skills; they tend to be disembodied and codified and hence easy to transfer. Specific assets, on the other hand, include highly differentiated system and firm-specific assets and skills. Specific assets and capabilities are typically embedded in the organization; or even if not embedded in the organization (like a specialized machine) are of reduced value in a different organizational context. In a sense, specific assets represent the firm's particular assemblage of physical assets and prior learning. Accordingly, they are difficult for competitors to replicate.

Thus, when imitation of aspects of a firm's technology is easy, it is essential for firms to be world-class—or to be linked to partners who are world-class—in the less imitatable complementary activities. Accordingly, the best defense against product imitators may well be the development of a less easily imitatable superior manufacturing process to make the product; or it may be the firm's superior service capability. In short, because a firm's comparative advantage in research does not necessarily coincide with an advantage in the relevant complementary assets, the expert performance of the innovator's contractual partners in certain key activities complementary to the easily imitatable activities is often essential if the innovator is to capture a portion of the profits that the innovation generates. The antitrust laws must be shaped so that they do not impair such beneficial linkages.

In this regard, many British and American firms responsible for important product innovations have captured very little value from innovations for which they have been responsible because of their weaknesses in manufacturing. Often competitors can quickly reverse engineer new products. Once the new product design is apparent to competitors, success in the marketplace is determined by manufacturing costs and quality. In these circumstances, firms that are excellent at manufacturing — and this excellence is often harder to replicate than a new product is to reverse engineer — can garner practically all of the profits associated with the new product designs. Hence it is critical that innovating firms protect themselves from such outcomes by developing or somehow uniquely accessing the requisite complementary assets. The next section explains why cooperation may be necessary for firms to perform this function.

GOVERNANCE ALTERNATIVES

The previous section has argued that innovation often requires firms to enter into complex contracts and relationships with other firms in order to bring technology to the market and to hold imitators at bay. This section considers in more detail the range of organizational alternatives available to the innovator to generate, coordinate, and control these complementary assets.

Consider first the price mechanism. Theoretical treatments generally assume that the requisite coordination and control can be achieved by the invisible hand. Efficient levels of investment in complementary assets are brought forward at the right time and place by price signals. Entrepreneurship is automatic and costless. This view is implicit in textbook presentations; in turn, the textbook view seems implicit in U.S. antitrust law.

However, many economists seem to have what Tjalling Koopmans calls an "overextended belief" regarding the efficiency of competitive markets as a means of allocating resources in a world characterized by ubiquitous uncertainty. Market failures are likely to arise because of the ignorance that firms have with respect to their competitors' future actions, preferences, and states of technological information (Koopmans, 1957). In reality, nothing guarantees that investment programs are made known to all concerned at the time of their inception. This uncertainly is especially high for the development and commercialization of new technology. Accordingly, innovating firms need to achieve greater coordination than the price system alone appears able to bring about.

A second mechanism for effectuating coordination is the administrative processes within the firm. A company's internal organization can serve to shore up some market imperfections and provide some of the necessary coordination. As Alfred Chandler (1977) has explained, the modern multidivisional business enterprise "took over from the market the coordination and integration of the flow of goods and services from the production of raw materials through the several processes of production to the sale to the ultimate consumer. . . . administrative coordination replaced market coordination in an increasingly large portion of the economy." Oliver Williamson (1985) has developed an elegant and powerful framework to explain the relative efficiencies of markets and administrative processes. However, one property of large integrated structures is that they have the potential to become excessively hierarchical and less responsive to market needs (Teece, 1989c). Accordingly, at least for some aspects of innovative activity, smaller organizations are often superior.

In between pure market and full administrative solutions are many intermediate and hybrid possibilities, including interfirm agreements. Interfirm agreements can be classified as unilateral (where A sells X to B) or bilateral (whereby A agrees to buy Y from B as a condition for making the sale of X, and both parties understand that the transaction will be continued only if reciprocity is observed). Such arrangements can also be multilateral.

An especially interesting interfirm agreement is the strategic alliance, which can be defined as a bilateral or multilateral relationship characterized by the commitment of two or more partner firms to a common goal. A strategic alliance typically includes a constellation of agreements involving (1) technology swaps, (2) joint R&D or co-development, and/or (3) the sharing of complementary assets, such as where one party does manufacturing and the other distribution for a co-developed product. If the common goal was simply price-fixing or market-sharing, such an agreement might constitute a cartel, especially if the agreement included substantially all members of an industry.

By definition, a strategic alliance can never have one side receiving cash alone; it is not a unilateral exchange transaction. Nor do strategic alliances include mergers because alliances by definition cannot involve acquisition of another firm's assets or controlling interest in another firm's stock. Alliances need not involve equity swaps or equity investments, although they often do. Strategic alliances without equity typically consist of contracts between or among partner firms that are nonaffiliated. Equity alliances can take many forms, including minority equity holdings, consortia, and joint ventures. Such interfirm agreements are usually temporary, and are assembled and disassembled as circumstances warrant. Typically, only a limited range of the firm's activities are enveloped in such agreements, and many competitors are excluded.

Strategic alliances, including consortia and joint ventures, are often an effective and efficient way to organize for innovation, particularly when an industry is fragmented. Interfirm cooperation preserves market selection and responsiveness; in a sense, it is the pure private enterprise solution. The case for planning and industrial policy recedes if a degree of operational and strategic coordination can be attained through private agreements. The benefits associated with less hierarchical structures can be obtained without incurring the disadvantages of insufficient scale and scope.

ANTITRUST TREATMENT OF INTERFIRM AGREEMENTS

The United States

Current U.S. antitrust law in the United States needlessly inhibits interfirm agreements designed to develop and commercialize new technology.[14] First, the legal standards for interfirm agreements are ambiguous. While it is generally true that rule of reason analysis—rather than per se rules—will be applied to contractual arrangements designed to advance innovation,[15] the elements of rule of reason analysis are quite muddled.[16] Some clarity exists for vertical arrangements, but horizontal and hybrid (elements of both vertical and horizontal) cooperative arrangements face greater uncertainty. This is primarily because the economics literature has not hitherto provided the courts with plausible theories of horizontal cooperation other than cartels. While simple "scale economy" or "risk reduction" theories are often discussed, these notions capture only a fraction of the variety of the circumstances where social benefits can arise from interfirm agreements.

First, current law does not recognize a market power-based safe harbor for horizontal contractual arrangements among firms with less than 20 percent market share, although it does for mergers and acquisitions.[17] A market power threshold — a burden on plaintiffs to demonstrate that defendants possess substantial market power in a relevant horizontal, upstream, or downstream market — that we propose below would clarify the legal treatment of cooperative arrangements by creating an objective test by which firms can prospectively gauge the legality of their plans. A market-power-based safe harbor approach would also bring analysis of cooperative arrangements into alignment with the approach taken in merger analysis and articulated in the Department of Justice's *Merger Guidelines*.[18] But as long as the parameters of rule of reason analysis are ambiguous and unstructured, the result is that uncertainty and unpredictability surround interfirm agreements, thereby chilling investment and cooperative arrangements to bring new products and processes to market.

Second, antitrust law permits private plaintiffs to engage in treble damage litigation against cooperative commercialization arrangements, even when the government has "signed off" on a venture. The Clayton Act permits private parties to sue for treble damages for alleged antitrust injuries, and allows state attorney generals to recover treble damages on behalf of persons residing in the state.[19] Successful plaintiffs can also recover attorneys' fees.[20] These remedies — available only in the United States — provide a powerful incentive for plaintiffs to litigate — and a powerful disincentive for business to form cooperative innovation arrangements and strategic alliances.

Treble damages and attorneys' fees are designed to deter anticompetitive conduct by giving plaintiffs an incentive to ferret out anticompetitive conduct, particularly when such conduct might be difficult to detect. In our view, these incentives are unwarranted in the context of cooperative innovation. While it is difficult to measure the missed opportunities for cooperative innovation caused by the threat of treble damage litigation, our judgment is that it is substantial, largely due to ingrained habits caused by a hostile antitrust tradition.

Congress has already recognized some of these concerns and has made small steps toward remedying the situation. Its response thus far has been the National Cooperative Research Act (NCRA) of 1984,[21] which has taken two significant steps to remove legal disincentives to cooperative innovation.[22] First, the NCRA provides that "joint research and development ventures" must not be held illegal per se, and that such ventures instead should be "judged on the basis of [their] reasonableness, taking into account all relevant factors affecting competition, including, but not limited to, effect on competition in properly defined, relevant research and development markets."[23] By adopting the rule of reason, Congress essentially removed any doubts about the inapplicability of per se rules.[24] Second, the NCRA establishes a registration procedure for joint research and development ventures,[25] limiting antitrust recoveries against registered ventures to single damages, interest, and costs, including attorneys' fees.[26] Thus, Congress eliminated the threat of treble damages for litigation challenging cooperative innovation arrangements, provided that the parties to the arrangement first register their venture.

Unfortunately, the substantive protection provided by the NCRA—guaranteed rule of reason treatment and reduction of damages—extends only to research and downstream commercial activity "reasonably required" for research[27] and is narrowly confined to marketing intellectual property developed through a joint R&D program.[28] Treatment of commercialization agreements is thus left uncertain, to be determined only by interpretation of the "reasonably required" standard.

In our view, the NCRA is not sufficiently permissive. The NCRA unwisely precludes joint manufacturing and production of innovative products and processes, which are often necessary to provide the cooperating ventures with significant feedback information to aid in further innovation and product development, and to make the joint activity profitable. Unfortunately, the NCRA seems to have adopted—at least implicitly—a "serial" view of the innovation process.

Moreover, the NCRA gives little guidance concerning the substantive content of its rule of reason approach.[29] While the act did require that markets be defined in the context of research and not the products that might result from it, the NCRA fails either to create a market power-based safe harbor or to specify factors to be considered within rule of reason analysis. It simply requires consideration of "all relevant factors affecting competition," paying no special attention to the special characteristics of the innovation process in a quickly changing industry.

Finally, while the NCRA's elimination of treble damages for registered ventures is an important step forward, cooperating firms are still not protected from antitrust litigation. The cost of defending antitrust suits is not materially reduced by the exceedingly narrow circumstances in which the act permits an award of attorneys' fees to prevailing defendants.[30] Moreover, single damages are still available. We believe that if an approval procedure existed under which procompetitive arrangements could obtain exemptions from further antitrust exposure to private damage actions, then many more competitively beneficial ventures would utilize the NCRA.[31]

In contrast to the picture we have sketched of U.S. antitrust law, Japan's and Europe's antitrust environments are more hospitable to strategic alliances and cooperative arrangements for innovation.

Japan

The basic Japanese attitude is that joint R&D activities are procompetitive and thus should not be touched by the Antimonopoly Act. Significantly, the term "R&D" in Japan includes joint commercialization.[32] The Fair Trade Commission (FTC) is responsible for executing and enforcing the Antimonopoly Act of 1947, which, like the Sherman Act, broadly prohibits unreasonable restraints of trade. While there is no specific legislative exemption for joint innovation arrangements under the act, the FTC has been able to exempt cooperative innovation efforts from the scope of the law by virtue of its power as the primary enforcer of the

act.[33] FTC policy states that if there are cases presented where competition allegedly is negatively impacted, the procompetitiveness benefits of innovation must
be balanced against any anticompetitive effects. Balancing will take place not
only within a particular market but also across markets because "there is a possibility of the emergence of competition at the intersection of industrial sectors as
a result of joint R&D between firms in different sectors."[34]

In considering anticompetitive effects of cooperative innovation arrangements, Japan's FTC analyzes market shares and market structure.[35] The FTC
specifically recognizes the needs of innovators and articulates procompetitive
justifications that include (1) the difficulty of single-firm innovation; (2) the
abbreviation of the time needed for innovation by cooperation and specialization
between joint participants; (3) the pursuit of innovation in new fields by utilizing
shared technology and know-how; and (4) enhancement of the technological
level of each participant through the interchange of technology.[36]

When the Ministry of International Trade and Industry (MITI) seeks to
promote cooperative R&D activities (for example, as authorized by the Act for
Facilitation of Research in Key Technology,[37] or the Research Association for
Mining and Manufacturing Technology Act),[38] the FTC is consulted in advance
concerning competition problems. Once the activities are cleared by the FTC, it
is extraordinarily unlikely that the FTC would pursue antitrust remedies at a
future time. Significantly, treble damages are not available to private parties
seeking to enforce Japanese antitrust laws.[39] Moreover, even private suits for
single damages under the act are very rare and usually unsuccessful.[40] Thus,
Japanese firms cooperating on innovation and commercialization of innovation
have little to fear from Japanese antitrust laws.

Under this type of antitrust environment, it is not surprising that there is
frequent collaboration for innovation. Although regular statistics are not kept in
Japan because there is no reporting requirement for collaborative research and
commercialization activities, the Fair Trade Commission report on "Research
and Development Activities in Private Enterprise and Problems They Pose in
Competition Policy" issued in 1984[41] contains statistics suggestive of the quantity
and variety of joint innovation activities in Japan. The survey results indicate
that joint R&D projects among corporations in the same industrial sector, which
might be classified as horizontal collaboration, represent 19.1 percent of total
projects.

The European Community

The antitrust environment shaping cooperation in the European Community is
also markedly different from the United States. In 1968, the European Commission issued a Notice of Cooperation between Enterprises which indicates that
horizontal collaboration for purposes of R&D normally is outside the scope of
antitrust concerns as defined in Articles 85 and 86 of the EEC Treaty. The
commission has consistently taken a favorable position on R&D agreements unless the large entities involved imply serious anticompetitive consequences.

In 1984, the European Commission adopted Regulation No. 418/85 (Reg.
418) expanding the favorable antitrust treatment of R&D. It provides blanket
exceptions for horizontal R&D arrangements, including commercialization—

which the commission views as "the natural consequence of joint R&D—up to the point of distribution and sales, for firms whose total market share does not exceed 20 percent."[42] In addition, under Article 85(3) the EEC Commission is authorized to grant exemptions for cooperative efforts that do not fall within the block exemption or safe harbor. Such exemptions may be granted when a horizontal agreement contributes to economic or technological progress in the research, production, or distribution of goods, and when procompetitive features outweigh anticompetitive aspects.

PROPOSED MODIFICATIONS TO U.S. ANTITRUST LAW

To insure that antitrust law is responsive to the needs of innovating firms and does not inhibit U.S. firms from competing effectively in global markets experiencing rapid technological change, we believe the following changes are in order.

First, the rule of reason should be clarified to take specific account of the appropriability regime, the pace of technological change, the diversity of sources of new technology, the need to access complementary assets and technologies, and the need to have cheek-by-jowl cooperation to manage the innovation process simultaneously rather than serially.

Second, a safe harbor defined according to market power should be expressly adopted that would shield from antitrust liability interfirm agreements that involve less than 20 to 25 percent of the relevant market.

Third, market definition should be tailored to the context of innovation, as described in Chapter 1, and should focus primarily on the market for know-how; specific product markets become relevant only when commercialization is included within the scope of the cooperative agreement. Even then, the extent of appropriability should be factored in when analyzing product market issues. The geographic market should be presumed to be worldwide, with the burden on the challenger to demonstrate otherwise.

Fourth, antitrust law should not bias the selection of interfirm organizational forms; at a minimum, integration by contract or alliance should be treated no less favorably than full mergers.

Fifth, the NCRA should be amended to include joint commercialization efforts to exploit innovation.

Sixth, an administrative procedure should be created, involving both the Justice and Commerce Departments, to allow evaluation and possible certification of cooperative arrangements among firms with higher market shares, when dynamic efficiency gains are likely and rivalry robust. We favor providing the opportunity for firms to either simply register and receive relief from treble damages as with the NCRA, or to apply for a certificate of exemption from the Justice and Commerce Departments that would provide even more protection. However, the quid pro quo would be greater disclosure and scrutiny of business plans. The firms themselves would choose which path to take.

Seventh, private antitrust suits challenging cooperative innovation arrangements should be limited to equitable relief, and attorneys' fees should be awarded to the prevailing party.

The first four of these proposals could be accomplished by courts interpreting the rule of reason and the National Cooperative Research Act. We hope courts will not hesitate to employ the tools of evolutionary, common law interpretation and development to achieve these changes. However, to achieve the complete package of substantive and procedural changes most quickly, and thus assure certainty and predictability, legislation is the best overall solution. At a University of California Berkeley Conference on "Antitrust, Innovation and Competitiveness" in October 1988, we distributed a draft of legislation that combined a "registration" and "certification" approach for cooperative commercialization ventures. (See Appendix following this chapter.) Shortly thereafter, Congressman Edwards (H.R. 1025) and Congressman Fish (H.R. 2264) advanced a "registration" approach to cooperative commercialization efforts and Congressmen Boucher and Campbell (H.R. 1024) proposed a "certification" approach. After three hearings on these bills, Chairman Jack Brooks of the House Judiciary Committee introduced and the Judiciary Committee passed the National Cooperative Production Amendments of 1990 (H.R. 4611). H.R. 4611 would amend the National Cooperative Research Act to extend its registration approach to joint production ventures.[43] At the same time, Attorney General Richard Thornburgh and Commerce Secretary Robert Mosbacher announced the Bush Administration's support of a registration approach for production joint ventures.[44]

As mentioned above, we support *both* a registration and certification approach. We do not see them as alternatives. Rather, we believe they should be combined into a single, two-track approach. Firms could choose the level and then the form of protection most appropriate for their joint activity. Greater disclosure could buy greater protection.

The case for these changes rests on three fundamental pillars. The first is that the innovation process is terribly important to economic growth and development because it yields social returns in excess of private returns, and because innovation is a powerful spur to competition. Hence, if antitrust policy is going to err, it ought to do so by facilitating innovation rather than inhibiting it. This principle is well-understood in Europe and Japan.

Second, economic theory tells us that if certain organizational arrangements are exposed to governmentally imposed costs while others are not, firms will substitute away from the burdened forms (in this context, interfirm agreements) in favor of the unburdened forms (in this context, hierarchy), even when the former are potentially economically superior. According to Aoki (1989), the slowdown in total factor productivity in the United States can be attributed in large part to a mismatch between organizational form and the requirements of new technology; in particular, he is concerned that hierarchical solutions are overused, at least in the United States. As we have explained at some length above, we are concerned that present antitrust laws do not give full recognition to the interorganizational requirements of the innovation process; failure to do so is damaging when innovation must proceed according to the simultaneous model.

Third, cartelization of industries experiencing rapid technological change, and which are open to international trade and investment, is very difficult. So long as these industries remain open and innovative, antitrust policy should err on the side of permitting rather than restricting interfirm contracts.

Beneficial cooperation will eventually expand if antitrust laws are revised along the lines we propose. The response may not be immediate, particularly with respect to consortia, since the experience base in U.S. industry in this area is thin because of our antitrust history, and because U.S. firms, at least in the postwar period, have been large relative to their foreign competitors. Accordingly, the need to cooperate has not been as powerful in the past as it is now. However, once organizational learning accumulates, we expect consortia to begin to flourish even in the absence of government funding. We also expect the reinforcement of bilateral alliances, already common in U.S. industry. In the following sections we briefly discuss the kinds of activities that might take place.

Cooperative Manufacturing and Commercialization

In a number of circumstances, cooperative activity beyond early stages will benefit innovating firms. As discussed, sometimes this is true because of scale, risk, and appropriability considerations. Sometimes it is true because prohibition of cooperative commercialization imposes a significant technology transfer problem, for instance, from the research joint venture (if there is one) back to the funding companies. In most cases firms will not wish to cooperate all the way from research through to commercialization. But in some instances they will, or they will wish to cooperate simply on a downstream production venture. When cartelization of the industry is not a threat, we see no reasons for antitrust restraints.

The now defunct U.S. Memories, Inc. consortium wanted to invest $500 million to $1 billion to develop and manufacture for its members and for the market advanced dynamic random access memories (DRAMs). With fabrication facilities costing hundreds of millions, acting alone is beyond the financial resources of many companies in this industry who might otherwise wish to have some control over their DRAM supply. This proposed consortium had to contend with a number of difficulties, including threats of third party litigation (Jorde and Teece, 1989b). While antitrust was not the main reason for the failure of this enterprise, the antitrust environment did nothing to help it succeed. A certification procedure would have provided important certainty to this venture and others like it. A registration procedure would provide less certainty, but still would be a significant advance over current antitrust law.

Similarly, in the area of superconductors, it is likely that the real challenges will come not in developing superconductors, but in their commercialization. Applying superconductors in systems like railroads, computers, and electricity distribution will require great amounts of time, resources, and capital—probably greater than any single business can muster internally. Accordingly, a public policy stance that treats only early stage activity as potentially requiring cooperation is misguided and will thwart both early and later stage activities. Most firms will not have much incentive to engage in early stage, joint development if later stage, stand-alone commercialization appears too expensive to accomplish profitably.

Cooperative Innovation Designed to Achieve Catch-Up

Cooperative activities in Japan and Europe have frequently been motivated by a desire to catch up with the world's technological frontier, which in the postwar years was usually the technology of U.S. firms. However, U.S. firms are increasingly slipping behind the frontier. For instance, U.S. firms are now behind in areas like ceramics and robotics, and in products like VCRs, facsimiles, and high definition televisions (HDTV). Just as foreign firms have found cooperative ventures useful for catch-up in the past, U.S. firms could utilize cooperation for this purpose. For example, U.S.-based firms, acting together and with foreign firms, may still have a slender chance of competing in the market for HDTV and related products expected to evolve in the 1990s. In the absence of cooperative interfirm agreements, we doubt that development of HDTV systems is possible in the United States. If America's potential "reentrants" to the consumer electronics business combine to attempt reentry, they cannot be sure of avoiding serious antitrust problems involving treble damages, particularly if they are successful.

At minimum, the legislative changes proposed would facilitate unfettered information exchange and strategic coordination with respect to reentry strategies. If such efforts facilitated profitable reentry into high technology businesses when reentering would otherwise not occur, or would occur in a more limited and unprofitable way, we do not see why antitrust concerns ought to interfere.

Cooperation in Response to Foreign Industrial and Technology Policy

In high technology industries, both European and East Asian nations have active industrial and technology policies that significantly impact market outcomes, both in their own countries and abroad. Airbus is a case in point. The dominant U.S. attitude is one of laissez-faire, and many economists are of the view that the United States should send a letter of thanks to foreign governments who subsidize exports to the United States. This view is insensitive to the dynamics of technological change, to the importance of cumulative learning, and to reentry costs.

Some U.S. policy makers, however, favor retaliation against foreign countries that have active industrial policies. We support a modification of U.S. antitrust laws which in some circumstances would permit a competitive response by U.S. industry acting collectively. The proposals we advance to encourage greater cooperation among U.S. firms do not require government expenditures nor do they involve the government "picking winners." Instead they would soften the tensions emerging in the United States between technology and antitrust and trade policies.

CONCLUSION

The past two decades has wrought significant changes in the business environment. Markets have become globalized, sources of new technology are increasingly pluralistic, and "simultaneous" systems of innovation have substituted linear, hierarchical ones. Moreover, the ability of foreign firms to utilize technology developed in the United States has increased markedly. Imitation is easier, not harder, in spite of recent court decisions which have strengthened patents.

Accordingly, innovative firms confront significant challenges in capturing value from new technology. Success in research and development does not automatically translate into financial success, even if the technology developed meets a significant market need. To succeed financially, innovative firms must quickly position themselves advantageously in the appropriate complementary assets and technologies. If they are not already integrated, the best solution often involves bilateral and multilateral cooperative agreements.[45]

U.S. antitrust policy, like so much of our economic policy, has been preoccupied with static rather than intertemporal concerns. Despite important recent developments, it is informed by naive theories of the innovation process and, in particular, is insensitive to the organizational needs of innovation. U.S. antitrust scholars still harbor suspicion of cooperative agreements among competitors and do not appreciate the benefits. This suspicion fuels uncertainty about how the courts would view interfirm arrangements to promote technological progress and competition.

The policy changes we advance are certainly no panacea for the severe problems the U.S. high technology industry is experiencing currently. But in bringing American antitrust policy closer to Europe and Japan, we will at least purge the influence of dogma that no longer deserves a place in U.S. industrial policy. In time, reduced antitrust exposure will help clear the way for beneficial cooperation, thereby reducing incentives for mergers and acquisitions.

The centennial decade of the Sherman Act would be a good occasion to set things right. The economics profession, which in the past has had a significant impact on the law of vertical restraints, can provide the intellectual leadership necessary to propel adjustments in the horizontal area, thereby helping to align U.S. policies with the technological and competitive realities of today's global economy.

NOTES

Portions of this chapter have been developed and published in Jorde and Teece, "Innovation, Cooperation and Antitrust: Balancing Competition and Cooperation," *High Technology Law Journal* 4:1 (1989); Jorde and Teece, "Acceptable Cooperation Among Competitors in the Face of Growing International Competition," *Antitrust Law Journal* 58:2 (Summer) (1989); and Jorde and Teece, "Innovation and Cooperation: Implications for Competition and Antitrust," *Journal of Economic Perspectives*, 4:3 (1990). This chapter also draws heavily on Teece (1986).

We are extremely grateful for financial support from the Alfred P. Sloan Foundation, the Smith-Richardson Foundation, the Pew Foundation, and the Sasakawa Peace Foundation. We wish to thank Joseph Stiglitz, Carl Shapiro, and Tim Taylor for valuable substantive and editorial comments. Bill Baxter, Oliver Williamson, and Dick Nelson made helpful comments on earlier drafts and oral presentations. We implicate none of the above in our conclusions.

1. For instance, cooperative R&D and related activities have been important to the success of the West German machine tool industry. The industry formed a strong association that has a research and teaching institute at Aachen. The West German industry has been described as "groups of clubs" (Collis, 1988, p. 95) because of the nature of the cooperation displayed. The Italian machine tool industry around Modena is similarly organized, as is the Italian textile industry and the Danish furniture industry. A review of examples of cooperative activity abroad is part of the authors' ongoing research.

2. There is no necessary conflict between promoting cooperation and competition, if the cooperation improves efficiency or advances innovation. As Schumpeter (1942, p. 85) pointed out, compared to competition among firms with similar products and technologies, the competition that counts "comes from the new commodity, the new technology, the new source of supply. . . . This kind of competition is as much more effective than the other as bombardment is in comparison with forcing a door, and so much more important that it becomes a matter of comparative indifference whether competition in the ordinary sense functions more or less promptly."

3. Recently, the House Judiciary Committee approved the "National Cooperative Production Amendments of 1990" (H.R. 4611), a bill that incorporates many of the changes we suggest in this article and which we have been advocating since 1988. We discuss the provisions of H.R. 4611 and additional antitrust changes that we believe would advance innovation and U.S. competitiveness.

4. Dosi (1988) provides an excellent review of the innovation literature.

5. This argument is presented at greater length in Teece (1989a).

6. This process also has been termed "cyclic" (Gomory, 1987, p. 72). The popular press has been begun to recognize and discuss the simultaneous nature of innovation and effective commercialization. See "A Smarter Way to Manufacture," *Business Week* (April 30, 1990), 110–117 (discussing "concurrent engineering").

7. Moreover, the linkage from science to innovation is not solely or even preponderantly at the beginning of typical innovations, but rather extends all through the process. "Science can be visualized as lying alongside development processes, to be used when needed" (Kline and Rosenberg, 1986). Design is often at the center of the innovation process. Research is often spawned by the problems associated with trying to get the design right. Indeed, important technological breakthroughs can often proceed even when the underlying science is not understood.

8. For a more complete statement of our own views on this, see Teece (1977; 1989b).

9. For a review of the characteristics of know-how, see Winter (1987) and Teece (1989b).

10. A related set of vertical relationships involving innovation has been remarked on by Rosenberg (1972, pp. 98–102) in his treatise on technology and American economic growth. The machine tool industry in the 19th century played a unique role both in the initial solution of technical problems in user industries, such as textiles, and as the disseminator of these techniques to other industries, such as railroad locomotive manufacture. Rosenberg's description suggests that the users played a role in the development of new equipment. He notes that before 1820 in the United States, one could not identify a distinct set of firms that were specialists in the design and manufacture of machinery. Machines were either produced by users or by firms engaged in the production of metal or wooden products. Machinery-producing firms were thus first observed as adjuncts to textile factories. However, once established, these firms played an important role as the transmission center in the diffusion of new technology.

11. Nalebuff and Stiglitz (1983) argue that the gains from competition may more than offset the losses from duplication. Also, Sah and Stiglitz (1989) show that in a model with ex post Betrand competition where there is knowledge of which research projects others are undertaking, the number and range of research projects undertaken will be a constrained Pareto optimum.

12. See Levin, Klevorick, Nelson, and Winter (1987). These researchers surveyed R&D managers in various industries. The survey shows that, on a seven-point scale (1 = not at all effective, 7 = very effective) for eighteen industry categories with ten or more respondents, managers in only chemical (specifically drugs, plastic materials, inorganic chemicals, and organic chemicals) and petroleum refining rated process patents effectiveness higher than 4 on the scale, and only these same chemical indus-

tries and steel mills rated product patents higher than 5. These findings make very clear that managers have little confidence that patents suffice as mechanisms to protect intellectual property from free riders. The results also show that other methods of appropriation such as first mover advantages (lead time and learning curve advantages), secrecy, and investment in sales or service support were more effective.

13. There has been almost no treatment in the economic literature of the concept of *complementary assets*. It does not map easily into the familiar concept of indivisibilities, which is perhaps the closest analogue. For a more complete treatment, see Teece (1986).

14. For a detailed treatment of the impact of U.S. antitrust law on cooperation among competitors, see Jorde and Teece (1989a).

15. See, e.g., Continental T.V. Inc. v. GTE Sylvania Inc., 433 U.S. 36 (1977); Broadcast Music Inc. v. CBS, 441 U.S. 1 (1979); NCAA v. Board of Regents of Univ. of Olka., 468 U.S. 85 (1984); Northwest Wholesale Stationers Inc. v. Pacific Stationery and Printing Co., 472 U.S. 284 (1985); FTC v. Indiana Federation of Dentists, 476 U.S. 447 (1986).

16. See, e.g., Assam Drug Co. v. Miller Brewing Co., 798 F.2d 311, 315 (8th Cir. 1986) ("The vertical nonprice restraint at issue in this case is plainly subject to evaluation under the rule of reason (citing Continental T.V. Inc. v. GTE Sylvania Inc., 433 U.S. 36 (1977). The rule of reason, however, is a vacuous standard and as such it provides little concrete direction for evaluating the competitive effects of challenged restraint."); Graphic Prods. Distribs. v. Itek Corp., 717 F.2d 1560, 1568 n.10 (11th Cir. 1983) ("Not called upon to apply the rule of reason to the facts at hand, the [*Sylvania*] Court merely recited the classical articulation of the rule by Justice Brandeis in Chicago Bd. of Trade v. United States, 246 U.S. 231 (1918). The exceedingly general nature of these factors, and the absence of an analytical framework for applying the rule of reason, has been discussed by commentators of every persuasion (references omitted)"); Valley Liquors Inc. v. Renfield Importers Ltd., 678 F.2d 742, 745 (7th Cir. 1982) ("The plaintiff in a restricted distribution case must show that the restriction he is complaining of was unreasonable because, weighing effects on both intrabrand and interbrand competition, it made consumers worse off. Admittedly, this test of illegality is easier to state than to apply").

Numerous commentators have reached the same conclusion. See, e.g., Zelek, Stern, and Dunfee (1980, p. 893): "[N]either *Sylvania* nor previous decisions offer much practical guidance to lawyers who must advise clients or to judges who must decide cases under the rule of reason, leaving the question of what analytical methods are appropriate largely unresolved." Sullivan (1987, pp. 835, 843): In Broadcast Music, "the majority give little guidance for balancing efficiency and harm once the record is expanded." Arthur (1986, p. 263). Clark (1985, pp. 1125, 1131): "In practice . . . the Rule of Reason has provided little coherency or guidance." Easterbrook (1984, pp. 1, 10): simplicity of per se rule has been undercut by requirement of showing of absence of procompetitive benefits to quality for per se condemnation. Brodley (1982, p. 1523): Under the rule of reason, "the ultimate question remains of such broad scope and generality that little predictive guidance is possible. The ultimate legal result continues to turn on judicial characterization of a complex factual transaction, a situation that leads to uncertainty and costly proceedings." Ginsburg (1979, pp. 635, 674): "the published sources of guidance to business people and their lawyers planning joint R&D ventures provide little basis upon which to plan with confidence that no adverse antitrust consequence will ensue."

17. To date, the Supreme Court has neither endorsed nor foreclosed a market power-based safe harbor approach. See *In Re* Arbitration Between First Texas Savings Ass'n and Financial Exchange, Inc., 55 Antitrust and Trade Reg. Rep. (BNA) at 340 (Aug.

25, 1988). The courts of appeals have not waited for the Supreme Court. The move toward a market power-based safe harbor can be seen most clearly in the cases involving vertical relationships, where the lack of substantial market power has been used to screen out numerous challenges to vertical restraints. In the vertical cases, the courts appear to be converging on a safe harbor definition that protects firms possessing less than a 20 to 25 percent market share in a relevant market. See, e.g., Assam Drug Co. v. Miller Brewing Co., 798 F.2d 311, 318 n.18 (8th Cir. 1986); O.S.C. Corp. v. Apple Computer Inc., 601 F. Supp. 1274, 1291, n.8 (C.D. Cal. 1985); Donald B. Rice Tire Co. v. Michelin Tire Corp., 483 F. Supp. 750, 761 (D.Md. 1980), *aff'd*, 638 F.2d 15 (4th Cir. 1980), *cert. denied*, 454 U.S. 864 (1981). See also Ryco Mfg. Co. v. Elden Servs., 823 F.2d 1215, 1231–32 and n.14 (8th Cir. 1987), *cert. denied*, 108 S. Ct. 751 (1988); Hind v. Central Trans. Inc., 779 F.2d 8, 11 (6th Cir. 1985); Graphic Prods. Distribs. v. Itek Corp., 717 F.2d 1560, 1568 n.10 (11th Cir. 1983).

More recently, courts have begun to apply a market power-based screen in horizontal cases, holding that under rule of reason analysis, plaintiffs must first establish that cooperating defendants possess substantial market power in a relevant market. See, e.g., Polk Bros. Inc. v. Forest City Enters. Inc., 776 F.2d 185 (7th Cir. 1985); General Leaseways Inc. v. National Truck Leasing Ass'n, 744 F.2d 588, 596 (7th Cir. 1984); Rothery Storage and Van Co. v. Atlas Van Lines, Inc., 792 F.2d 210, 217 (D.C. 1986); *In Re* Arbitration Between First Texas Savings Ass'n and Financial Interchange Inc., 55 Antitrust and Trade Reg. Rep. (BNA) at 340, 350 (Aug. 25, 1988). However, the courts have not yet clarified the boundaries of a safe harbor for horizontal cases.

18. 49 Fed. Reg. 26,823 (June 29, 1984), reprinted in 4 Trade Reg. Rep. (CCH) ¶ 13,103.
19. 15 U.S.C. § 15c.
20. 15 U.S.C. § 15.
21. 15 U.S.C. § 4300 et seq.
22. For a general discussion of the legislative history of the NCRA, see Wright (1986: 133, 137–144). See also, H.R. Rep. No. 1044, 98th Cong., 2d Sess. 14, reprinted in *U.S. Code Cong. and Admin. News*, 3131, 3139 ("a pre-eminent purpose of this bill is to clarify the antitrust analysis of joint R&D ventures.").
23. 15 U.S.C. § 4302.
24. See Wright (1986), at 178.
25. 15 U.S.C. § 4305(a)–(b).
26. 15 U.S.C. § 4303(a). The Act allows prevailing defendants to recover attorney's fees only "if the claim, or the claimant's conduct during the litigation of the claim, was frivolous, unreasonable, without foundation, or in bad faith." 15 U.S.C. § 4304(a)(2).
27. The NCRA's substantive protections extend only to "joint research and development ventures," defined as "any group of activities" undertaken for the purpose of theoretical analysis, experimentation, development or testing of engineering techniques, conversion of scientific or technical theories into practical applications, or collection or exchange of research information. 15 U.S.C. § 4301(a)(6).
28. 15 U.S.C. § 4302. The legislative history of the NCRA contains statements both that ancillary restraints are not covered, see 130 *Congressional Record H10566* (Oct. 1, 1984) (statement of Rep. Rodino), and that they should be, see *S. Rep. No. 427*, 98th Cong. 2d Sess. 16, reprinted in 1984 *U.S. Code Cong. and Adm. News*, 3105, 3112–13 ("Marketing this intellectual property may be the ultimate goal and a key financial aspect of a joint R&D program and is rightfully viewed as an integral part of it.") See Wright (1986) at 161, 180–81. The NCRA expressly excludes from coverage (1) exchanges of information about costs, sales, profitability, prices, marketing or distribution that are "not reasonably required to conduct the research and develop-

ment," 15 U.S.C. § 4301(b)(1); (2) agreements regarding production or marketing of any product, process or service other than "proprietary information" developed through the venture, 15 U.S.C. § 4301(b)(1); and (3) agreements (if not "reasonably required to prevent misappropriation of proprietary information") restricting or requiring participation in other R&D in the sale of developments not developed through the venture. 15 U.S.C. § 4301(b)(3).

29. See Grossman and Shapiro (1986) at 316 ("Although Congress undoubtedly has diminished the antitrust risks facing potential ventures, considerable uncertainties remain, not the least of which concerns the interpretation of the new law's broad rule-of-reason approach").

30. See note 26, *supra.*

31. Businesses seem to have recognized the limited nature of the steps taken by the NCRA. Not surprisingly, only 111 separate cooperative ventures registered under the NCRA between 1984 and June 1988. Our review of these filings indicates that they are very modest endeavors that are aimed at solving industry problems and are not of great competitive moment.

32. Indeed, the literal Japanese translation of "R&D" — *Kenkyu Kaihatsu* — implicitly includes commercialization; there is no semantic distinction between the concepts of R&D and commercialization.

33. The basic administrative policy outlining the standards by which such joint innovation efforts are to be scrutinized is contained in Fair Trade Commission (Japan) (1984, pp. 37–39) [hereinafter FTC (Japan), Research and Development Activities]. The report states that the evaluation of the anticompetitive effect of joint R&D at the product market stage will depend significantly "on the competition and market shares among the participants and the market structure of the industry to which the participants belong. . . . In cases where the market shares of the participants are small . . . the effects will be small." Although "small" is not defined in the report, Japan's Merger Guidelines state that the FTC is not likely to closely examine cases in which the combined market share of the merging parties is less than 25 percent. See Iyori and Yesugi (1983, pp. 86–88). Our discussions with MITI and FTC officials confirm that the horizontal merger safe harbors would be equally applicable to cooperative contractual arrangements.

34. FTC (Japan), Research and Development Activities, *supra* note 33.

35. *Ibid.*

36. *Ibid.*

37. Kiban Gijutsu Kenkyu Enkatsuka No Law, No. 65 of 1985 (Japan).

38. Kokogyo Gijutsu Kenkyu Kumiai No Law, No. 81 of 1961 (Japan).

39. See *supra*, note 33.

40. A recent case shows the difficulty of private suits. A group of consumers sued oil refining companies for damages caused by the formation of an oil cartel that had been successfully sued by the FTC for price-fixing. See Japan v. Itemitsu Kosan Co. Ltd., 38 Case 1287 (Sup. Ct. 2d P.B., Feb. 24, 1984). The Supreme Court rejected the private claim on the grounds that there was no proof that lower prices would have prevailed in the absence of the cartel. See also Kai v. Cosmo Oil Co. Ltd., 1239 Hanrei Jiho 3 (Sup. Ct. 1st P.B., July 2, 1987).

41. FTC (Japan), Research and Development Activities, *supra* note 33, at 25. Questionnaires were sent to 484 manufacturing corporations in the fields of electronics, telecommunications, automobiles, chemicals, ceramics, steel, and nonferrous metals, whose stocks were listed in Tokyo and Osaka Stock Exchanges. Two-hundred forty-two corporations provided data on their activities. These represent 1.9 percent of the total manufacturing industry that engage in R&D activities in terms of the number of

corporations and 16.7 percent in terms of sales. *Ibid.* at 3, 4. As to the nature of the joint R&D projects, 54.3 percent of the total cases were developmental research. Basic and applied research were 13.6 and 32.1 percent respectively. In the case of large corporations with capital of more than 10 billion yen, the total basic and application research amounted to 52.1 percent.

42. Regulation No. 418/85 of 19 December 1984 on the application of Art. 85(3) of the Treaty to categories of research and development agreements, *O.J. Eur. Comm.* (No. L 53) 5 (1985), entered into force March 1, 1985, and applicable until December 31, 1997. The statutory framework of Reg. 418 is complex and can best be illustrated by highlighting its most important features. It applies to three categories of agreements involving R&D: (1) joint research and development of products or processes and joint exploitation of the results of that R&D; (2) joint exploitation of the results of R&D product or processes pursuant to a prior agreement between the same parties; and (3) joint research and development of products without joint exploitation should the agreement fall within the purview of Art. 85(1). Under Reg. 418, joint exploitation is interpreted to mean joint manufacturing and licensing to third parties. Joint distribution and sales, however, are not covered and require individual exemptions pursuant to Art. 85(3).

43. Professor Jorde testified on July 26, 1989, in favor of both a registration and certification approach. See Jorde and Teece (1989c). Legislation advancing a registration approach for production joint ventures has also been introduced in the Senate by Senators Patrick Leahy (D-VT) and Strom Thurmond (R-SC) (S.1006). Three aspects of H.R. 4611 bear noting. First, relevant market definition under rule of reason analysis would specifically consider the worldwide capacity of suppliers. Second, foreign participation in a production joint venture would be limited to 30 percent of the voting securities or equity interests, and all production facilities would have to be located in the United States or its territories. Third, apparently production joint ventures would not be limited to efforts designed to commercialize joint R&D, nor need they be related to innovation.

44. See Department of Justice release, "Thornburgh Mosbacher Send Revision Legislation to Congress" (May 7, 1990) (supporting and detailing "legislation designed to facilitate joint production ventures"), reported at *Antitrust and Trade Regulation Report* 58, no. 1465 (May 10, 1990), p. 701.

45. As Richard Nelson (1990) notes, a wide variety of new kinds of organizational arrangements is emerging to support innovation. He predicts, and we concur, that some will succeed, and some will not. Our concern is that because the requirements of innovation are not well understood in mainstream economics and in contemporary antitrust analysis, there is significant danger that the performance of U.S. firms will be impaired by outdated antitrust law.

REFERENCES

Aoki, M. 1989. "Global Competition, Firm Organization, and Total Factor Productivity: A Comparative Micro Perspective." Paper presented at the International Seminar on the Contributions of Science and Technology to Economic Growth, OECD, Paris (June).

Arrow, Kenneth J. 1962. "Economic Welfare and the Allocation of Resources for Invention." In National Bureau of Economic Research, ed. *The Rate and Direction of Inventive Activity*. Princeton: Princeton University Press, pp. 609–625.

Arthur, Thomas C. 1986. "Farewell to the Sea of Doubt: Jettisoning the Constitutional Sherman Act." *California Law Review* 74:263–376.

Brodley, Joseph F. 1982. "Joint Ventures and Antitrust Policy." *Harvard Law Review* 95: 1523–1590.

Buzzell, Robert D., and Paul Ferris. 1977. "Marketing Costs in Consumer Goods Industries." In Hans Thorelli, ed. *Strategy + Structure = Performance.* Bloomington: Indiana University Press.

Chandler, Alfred D. 1977. *The Visible Hand: The Managerial Revolution in American Business.* Cambridge: Harvard University Press.

Clark, Nolan Ezra. 1985. "Antitrust Comes Full Circle: The Return to the Cartelization Standard." *Vand. Law Review* 38:1125–1197.

Collis, David. 1988. "The Machine Tool Industry and Industrial Policy, 1955–1982." In A. Michael Spence and Heather A. Hazard, eds. *International Competitiveness.* Cambridge, MA: Ballinger.

Davis, Dwight B. 1985. "R&D Consortia: Pooling Industries' Resources." *High Technology* Vol 5 no. 10 (October):42–47.

Dertouzos, Michael L., Richard K. Lester, and Robert M. Solow. 1989. *Made in America: Regaining the Productive Edge.* Cambridge: MIT Press.

Dosi, Giovanni. 1988. "Sources, Procedures, and Microeconomic Effects of Innovation." *Journal of Economic Literature* 26 (September):1120–1171.

Easterbrook, Judge Frank. 1984. "The Limits of Antitrust." *Texas Law Review* 63:1–40.

Fair Trade Commission (Japan). 1984. *Research and Development Activities in Private Enterprises and Problems They Pose in the Competition Policy (Minkan kigyo ni okeru kenkyu kaihatsu katsudo no jttai to kyoso seidaku jo no kaidai).*

Ginsburg, Douglas H. 1979. "Antitrust, Uncertainty, and Technological Innovation." *Antitrust Bulletin* 24:635–686.

Gomory, Ralph E. 1987. "Dominant Science Does Not Mean Dominant Product." *Research and Development* 29 (November):72–.

Grossman, Gene M., and Carl Shapiro. 1986. "Research Joint Ventures: An Antitrust Analysis." *Journal of Law and Economics* 2:315–337.

Imai, Ken-chi, and Yasunori Baba. 1989. "Systemic Innovation and Cross Border Networks." Paper presented at the International Seminar on the Contributions of Science and Technology to Economic Growth, OECD, Paris (June).

Iyori, Hiroshi and Akinori Uesugi. 1983. *The Antimonopoly Laws of Japan.* New York: Federal Legal Publications.

Jorde, Thomas M., and David J. Teece. 1989a. "Innovation, Cooperation, and Antitrust: Balancing Competition and Cooperation." *High Technology Law Journal* 4 (Spring):1–112.

Jorde, Thomas M., and David J. Teece. 1989b. "To Keep U.S. in the Chips, Modify the Antitrust Laws." *Los Angeles Times*, 24 July.

Jorde, Thomas M., and David J. Teece. 1989c. "Legislative Proposals to Modify the U.S. Antitrust Laws to Facilitate Cooperative Arrangements to Commercialize Innovation." *Hearings Before the Subcommittee on Economics and Commercial Law*, Committee on the Judiciary, U.S. House of Representatives (July 26).

Kline, Stephen J., and Nathan Rosenberg. 1986. "An Overview of Innovation." In Nathan Rosenberg and Ralph Landau, eds. *The Positive Sum Strategy.* Washington, D.C.: National Academy Press 275–285.

Koopmans, Tjalling. 1957. *Three Essays in the State of Economic Science*, part 2. New York: Kelley Press.

Levin, Richard C., Alvin K. Klevorick, Richard R. Nelson, and Sidney G. Winter. 1987. "Appropriating the Returns from Industrial Research and Development." *Brookings Papers on Economic Activity* 3:783–831.

Lieberman, Marvin B., and David B. Montgomery. 1988. "First- Mover Advantages." *Strategic Management Journal* 9:41–58.

Mansfield, E., A. Romeo, M. Schwartz, D. Teece, S. Wagner, and P. Brach. 1982. *Technology Transfer, Productivity, and Economic Policy*. New York: W. W. Norton.

Merges, Robert P., and Richard R. Nelson. 1990. "On the Complex Economics of Patent Scope." *Columbia Law Review* 90:839–916.

Nalebuff, Barry, and Joseph Stiglitz. 1983. "Information, Competition and Markets." *American Economic Review* 72 (May):278–284.

Ordover, J., and R. Willig. 1985. "Antitrust for High Technology Industries: Assessing Research Joint Ventures and Mergers." *Journal of Law and Economics* 28 (May): 311–333.

Rosenberg, Nathan. 1972. *Technology and American Economic Growth*. Armonk, NY: M. E. Sharpe.

Sah, Raja, and Joseph Stiglitz. 1989. "Technological Learning, Social Learning and Technological Change." In S. Chakravarty, ed. *The Balance between Industry and Agriculture in Economic Development*. London: Macmillan Press/International Economic Association, pp. 285–298.

Schumpeter, Joseph A. 1942. *Capitalism, Socialism and Democracy*. New York: Harper Brothers.

Stiglitz, Joseph E. 1987. "Technological Change, Sunk Costs, and Competition." *Brookings Papers on Economic Activity* 3.

Sullivan, Lawrence A. 1987. "The Viability of the Current Law on Horizontal Restraints." *California Law Review* 75:835–891.

Teece, David J. 1977. "Technology Transfer by Multinational Firms: The Resource Cost of Transferring Technological Know-how." *The Economic Journal* 87 (June):242–261.

Teece, David J. 1980. "Economies of Scope and the Scope of the Enterprise." *Journal of Economic Behavior and Organization* 1:223–247.

Teece, David J. 1982. "Towards an Economic Theory of the Multiproduct Firm." *Journal of Economic Behavior and Organization* 3:39–63.

Teece, David J. 1986. "Profiting from Technological Innovation." *Research Policy* (December): 15:285–305.

Teece, David J. 1989a. "Inter–organizational Requirements of the Innovation Process." *Managerial and Decision Economics* 10:135–42.

Teece, David J. 1989b. "The Strategic Management of Intellectual Property." Unpublished manuscript. Center for Research in Management, University of California at Berkeley.

Teece, David J. 1989c. "Innovation and the Organization of Industry." Unpublished working paper. Center for Research in Management, University of California at Berkeley.

Tirole, Jean. 1988. *The Theory of Industrial Organization*. Cambridge: MIT Press.

U.S. Department of Justice, Antitrust Division. 1984. *U.S. Department of Justice Merger Guidelines*, June 14. Washington, D.C.

von Hippel, Eric. 1988. *The Sources of Innovation*. New York: Oxford University Press.

Williamson, Oliver E. 1985. *The Economic Institution of Capitalism: Firms, Markets, Relational Contracting*. New York: Free Press.

Winter, Sidney J. 1987. "Knowledge and Competence as Strategic Assets." In D. J. Teece, ed. *The Competitive Challenge*. Cambridge, MA: Ballinger.

Wright, Christopher O. B. 1986. "The National Cooperative Research Act of 1984: A New Antitrust Regime for Joint Research and Development Ventures." *High Tech. Law Journal* 1:133–193.

Zelek, Eugene F., Louis W. Stern, and Thomas W. Dunfee. 1980. "A Rule of Reason Decision Model After *Sylvania*." *California Law Review* 68:813–47.

Appendix: National Cooperative Research and Commercialization Act (NCRCA)

Legislative Proposal by Professor Thomas M. Jorde and Professor David J. Teece, University of California at Berkeley

(As amended from National Cooperative Research Act (NCRA), 15 U.S.C. §§ 4301–4305 (Supp. 1986). Where possible, the NCRCA retains the language and structure of the NCRA.)

SECTION 4301. PURPOSES

(a) THE CONGRESS FINDS THAT—

(1) technological innovation and its profitable commercialization are critical components of the United States' ability to raise the living standards of Americans and to compete in world markets;

(2) cooperative arrangements among nonaffiliated firms in the private sector are often essential for successful technological innovation and commercialization;

(3) the antitrust laws tend to inhibit cooperative innovation arrangements because of uncertain legal standards and the threat of private treble damage litigation;

(4) cooperative innovation efforts present little or no threat to competition when cooperating firms lack substantial market power, or when cooperative activity takes place in industries experiencing rapid technological change;

(5) the uncertainty of substantive antitrust standards and the potential delays of antitrust litigation are especially troublesome in fast paced industries experiencing rapid technological change; and

(6) present antitrust law unwisely treats mergers more favorably than more flexible, less permanent contractual and strategic relationships.

(b) It is the purpose of this Act to promote innovation and profitable product commercialization, facilitate trade, and strengthen the competitiveness of United States based firms in world markets by clarifying the legal standards applicable to cooperative innovation arrangements and by establishing a procedure by which firms may seek approval for their cooperative innovation arrangements from the Department of Justice, in consulta-

A detailed explanation of the proposed legislation can be found in *High Technology Law Journal,* 4:1 (1989): 62–80.

tion with the Secretary of Commerce, and thereby obtain exemption from criminal anti-trust actions or civil antitrust damage actions.

SECTION 4301a. DEFINITIONS

(a) FOR THE PURPOSES OF THIS CHAPTER:

(1) The term "antitrust laws" has the meaning given it in subsection (a) of section 12 of this title, except that such term includes section 45 of this title to the extent that section 45 applies to unfair methods of competition.

(2) The term "DOJ" means Department of Justice and the term "FTC" means Federal Trade Commission.

(3) The term "Secretary" means the Secretary of Commerce.

(4) The term "person" has the meaning given it in subsection (a) of section 12 of this title.

(5) The term "State" has the meaning given it in section 15g(2) of this title.

(6) The term "cooperative innovation arrangement" means any group of activities, including attempting to make, making, or performing a contract, by two or more persons for the purpose of —

(A) theoretical analysis, experimentation, or systematic study of phenomena or observable facts,

(B) the development or testing of basic engineering techniques,

(C) the extension of investigative findings or theory of a scientific or technical nature into practical application for experimental and demonstration purposes, in-cluding the experimental production and testing of models, prototypes, equipment, materials, and processes,

(D) the collection, exchange, and analysis of research information,

(E) manufacturing, producing, marketing, distributing, or otherwise commercial-izing products, processes, or information developed jointly through activities (A)-(E) or by one or more of the persons in the arrangement, or

(F) any combination of the purposes specified in subparagraphs (A), (B), (C), (D), and (E),

and may include: the integration of existing facilities or the establishment and operation of new facilities for the conducting of cooperative work, the conducting of such venture on a protected and proprietary basis, and the prosecuting of applications for patents and the granting of licenses for the results of such venture.

(7) The term "market share" means the percentage of total market sales represented by a single market participant in a relevant market.

(8) The term "market power" means the ability to restrict output and/or increase prices above competitive levels in a relevant market.

(9) The term "Herfindahl–Hirschmann Index" (HHI) means the total of the squares of the market shares of all actual competitors in a relevant market.

(b) The DOJ or FTC, with the concurrence of the Secretary, may by regulation further define any term defined in subsection (a).

SECTION 4302. JUDICIAL STANDARDS TO BE APPLIED TO COOPERATIVE INNOVATION ARRANGEMENTS

(a) RULE OF REASON

Cooperative innovation arrangements remain subject to the antitrust laws. However, in any action under the antitrust laws, or under any State law similar to the antitrust laws, the conduct of any person in carrying out, or in making or performing a contract to carry out, all or any part of a cooperative innovation arrangement shall not be deemed illegal per se. Such conduct shall be judged on the basis of its reasonableness, determined as specified under subsections (b) through (e) of this section.

(b) PRIMA FACIE CASE

(1) In any action subject to subsection (a), the plaintiff shall have the burden of showing that the defendants have, or threaten to have as a result of the challenged conduct, substantial market power in one or more relevant market(s). Plaintiff may fulfill this burden by—

(A) demonstrating—

(i) that the Herfindahl–Hirschmann Index (HHI) of any relevant market (including within that market, as a single firm, the cooperative innovation arrangement) is, or imminently threatens to become, greater than 1800, and

(ii) that the formation of such arrangement increased, or imminently threatens to increase, the HHI of such market by more than 50; or

(B) demonstrating that the market shares of firms in a relevant market cannot be measured by reasonably obtainable data, and that there are only five or fewer firms (including the arrangement) currently participating in each relevant market that are capable, alone or cooperatively, of engaging in the type and scope of innovation and commercialization undertaken by the cooperative innovation arrangement in such market; and/or

(C) demonstrating that the conduct of the cooperative innovation arrangement has actually harmed competition and consumers by reducing output or increasing prices of products in any relevant market.

(2) In any action subject to subsection (a), if the plaintiff makes the showing required by paragraph (1), the defendants may introduce evidence that the plaintiff defined any relevant market in a manner inconsistent with subsection (c), and that such inconsistency resulted in an erroneous conclusion as to the applicable Herfindahl–Hirschmann Index, market shares, or number of firms in such market.

(c) MARKET DEFINITION

In any action subject to subsection (a)—

(1) relevant markets shall be defined in a manner that reflects commercial realities, and will often involve know-how markets and product markets,

(2) relevant markets shall be defined in a manner takes account of the actual and potential competitors, both foreign and domestic, who, either alone or cooperatively, are capable of timely engaging in similar innovation and commercialization efforts,

(3) relevant markets shall be drawn with sensitivity to product features and performance characteristics, in addition to price elasticities, and

(4) relevant markets involving innovation are presumed to be global, unless evidence demonstrates a more narrow market is appropriate.

(d) REBUTTAL; DEFENSES

(1) In any action subject to subsection (a), if the plaintiff makes the prima facie showing required by paragraph (b)(1), the defendant or defendants may introduce evidence—

(A) that the cooperative innovation arrangement will produce procompetitive benefits and efficiencies, and that any specifically challenged contractual provisions are justified because they are logically related to successful innovation and commercialization, and/or

(B) that the existence of potential competitors in any relevant market in which the cooperative innovation arrangement is shown to possess market power precludes potential anticompetitive effects that might otherwise be inferred from present market power.

(2) Evidence introduced under subparagraph (1)(A) of procompetitive benefits and efficiencies and their logical relationship to specific contractual restraints may include, but is not limited to, evidence—

(A) that the innovation sought by the arrangement will, if achieved, be inadequately protected under the patent, trade secret, or other intellectual property laws, and that contractual restraints, including the challenged conduct, are necessary in order to secure appropriability and prevent free-riding by rivals and opportunistic behavior by parties to the arrangement or by rivals,

(B) that the innovation sought by the arrangement is of such a character or magnitude that a cooperative arrangement will help achieve the economies of scale and scope necessary to mount a successful research and commercialization effort,

(C) that successful innovation sought by the arrangement will be aided by cooperative or integrated commercialization, including the challenged conduct,

(D) that the arrangement will compete in a market or markets that are characterized by rapid technological change, or will be so characterized by the arrangement or others like it, and/or

(E) that the innovation sought by the arrangement will compete with other technologies in a preparadigmatic stage of competition for particular products or processes.

(e) ULTIMATE BURDEN OF PROOF

(1) In any action subject to subsection (a), the plaintiff shall have the ultimate burden of proving that the challenged conduct is unreasonable. In attempting to fulfill this burden, such plaintiff may, without limitation upon other approaches—

(A) rebut any evidence introduced by the defendants under subsections (c) and (d); and/or

(B) introduce additional evidence of the defendants' market power in any relevant market, or of anticompetitive harms caused by the challenged conduct, and/or

(C) introduce evidence that profitable commercialization, or procompetitive benefits or efficiencies offered by the defendants under subsection (d) could be achieved—

(i) by an existing firm or viable combination of firms with substantially less market power than that exercised by the cooperative innovation arrangement in question in any relevant market, and/or

(ii) by the parties to the cooperative innovation arrangement in an obviously and substantially less restrictive manner, and/or

(D) introduce evidence that the anticompetitive harms caused by the cooperative innovation arrangement outweigh the procompetitive benefits and efficiencies generated.

SECTION 4303. ATTORNEY'S FEES

(a) AWARD OF FEES TO PREVAILING CLAIMANT OR DEFENDANT

Notwithstanding sections 15 and 26 of this title, in any claim under the antitrust laws, or any State law similar to such laws, subject to section 4302, the court shall, at the conclusion of the action, award to the substantially prevailing party the cost of suit attributable to such claim, including a reasonable attorney's fee, except as specified in subsection 4304(d).

(b) OFFSET OF AWARD

The award made under subsection (a) of this section may be offset in whole or in part by an award in favor of any other party for any part of the cost of suit, including a reasonable attorney's fee, attributable to conduct during the litigation by any prevailing party that the court finds to be frivolous, unreasonable, without foundation, or in bad faith.

SECTION 4304. APPROVAL OF COOPERATIVE INNOVATION ARRANGEMENTS

(a) WRITTEN APPLICATIONS; FILING

(1) Any party to a cooperative innovation arrangement, acting on such arrangement's behalf, may, not later than 90 days after entering into a written agreement to form such arrangement or not later than 90 days after [EFFECTIVE DATE OF BILL], whichever is later, file simultaneously with the DOJ and FTC a written application disclosing—
  (A) the identities of the parties to the arrangement,
  (B) the nature and objectives of the arrangement, including description of procompetitive benefits and efficiencies to be achieved by the arrangement,
  (C) the current market shares, in all relevant markets, of all parties to the arrangement,
  (D) the estimated or predicted market share, in all relevant markets, of the arrangement, and the basis for the estimate or prediction (including an estimate of the effect of potential competitors on current or future market shares),
  (E) the estimated concentration of all relevant markets, expressed in terms of the Herfindahl–Hirschmann Index; or, if market shares of participants in a relevant market cannot be measured by reasonably obtainable data, then in terms of the number of firms (including the arrangement) currently participating in each relevant market that are capable, alone or cooperatively, of engaging in the type and scope of innovation and commercialization proposed by the applicant, and
  (F) the estimated or anticipated duration of the arrangement.
(2) Within ten days after an application submitted under paragraph (1) is received by the DOJ and FTC, the DOJ shall publish in the Federal Register a notice that announces that an application has been submitted, identifies each person submitting the application, and describes the cooperative innovation arrangement for which the application is submitted, subject to the limitations specified in subsection (g).

(b) APPROVAL OF APPLICATIONS; FILING

(1) Market power safe harbor. The DOJ and FTC shall decide within 5 days of filing which agency shall conduct approval procedures. The DOJ or FTC shall approve an application filed under subsection (a) if it determines, with the concurrence of the Secretary—
  (A) that the arrangement will not possess substantial market power in any relevant market, and

(B) that the duration of the arrangement will not exceed limits reasonably required to accomplish the objective of the arrangement, and in any event will not exceed seventeen years.

(2) The DOJ or FTC may approve an application filed under subsection (a) if it determines, with the concurrence of the Secretary that, notwithstanding that the arrangement will possess substantial market power in a relevant market,

(A) the arrangement is reasonable, because the procompetitive benefits outweigh any anticompetitive harms, as determined under paragraph (5), and

(B) the scope and duration of the arrangement will not exceed limits reasonably required to accomplish the objective of the arrangement, and in any event will not exceed seventeen years.

(3) For the purposes of this section, the DOJ or FTC shall find that the arrangement possesses substantial market power in a relevant market if—

(A) the Herfindahl–Hirschmann Index of the relevant market (including within that market, as a single firm, the cooperative innovation arrangement) is, or imminently threatens to become, greater than 1800, and the formation of the arrangement increased, or imminently threatens to increase, the Herfindahl–Hirschmann Index of such market by more than 50; or

(B) the market shares of firms in the relevant market cannot be measured by reasonably obtainable data, and there are only five or fewer firms (including the arrangement) currently participating in each relevant market that are capable, alone or cooperatively, of engaging in the type and scope of innovation and commercialization undertaken by the cooperative innovation arrangement in such market.

(4) For the purposes of this section, the DOJ or FTC shall, when defining relevant markets, consider the factors set forth in subsection (c) of section 4302.

(5) For the purposes of this section, the DOJ or FTC shall, in determining whether a cooperative innovation arrangement is reasonable, consider the following factors—

(A) the degree of market power possessed by the arrangement;

(B) whether the arrangement will harm competition and consumers by reducing output or increasing prices of products in a relevant market;

(C) whether the arrangement will produce, and whether there is a logical relationship between specific contractual restraints embodied in the arrangement and the achievement of, procompetitive benefits and efficiencies, evidence of which may include, but is not limited to, evidence—

(i) that the innovation sought by the arrangement will, if achieved, be inadequately protected under the patent, trade secret, or other intellectual property laws, and that specific contractual restraints are necessary in order to secure appropriability and prevent free-riding and opportunistic behavior,

(ii) that the innovation sought by the arrangement is of such a character or magnitude that a cooperative arrangement will help achieve the economies of scale and scope necessary to mount a successful research and commercialization effort,

(iii) that successful innovation sought by the arrangement will be aided by cooperative or integrated commercialization, including specific contractual restraints,

(iv) that the arrangement will compete in a market or markets that are characterized by rapid technological change, and/or

(v) that the innovation sought by the arrangement will compete with other technologies in a preparadigmatic stage of competition for particular products or processes;

(D) whether such procompetitive benefits and efficiencies could be achieved—

(i) by an existing firm or viable combination of firms with substantially less market power than that exercised by the arrangement in any relevant market; and/or

(ii) by the parties to the arrangement in an obviously and substantially less restrictive manner; and

(E) whether the existence of potential competitors in any relevant market in which the arrangement possesses substantial market power precludes potential anticompetitive effects that might otherwise be inferred from such market power.

(6) If the DOJ or FTC, with the concurrence of the Secretary, determines that approval is unwarranted under paragraphs (1) and (2), it may (with the concurrence of the Secretary) either deny approval or grant an approval conditioned on modification of the terms, scope, membership, and/or duration of the arrangement.

(7) The DOJ or FTC may, to assist in making any determination required by this subsection, hold, after publishing appropriate notice in the Federal Register, a hearing at which the applicant may present evidence pertinent to the determination in question.

(c) PUBLICATION; EFFECTIVE DATE OF APPROVAL

(1) Except as provided in subsection (h), not later than 60 days after receiving an application filed under subsections (a) or (f), the DOJ or FTC, with the concurrence of the Secretary, shall publish in the Federal Register a statement of the approval or denial of the application. Prior to its publication, the contents of such notice shall be made available to the parties to the arrangement. If the application is approved under paragraphs (b)(2) or (b)(6), such notice shall also include a summary of the DOJ or FTC's reasoning, a description of the terms of the approval, and a description of the activities and conduct within the scope of the approval.

(2) The DOJ or FTC may, prior to the expiration of the 60-day period specified in paragraph (1), require the submission of additional information or documentary material relevant to consideration of the factors set forth in subsection (b). If such information or material is requested, the period after which the DOJ or FTC must publish notice of approval or denial of the application shall be extended by 30 days.

(3) Approval of applications filed under subsections (a) or (f) shall take effect 30 days after notice is published under paragraph (1) or (2), except as specified in paragraph (4).

(4) If subjected to acceptance of conditions imposed by the DOJ or FTC under paragraph (b)(6) or judicial review (of the DOJ or FTC's denial of a petition for revocation pursuant to subsection (e)) under subsection (i), approval of applications filed under subsections (a) or (f) shall take effect —

(A) on the date on which a final judgment upholding such approval is announced, or

(B) if such approval is conditional or is modified by the court, on the date on which any party to the cooperative innovation arrangement submits to the court in writing a statement of its acceptance of all modifications required by the DOJ or FTC or the court.

(d) EFFECT OF DOJ OR FTC'S APPROVAL

No damages, interest on damages, costs, or attorney's fees may be recovered in any criminal or civil action based in whole or in part on conduct within the scope of a cooperative innovation arrangement approved by the DOJ or FTC (as upheld and/or modified by the court under subsection (i)) under the antitrust laws, or any State laws similar to the antitrust laws, if such approval was in effect at the time of the conduct.

The remedy of injunctive relief, available under section 16 of the Clayton Act (15 U.S.C. 26), shall be available to challenge conduct that is outside the scope of the approval granted by the DOJ or FTC.

(e) REVOCATION

(1) At any time during which an approval granted by the DOJ or FTC is in effect, the DOJ or FTC, on its own initiative or after receiving complaints from the public, may investigate and review whether the approved cooperative innovation arrangement or any part thereof remains within the scope of and standards for approval under subsection (b). The review performed by the DOJ or FTC shall be informal and shall not include any public hearing.

(2) The DOJ or FTC shall revoke an approval granted under subsection (b) only—

(A) with the concurrence of the Secretary, and

(B) if it determines that the cooperative innovation arrangement in question, or any part thereof, has—

(i) utilized the approval to abuse a dominant market position, or

(ii) become unreasonable, as determined under paragraph (b)(5), and

(C) after notifying the parties to the cooperative innovation arrangement in question, providing such parties with a reasonable opportunity to present evidence relevant to the determinations made under subparagraph (B), and determining that such evidence fails to eliminate all grounds for revocation.

(3) If a revocation is granted under paragraph (2), the DOJ or FTC shall publish notice in the Federal Register of the revocation, including a statement of reasons therefore. Prior to publication of any notice published under this subsection, the contents of such notice shall be made available to the parties to the cooperative innovation arrangement in question.

(4) Revocations granted under paragraph (2) shall take effect 30 days after notice is published, except as subjected to judicial review under subsection (i). If subjected to judicial review, revocation shall take effect on the date on which a final judgment upholding such revocation is announced.

(f) DURATION OF APPROVAL; APPLICATIONS FOR RENEWAL

The approval of cooperative innovation arrangements under this section shall, unless revoked pursuant to subsection (e), remain in effect for seventeen years, or a lesser term specified by the DOJ or FTC or a reviewing court, after which any party to such arrangement may submit an application for renewal. The application shall provide the information, updated, required under subsection (a), and shall be approved or denied pursuant to the procedure set forth in subsections (b) and (c). The protections afforded by the initial approval shall continue in effect until the date on which notice of approval or denial of the application for renewal is published.

(g) EXEMPTION; DISCLOSURE; INFORMATION

(1) Information submitted by any person in connection with applications for approval or petitions for revocation shall be exempt from disclosure under section 552 of title 5, United States Code.

(2) Except as provided in paragraph (c)(1) or as provided in paragraph (3), no officer or employee of the United States shall disclose financial, commercial, or technical information submitted in connection with applications for approval or petitions for revocation if the information is privileged or confidential and if disclosure of the information would cause harm to the person who submitted the information.

(3) Paragraph (2) shall not apply with respect to information disclosed—

(A) upon a request made by the Congress or any committee of the Congress,

(B) in a judicial or administrative proceeding, subject to appropriate protective orders,

(C) with the consent of the person who submitted the information,

(D) in accordance with any requirement imposed by a statute of the United States, or

(E) in accordance with any rule or regulation promulgated under subsection (k) permitting the disclosure of the information to an agency of the United States on the condition that the agency will disclose the information only under the circumstances specified in subparagraphs (A) through (D).

(h) WITHDRAWAL OF APPLICATIONS

Any person who files an application under this section may withdraw such application before notice of approval or denial of the application is published under subsection (c). Any application so withdrawn shall not confer the protections of subsection (d) on any person with respect to whom such application was filed.

(i) JUDICIAL REVIEW OF ACTION BY THE DOJ OR FTC

(1) If the DOJ or FTC approves, denies, or revokes any application filed under this section, any person aggrieved by such action may, within 30 days of publication of notice announcing such action, obtain a review of such decision in any United States court of appeals in the circuit wherein such person resides or transacts business, or in the United States Court of Appeals for the District of Columbia, by filing in such court a written petition praying that the action of the DOJ or FTC be modified or set aside.

(2) If, in any suit brought under paragraph (1), the court finds that the action of the DOJ or FTC is unsupported by substantial evidence on the record considered as a whole, it shall modify such action to bring it into compliance with the requirements of this section, unless doing so would materially alter the scope or structure of the cooperative innovation arrangement in question. The record shall include all evidence introduced by any party or collected by the DOJ or FTC in the course of approving such arrangement and considering the applicable petition for revocation.

(3) Rules and regulations promulgated by the DOJ or FTC under subsection (k) shall be subject to the requirements set forth under chapters 5 and 7 of title 5, United States Code.

(4) Except as specified under paragraphs (1), (2), and (3), no action by the DOJ or FTC taken pursuant to this section shall be subject to judicial review.

(j) ADMISSIBILITY OF EVIDENCE

(1) Except as provided in paragraph (2), for the sole purpose of establishing that a person is entitled to the protections of subsection (d) of this section, the fact of application under subsection (a) and the fact of approval under subsections (b) and (c) shall be admissible into evidence in any judicial or administrative proceeding.

(2) No action by the DOJ or FTC taken pursuant to this section shall be admissible into evidence in any such proceeding for the purpose of supporting or answering any claim under the antitrust laws or under any State laws similar to the antitrust laws.

(k) RULEMAKING

The DOJ or FTC, with concurrence of the Secretary, shall promulgate such rules and regulations as are necessary to implement the requirements of this section.

SECTION 4305. DISCLOSURE OF COOPERATIVE INNOVATION ARRANGEMENTS; LIMITATION ON RECOVERY

(a) WRITTEN DISCLOSURES; FILING

Any party to a cooperative innovation arrangement, acting on such arrangement's behalf, may not later than 90 days after entering into a written agreement to form such arrangement or not later than 90 days after [EFFECTIVE DATE OF BILL], whichever is later, file simultaneously with the DOJ and FTC a written notification disclosing —

(1) the identities of the parties to the arrangement, and

(2) the nature and objectives of the arrangement.

Any party to the arrangement, acting on the arrangement's behalf, may file additional disclosure notifications pursuant to this section as are appropriate to extend the protections of subsection (c). In order to maintain the protections of subsection (c), the arrangement shall, not later than 90 days after a change in its membership, file simultaneously with the DOJ or FTC a written notification disclosing such change.

(b) PUBLICATION OF NOTICE

Except as provided in subsection (e), not later than 30 days after receiving a notification filed under subsection (a), the DOJ or FTC shall publish in the Federal Register a notice that identifies the parties to the arrangement and that describes in general terms the area of planned activity of the arrangement. Prior to its publication, the contents of such notice shall be made available to the parties to such venture.

(c) EFFECT OF NOTICE

(1) If, with respect to a notification filed under subsection (a) of this section, notice is published in the Federal REgister, then such notification shall, notwithstanding section 15 of this title and in lieu of the relief specified in such section, operate to limit the recovery of any person or State entitled to recovery on a claim under the antitrust or similar State laws to the actual damages sustained by such person, interest calculated at the rate specified in section 1961 of Title 28 on such actual damages as specified in paragraph (2), and the cost of suit attributable to such claim, including a reasonable attorney's fee pursuant to section 4303 of this title if such claim —

(A) results from conduct that is within the scope of the notification, and

(B) is filed after such notification becomes effective pursuant to paragraph (4).

(2) Interest shall be awarded on damages recovered under paragraph (1) for the period beginning on the earliest date for which injury can be established and ending on the date of judgment unless the court finds that the award of all or part of such interest is unjust in the circumstances.

(3) This section shall be applicable only if the challenged conduct of a person defending against a claim is not in violation of any decree or order, entered or issued after [EFFECTIVE DATE OF BILL], in any case or proceeding under the antitrust or any similar State laws challenging such conduct as part of a cooperative innovation arrangement.

(4) The protections conferred by paragraph (1) shall take effect as of the earlier of —

(A) the date of publication of notice under subsection (b) of this section, or

(B) if notice is not published within the time required by subsection (b), after the expiration of the 30-day period beginning on the date the DOJ or FTC receives the applicable information described in subsection (a).

(d) EXEMPTION; DISCLOSURE; INFORMATION

Except with respect to the information published pursuant to subsection (b) —

(1) all information and documentary material submitted as part of a notification filed pursuant to this section, and

(2) all other information obtained by the DOJ or FTC in the course of any investigation, administrative proceeding, or case, with respect to a potential violation of the antitrust laws by the cooperative innovation arrangement with respect to which such notification was filed,

shall be exempt from disclosure under section 552 of Title 5 and shall not be made publicly available by any agency of the United States to which such section applies except in a judicial or administrative proceeding in which such information and material is subject to any protective order.

(e) WITHDRAWAL OF NOTIFICATION

Any person who files a notification pursuant to this section may withdraw such notification before notice of the cooperative innovation arrangement involved is published under subsection (b). Any notification so withdrawn shall not be subject to subsection (b) and shall not confer the protections of subsection (c) on any person with respect to whom such notification was filed.

(f) JUDICIAL REVIEW; INAPPLICABLE WITH RESPECT TO NOTIFICATIONS

Any action taken or not taken by the DOJ or FTC with respect to notifications filed pursuant to this section shall not be subject to judicial review.

(g) ADMISSIBILITY INTO EVIDENCE

(1) Except as provided in paragraph (2), for the sole purpose of establishing that a person is entitled to the protections of subsection (c), the fact of disclosure of conduct under subsection (a) and the fact of publication of a notice under subsection (b) shall be admissible into evidence in any judicial or administrative proceeding.

(2) No action by the DOJ or FTC taken pursuant to this section shall be admissible into evidence in any such proceeding for the purpose of supporting or answering any claim under the antitrust laws or under any State law similar to the antitrust laws.

Antitrust: Source of Dynamic *and* Static Inefficiencies?

WILLIAM J. BAUMOL
AND JANUSZ A. ORDOVER

This paper undertakes to reexamine some of the efficiency consequences of the antitrust laws. It will offer a variety of grounds suggesting that matters in this area are more complex than conventional views of the subject may suggest. We will not emerge with categorical conclusions on the evaluation that these laws have earned on balance, but we will offer a number of policy suggestions that can plausibly be expected to improve their performance.

If there is any one prevailing view on the merits and demerits of antitrust legislation as a stimulus to economic efficiency it would appear, very roughly, to hold that on the static side, by discouraging the exercise of monopoly, these laws have served unambiguously to promote economic welfare. Nevertheless, there has been a trade-off for social welfare, in that at least in the past antitrust rules have discouraged joint research efforts, have exacerbated the innovator's free-rider problems through restrictions on the scope of the licensing contracts, and may have impeded the attainment of the firm sizes needed to mount the most effective research and innovation efforts.[1] Not everyone agrees that the last point is a problem in reality, but there does seem to be a consensus that if antitrust falls short anywhere, the problems are most likely to take the form of impediments to *growth* in productivity.

Although we will *emphatically not* take the opposite view, it will be suggested here that there are two sides to the story, both in its static and dynamic components, and that the standard list of sources of inefficiencies possibly deriving from antitrust activities is not quite complete. First, we will try to show that antitrust can and probably often does serve as a vehicle for rent seeking and as a means to prevent "unfair competition," meaning any competition that threatens to make life too uncomfortable for rivals, as true and effective competition should do. To this extent, rather than promoting static efficiency, antitrust legislation may serve to undermine it.

The opposite may be true on the dynamic side, where antitrust may contribute more to efficiency than it has been given credit for. Those entrepreneurs who do not concern themselves overly about the avenues they use to pursue wealth, power, and prestige will tend to seek the course of least resistance to the achievement of their goal. As Schumpeter pointed out in 1911, the creation of monopolies is one of those avenues. To the extent that antitrust legislation is an effective impediment to the use of monopolization for the entrepreneur's purposes, other avenues such as productive innovation may become more attractive alternatives. Where this occurs, antitrust legislation can contribute materially to dynamic efficiency.

ANTITRUST AND THE TWO TYPES OF EFFICIENCY: THE CONVENTIONAL MODEL

Analyses of the efficiency consequences of the Sherman Act tend to take the law at face value. The implicit point of departure is the act's rules against monopolization and restraint of trade—that is, it is assumed for purposes of analysis that its main effect is to extend the domain over which competition holds sway, and to reduce the size of the arena in which monopoly power is exercised. Monopolistic influences, in turn, are shown by the standard static analysis to entail welfare losses that can be substantial.

But while monopoly is rightly recognized as an enemy of static efficiency, there are a number of reasons why it is suspected that its effects on intertemporal efficiency are not so clearly one-sided. Because both large firm size and the possession of market power can, in this view, be helpful to innovation and productivity growth, it is sometimes suggested that antitrust activity, as the enemy of market power and even of large firm size, can serve as an impediment to growth and, by enhancing its cost, as a source of intertemporal inefficiency. Furthermore, when antitrust rules create barriers to efficient interfirm cooperation in research and development and in the exploitation of the fruits of such activity, the adverse consequences from intertemporal efficiency are further exacerbated.

We can define dynamic efficiency to consist of the Pareto-optimal allocation of resources between present and future. On this foundation, one can immediately recognize (at least) three ways in which monopoly elements, or at least large firm size, can conceivably help to promote dynamic efficiency. All of them have, of course, been emphasized or noted in the pertinent literature.

1. Perhaps the overriding impediment to dynamic efficiency, and certainly the one that economists have emphasized, is the public-goods character of research and invention, with the attendant free-rider problems. It is difficult to prevent new ideas from benefiting anyone other than the individuals who have borne the costs of generating the ideas. This means that when an innovator has many rivals who can readily absorb the ambient spillovers from its R&D expenditures, the amount invested in the creation of productive knowledge and in the development of the means for its effective utilization will tend to be less than the optimal amount. This problem is apt to be particularly severe when the innovator and the beneficiaries of new productive knowledge are highly competi-

tive with each other. Monopoly can improve appropriability because its presence means that an innovator has no actual competitors who can receive and use the spillovers. But, of course, even a "monopolist" can produce spillovers for *potential* entrants and thus also needs to keep in mind the competitive effects of its R&D.

Even oligopoly can improve matters here, if cooperation in research is feasible, because then the industry beneficiaries can apportion the costs among themselves, and, if there are no free riders outside the industry, this can internalize the innovation externality altogether.

2. The Schumpeterian analysis tells us that the innovator obtains its reward via the temporary (and generally desirable) monopoly power that priority can confer on it by permitting it to outperform its rivals until they are able to respond through imitation or by some other means. Obviously, patents are a means to increase this incentive by providing legal support for such monopoly power and, perhaps, by extending the period during which it endures. Consequently, restrictions on the innovator's exercise of monopoly power stemming from the innovation can weaken appropriability and can constitute a disincentive for investment in productive innovation.[2]

3. Schumpeter also emphasized the economies of scale in the use of innovations and the large sunk costs that may be entailed in attaining the requisite knowledge, and in putting it to practical use. On both counts, he argued, firms that are monopolistic and large, with their (presumably) abundant financial resources, are likely to be more effective innovators.

The upshot of all this is that if the antitrust laws achieve their objectives and do reduce the attainment and exercise of monopoly, they may thereby impede dynamic efficiency in any or all of the ways that have just been described. On this view of the matter, then, there is a clear trade-off, with antitrust promoting one efficiency goal at the expense of the other.

DIGRESSION: CONTESTABILITY AS OPTIMAL COMPROMISE FOSTERED BY ANTITRUST?

It is clear that neither competition nor monopoly emerge with an enviable reputation from the preceding summary of "the standard evaluation." Because of the association of the present authors with the theory of contestable markets, it may well be expected of us to suggest this recently formalized market structure as an ideal compromise, capable (*in theory*) of performing optimally in static terms, and of doing better than either perfect competition or monopoly in dynamic performance. However, that is *not* our purpose here; indeed, we will argue presently that perfect contestability is, at best, a rather imperfect, if not a rather shabby ideal in terms of intertemporal efficiency.

This is all pertinent to the central theme of this book because there are good grounds for arguing that antitrust has, without knowing it, been promoting something at least approximating contestability rather than anything approaching perfect competition. Moreover, there is some reason for arguing that it is right and proper for antitrust to have taken contestability as its abstract goal.

We will elaborate in a few paragraphs about the association of antitrust and contestability, but some words need first be said about the dynamic efficiency properties of the latter.[3] We will see that even the imaginary case of the *perfectly* contestable market is apt to exhibit some shortcomings in this arena, and that the magnitude of the social costs of these shortcomings seems far from obvious. Thus, even if it is agreed that contestability is the secret love of the antitrust establishment, this does not immunize the latter from the problems to which this paper calls attention.

The empirical evidence does seem to suggest the character of the industry structure that is most conducive to technical advance. It is neither pure monopoly nor perfect competition that appears to come off with the honors. It is intermediate-sized, not giant-sized, firms that are the most propitious for R&D investment, while strong competitive pressures stimulate rapid dissemination and widespread adoption of successful innovative steps. Contestability thus *seems*, at first glance, to be tailor-made to satisfy both these desiderata. It certainly is consistent with largeness of firms relative to the size of the market, although not *requiring* them to be gigantic, and it brings with it effective competitive pressures, almost perfectly analogous with those associated with perfect competition while, unlike the latter, not requiring industry to be populated exclusively by midget enterprises.

This is good for dynamic efficiency but, unfortunately, it is not the end of the story. Contestability, of course, does nothing to weaken the public-goods properties of knowledge production and innovation—the free-rider problem which economists seem, with good reason, to consider the most potent impediment to dynamic efficiency. The reason contestability makes no contribution here is that at bottom the problem is an externality, a warp in the price mechanism, which perfect competition also cannot correct unless the means are found to eliminate the gap in the price mechanism's coverage. But it is more than that. By entailing complete absence of barriers to entry, perfect contestability, again like perfect competition, threatens to rule out entirely the reward mechanism that elicits the Schumpeterian innovation process. This mechanism, as we have seen, rests on the innovator's supernormal profits, which are permitted by the temporary possession of monopoly power flowing from priority in innovation. Since perfect contestability rules out all market power, that is, since it permits immediate entry of imitators of any innovation, the market mechanism's main reward for innovation is destroyed by that market form. In short, it is clearly no panacea that can claim to bring dynamic and static efficiency at the same time.

We return now to the second topic of this section: our suggestion that perfect contestability, rather than perfect competition, has in practice been the unrecognized ideal of antitrust activity.[4] We may note first that antitrust rarely concerns itself with industries characterized by the constant or diminishing returns to scale that alone can permit very small firms (and only very small firms) to survive and prosper. But in industries whose technology is characterized by economies of scale and scope (which include most of those likely to attract the attention of the antitrust agencies), small firms—that indispensable requirement of perfect competition—neither can nor should prevail since, by definition, that entails high and unnecessary costs that must render small firms vulnerable to the rivalry of larger enterprises and must, at the same time, reduce consumer welfare.

Accordingly, even when the Department of Justice or the Federal Trade Commission has been at its most active, neither has sought to split dominant enterprises into thousands of diminutive firms. Rather, in those instances when structural relief was contemplated, the goal was to create a modest number of companies at most, all of these firms of sufficient size to make survival a realistic possibility.[5] With that goal, the antitrust community implicitly chose to forgo all use of perfect competition as its guiding ideal. At the same time, the antitrust agencies have generally taken a stand opposing the erection of barriers to entry, and have even sought to demolish barriers already erected, presumably treating freedom of entry as an effective, if perhaps second-best, substitute for the numbers of actual competitors.[6] But it is more than that. The Department of Justice has repeatedly announced its commitment to what amounts to a reward for an industry's eschewal of barriers to entry. The merger guidelines tell us emphatically that the DOJ will generally refrain from opposing merger projects in industries into which entry is sufficiently easy. We conclude from all this that the sort of competition that the antitrust agencies really seek to promote is closer to the variety associated with the theoretical concept of perfectly contestable markets, one which bears little family resemblance to the perfect competition of more venerable economic theory. Once again it must be emphasized that this is not *necessarily* a desirable development; but we suspect that it is a reasonably good approximation to the facts.

ANTITRUST REGULATION AS A SOURCE OF IMPEDIMENTS TO STATIC EFFICIENCY?

We come now to one of our two central themes — that antitrust activity may not be as categorically advantageous for static efficiency as is apt to be believed. The standard view of antitrust and efficiency holds that this activity is largely beneficial in the static arena. Yet, few careful observers of antitrust activity in practice will have failed to notice the rent-seeking opportunities that it offers, and the fact that it lends itself to distortion as an instrument for the prevention of excessive vigor in the competitive process. In this way, then, it can contribute to static inefficiency, offsetting, at least in part, the benefits it offers in that area.

This is particularly true of private antitrust suits.[7] But these suits, as is true of many of the other institutions that give rise to rent-seeking opportunities, also have a significant beneficial side to them, which is precisely why the problem does not lend itself to simple remedies.

Yet it remains true that a variety of legal institutions and developments seem to have enhanced the incentives for the bringing of antitrust suits that have relatively little merit. First, there is the fact that even a plaintiff whose case is ultimately found to be without merit is only on rare occasions assessed a share of the defendant's litigation costs.[8] Second, less scrupulous attorneys may actively foster litigation in the hope of collecting large contingency fees from somewhat questionable suits that may well be settled before the defendant subjects itself to the degree of risk entailed in proceeding to a final judgment. Third, and more important, automatic trebling of antitrust damages raises the prospective benefits to the plaintiff from such a suit and significantly increases the defendant's costs of losing, thereby threatening to elicit indefensible and excessively frequent settlements. Fourth, certification of a class — a process that in and of itself can sometimes produce questionable results — further increases the incentives to settle, even when the facts of the case may favor the defendant(s). And, finally, the rules of joint and several liability create incentives for plaintiffs to implicate firms that may well be innocent in the hope of eliciting quick settlements and extracting additional money.[9] The temptation to bring suit in hope of making an easy killing may at times be all but irresistible. This temptation can be enhanced further by the observation that in the hands of a jury when a case is brought by a small plaintiff from a neighboring location against a large firm with no significant local connections, a heavy handicap is borne by the latter.[10]

There is no need to expand the list further. The point is clear. The arena constantly offers an abundance of attractive targets to a firm seeking an easy way to add to its wealth without investing additional effort and resources in any productive activities. In short, the antitrust laws constitute an opportunity for rent seeking and, as we know, this is generally in direct conflict with the requirements of economic efficiency. It diverts valuable resources that might have been used for productive purposes. Instead, it forces firms to take measures not called for by some productive purpose, but as a means to protect themselves from the attempts of others to enrich themselves.[11] Opportunities like those under discussion can also lead to competition among the rent seekers, but here competition, rather than protecting the interests of consumers, merely multiplies the ensuing waste of resources.

While rent seeking seems to be associated most directly with *private* antitrust activity, the hobbling of competition can be contributed either by private or by public antitrust intervention. The competitive process is one that is not calculated to be pleasant for the firms that are subject to its pressures and, as Adam Smith emphasized repeatedly, it is natural for those who suffer under its sway to seek whatever means they can to free themselves from it or, at least, to reduce the harshness of its regime.[12] In practice such predictable responses to competition, which threaten to become threateningly effective in their effects on the runner-up, are commonplace. Public relations specialists are adept at putting a procompetitive face on such anticompetitive endeavors. Terms such as "unfair competition," "destructive pricing" and "predatory innovation" are regularly displayed, particularly in circumstances where there is little substance to their implied contention. The purpose of such charges is to usher in a reign of "fair competition," by which is meant virtually no competition at all. Where such attempts succeed, and it can be argued that they sometimes have in the past, the antitrust institutions are effectively subverted into providing a protective umbrella to inefficient suppliers; thereby, in the words of the courts, promoting the interests of competitors at the expense of competition. It can also be argued that the antitrust agencies have sometimes allowed themselves to be used for such purposes, that is, to grant a degree of immunity from the rigors of competition to the runners-up in a competitive race.[13]

Once again it should be clear that when and if they work in this way the antitrust institutions serve to impede static efficiency. Of course, this must all be balanced against their genuine contributions to competitiveness, and we are not prepared to deny that the balance will usually come down in their favor. We are merely contending that there is more than one side to the matter.

We should also make clear our recognition of the fact that institutions such as contingency fees, class action suits, and trebling of damages all have very valuable and very legitimate purposes in many cases. Without the last of these monopolistic acts would become actuarially profitable gambles, viewed *ex ante* in light of the nonzero probability of escaping punishment. And without contingency fees and class action suits the less-affluent victims of monopoly and monopolization would be left with much less protection. These considerations make it clear that there are no simple and socially costless solutions to the problem of rent seeking engendered by antitrust. We certainly would oppose abolition of the institutions just cited as sources of the problem because the cost to the public would in our view be unacceptable. But that hardly justifies unwillingness to recognize the social costs of the rent seeking they stimulate or to consider the desirability of *some* modifications in the current arrangements.

ANTITRUST REGULATION AND INTERTEMPORAL EFFICIENCY

We come next to our second main contention—that is, antitrust may be helpful to intertemporal efficiency in ways that are not always recognized. As we have noted, when it comes to dynamic efficiency, the conventional view is very different from that described in the preceding section. While some of the more extreme of the Schumpeterian conjectures about the ways in which bigness of enterprise and even monopoly contribute to growth, the balance of opinion still seems to favor the conclusion that there is a genuine trade-off between static and intertemporal efficiency, and the moves that enhance competitiveness, while they will promote the former, may often do so at the expense of the latter. There is no need to repeat the well-known arguments here, since most of them already were suggested earlier in this paper.

This conclusion has the corollary, already noted, that the antitrust laws and their execution can well constitute an impediment to *growth* in productivity and output per capita. Aside from the general grounds for this conclusion, a number of particular propensities of the antitrust agencies and policies have been questioned on these grounds. But perhaps the main source of the problem is the fact that the design of defensible antitrust policy for dynamic industries, meaning industries in which product and process innovation constitute key market activities, raises significant methodological difficulties. These difficulties arise precisely because, when narrowly perceived, antitrust policies seem excessively preoccupied with static market power and competition at the expense of intertemporal considerations.

Closer scrutiny reveals that this view, while not without some justification, is not entirely correct.[14] To begin with, at least over the past fifteen years, many, albeit not all, courts have resisted condemnation of any technological moves, even by firms with substantial market shares.[15] This is on the whole a salutary development, particularly because technologically successful firms — such as IBM, AT&T, or Kodak — often constitute an inviting target for antitrust action. Nevertheless, antitrust considerations probably continue to influence R&D decisions of firms. Crucial decisions — such as those determining the design of interfaces and the degree of compatibility among the components of computer or telecommunications systems; like those on the timing of announcements of new products that will divert sales from the products of smaller rivals; and those on the time path of prices that can damage rivals which have not yet had a chance to benefit from learning-by-doing — all invite scrutiny with an eye to their effects on competitors and competition. There is no doubt that business fear of such scrutiny, whether justified or not, has engendered some degree of conservatism, which may be detrimental to the entire process of invention, innovation, and dissemination.

High technology industries, with their emphasis on investments in R&D that are characterized by imperfect appropriability and excludability, provide fertile ground for cooperation among potential competitors that may well prove socially beneficial. Such cooperation frequently is likely to prove procompetitive since it can increase returns to innovation through improved appropriability, encourage dissemination of innovations, facilitate exploitation of economies of scale and scope in the creation of new knowledge, and permit better spreading of the risks associated with investments in R&D when market mechanisms for risk sharing perform inadequately.[16] Yet antitrust policies have built into them an aversion toward coordinated and cooperative use of assets that are under separate ownership, and this aversion can exert a chilling effect on prospective cooperation in the innovation process in high technology industries, even if the courts exercise considerable restraint in interfering in the process.

The recently enacted National Cooperative Research Act of 1984 (NCRA)[17] reflects the changing antitrust climate in this area. The act recognizes the importance of economic progress of cooperative research activities among noncompetitors and competitors alike, as well as for continued economic vitality and viability of American firms in intensely competitive world markets in technology-based products and services. Research joint ventures contribute to dynamic efficiency by enabling the participating firms to reduce the free-rider problems that bedevil production of new knowledge. In this way, they raise returns to innovative activity by lowering its costs and increasing the pool of effective knowledge that is available to firms.

Research joint ventures are not, however, a panacea for the lack of technological drive that can infest some firms or entire industries. In addition, research joint ventures are at times subject to internal conflicts that undermine even the best-laid plans and cause participating firms to pursue their own independent research intensively, while withholding superior scientific and engineering talent from the joint venture. Finally, there is the possibility, even if remote, that the joint venture will curtail investments in R&D below the level that would emerge with less coordination and that it will reduce effective dissemination of knowledge by exclusionary licensing policies. Looked at in this way, then, research joint ventures and other consortia of firms of this type are properly viewed as socially valuable institutions that should be encouraged but which carry some competitive risks that are best handled through a rule of reason, as is explicitly recognized in NCRA.

We have, thus, no quarrel with the conventional view that antitrust policies and private litigation can conceivably weaken the incentives to invest in R&D and disseminate newly created knowledge to the detriment of dynamic efficiency. Indeed, we ourselves have recently taken similar positions in another paper.[18] We do, however, feel that it is not the entire story. For, as will be argued next, the preceding discussion does not encompass some contributions that antitrust *does* make to the enhancement of dynamic efficiency; at the same time, it leaves out of consideration other ways in which the institution impedes efficiency of this variety. Both of these relate to the manner in which antitrust activity affects the exercise of entrepreneurship.

The entrepreneur has been cited often enough as a key player in the orchestration of economic growth. As the innovator who introduces new products, new technology, new marketing and organizational techniques this individual is constantly taken to be a crucial contributor to the growth process. When a nation's growth falters, one surmises that a major source of the difficulty is a drying-up of the entrepreneurial spirit, or the erection of impediments to its exercise; when the growth of an economy blossoms, one tends to seek evidence of an outburst of entrepreneurial activity as a significant contributory cause.

This view of the matter seems to treat the exercise of entrepreneurship as a variable that is largely exogenous. But we believe that this interpretation is misleading. Entrepreneurship, in our view, is an input, whose supply and allocation, like those of other inputs, is determined in part by economic circumstances. If we define entrepreneurs as the individuals who are prepared to depart from the conventional modes of economic operation in the pursuit of wealth, power, and prestige, then one can expect them to follow the line of least resistance in pursuit of these goals. Entrepreneurs presumably being no more or less dedicated to morality than are lawyers, landlords, doctors or professors, there will be at least a number among them who are prepared to be flexible in their choice of economic activity, preferring a line of endeavor that contributes to productivity only if it happens to be the most promising way toward the acquisition of wealth and the entrepreneur's other personal objectives.

Along these lines, Schumpeter himself listed the formation of monopoly as among the sorts of (organizational) innovation an entrepreneur will sometimes seek to undertake. Similarly, the introduction of new wrinkles into "risk arbitrage," as was done by Ivan Boesky, was surely an entrepreneurial act, albeit one not likely to contribute much to production. The same is true of the inauguration of a legal gambit that permits the individual to use the regulatory agencies or the courts more effectively than before as instruments of rent seeking. The point is that when such avenues for rent seeking are effectively closed or their use is rendered more difficult, such entrepreneurs will be driven, *faute de mieux*, to productive innovation as the most promising means for the achievement of wealth, power, and prestige. We believe, in sum, that contrary to what is implied by the common view of the matter, entrepreneurs do not have a propensity to disappear suddenly and mysteriously. Rather, as the identity of their most promising opportunities changes, they reallocate themselves accordingly, sometimes with striking rapidity. This reallocation all too often entails their withdrawal from the arenas in which they can most effectively contribute to growth and moves them into economic activities that sometimes add little to growth and sometimes actually impede it.

It should now be clear how antitrust fits into this story. To the extent that it prevents or impedes monopolization or reduces its profitability, it can discourage entrepreneurs from embarking on such ventures and cause them to reallocate their talents and efforts into production-enhancing innovation. On the other hand, to the extent that antitrust activity is carried out in ways that facilitate rent seeking (in the manner that was discussed earlier), it can redirect entrepreneurship the other way, at the expense of productivity growth. Thus, facilitation of rent seeking would appear to have a double cost to society, one static and the other dynamic. Since antitrust contributes to all of this, it bears a substantial burden of responsibility for intertemporal inefficiency, in addition to those factors that are conventionally suggested.

CONCLUSION: POLICY IMPLICATIONS

Despite the very general character of many of the considerations that have been raised in this chapter they do suggest a number of conclusions relating to policy, some of them rather specific. But first let us offer two general observations. The first is a rather obvious point. Despite the reservations that have just been expressed about the nature of the proper trade-off between static and intertemporal efficiency, it remains clear that society retains an interest in simultaneous promotion of both of these, and in the enhancement of either if it can be done in a way that does not impede the other. The ways in which antitrust can impede the pursuit of these two objectives, then, virtually become a list of items whose amendment will constitute the bulk of our policy recommendations. Our second preliminary observation is that those who design antitrust policy would do well to recognize overtly that something like perfect contestability, and not perfect competition, constitutes the proper ideal that should (and to a considerable extent already does) guide their activities. By recognizing this explicitly, as will be seen from the discussion that follows, the door will be opened to a number of improvements in at least the details of the design of their policies, modifications in detail which may nevertheless promise considerable benefits.

Let us then proceed to a list of illustrative policy proposals. It is hardly necessary to say that they are mostly preliminary, that most of them require considerable further exploration, and that they are by no means meant to be exhaustive. In any event, the brevity of our discussion of each proposal will by itself suggest how much more investigation of their details and implications remains to be done.

We group the proposals into three broad categories: (1) measures designed to prevent misuse of antitrust and regulation as protective instruments that weaken the competitive process; (2) measures that inhibit their use for rent-seeking purposes; and (3) measures that address themselves to the conventional concerns about antitrust and intertemporal efficiency.

1. Prevention of use of antitrust and regulation to inhibit competition. It is in the arena of misuse of antitrust and regulation by runners-up who hope to shield themselves from the effectiveness of competition that the contestability goal can make its main contribution. The ideal of perfect competition has long been recognized as something so far removed from the practicalities of the pertinent economic arenas that it was largely ignored in the design of policy. But, taken as an ideal to be emulated, the contestability model is more suitable. It retains the virtue of compatibility with static economic efficiency and, despite the reservations expressed earlier, it seems to comport workably, if imperfectly, with intertemporal efficiency, while not requiring industries to be transformed into collections of diminutive enterprises that are inconsistent with and are rendered undesirable by the presence of economies of scale and scope. Once it is agreed that the proper role of regulation and antitrust is to promote competitiveness where it is prospectively viable, and to act as a surrogate for competition where it is not, a general course of action recommends itself. The standard of acceptable conduct by the firms at issue becomes what their behavior would have been if they had been operating in a market that was (hypothetically) perfectly contestable.[19] Such behavior must be expected of all firms subject to antitrust or regulatory scrutiny. But they must never be constrained further, since any additional circumscription of the range of decisions open to them would represent governmental intrusion that threatens efficiency by requiring firms to act differently from the ways in which effectively competitive market forces would require them to behave. Three specific examples will illustrate the policy implications of these observations.

A. Abandonment of fully distributed cost as a guide to price evaluation. The history of regulation and antitrust is replete with the use of fully distributed cost calculations by protection-seeking competitors. They have proposed these costs as a price floor, arguing that prices lower than this are destructive or predatory. Similarly, firms seeking to extract subsidized inputs have urged the use of these costs as ceilings, claiming that prices higher than this are unfair. But economic analysis shows that neither perfect contestability, nor even perfect competition, calls for firms to satisfy these arbitrary standards. Market forces simply make no rules linking prices to fully distributed costs, which are also, demonstrably, an impediment to economic efficiency of any sort. An explicit commitment to eschew any and all further reliance on fully distributed cost in antitrust cost in antitrust actions related to pricing and in regulation of rates would close off an important avenue for subversion of the antitrust laws by those who would use them to reduce the severity of the competitive process.

B. Use of Areeda–Turner-like rules. The obverse of the preceding point is that criteria of acceptable pricing behavior should be derived from careful economic analysis of the behavior of competitive and contestable markets. The Areeda–Turner criterion of predatory pricing, despite all the criticism to which it has been subjected, and all the modifications that have been proposed by very competent economists, is recognized as a very commendable starting place for evaluating pricing decisions, particularly in markets protected by significant entry barriers.

C. Incremental cost floors and stand-alone cost ceilings. A further step in this direction was taken by the Interstate Commerce Commission in 1985 when it adopted what it called "constrained market pricing" as its guide for the regulation of rates for the transportation of coal by railroads.[20] Here, explicitly acknowledging contestability analysis as the basis for its decision, it adopted the incremental cost of any type of shipment as the proper floor for its price, and stand-alone cost (the price that would make entry just barely profitable in a market from which entry barriers were totally absent) as the corresponding ceiling. The point is that in a perfectly contestable market, depending on demand conditions, price can sometimes go as low as incremental cost, and sometimes as high as stand-alone cost, but any price that is below the former or above the latter will rapidly be undermined by market forces. These rules can be shown to be compatible with the requirements of at least static efficiency, and surely contribute to intertemporal efficiency by discouraging the diversion of entrepreneurship into attempts to use antitrust regulation as a means to protect their firms from effective competition.

2. *Discouragement of use of antitrust action for rent-seeking purposes.* We can be briefer in the discussion of the second category of our policy suggestions, since the points are fairly straightforward and have been discussed elsewhere in the literature. The essence of the matter is to take steps to discourage the use of private antitrust actions as prospective cash cows, ready for milking by rent seekers. Here, at least four obvious steps seem clearly to merit consideration.

A. *Symmetry of responsibility for costs imposed on the victor.* As currently arranged, the defendant in an antitrust case can be required to bear the costs incurred by the plaintiff in bringing the suit, if the defendant is found guilty of violating the antitrust laws. But if the suit is found to have no merit the defendant generally cannot recover its costs from the plaintiff. This arrangement is a clear incentive for rent seeking and a change seems to be warranted.

B. *Restriction of contingency arrangements with lawyers.* The argument for an amendment in the rules that restricts the use of contingency arrangements by attorneys in private antitrust suits is similar. There may be exceptional cases in which such arrangements are indispensable, but these should be spelled out clearly and restricted narrowly. Perhaps a simple ceiling on contingency fee payments, restricting them, for example, to one million dollars, would preserve this instrument for use by less-affluent clients, while making it unavailable to a mega-case treasure hunt.

C. *Definition of the appropriate basis for granting of class action designation.* The class action suit has a very legitimate social purpose and it sometimes contributes to the efficiency of the legal process. However, the basis on which class action designation is granted or denied is far from clearly spelled out, and it can also be granted where it serves no discernible social purpose. Moreover, it may serve as an instrument of what is not quite blackmail by the rent seeker, who uses the enormous risk borne by the defendant in a class action case to extract a lucrative settlement. The implication is that some effort needs to be devoted to a reexamination of the logic of class actions to determine the circumstances in which they serve the public interest and those where they do not; corresponding amendment and spelling out of the pertinent legal rules should also be given serious consideration.

D. Uncoupling of trebled damages. Since it is clear that violators of antitrust rules do sometimes succeed in escaping detection, prosecution, or punishment, it would not provide an adequate deterrent to make them subject to payment of only the amount of damage their conduct has caused. Effective deterrence, therefore, does require some multiplication of the damage figure as the amount for which they are liable if found guilty, even if the use of the number three for this purpose is a bit arbitrary. But trebled damages also serve as an incentive for rent-seeking private antitrust suits. The compound goal of effective deterrence without encouragement of rent seeking can be served by continuing the trebled damages as the amount for which the defendant is liable if found guilty, but with the amount the plaintiff is permitted to recover limited to actual damages plus, perhaps, some small addition. The resulting surplus could then go to the federal government. In addition, there are strong reasons for detrebling damages for antitrust violations resulting from activities falling in the category of joint R&D — as has already been done by the NCRA — and production joint ventures set up to exploit the results of such joint R&D.

3. Measures to reduce inefficiencies more commonly attributed to antitrust regulation. These measures build on one common foundation — recognition that social rates of return to investments in R&D tend to exceed private rates of return in such activities. Consequently, antitrust policies should be designed carefully to avoid increasing the gap even further.

A. Antitrust attention in dynamic industries should focus on the markets in technology. The static focus of antitrust tends to lead the analyst to particularly close scrutiny of "downstream" or product markets. In high technology industries, the "upstream" markets — the markets for technology — which include the R&D stage, are likely to be of greater consequence for competition, particularly in the longer run. These upstream markets are more likely to be international in scope, less protected by entry barriers, and are apt to be characterized by greater fluidity in market shares. Accordingly, less weight should be assigned to the current market status of a firm, or group of firms in technologically evolving industries, when analyzing the implications of unilateral conduct and interfirm cooperation for the state of competition. The analysis should also recognize the critical links between the "upstream" and "downstream" markets. Thus, technological races that produce only one winner can lead to concentrated product markets. Such outcomes may be inevitable and, if so, then should generally not be discouraged by antitrust policies.

B. Dominant firms should be afforded significant latitude in their technological decisions. Dominant firms can manipulate technological competition to their advantage against actual and potential rivals. However, in many circumstances these decisions are unlikely to be harmful to dynamic efficiency. Consequently, stringent filters must be used before unilateral technological decisions by firms with current market power are found to be anticompetitive.

C. Antitrust rules should take account of benefits from cooperation in technology production. Research joint ventures, research consortia, and even mergers in high technology industries are frequently a socially optimal response to market failures that beset the production and dissemination of knowledge. Accordingly, a relaxed rule-of-reason approach to interfirm coordination is the approach that seems best to balance the various concerns apt to be raised by such coordination. In this process consortia, joint ventures, and even mergers of firms with substantial current market shares in high technology industries can be judged to be conducive to dynamic efficiency—more so than in industries that are less driven technologically.

D. *Antitrust policy should not exacerbate contractual problems in the dissemination of information.* Firms should be permitted great latitude in their patent licensing policies in order to increase returns to innovative effort and facilitate dissemination. Consequently, licensing schemes employed by patent holders must not be subject to more stringent antitrust constraints than those that attach to exploitation of other property rights. Indeed, when the licensor is not vertically integrated into the downstream market, its choice of licensing scheme should be virtually free from antitrust scrutiny, with only two provisos: that the licensing scheme not erect undue barriers to entry into the upstream market; and that the license not be used as a collusion-facilitating mechanism in the downstream market.

The preceding discussion does not pretend to be a coherent and exhaustive program for the future directions of antitrust activities. It does, however, show that consideration of the connection between antitrust and the goals of static and intertemporal efficiency does suggest concrete directions that promise to contribute to the public welfare and which, at the very least, merit further and more careful examination.

NOTES

The authors are grateful to the C. V. Starr Center for Applied Economics at NYU for its support. They also want to thank Professor Joseph F. Brodley and other commentators, at the conference at which this paper was presented, for their very valuable comments. We obviously did not agree with all of these comments, but they all merited serious consideration, and certainly led to modifications in our text.

1. The evidence on the relationship between firm size and innovativeness is inconclusive. The most plausible relationship is probably U-shaped. See Baldwin and Scott (1987).
2. In this context, see, e.g., Ordover (1984), and Ordover and Baumol (1988) for a discussion of restrictions on patent licensing agreements.
3. We leave for another occasion a more complete discussion of the idea of contestability in technology-driven industries.
4. In offering this hypothesis we do not mean to imply that the antitrust agencies consider potential entry to be a constraint upon market power or monopolization that is as powerful as the actual presence of current competitors. We are merely speaking of the theoretical state of *perfect* contestability as the (unattainable) performance goal toward which the authorities implicitly aspire, given the impossibility of achievement and survival of any number of firms approaching that required for perfect competition in those realms where scale economies are present—the very realms that are most likely to attract the attention of those authorities.
5. Thus, the 1969 dissolution plan worked out between the government and United Shoe still left the firm with one third of its market share. In the Alcoa case, structural remedy was not granted by the district court judge despite Alcoa's large share of domestically produced virgin ingot. See the classic article by Hale (1940), for a discus-

sion of the effectiveness of remedies in the main cases brought by the United States against the "trusts" formed during the merger movement.

6. Here, one needs only to cite the two grand antitrust cases brought under the Sherman Act, viz., United States v. United Shoe Machinery, Corp., 110 F. Supp. 295, 345 U.S. 521, and United States v. Aluminum Co. of America, 148 F.2d 416 (2d Cir. 1945). Speaking broadly, the antitrust law's concern with exclusionary behavior as such reflects the sound policy view that the mere possibility of entry tends to constrain the exercise of market power by a dominant incumbent. It is also fair to say that courts, legal and economic scholars, and enforcement agencies have been modifying their views as to what constitutes barrier-raising exclusionary conduct.

7. The papers in White (1988) provide a comprehensive theoretical, empirical, and public policy discussion of many of the points raised in this section.

8. In no instance does the losing plaintiff have to compensate the defendant for costly disruption of business activities, which can be far higher than the litigation costs. Here it is interesting that defendants tend to spend more on their side of the case than do private plaintiffs. See Teplitz (1988).

9. See Benston (1988) for a comprehensive discussion of some of these issues.

10. This handicap does not carry to the appeals stage, however, where some of the lower court decisions are apt to be reversed.

11. Of course antitrust is hardly the only arena in which litigation provides opportunities for rent seeking.

12. This also includes firms that seek to protect themselves from the rigors of foreign competition and who place the blame for their poor showing in the marketplace on the allegedly hobbling antitrust provisions.

13. But regulatory agencies appear also to have been captured to a degree by the incumbents who dread having their bailiwicks challenged by new firms.

14. See Ordover and Baumol (1988).

15. See Areeda and Hovenkamp (1987), ¶¶ 738.1–4, for a discussion of recent judicial developments.

16. See Katz and Ordover (1990), for the analysis of competitive effects of research joint ventures.

17. 15 U.S.C. ¶¶ 4301–5.

18. See Ordover and Baumol, op. cit., p. 11.

19. Though a number of critics have raised questions about the frequency with which approximations to perfect contestability are to be found in reality, and about the desirability of the performance to be expected of firms and industries in markets that are imperfectly contestable, no one, to our knowledge, has raised doubts about the desirability of the use of perfect contestability as a policy benchmark in the manner described here.

20. Interstate Commerce Commission, "Coal Rate Guidelines, Nationwide," Ex Parte No. 347 (Sub-No. 1) (Washington, D.C.: August 3, 1985).

REFERENCES

Areeda, P., and Hovenkamp. 1987. *Antitrust Law*, Supplement. Boston: Little, Brown.

Baldwin, W. L., and J. T. Scott. 1987. *Market Structure and Technological Change*, vol. 17. In J. Lesourne and H. Sonnenschein, eds. *Fundamentals of Pure and Applied Economics*. Harwood.

Benston, G. J. 1988. "A Comprehensive Analysis of the Determinants of Private Antitrust

Litigation, with Particular Emphasis on Class Action Suits and the Rule of Joint and Several Damages." In White, ed. *Private Antitrust Litigation*, pp. 271–328.

Hale, G. E. 1940. "Trust Dissolution: 'Atomizing' Business Units of Monopolistic Size." *Columbia Law Review* 40:615–73.

Interstate Commerce Commission. "Coal Rate Guidelines, Nationwide." Ex Parte No. 347 (Sub-No. 1). Washington, D.C., August 3, 1985.

Katz, M., and J. A. Ordover. 1990. "R&D Cooperation and Competition." *Brookings Papers on Economic Activity: Microeconomics*. forthcoming.

Ordover, J. A. 1984. "Economic Foundations and Considerations in Protecting Industrial and Intellectual Property." *Antitrust Law Journal* 53:503–18.

Ordover, J. A., and W. J. Baumol. 1988. "Antitrust Policy for High Technology Industries." *Oxford Review of Economic Policy* 4 (Winter) 13–34.

Teplitz, P. V. 1988. "Georgetown Project: Overview of Data Set and Its Collection." In White, ed., pp. 60–81.

White, L. J., ed. 1988. *Private Antitrust Litigation: New Evidence, New Learning*. Cambridge: MIT Press.

Agreements Between Competitors

RICHARD SCHMALENSEE

The per se rule against "horizontal restraints"—agreements between competitors that serve to restrain rivalry—is almost as old as the Sherman Act itself. This rule is commonly held to have originated with William Howard Taft's 1898 *Addyston Pipe* opinion, to have reached its majority with the 1927 *Trenton Potteries* decision, and to have attained full maturity with Justice Douglas's opinion in *Socony-Vacuum*.[1]

Thus generations of lawyers and economists have discussed the apparent economic inconsistency between the evaluation of horizontal mergers by their likely economic effects under Section 2 of the Sherman Act (and later under the Clayton and Celler–Kefauver Acts) and the courts' refusal to consider economic effects in applying the per se rule under Section 1 to less durable horizontal restraints. It has long been a provocative and entertaining classroom device to point out that two executives considering a legal horizontal merger would commit a felony if they decided instead simply to coordinate their pricing. The much-discussed hypothesis that the merger wave around the turn of the century was triggered by the birth of the per se rule illustrates nicely the apparent tension between these two parts of the antitrust law.[2]

Until the 1980s, however, most post-*Socony-Vacuum* discussions of the per se rule seem to have stressed its procedural strengths rather than its substantive weaknesses. In his 1969 *Container Corp.* dissent, Justice Marshall expressed well the traditional case for per se rules:

> Per se rules always contain a degree of arbitrariness. They are justified on the assumption that the gains from imposition of the rule far outweigh the losses and that significant administrative advantages will result. In other words, the potential competitive harm plus the administrative costs of determining in what particular situations the practice may be harmful must far outweigh the benefits that may result. If the potential benefits in the aggregate are outweighed to this degree, then they are simply not worth identifying in individual cases.[3]

In 1969 and earlier, most lawyers and economists would have agreed that this test was passed by the traditional per se rule against horizontal restraints and that it would clearly not be passed by a per se rule against horizontal mergers. Joint ventures and information exchange activities were generally assigned to the rule of reason.

Nonetheless, on the eve of the Sherman Act's centennial, the venerable per se rule has come under strong attack. There have been earlier attacks, of course. As early as 1918, in *Chicago Board of Trade*, the Supreme Court declined to apply the per se rule to an agreement among competing grain traders not to buy or sell outside normal exchange hours except at the previous day's closing price.[4] Instead, the Court found that price-related horizontal restraint to be lawful under the rule of reason. Although this case was distinguished in *Trenton Potteries* and *Socony-Vacuum*,[5] it has never seemed clear (at least to a nonlawyer) exactly what limits, if any, the sensible *Chicago Board of Trade* decision set on the scope of the per se rule.[6] On the academic front, many observers have noted that using the per se rule to prohibit fixing maximum selling prices has doubtful economic effects at best.[7]

But the most serious assault on the per se rule seems to have begun with the Supreme Court's 1979 *BMI (Broadcast Music, Inc.)* decision.[8] By 1984, the Court could assert in its *NCAA (National Collegiate Athletic Association)* decision that "there is often no bright line separating per se from rule of reason analysis."[9] And in 1986, in the majority opinion in *Rothery*, Judge Bork asserted that this assault had succeeded completely: "In *BMI, NCAA*, and *Pacific Stationery*, the Supreme Court returned the law to the formulation of *Addyston Pipe & Steel* and thus effectively overruled *Topco* and *Sealy* as to the per se illegality of all horizontal restraints."[10] While this assertion may be a bit strong,[11] it seems safe to assume, as I do in what follows, that the traditional per se rule no longer dictates the antitrust treatment of horizontal restraints. My main concern in this essay is with the obvious question this assumption raises: What policy toward horizontal restraints should replace the traditional per se rule?

One fairly discouraging description of the possible answers to this question was given by Justice Marshall, writing for the majority in the 1972 *Topco* case:

> Without the per se rules, businessmen would be left with little to aid them in predicting in any particular case what courts will find to be legal and illegal under the Sherman Act. Should Congress ultimately determine that predictability is unimportant in this area of the law, it can, of course, make per se rules inapplicable in some or all cases, and leave courts free to ramble through the wilds of economic theory in order to maintain a flexible approach.[12]

Is, as Justice Marshall suggests, the only alternative to the traditional per se rule an unstructured rule-of-reason standard? If so, and if every horizontal restraints case must become an aimless "ramble through the wilds of economic theory," even economists, wealthy as many would become, might long for a return to the simpler world of *Sealy* and *Topco*. Alternatively, is it possible to devise a structured rule of reason that represents an acceptable trade-off between predictability and economic rationality?

I begin by discussing the passing of the traditional per se rule in more detail in the next section. The section "Proposed Policies" then considers a number of structured rules of reason that have been offered as replacements for the traditional rule. Following this, the section "Another Proposal" presents my own preferred framework for the analysis of horizontal restraints, and the last section offers a few concluding comments.

THE PASSING OF THE PER SE RULE

Contemplation of the results produced by the per se rule in the *Sealy* and *Topco* cases in 1967 and 1972, respectively, may have served to reduce the enthusiasm of that rule's defenders. *Sealy* involved what was in effect a joint venture among about thirty manufacturers of bedding products that had agreed to share the Sealy trademark. The joint venture fixed prices and assigned exclusive territories; the Supreme Court found both practices illegal per se. But *Sealy* clearly did not involve a cartel arrangement: Sealy's market share was less than 20 percent, and it made no attempt to include its major rivals. Instead, by concentrating on maintaining nationwide distribution of the Sealy trademark, this joint venture permitted a set of relatively small firms to take advantage of economies of national advertising. Price fixing and market division seem likely to have served mainly to align the interests of the participating sellers by making it impossible for them to "free-ride" on each other's promotional activity, thus serving to strengthen the joint venture in the competitive arena.[13]

Topco was a cooperative association of twenty-five regional supermarket chains that functioned as a purchasing agent for private label products and enabled its members to exploit scale economies in purchasing. The average regional market share of Topco's members was about 6 percent; about 10 percent of their sales were of private label products bearing the Topco name. The per se rule came into play in this case because Topco members agreed to sell Topco-brand products in designated territories, which were usually exclusive. Despite a finding that private labeling could be procompetitive and beneficial to consumers, the Court found that Topco's use of exclusive territories was sufficient for a finding of per se illegality. It is clear, however, that without exclusivity, individual members would not have been able to reap the full benefits of promoting Topco products; they would have been vulnerable to price-cutting by other members of the association.

Thus while both these cases involved market division, and *Sealy* involved price-fixing, neither bore more than the most superficial resemblance to the cartel arrangements that are the real target of Section 1. In both cases it seems likely that overall economic efficiency was enhanced by—and even that consumers benefited from—the arrangements that were declared per se illegal by the Court.[14]

Of course, two socially undesirable decisions do not by themselves make much of a case for abandoning the per se rule. As Justice Marshall noted in the passage in his *Container Corp.* dissent quoted earlier, one should support the per se rule despite occasional undesirable outcomes if one believes both that cases that would produce such outcomes are rare and that such cases would be difficult for courts to identify reliably. Perhaps the main reason for the demise of the per se rule is that these beliefs are not nearly as widely held as they once were. The climate of opinion among economists and lawyers as regards contractual restraints—both horizontal and vertical—has shifted substantially in recent years.

This shift in opinion has been clearest in the vertical area, where a variety of more or less plausible mechanisms through which vertical restraints could in theory enhance economic efficiency and benefit consumers have been identified.[15] Not only do actual vertical arrangements sometimes seem to mirror those studied in theoretical research, but that research has provided tools that can be used in analyzing particular cases or, with the addition of facts or presumptions regarding economywide market conditions, in formulating general rules. There remains essentially no academic support for the per se illegality of nonprice vertical restraints and very little support for per se illegality of resale price maintenance. Indeed, some influential commentators have argued for nearly per se legality of all vertical restraints.[16]

Although less has been written about horizontal restraints in the academic economics literature, many of the theoretical arguments that have been persuasive in the vertical area apply there as well. This reflects, in part, the fact that the horizontal/vertical distinction is often not nearly as sharp in practice as it sometimes seems in the classroom. It is thus troublesome that this distinction was so critical in determining legality under the traditional per se rule. For instance, if Topco had been an independent supplier rather than a creature of potentially competing retailers, its territorial exclusivity would have been a vertical nonprice restraint subject to the rule of reason.

Judge Bork's discussion of the free-rider problem in his majority opinion in *Rothery* provides a good example of the close intellectual link between the economics of horizontal and vertical restraints. The case involved Atlas Van Lines, the sixth largest household goods carrier in the United States. Atlas employed 490 independent moving companies, including Rothery, as its agents to provide nationwide service. Atlas and its carrier agents, several of whom sat on its board of directors, accounted for about 6 percent of interstate carriage of used household goods. In all, the industry consisted of at least 1100 interstate carriers employing about 8000 agents; the Herfindahl–Hirschmann Index (HHI) was about 520. Atlas required its agents to carry household goods only on its account (although it permitted them to set up separate corporations to carry goods on their own accounts) and terminated the contracts of those agents that did not comply.

Judge Bork argued that this was clearly a horizontal restraint, if only because Atlas's agents were represented on its board, but, citing *BMI, NCAA*, and *Pacific Stationery* for authority, he did not apply the per se rule. After arguing that Atlas lacked market power and was clearly not a cartel, he argued affirmatively that the arrangements complained of served to enhance efficiency. Also noting that Atlas provided its carriers a "national image" and a variety of specific services (including dispatching, training, some equipment, and support for advertising and painting trucks), he reasoned as follows:

> If the carrier agents could persist in competing with Atlas while deriving the advantages of their Atlas affiliation, Atlas might well have found it desirable, or even essential, to decrease or abandon many [of the] services [it provided to them]. See

Continental T.V. Inc. v. GTE Sylvania Inc., 433 U. S. 35, 55 (1977) ("Because of market imperfections such as the so-called 'free-rider' effect, [certain] services might not be provided . . . in a purely competitive situation. . . . "). . . . On the other side, the firm receiving a subsidized good or service will take more of it. . . . Carrier agents . . . will increase the use of Atlas' services, etc., on interstate carriage for their own accounts, over-consuming that which they can obtain at less than its true cost. In this way, free riding distorts the economic signals within the system so that the van line loses effectiveness in serving customers. The restraint at issue in this case, therefore, is a classic attempt to counter the perceived menace that free-riding poses.[17]

Thus Bork plausibly employed exactly the same economic arguments used by the Supreme Court in its rule-of-reason analysis of *vertical* territorial restrictions in *Sylvania*.[18]

Similarly, the economic arguments used by the Supreme Court to analyze horizontal restraints in *BMI, NCAA*, and *Pacific Stationery* bear at least a family resemblance to arguments that have been made in the vertical arena. *BMI* involved the joint determination by composers and publishing houses of the prices for blanket licenses for the use of copyrighted musical compositions. In finding the per se rule inapplicable to this horizontal restraint, the Court stressed the reduction in transaction costs and the exploitation of scale economies that it found blanket licensing to have permitted.

> ASCAP [a defendant along with BMI] reduces costs absolutely by creating a blanket license that is sold only a few, instead of thousands, of times, and that obviates the need for closely monitoring the [television] networks to see that they do not use more than they pay for. ASCAP also provides the necessary resources for blanket sales and enforcement, resources unavailable to the vast majority of composers and publishing houses. Moreover, a bulk license of some type is a necessary consequence of the integration necessary to achieve these efficiencies, and a necessary consequence of an aggregate license is that its price must be established.[19]

At issue in *NCAA* were restrictions imposed by the NCAA, a nonprofit organization with policies set by its 850-member colleges, on the telecasting of football games. The basic rationale for applying the rule of reason to these arrangements was the finding that *some* horizontal restraints were clearly necessary in order to produce the final product at issue.

> What the NCAA and its member institutions market in this case is competition itself—contests between competing institutions. Of course this would be completely ineffective if there were no rules on which the competitors agreed to create and define the competition to be marketed. . . . Thus the NCAA plays a vital role in enabling college football to preserve its character, and as a result enables a product to be marketed which might otherwise be unavailable.[20]

The Court went on to cite *Sylvania* for the proposition that "a restraint in a limited aspect of a market may actually enhance market-wide competition."[21] The attractiveness of the per se rule was not enhanced by the Court's apparent ability to decide, without a "ramble through the wilds of economic theory," that the particular arrangements at issue were unreasonable—and thus unlawful—because they did not in fact promote efficiency.[22]

Finally, *Pacific Stationery* involved a wholesale purchasing cooperative, Northwest Wholesale Stationers, that redistributed its profits to members, thus enabling them to buy stationery more cheaply than nonmembers. Pacific argued that its expulsion from that cooperative without prior notice or explanation after the fact amounted to a group boycott that was subject to the per se rule. But the Court disagreed because the cooperative lacked market power, and it again discussed likely efficiencies.

> The [cooperative purchasing] arrangement permits the participating retailers to achieve economies of scale in both the purchase and warehousing of wholesale supplies, and also ensures ready access to a stock of goods that might otherwise be unavailable on short notice. The cost savings and order-filling guarantees enable smaller retailers to reduce prices and maintain their retail stock so as to compete more effectively with larger retailers. . . . Wholesale purchasing cooperatives must establish and enforce reasonable rules in order to function effectively. . . . Unless the cooperative possesses market power or exclusive access to an element essential to effective competition, the conclusion that expulsion is virtually always likely to have an anticompetitive effect is not warranted.[23]

It is difficult to quarrel with this reasoning on economic grounds.

Generally, then, the economic argument in favor of removing the per se illegality of horizontal restraints is virtually identical to the argument that has prevailed (at least for nonprice restraints) in the vertical area. In both areas, economic theories (sometimes the same theories) indicate that contractual restraints can improve consumer welfare. And in both areas the courts have been able to use the insights provided by theory to identify, relatively easily, cases in which contractual restraints seem likely to have procompetitive effects. Thus not only are horizontal restraints sometimes productive of economic efficiency in theory, cases in which they are likely to be beneficial in practice seem to occur with some frequency and seem to be identified easily enough by courts that making horizontal restraints illegal per se would impose significant costs on society.[24]

But there is an obvious and critical difference between horizontal and vertical restraints: in theory and in practice, cooperation between rivals is noticeably less likely to be socially desirable than cooperation between buyers and sellers. In most antitrust cases involving horizontal restraints, those restraints seem to constitute more or less pure cartel arrangements, which are virtually certain to harm consumers and very unlikely to enhance overall economic efficiency. A policy of per se legality toward vertical restraints has many advocates; to my knowledge nobody has stepped forward to argue for the per se legality of horizontal restraints.

The key to a sound general policy toward horizontal restraints is thus a workable procedure for distinguishing desirable restraints from undesirable ones. Any such policy must have two parts. First, it must specify the residual domain of application—if any—of the per se rule. That is, it must specify what sorts of restraints, if any, are to be condemned without a detailed inquiry into their actual or likely effects. Second, it must say something about the analysis to be applied in the remaining, rule-of-reason cases. At the very least the policy must state the general criteria the courts are to employ, and it must say more about the structure of the analysis if unnecessary "rambles through the wilds of economic theory" are to be minimized.

PROPOSED POLICIES

As the traditional per se rule has come under attack by courts and commentators, several replacements for it have been offered. In this section, I describe and discuss a number of proposed general policies toward horizontal restraints.[25] I focus on economic issues and leave it to those with appropriate training to discuss the consistency of these proposals with the relevant precedents.[26]

The Bork Proposal

Robert Bork, in his majority opinion in *Rothery* and, earlier, in his book *The Antitrust Paradox*,[27] has proposed a policy toward horizontal restraints that is based on the distinction between "naked" and "ancillary" restraints advanced in William Howard Taft's *Addyston Pipe* decision.

As Bork interprets Taft, naked restraints are those that only serve to limit competition, while ancillary restraints serve to make a legitimate (and thus presumptively socially desirable) "primary" transaction more effective. An agreement that involved only bid-rigging would thus be a naked restraint. Taft's classic discussion of restrictions on the partners' ability to compete with a partnership provides the classic example of an ancillary restraint, the primary transaction in this case being the functioning of the firm.

> [W]hen two men become partners in a business, although their union might reduce competition, this effect was only an incident to the main purpose of a union of their capital, enterprise, and energy to carry on a successful business, and one useful to the community. Restrictions in the articles of partnership upon the business activity of the members, with a view to securing their entire effort in the common enterprise, were, of course, only ancillary to the main end of the union, and were to be encouraged.[28]

Bork would retain the per se rule for naked restraints and apply a structured rule of reason—discussed below—to ancillary restraints. While I think the naked-ancillary distinction has some utility, it also has important limitations.

Taft's terminology suggests the basic problem. Naked restraints are a bit like pornography: we all know them when we see them, but a workable general classification rule is somewhat elusive. It is clear from the cases discussed above that one cannot simply test for the presence of price-fixing, market division, or collective refusal to deal, as all of these practices were present in arrangements that were likely to have been beneficial on balance. One must look at the total package of horizontal restraints in any particular case and ask whether that package constitutes a naked restraint of trade. The outcome of any such inquiry within Bork's framework will then turn in at least some cases on the standards for judging the presence of a legitimate primary transaction.

If, at one extreme, naked restraints are defined as those contractual arrangements for which efficiency gains cannot be proven, the first stage of many horizontal cases may come to involve protracted, relatively unpredictable rule-of-reason inquiries into claimed efficiencies. However, at the other extreme, if naked restraints are defined as arrangements for which no superficially plausible argument for efficiencies can be concocted, because absolutely no coordination of productive activity is involved, the apparent incidence of nudity in this area might decrease significantly over time.

Consider, for instance, a market division scheme in the cement industry. Such a scheme may both raise prices and prevent a good deal of wasteful cross-hauling. Is it naked because there is no explicit coordination of shipments, or is it ancillary to avoiding waste and improving the ability of cement to compete with other building materials? Or, consider a steel cartel that allocates production among its members to minimize costs and shares profits in some fashion after the fact. This rationalization scheme can enhance overall economic efficiency if the firms' costs differ enough, although consumers will generally be harmed (see note 14, *supra*). Is the collective determination of total output a naked restraint, or is it ancillary to reducing the cost of steel and thus enhancing the industry's ability to compete with other materials and to meet foreign competition? If a very strict definition of naked restraints (no facially plausible efficiency defense) was adopted, one would expect some cartels to succeed in wrapping output restriction in the cloth of efficiency enhancement.

As the examples above indicate, the distinction between primary and ancillary provisions of a complex agreement is somewhat blurry and is not particularly useful in distinguishing between harmful and beneficial restraints. As an economic matter, if a contract or other agreement has multiple provisions and multiple effects, there is no rigorous, general way to decide what is "primary" and what is "ancillary." It is the total package that matters — both to the parties and to society as a whole. Thus the primary/ancillary distinction seems to invite formal, scholastic analysis, lacking economic substance, of contractual terms; economically empty debates over the "proper" allocation of joint and common costs in public utility ratemaking come to mind.

Now let me consider the structured rule of reason that Bork proposes for application to restraints found to be "ancillary." In *The Antitrust Paradox*, Bork advocates a two-stage approach.

1. Is the restraint "essential" if the primary activity involved (the activity to which it is ancillary) is to be carried on? If so, it is legal. If not, we go to the second tier.
2. Are *all three* of the following conditions met? If so, the restraint is legal; if not, it is not.
   (a) "The agreement fixing prices or dividing markets is ancillary to a contract integration; that is, the parties must be cooperating in an economic activity other than the elimination of rivalry, and the agreement must be capable of increasing the effectiveness of that cooperation and no broader than is necessary for that purpose.
   (b) "The collective market share of the parties does not make the restriction of output a realistic danger (judged by rational horizontal merger standards).

   (c) "The parties must not have demonstrated a primary purpose or intent to
       restrict output."[29]

Bork goes on to argue that, "Where there is no coordination of productive
activity, [condition (a), above] is violated; such an agreement is naked rather
than ancillary and should be illegal per se."[30]

I have three specific problems with this structured rule of reason. First, I am
skeptical that the first stage's "essentiality" test can be made rigorous or predictable. As the Supreme Court recognized in *NCAA*, for instance, some cooperation between competitors clearly is "essential" to produce competitive sports. But
it is hard to see how one could ever hope with any confidence to sort the multiple
contractual elements of a real, complex league arrangement into those that are
"essential" and those that are merely very useful. Again, it is the total package
that matters.

Second, the second stage's condition (a) is simply the naked-ancillary distinction all over again, with the added complication that the court must decide if the
restraint at issue is "no broader than is necessary." As the discussion above might
suggest, I do not think the naked/ancillary distinction is sharp enough to make
two different, useful cuts in the same case, even with the added "no broader than
is necessary" test. And the ability of judges or juries — or for that matter anyone
not intimately familiar with the relevant commercial realities — to predict accurately the likely effects of altering specific provisions of complex contractual
schemes is at the very least doubtful. Decisions that turn on this test often seem
rather arbitrary and forced.

Third, I have serious doubts about the potential importance of evidence
regarding "primary purpose or intent" under Bork's proposal. Firms often have
multiple objectives when entering into contractual arrangements; how can one
decide which of these is "primary"? Moreover, it is common knowledge even
among economists that it is difficult to predict what will result from a judicial
inquiry as to the collective intent of a set of diverse individuals in a single firm.
Intent seems considerably more elusive in a multifirm context; how can any firm
know what damning language lurks in memoranda in the files of another firm's
middle managers?

In Judge Bork's *Rothery* opinion, this analytical machinery does not seem
to have been fully deployed. Neither essentiality nor intent are discussed at any
length. Rather, Bork seems to place most weight on the market power test implicit in the use of "rational horizontal merger standards" in condition (b), above.
And, as I discuss later in the section "Another Proposal," I think this is completely appropriate.

The Calvani Proposal

Writing for the Federal Trade Commission in *Massachusetts Board*, Commis-
sioner Calvani offers a structured approach with three stages.

   1. "First, we ask whether the restraint is 'inherently suspect.' In other words, is the
      practice the kind that appears likely, absent an efficiency justification, to 'restrict
      competition and decrease output'? For example, horizontal price-fixing and mar-

ket division are inherently suspect because they are likely to raise price by reducing output." If the answer is no, "the traditional rule of reason, with attendant issues of market definition and power, must be employed." If the answer is yes, we move to the second tier.

2. "Is there a plausible efficiency defense for the practice? That is, does the practice seem capable of creating or enhancing competition . . . ? Such an efficiency case is plausible if it cannot be rejected without extensive factual inquiry." If the answer is no, "the restraint can be quickly condemned." If the answer is yes, we move to the third tier.

3. At this level the court must engage in a thorough factual inquiry to ascertain "whether the [efficiency] justification is really valid. If it is, it must be assessed under the full balancing test of the rule of reason." If it is not, "the practice is unreasonable and unlawful under the rule of reason without further inquiry — there are no likely benefits to offset the threat to competition."[31]

Note first that while Bork focuses primarily on evidence relating to market power, without a detailed inquiry into claimed efficiencies, Calvani stresses the analysis of efficiency effects and the need in some cases to balance the two. In particular, Calvani's proposal lacks the "safe harbor" provided to firms with negligible collective market power by stage 2(b) of the Bork proposal.

Bork explicitly denies that balancing efficiency gains and market power losses is ever necessary. "All the court need do is decide that an economic integration capable of producing efficiencies is before it, determine whether the restraint . . . is capable of adding to the efficiencies, and then decide the case on the basis of market power and intent rather than a per se proscription."[32] It is difficult to see, however, how courts could reach economically rational decisions in cases in which both market power and efficiency effects are clearly present without employing what Calvani terms "the full balancing test of the rule of reason."

Calvani's first two stages seem to involve, in part, Bork's test for per se illegality. Presumably "inherently suspect" restraints that lack "a plausible efficiency defense," which Calvani states should be "quickly condemned," would be classed as naked restraints by Bork. Calvani's use of alternative, less familiar language has both costs and benefits. It is less familiar to lawyers and judges than the naked-ancillary terminology, but it is weighed down with less historical baggage. At least to an economist who has tried to read *Addyston Pipe*, the benefits seem quite substantial.

Regarding the first stage of Calvani's proposal, it is unclear if courts are to decide whether an individual restraint or contractual provision is inherently suspect in isolation, or if judgment is to be passed only on an agreement between competitors as a whole. Was the agreement in *BMI* inherently suspect because it involved price-fixing, or was it not because it involved more? Only by considering an agreement as a whole can its likely effects be intelligently evaluated.

It would appear that Calvani expects judgments regarding inherent suspiciousness to be reached after a relatively brief inquiry. It seems odd then that all restraints that pass this screen are to be subjected to "the traditional rule of reason." If an agreement between competitors seems unlikely to raise the probability of effective collusion, why should this trigger an extensive and expensive rule-of-reason analysis of "market definition and power"? It would seem that a structured examination of the likely effects of challenged horizontal restraints would be in order before submitting the parties to the mercies of the unstructured rule of reason. If no adverse effects appear in this examination, there is no need to proceed further.

Finally, Calvani provides no guidance regarding the application of "the traditional rule of reason" beyond the necessity to examine "market definition and power." It is unclear in this proposal what questions are to be asked or how the answers received are to be integrated into a final judgment.

The Areeda Proposal

In his treatise on antitrust law, Professor Areeda argues that one should think of per se rules in general as the result of applying rule of reason analysis on a class basis, not as a distinct species of policy. He accordingly avoids using per se language in his proposed framework for the analysis of horizontal restraints.

1. "The plaintiff must show by argument that the challenged activity is of a type that restrains trade within the meaning of the Sherman Act"—that is, that it tends to impair competition.
   (a) If the restraint "is of the kind that has been regarded as very serious and usually without recognized redeeming virtue, it may be condemned on this showing alone."
   (b) The defendants may nevertheless trigger further inquiry by claiming "justification of the kind which a 'quick look'—usually at the arguments alone—shows to be legitimate in principle and capable of being proved satisfactorily."
2. If further inquiry is thus triggered, plaintiff must show "actual detrimental effects, such as a reduction in output," or, as a surrogate, market power. If this cannot be shown, the restraint is lawful.
3. If plaintiff prevails at stage 2, defendants must then show "that the justifications claimed are legitimate in principle and are actually promoted significantly by the restraint." If this cannot be shown, the restraint is unlawful.
4. If efficiencies are thus established, plaintiff has the burden of showing that "the legitimate objective can be achieved nearly as well by a significantly less restrictive alternative." If plaintiff meets this burden, the restraint is unlawful.
5. Otherwise, the court must balance the pro- and anti-competitive effects of the restraint.[33]

Stage 1 can be viewed in traditional language as defining the residual scope of the per se rule as facially suspect restraints for which plausible efficiency arguments cannot be constructed.[34] One thus takes a "quick look" at the plausible anti- and procompetitive effects of the challenged conduct; restraints that are likely to diminish competition and for which no plausible efficiency rationales can be offered—"naked" restraints of trade in the usual language—are condemned without a detailed factual inquiry.

Unlike Bork and Calvani, Areeda makes inquiry into competitive effects or market power the next step in the analysis. His framework thus provides for what Jorde and Teece have called a "market-power-based safe harbor":[35] horizontal restraints for which a plausible efficiency rationale can be advanced are legal if neither detrimental effects nor market power can be demonstrated, since they can have no anticompetitive effects. An important virtue of proceeding in this order is that economists, enforcement agencies, and courts have considerably more experience in the analysis of market power than in the assessment of the efficiency effects of actual horizontal restraints or hypothetical "less restrictive" alternatives.[36]

Stage 3 is central to all rule of reason analyses in this area. If a horizontal restraint is likely to impair competition, it should be condemned under the antitrust laws unless defendants can show that it is also likely to produce offsetting procompetitive benefits. Stage 4, on the other hand, is somewhat controversial. As I discuss further in the section "Another Proposal," it is unclear whether the analysis of hypothetical, less restrictive alternative arrangements can be carried out with the sort of precision that seems required here.

Finally, it is worth noting that Areeda, like several other commentators, argues for the use of "a kind of 'sliding scale' which demands more proof of power when the benefit seems clear or more proof of benefit or the absence of a less restrictive alternative when the harm appears serious."[37] This policy seems sensible both prescriptively and descriptively.

Current Enforcement Policy

The recently issued Department of Justice *Antitrust Enforcement Guidelines for International Operations* (hereinafter *Enforcement Guidelines*) contains a statement of general enforcement policy that can usefully be compared with the specific proposals discussed above.[38] The Department begins by defining the proper scope of the per se rule.

> The Department condemns as per se unlawful "naked" restraints of trade that are so inherently anticompetitive and so rarely beneficial that extensive analysis of their precise competitive effects is unnecessary. The Department considers a restraint to be naked if it is a type of restraint that is inherently likely to restrict output or raise price and is not plausibly related to some form of economic integration (by contract or otherwise) of the parties' operations that may generate procompetitive efficiencies. The most common examples of naked restraints of trade are price-fixing and bid-rigging schemes among competitors.[39]

In a footnote to the last sentence in this quote, the Department notes that at this first stage in the analysis it does not attempt to determine if efficiencies actually would be produced: "It is enough if the form of integration involved in general generates efficiencies."[40] This first stage thus follows Areeda: the potential of the challenged restraint to facilitate the exercise of market power is first examined, and, if such potential is found, plausible efficiency arguments are sought. If no such arguments are advanced, the restraint is condemned; otherwise the rule of reason is brought to bear.

The *Enforcement Guidelines* describe the Department's general approach to rule-of-reason analysis as follows:

> [T]he Department's first question is whether the transaction or conduct would likely create, enhance, or facilitate the exercise of market power in any relevant market.

. . . If the Department concludes that a particular transaction or course of conduct would not be anticompetitive, the Department will not challenge it, regardless of whether the transaction or conduct actually would result in significant procompetitive efficiencies. . . . If the department does conclude that [there is a market power problem], then the Department considers whether the risk of anticompetitive harm is outweighed by procompetitive efficiencies that the parties claim will result from the transaction or conduct. . . . Of course, if it is clear that equivalent efficiencies can be achieved by means that involve no anticompetitive effect, then the Department would not recognize the parties' efficiencies claim.[41]

Like Areeda, the Department considers market power and anticompetitive effects before turning to the analysis of efficiencies. It thus offers a "safe harbor" to defendants who collectively lack market power. In considering efficiencies, the Department appears to apply a stricter standard to arguments regarding less restrictive alternatives than Areeda: it must be "clear that equivalent efficiencies can be achieved" (not just that "the legitimate objective can be achieved nearly as well") by "means that involve no anticompetitive effect" (not just by "a significantly less restrictive alternative").

I believe that this general enforcement policy, which closely resembles the Areeda proposal, constitutes a sound framework to which the details of an economically rational antitrust policy toward horizontal restraints can be readily attached. In the next section, I discuss a few important details of this sort, beginning with those relevant to the scope of the per se rule and then considering the proper conduct of rule-of-reason analysis.

ANOTHER PROPOSAL

Terminology and fine distinctions aside, all the proposals discussed above agree about the proper scope of the per se rule. In essence, per se treatment is reserved for agreements between competitors that are likely to do nothing but facilitate the exercise of market power—agreements that Bork would quickly classify as "naked" because the parties are plainly not "cooperating in an economic activity other than the elimination of rivalry," for which Calvani would find no "plausible efficiency defense," and which the Department of Justice would find not to be "plausibly related to some form of economic integration . . . that may generate procompetitive efficiencies." Five points should be made regarding this initial "quick look" test.

First, as I have argued above, in order to reach an economically sound judgment regarding the applicability of the per se rule, even at this initial stage, one must look at all the provisions and likely effects of a challenged arrangement and judge that arrangement as a whole. Thus, under this policy, Topco would not be subject to the per se rule simply because it assigned exclusive territories. Rather, it would be made subject to the rule of reason because it did more.

Second, whether or not per se terminology is ultimately retained, it should be clearly understood that arguments that a challenged horizontal restraint produces legitimate procompetitive efficiencies are always admissable; the initial "quick look" should be more than a casual glance. If plausible procompetitive efficiency arguments are advanced, they should trigger a more detailed (rule-of-reason) inquiry.

Third, in the interest of clarity and efficiency, some general guidance must be provided as to the sorts of arrangements that are likely to fail this threshold test. The *Enforcement Guidelines* note only that price-fixing and bid-rigging schemes are the most common examples of such schemes and omit the sensible clarification, present in an earlier draft, that price-fixing may involve, "[f]or example, agreements among competitors to raise their individual prices by a specified amount, to maintain a specified profit margin, or to notify one another before reducing price."[42]

I would add territorial or customer restrictions to the list of inherently suspect practices and subtract price-fixing schemes that have the likely effect of *lowering* prices received or *raising* prices paid. Applying the test outlined in *BMI*,[43] along with basic economic principles, the latter practices do not "facially" appear to be ones that "would always or almost always tend to restrict competition and decrease output"—although a detailed rule-of-reason analysis may subsequently detect such effects in particular cases. This policy would thus place the arrangements in *Kiefer-Stewart* outside the domain of the per se rule. Finally, the *Pacific Stationery* discussion of collective refusals to deal, quoted earlier, would seem to place such practices correctly outside the scope of the per se rule, since likely competitive consequences must be analyzed.

Fourth, as I argued in the section "The Bork Proposal," one might expect a policy of this sort to produce attempts, some of which will no doubt succeed, to disguise cartels as efficiency–enhancing contractual arrangements. Such attempts are, I fear, an inevitable consequence of any limitation of the scope of the per se rule; some potential defendants will try to follow any new path leading to the rule of reason. But this sort of disguise may not even be attempted in the great majority of cases. Clear violations of any conceivable current interpretation of the per se rule, violations disguised only by secrecy, seem to be uncovered almost daily. The difficulty of devising and sustaining even simple collusive arrangements may in most cases deter cartel members from even attempting the more complex task of devising a disguise that might work in public.

Moreover, the enforcement agencies could reduce this problem by being aggressively willing to provide advisory opinions on the per se illegality of proposed agreements between competitors.[44] The "quick look" test described above would surely take much less time to perform in most cases than the evaluation of a typical proposed merger. Pure cartels would be unlikely to come to the agencies openly. Not only are good disguises not easy to devise, as noted above, but an unfavorable official opinion would be expected to subject the industry to subsequent antitrust scrutiny that might well detect a covert cartel. Thus the Department's current practice of taking covert behavior as an indicator of per se illegality (and, indeed, of criminal intent and behavior) would be quite appropriate under this policy.[45] That is, firms could be encouraged to seek advisory opinions by providing explicit immunity from criminal prosecution for those that prenotify, regardless of the Department's opinion of the restraint involved. Firms actually attempting to use contractual restraints to enhance their efficiency would then have both the incentive and ability to design an arrangement that would pass the agencies' per se screen in order to reduce the likelihood of subsequent private or public enforcement actions.

Fifth, it must be admitted that the version of the per se rule advanced here and in the proposals discussed in the section "Proposed Policies" does not fully resolve the economic tension between the antitrust treatments of mergers and of horizontal restraints. Under all these standards, two tiny firms in an unconcentrated market with no entry barriers would still violate the law if they agreed simply to fix prices, even though no economic harm could conceivably result, and a merger between the two firms would be perfectly lawful. I find Bork's discussion of this example persuasive.

> There being no possibility of efficiency, nothing is lost to society by outlawing the agreement. If these parties were allowed to prove lack of market power, all parties would have that right, thus introducing the enormous complexities of market definition into every price-fixing case. . . . [T]he only result would be to make the prosecution of output-restricting cartels more difficult, rendering the law less effective. Very few firms that lack power to affect market prices will be sufficiently foolish to enter into conspiracies to fix prices. . . . There is no unfairness in applying the per se rule to parties whose agreement was useless, since their intent was wrongful.[46]

This argument gains force if per se treatment is confined narrowly to "totally naked" restraints for which no plausible efficiency defense is advanced.

Let me now turn to the rule-of-reason analysis of horizontal restraints for which plausible efficiency arguments are advanced. Broadly following the Areeda framework and the Department of Justice *Enforcement Guidelines*, I would apply a two-stage procedure to analyze such agreements between competitors.

1. Does the agreement, taken as a whole, significantly facilitate the exercise of market power? If no, it is legal, since regardless of intent or efficiencies, it can do no harm. If yes, we proceed to the second tier.
2. Does the agreement produce important static or dynamic economies that could not readily be achieved by an obvious alternative arrangement with no anticompetitive potential? If no, the agreement is illegal, since there are no benefits to balance against the costs of market power.
3. If yes, the court must bite the bullet and perform Calvani's "full balancing test of the rule of reason."

The first stage involves analysis of both the inherent nature of the agreement at issue and the collective market power of the firms involved. The defendants could escape at this level by showing that the agreement involved would be unlikely to facilitate the exercise of market power even if it is assumed, for the sake of argument, that a merger between the parties to the agreement would have this effect. This defense might well have saved the cooperative purchasing agreement in *Pacific Stationery*, the exchange rules at issue in *Chicago Board of Trade*, and the fixing of maximum selling prices in *Kiefer-Stewart*.

Alternatively, defendants could escape at the first level by showing, along the lines of the current *Merger Guidelines*,[47] that they collectively lack market power. The basic economic soundness of the *Merger Guidelines* and the experience with their application to horizontal mergers in both the legal and economic communities argues strongly for considering questions of market power before attempting a detailed analysis of efficiency benefits.[48] Relevant evidence under this framework would include "[t]he collective market share of the parties," to which Bork points, but it would also encompass market concentration levels, barriers to entry, and the other factors discussed in the *Enforcement Guidelines*. As under the *Enforcement Guidelines*, no inquiry into intent would be necessary.[49] Since partial integration by contract is generally reversible, it would be appropriate to require plaintiff to prove more substantial market power risks than would be necessary in a merger case. This safe harbor would surely have saved the arrangements in *Sealy, Topco,* and *Rothery*, and it would have made the analysis of efficiencies in the latter case superfluous.

Moreover, the availability of this second defense would serve, at least in part, to unify the treatment of horizontal restraints and horizontal mergers. It certainly makes economic sense to allow firms that could legally merge to enter into less durable contractual relationships that are not obviously objectionable and that may enhance efficiency.

The language used in describing the second stage of this policy is designed to imply relatively heavy burdens of proof, first on defendant and then on plaintiff. Since possible efficiency gains are often easy to imagine—as in the hypothetical cement and steel cases discussed in the section "The Bork Proposal"—it seems sensible to require defendants to do substantially more than assert theoretical possibilities to offset proof of market power risks.[50] The phrase "important economies" is thus intended here to suggest something approaching (but not reaching) Bork's essentiality test. Since it is usually difficult to show rigorously that consumers will necessarily benefit from any particular agreement or that economic welfare will be enhanced (see note 14, *supra*), defendants should be able to meet their burden here by showing that the arrangement actually involves coordination of productive activity and that it produces important private economies. Ideally, but not necessarily, those economies would be significant enough to support a reasonable inference that some product or service could not be offered if they were not exploited.[51]

The burden would shift if the defendant could establish the existence of important economies. It also seems to be easy—particularly if one is well trained in modern economic theory and does not know the business involved well—to imagine a host of alternative contracts that seem on the surface to produce the same efficiencies. I would thus follow the *Enforcement Guidelines* and require the plaintiff to demonstrate that obvious alternative arrangements exist that would yield equivalent efficiencies but involve no market power risks in order to prevent application of the full balancing test and thus to produce an immediate finding of illegality under the rule of reason.[52] Such proof would most likely take the form of evidence that such alternatives produce equivalent results in related or geographically distinct markets or convincing testimony from individuals who know well the relevant commercial realities.

Finally, the third stage of the approach proposed here seems necessary as a logical matter if cases with both market power costs and efficiency benefits clearly present are to be intelligently decided. I would not expect many decisions to involve explicit balancing of costs and benefits, however.[53] Since the existence of both costs and benefits is likely to be at issue in most cases, I would expect courts to use a "sliding scale" in stages 2 and 3; that is, to require stronger evidence on market power when efficiencies are clearly present and to require stronger evidence on efficiencies when market power is a clear danger.[54] Thus decisions are likely to continue to be written in terms of the existence of costs or benefits, rather than their magnitude.

CONCLUDING COMMENTS

I applaud the passing of the traditional per se rule against horizontal restraints. Its demise, however, presents both a challenge and an opportunity. The challenge is to devise an alternative policy with enough structure to maintain acceptable predictability and to avoid unnecessary and unproductive rambles through the wilds of economic theory. The opportunity is the chance to reduce the incidence of undesirable outcomes, like those in *Sealy* and *Topco*, that were produced by the traditional rule.

I have argued in this essay that the challenge can be met and the opportunity can be seized by policies that have the effect of confining the per se rule narrowly to utterly naked restraints of trade with no plausible efficiency benefits, that employ a rule-of-reason analysis of the remaining cases, and that rely heavily on the same market power tests that have come to dominate the evaluation of proposed mergers. I realize, of course, that antitrust policy is ultimately made by judges on the field as they decide particular cases, not by economists' shouts from the sidelines. I can only hope that the analysis here contributes to what is very likely — given the historic rate at which the practical meaning of the Sherman Act's constitutional language has evolved — to be a policy development process that will occupy judges, lawyers, and even economists for years, if not decades, to come.

NOTES

I am indebted for useful comments to participants in the Eighth Annual NERA Antitrust Seminar and in the Berkeley Conference, particularly Phillip Areeda, William Baxter, Joe Brodley, Jerry Hausman, Howard Kitt, Charles Rule, and the editors. This essay reflects only the author's opinions, not necessarily those of the Council of Economic Advisers, and only the author is responsible for its defects.

  1. United States v. Addyston Pipe & Steel Co., 85 F. 271 (6th Cir. 1898), aff'd, 175 U.S. 211 (1899); United States v. Trenton Potteries Co., 273 U.S. 392 (1927); United States v. Socony-Vacuum Oil Co., 310 U.S. 150 (1940).
  2. For a recent discussion of this hypothesis, see G. Bittlingmayer, "Did Antitrust Policy Cause the Great Merger Wave?" *Journal of Law and Economics* 28 (1985): 77.
  3. United States v. Container Corp. of America, 393 U.S. 333, 341 (1969).
  4. Chicago Board of Trade v. United States, 246 U.S. 231 (1918).
  5. 273 U.S. 392, 401 (1927); 310 U.S. 150, 217 (1940).
  6. In particular, the often-cited dictum that "the test of legality is whether the restraint imposed is such as merely regulates and perhaps thereby promotes competition or whether it is such as may suppress or even destroy competition" (246 U.S. 231, 238

[1918]) does not shed much light on central issues in later cases. One can also note the difficulties raised, at least until *Socony-Vacuum*, by Appalachian Coals v. United States, 288 U.S. 244 (1933).

7. This was done, for instance, in Kiefer-Stewart Co. v. Joseph E. Seagram & Sons, 340 U.S. 211 (1951).

8. Broadcast Music, Inc. v. CBS, 441 U.S. 1 (1979).

9. NCAA v. Board of Regents of the University of Oklahoma, 468 U.S. 85, 104 n. 26 (1984).

10. Rothery Storage & Van Co. v. Atlas Van Lines, Inc., 792 F.2d 210 (D.C. Cir. 1986), *cert. denied*, 107 U.S. 880 (1987). The cases cited here but not above are, in order: Northwest Wholesale Stationers, Inc. v. Pacific Stationery & Printing Co., 105 S. Ct. 2613 (1985), Topco Associates, Inc. v. United States, 405 U.S. 596 (1972), and United States v. Sealy Corp., 388 U.S. 350 (1967).

11. As *Chicago Board of Trade* illustrates, it is unlikely that *all* horizontal restraints were ever per se illegal, and it is unclear that *Topco* and *Sealy* were overruled—since the Court continues to cite them—although they would probably be decided differently today.

12. 405 U.S. 596, 609 n. 10 (1972).

13. The "free-rider" problem is discussed further below.

14. It should be noted for the sake of clarity that, despite implicit assertions to the contrary by some lawyers of the Chicago School, consumer welfare and economic efficiency are rather different standards. Economic efficiency involves the sum of consumer and producer welfare (profit). Consumer welfare might seem to be the stricter standard, since firms rarely take actions to lower their own profits, but a firm may sometimes lower its rivals' profits by more than it increases its own so that total producer welfare falls. Profitable entry into a monopolized market by a high-cost producer, for instance, can enhance consumer welfare but reduce economic efficiency; a subsequent merger between these firms can have the opposite effects. (See R. Schmalensee, "Is More Competition Necessarily Good?" *Industrial Organization Review* 4 [1976]: 120, and "Competitive Advantage and Collusive Optima," *International Journal of Industrial Organization* 5 [1987]: 351.) The multiplication of examples of this sort by recent theoretical research suggests that neither standard can be rigorously employed on a case-by-case basis; in practice one must often rely heavily on the presumption that vigorous competition is more likely to enhance both consumer welfare and overall efficiency than any other alternative pattern of behavior.

15. An early and influential contribution, which introduced the free-rider problem as an efficiency rationale for vertical restraints, is L. G. Telser, "Why Should Manufacturers Want Fair Trade?" *Journal of Law and Economics* 3 (1960): 86. Surveys of the now voluminous theoretical literature on vertical restraints are provided by J. Tirole, *The Theory of Industrial Organization* (Cambridge: MIT Press, 1988), ch. 4, and M. Katz, "Vertical Marketing and Franchising Arrangements," in R. Schmalensee and R. D. Willig, eds., *Handbook of Industrial Organization* (Amsterdam: North-Holland, 1989). Since the markets modeled in this literature are imperfectly competitive, welfare outcomes tend to be ambiguous; it is generally shown that privately profitable vertical restraints that do not promote collusion may, but need not, enhance economic efficiency and even benefit consumers.

Considerably less empirical work has been done in this area. Most is broadly supportive of the notion that vertical restraints often serve legitimate business purposes; there is little analysis of ultimate effects on consumers or overall efficiency. See, for instance, R. N. Lafferty, R. H. Lande, and J. B. Kirkwood, eds., *Impact Evaluation of Federal Trade Commission Vertical Restraints Cases* (Washington,

D.C.: U.S. Federal Trade Commission, 1984), and T. W. Gilligan, "The Competitive Effects of Resale Price Maintenance," *Rand Journal of Economics* 17 (1986): 544.

16. See, for instance, R. Posner, "The Next Step in the Antitrust Treatment of Restricted Distribution: Per Se Legality," *University of Chicago Law Review* 48 (1981): 6.

17. 792 F.2d 210, 222–3 (1986).

18. It is interesting to note that the *Sylvania* Court, writing only two years before *BMI* was decided, explicitly asserts (n. 28) that "there is no doubt that [horizontal restrictions originating in agreements among the retailers] would be illegal per se" and goes on to cite *Topco*. It is also worth noting that the economic arguments in *Sylvania* and *Rothery* deal directly only with efficiency gains accruing to parties to the litigation; no explicit attempt is made to analyze net benefits to consumers or to society as a whole. This thinking reflects a point made in note 14, *supra*: courts must generally rely on the presumption that effective competition serves the public interest, rather than on formal applications of the economic efficiency or consumer welfare standard.

19. 441 U.S. 1, 21 (1979).

20. 468 U.S. 85, 101–2 (1984).

21. 433 U.S. 36, 51–57 (1977).

22. Similarly, in *Indiana Federation of Dentists* the Court cited *BMI* for the proposition that "we have been slow . . . to extend per se analysis to restraints imposed in the context of business relationships where the economic impact of certain practices is not immediately obvious" (F.T.C. v. Indiana Federation of Dentists, 476 U.S. 447, 458–9 [1986]), but went on to find for the plaintiff because "no credible arguments were advanced for the proposition that [the challenged restraint] has any . . . procompetitive effect" (*Id.* at 459).

23. 105 S. Ct. 2613, 2620–1 (1985).

24. This apparently widely held belief, which I admit to sharing, does not rest on a body of empirical research nearly as substantial as even the rather thin empirical literature on vertical restraints. It apparently rests instead on the general persuasiveness of theoretical analysis that at least shows that vertical and horizontal restraints can serve legitimate business purposes (even though their effects on consumer welfare or efficiency are often ambiguous) and the apparent confirmation of this theory in a relatively small sample of cases.

25. For an interesting general discussion of appropriate policy in this area that does not propose a specific alternative of the sort considered below, see L. Sullivan, "The Viability of the Current Law on Horizontal Restraints," *California Law Review* 75 (1987): 835.

26. This discussion overlaps to some extent with the valuable analysis of alternative policies in T. M. Jorde and D. J. Teece, "Innovation, Cooperation, and Antitrust" (see Chapter 3 in this volume). Jorde and Teece focus on cooperative innovation and consider the precedential implications of recent Supreme Court decisions in this area and the interpretation of those decisions by lower courts. Although our foci thus differ, we reach similar conclusions on a number of issues—notably the value of a "safe harbor" based on market power.

27. R. Bork, *The Antitrust Paradox: A Policy at War with Itself* (New York: Basic Books, 1978). See also R. Bork, "The Rule of Reason and the Per Se Concept: Price Fixing and Market Division," Part 1, *Yale Law Journal* 74 (1965): 775, and Part 2, *Yale Law Journal* 75 (1966): 373.

28. 85 F. 271, 280 (6th Cir. 1898). This discussion is cited by the Court as providing support for its *BMI* decision.

29. *Antitrust Paradox, supra* note 27, at 278–79.

30. *Id*. at 279.

31. *Massachusetts Board of Registration in Optometry*, Docket 9195, announced June 21, 1988 (CCH Trade Cases ¶22,555, 6-28-88, at p. 22,243).

32. *Antitrust Paradox, supra* note 27, at 278.

33. P. Areeda, 7 *Antitrust Law* (Boston: Little, Brown and Company 1986), ch. 15, pp. 428–30.

34. Areeda (*Id*. at 414–16) notes that confusion has been produced by applying the per se label in antitrust to actual or proposed rules that exclude arguments on three very different issues: reasonability, market power, and justification. For instance, both price-fixing and tying contracts are commonly said to be per se illegal, even though arguments on market power are critical in tying cases but excluded in price-fixing litigation. Areeda's approach excludes reasonability and specifies how market power and justification are to be considered.

35. *Supra* note 26.

36. For this reason I prefer the Areeda framework to the alternative sketched by Professor Kauper ("The Sullivan Approach to Horizontal Restraints," *California Law Review* 75 [1985]: 893, 913–15), in which detailed inquiry into efficiencies and less restrictive alternatives (Areeda's third and fourth stages) precedes detailed analysis of market power.

37. *Supra* note 33, at 402.

38. 55 *Antitrust & Trade Regulation Report* No. 1391 (Special Supplement, 11-17-88).

39. *Id*. at S-6. In an earlier footnote (*Id*. at S-6, n. 45), the Department indicates that "all references in these Guidelines to raising price should be read to include depressing price where the concern is with the exercise of market power by buyers."

40. *Id*. at S-6, n. 47.

41. *Id*. at S-6, 7.

42. 53 *Federal Register* 21584, 21588 (June 8, 1988).

43. 441 U.S. 1, 19–20 (1979).

44. The Department of Justice has, of course, provided such opinions through the Business Review procedure, and it seems to have been widely expected at its creation that the Federal Trade Commission would routinely provide judgments of this sort to the business community.

45. *Supra* note 38, at S-7. See also C. F. Rule, Assistant Attorney General, Antitrust Division, "Criminal Enforcement of the Antitrust Statutes: Targeting Naked Cartel Restraints," Remarks before the 36th Annual ABA Antitrust Section Spring Meeting, March 24, 1988.

46. *Antitrust Paradox*, note 27 *supra*, at 269.

47. *U.S. Department of Justice Merger Guidelines*, June 14, 1984; reprinted in 2 *Trade Regulation Reports* [CCH] ¶¶4491–95.

48. For a set of economic evaluations of the *Merger Guidelines* and their application to horizontal mergers, see S. Salop et al., "Symposium: Horizontal Mergers and Antitrust," *Journal of Economic Perspectives* 1 (1987): 3. I am sympathetic to the argument of Professors Jorde and Teece (see Chapter 3 in this volume) that the *Merger Guidelines* do not provide a fully acceptable framework for assessing market power in innovation–intensive industries. The problem is that industrial organization economics has yet to produce such a framework, nor has it yet provided much guidance for the assessment of likely dynamic efficiencies.

49. As Areeda suggests (*supra* note 33, ¶1506), evidence on intent would seem to be useful primarily in assisting the analysis of efficiency claims. Evidence that asserted efficiency gains were discovered after the fact and did not motivate defendants' decisions must lower the probability of their existence.

50. In particular, merely having obtained a favorable advisory opinion from the enforcement agencies should not serve to meet defendant's burden here. The test for per se illegality is the absence of a facially plausible efficiency defense; the requirement here is for an affirmative demonstration of real efficiencies. See also Oliver Williamson's convincing arguments regarding agencies' and courts' recent excessive readiness to accept theoretical "free rider" arguments in lieu of real proof of efficiencies (see Chapter 7 in this volume).

51. Of course, if defendants can actually establish that some good or service would not be provided but for the challenged restraint, if all obvious alternatives that would produce the same result would also entail market power risks, and if the only market power dangers involve the newly created market, the restraint should be lawful. Consumers are clearly no worse off if a new product is made available, even if it is effectively monopolized.

52. Even though Areeda proposes an apparently lighter burden on this point, his discussion of the difficulties of analyzing alternative contractual arrangements would seem to favor the position taken here. See Areeda, *supra* note 33, ¶1505.

53. Professor Kauper also makes this point (*supra* note 36, at 915).

54. See Areeda, *supra* note 33, at 402.

6

Ignorance and Antitrust

FRANK H. EASTERBROOK

The hallmark of the Chicago approach to antitrust is skepticism. Doubt that we know the optimal organization of industries and markets. Doubt that government could use that knowledge, if it existed, to improve things, given the ubiquitous private adjustments that so often defeat public plans, so that by the time knowledge had been put to use the world has moved on.[1] Efforts to improve markets through law aim at a moving target, with a paradox: if an economic institution survives long enough to be studied by scholars and stamped out by law, it probably should be left alone, and if an economic institution ought to be stamped out, it is apt to vanish by the time the enforcers get there. No wonder Chicago does not have a stirring program for aggressive antitrust enforcement.[2] To have such a program is to deny one or more of the premises underlying the analysis.

I

If the program implied by Chicago's analysis – clobber cartels and mergers to monopoly but treat with great skepticism proposals to do anything else – has not converted all judges and political actors as fully as it has convinced the Antitrust Division, Chicago's analytical lens is at least in wide use. Everyone at this conference believes that antitrust analysis means economic analysis. So does almost every judge. All have accepted the proposition that antitrust policy divorced from economics would be a calamity, and an antitrust policy conjoined with some inconsistent social policy would be incoherent and ineffectual.[3] To keep prices down and efficiency up, in the interests of consumers and the economy as a whole, courts and other enforcers must think like economists.

Which is easier said than done. Economic method entails more than recognizing that demand schedules slope downward and that people make decisions on the margin. To learn anything valuable about an industry or market the economist must collect facts, formulate hypotheses about the effects that are likely if the conduct is monopolistic, use data to search for these effects, and present the results to the scholarly community for the inevitable critique and refinement (sometimes disproof). This process of hypothesis-testing is alien to those trained in law and requires mathematical and statistical skills that lawyers and judges lack; it takes data (often unavailable, always costly) and time (often too much for the judicial system), and the results are not "truths" but estimates of probabilities.

Many of the old cases establishing per se rules were based on the belief that judges could not figure out the economic effects of business practices. The Supreme Court told us in *Standard Stations* that requiring the court to learn the economic effects of a practice would set up "a standard of proof, if not virtually impossible to meet, at least ill-suited for ascertainment by courts."[4] Again in *Topco*: "courts are of limited utility in examining difficult economic problems."[5] Yet again in *Illinois Brick*, where the Court described the obstacles to even so "simple" an exercise as determining the difference between the actual and competitive price, on the assumption that there was a cartel.[6] The Court recoiled in horror from the prospect of computing elasticities of demand and supply, as well it should have. Computing elasticities is only one of the many steps required for a full economic assessment of a novel business practice, however. Difficulties of collecting and interpreting data lead courts to ignore the theory of second best and to disregard in merger cases claims that the union will produce efficiencies greater in magnitude than the overcharge, although in principle such savings could justify mergers that create or augment market power.[7] Courts and the FTC could not even compute costs of service to implement the cost-justification defense under the Robinson-Patman Act; what are they to make of more complex disputes?

In designing legal rules courts can draw on the accumulated wisdom of the economic profession. Judges can examine hundreds of theories, models, arguments, and studies, subjected through the years to professional testing by other economists. Even when built on this base, rules may be flawed. Getting things right at the level of rules is much more likely than the chance that the court can start from scratch and determine, under the vacuous standard of *Chicago Board of Trade*,[8] whether a novel practice in particular circumstances satisfies the rule of reason.

That rules dominate case-by-case assessments of consequences is a lesson learned in other corners of the law. Think of the business judgment rule in corporate law: judges who do not hesitate to create rules of general application quail at the thought of examining any particular business decision. They haven't the data to make better decisions, and even if they did the consequences of awarding damages whenever bad decisions hurt investors would be frightening— managers, risk averse because they cannot hold diversified portfolios of employment, would respond by becoming Milquetoasts, even though risk-taking may be most desirable for investors and the economy. If judges had the data, we would not trust them to make good decisions. The business world relies on financial incentives to encourage managers to make the best use of knowledge and to weed out those who, despite their best efforts, cannot do as well as others. Judges do not profit from making astute business decisions and are not let go for making bad ones.

Next think of tort law. Engineers spend years designing cars and other complex machines (or drugs) to achieve a sensible balance of safety, efficacy, and cost. The interactions are subtle and often hard to trace. Regulatory agencies study many of these compromises to determine whether safety has received adequate weight in the process. We then allow judges and juries to second-guess the outcome in "design defect" tort cases, putting high school dropouts in judgment both of teams of engineers and of consumers (who may prefer cheaper but more risky products to those with maximum safety). Do juries beat producers, consumers, and regulators at determining whether cars should have airbags, or whether the Sabin live-virus polio vaccine is preferable to the Salk killed-virus vaccine? Although many thoughtful persons believe that the compensatory functions of tort law are worth the costs of the process, few are willing to defend the technical accuracy of verdicts, and many believe that case-by-case decisionmaking in such complex questions is a disaster.[9] Is case-by-case decisionmaking in antitrust fundamentally different?

To the extent judges make economic decisions in antitrust cases, they are making predictions about tomorrow's effects of today's practices. This is problematic under the best of circumstances. Economists start from existing practices and try to explain why they exist and survive. Even when all agree about the effects so far, they disagree about impending effects under changed conditions. Experts will take diametrically opposed positions. Any competent economist can construct a model showing that almost any practice injures consumers when certain assumptions hold. *Whether* they hold is an empirical question on which the economist will express a longing for data and a certitude that is not necessarily linked to available knowledge. To say this is not to question the ethics of the profession, for there is genuine difficulty in predicting the future even when we know all about the present — which we don't.

Consider this: *every* scholar working in antitrust and industrial organization believes that a *majority* of other scholars do not understand — even hold perverse views on — the topics about which he knows the most. If you do not believe it, reread the papers delivered at this conference. I need not draw out implications for the ability of generalist judges to give correct answers to knotty questions arising out of novel business practices.

None of this is the least bit surprising; disagreement and uncertainty is an outcome of the division of labor among scholars. No one can be "up" on even a large fraction of the work going on in industrial organization. Ronald Coase has observed that theories (the glorified name for arguments) always run well ahead of data.[10] You need a model to know what to look at (and for); without one the world is cacophony. That arguments outstrip knowledge in scientific endeavor is not only inevitable but also desirable: it is how progress occurs. What is desirable in science is not so attractive in law. Social and physical scientists use their models to improve the state of human understanding. Judges acting on models impose fines, put people in jail, and forbid conduct that may well be beneficial. That's different business, not so easy to justify on the basis of arguments, however plausible they seem to generalists.

Translation from social science to law should be a process of conserving on the costs of error and information. We wish to hold to a minimum the sum of

(a) the welfare losses from inefficient business arrangements; (b) the welfare losses from efficient business arrangements condemned or discouraged by legal rules; and (c) the costs of operating the legal system. How? The judge must decide between approaches before the economics profession is confident which is best, and in the process increases all three of these kinds of cost. A century of antitrust law, and the profession is *still* debating the merits of almost every practice except cartels and mergers to monopoly—and dissenting voices are being heard even on those subjects.

Take, for example, the problem of vertical restrictions on distribution. The data are Janus-faced, showing that these restrictions lead to higher prices (on which plaintiffs seize) and greater output (on which defendants seize). In all likelihood you can't have one without the other, for the higher prices are what induce dealers to supply additional services to customers, modifying "the product" from consumers' perspective to be a product-plus-service bundle. (A different product, just as a computer with a graphical interface and ease-of-use built in is a different product from one that is command-line based and requires more training.)

You need a theory to help decipher the facts, yet the profession cannot settle on a theory.[11] Neoclassical microeconomics does very well indeed for some common practices, such as cartels and mergers. Success in explaining the practices and their effects has led to the dominance of the economic approach to antitrust. Yet this is not where the action is in litigation. Forces that influence the decision when to settle and when to litigate ensure that more problematic practices dominate litigation. These unusual practices come to court before there is any theory at all, let alone competing theories.

Aspen Skiing is an excellent example.[12] The larger of two firms in the ski business in Aspen, Colorado, refused to cooperate with its rival in offering joint lift tickets. Perhaps this raised its rival's costs of doing business, allowing the larger firm to raise its own prices (if Aspen is a market). Perhaps this prevented its rival from taking a free ride on customers lured to Aspen by the larger firm's services and ads. No one has offered an attractive way to organize observations about such conduct; at all events, the parties did not collect the data needed to test conflicting hypotheses about the conduct, and the judge punted by giving the jury instructions so vague that it was left to assess the morality rather than the efficiency of the conduct.[13]

Aspen is the rule, not the exception. Try to think of any subject in the domain of antitrust—other than cartels and mergers to monopoly—in which you are confident that the decision of a lawyer-judge and twelve jurors with high school educations, guided by the economic analysis of two lawyers and some economic witnesses, will systematically beat the market in coming up with "good" results. Where are the triumphs of the judicial process in preceding the economic profession to an understanding of the effects of business practices?

Take as an example the subtheme of this conference: the relation between antitrust and innovation. An antitrust policy that reduced prices by 5 percent today at the expense of reducing by 1 percent the annual rate at which innovation lowers the costs of production would be a calamity. In the long run a continuous rate of change, compounded, swamps static losses. So what is the relation between concentration and cooperation, the bugbears of antitrust policy, and cost reduction (equivalently, the creation of improved products at the same cost) through innovation? Professors Jorde and Teece employ Joseph Schumpeter's approach to the problem and look sympathetically on claims that cooperation, if not concentration *simpliciter*, promotes innovation.[14] This is a logical proposition because the inventor cannot capture all of the benefits of new information unless it is a monopolist, collects royalties (or some equivalent return) from other manufacturers, or both. Yet what is logical is not always true. For decades economists have tried to confirm or refute Schumpeter's views of the relation between innovation and concentration, without success. One survey after another reports: "We don't know."[15] We don't know on average, aggregating all industries. We know even less about the relation in particular industries, or the effects of particular arrangements, which would be the subject of litigation.[16] How can antitrust cope, when concentration and cooperation have dangers of uncertain magnitude and a legal rule inhibiting concentration and cooperation may have costs of still larger magnitude? If, with Jorde and Teece, we allow cooperation, but only if the cooperating firms lack market power, we give up at the outset most of the potential gains — for when the cooperating firms lack market power they face the free-riding on innovation that they wanted to curtail by cooperating. If a rule allowing cooperation but limiting the market share of the cooperators is optimal, can courts implement it? The relevant market structure is the one that will prevail *after* the innovation is brought to market, because only then will it be possible to collect monopoly profits on the basis of the joint research. Yet this is the datum least likely to be known.

II

Let me give you just a few illustrations of the difficulty of using economics case-by-case to settle the question whether a novel practice is efficient (or, if you prefer, beneficial to consumers). I participated as lawyer in two of these cases and as judge in one, so you may discount for bias. You might conclude alternatively that if even deep study of a case does not yield a confident view of the economic consequences, something is amiss.

My first example is *Jefferson Parish Hospital District No. 2 v. Hyde*,[17] a tie-in case. A hospital granted to a group of anesthesiologists the exclusive right to that medical specialty within its walls. An anesthesiologist based at another hospital sued, contending that this contract monopolized by tying anesthesia to such services as recovery rooms and bedpans. Hyde, the plaintiff, contended that he could furnish better anesthesia to his patients more cheaply than the hospital's group could. The hospital replied that the exclusive contract eliminated free riding on the emergency, training, and supervisory services of the resident group (which furnished anesthesia twenty-four hours a day and ran the hospital's department, including making the choice between physicians and nurse-anesthetists as providers of services). If there was market power vis-à-vis patients, the hospital said, *it* possessed that power and had no reason to cede profits to the resident anesthesiologists but would instead buy those services as cheaply as it could (per unit of quality).

The dispute between the parties about the consequences of the practice may have been important to the Court's decision to moderate the *per se* rule that it formerly applied to tie-ins. After *Hyde* the plaintiff must establish market power in the tying and tied products and must show "forcing," which seems to require inquiry into whether informed consumers would approve of the practice — which they would if it is efficient. Yet how can a court tell? One cannot measure "efficiency" with a micrometer or barometer. The plaintiff's tale of monopoly implies that hospitals with exclusive contracts for anesthesiology (and other services such as radiology and pathology) charge higher prices for these services than those who do not. The defendants' reply that the exclusive is efficient does not necessarily imply lower prices (efficiency could lie in higher quality for the same price), and anyway what price serves as a benchmark? It would be hard to address the question without nationwide data on the market shares and exclusive contracts of hospitals, plus the price and effectiveness of anesthesiology at each. These are hard to come by — the duration of the litigation in *Hyde* was not nearly long enough, and some of the information (such as the quality of services rendered) is not available at all.

Hyde reached the Supreme Court long before the necessary data had been assembled. Three years after the Court's decision, the first useful information was published, by an economist who got a head start as a consulting expert in the case.[18] William Lynk obtained data on market shares and hospitals' use of exclusive contracts, but not on price or quality, and formulated a hypothesis to milk answers from these limited data. He reasoned that if exclusive contracts create or exploit market power, they should be used more often as concentration in the market increases; if they increase efficiency in production, there should be no relation with market concentration, but larger hospitals (holding aggregate concentration constant) would be more likely to use exclusives, because hospitals using efficient methods of production would grow relative to others (or perhaps because the larger the hospital the greater is the need to avert free riding in its "internal market"). The data Lynk assembled show that exclusives are somewhat less likely to be used as market concentration increases, but holding concentration constant exclusives are somewhat more likely to be used in the larger hospitals. Lynk concluded that these data refute the monopoly hypothesis, at least on average, without necessarily confirming his (or any particular) efficiency hypothesis. So some years after *Hyde* the economics profession took a step toward understanding the phenomenon, but too late to help in the litigation and still too uncertain to be a firm basis for deciding tomorrow's cases.

Example No. 2 is *NCAA v. Board of Regents of the University of Oklahoma*.[19] The NCAA controlled the telecasting of football games, limiting both the number of times per year any university could appear on national TV and the number of games available for telecasting. From one perspective the NCAA is a cartel, an association of producers that agreed to cut back output, driving price up and producing monopoly profits. From another perspective the NCAA is a joint venture, making a product (competitive football) that is beyond any one school's power, and without market power given the vast number of televised entertainments available from other sources. The NCAA portrayed itself as granting exclusive and limited rights in order to spread appearances among schools, which affected recruiting (an indirect form of talent-sharing similar in effect to the pro football draft) and maintained competitiveness, among other effects. How can one tell which explanation is correct? The Supreme Court thought it could be done by looking at output. True in the sense that cartels cut back on output while efficient competition increases output. But output *of what*? The Court thought that number of games shown is the measure of output, and by that standard the NCAA had to lose. Yet every TV producer controls output (there are no more than twenty-four episodes of "The Cosby Show" per year), and grants exclusive contracts (reruns of "Star Trek" are limited to one station in each market), and it does not follow that everyone is monopolizing. If Papermate makes pens that write twice as long and so sells fewer, it is not thereby trampling on Senator Sherman's handiwork.

There are other, more interesting measures of output: viewership and advertising revenues. Television stations "sell" viewers to advertisers, the real buyers of time; they use college football and other programs to attract viewers for advertisers' benefit. Advertisers value three things about viewers: the raw number, the demographic characteristics (wealthy viewers have more money to spend on the products), and the concentration of these characteristics in an audience (beer producers want audiences of beer drinkers, perfume producers of perfume buyers, and so on). College football is a valuable commodity because it produces large audiences with relatively high incomes (many viewers are college graduates), and with substantial homogeneity. But professional football does better in each of these criteria, and many other programs—from game shows to reruns of *Citizen Kane*—also attract large and desirable audiences. College football on all available channels may be less attractive to advertisers than college football on one channel, a good movie on a second, and different programs on the remaining frequencies.

From this perspective, the NCAA has market power only if its programs yield a higher price per (quality-adjusted) viewer than they could fetch if colleges sold TV rights independently. If the NCAA has a small share in the "viewership market"—and it does—an inference of market power is implausible, although still conceivable if there is a pool of viewers uniquely attracted to college football and uniquely responsive to the blandishments during the games (the former by no means implies the latter). If however the NCAA is not fundamentally different from the NFL, from Mary Tyler Moore Productions, and from re-releases from Disney Studios, in its ability to scare up the viewers advertisers value, then we should be more willing to infer that the NCAA's rules are beneficial because they make college football a better competitor to these other entertainments.

How, exactly, is a court to tell? Measuring price per *quality-adjusted* viewer is exceedingly difficult. So too is predicting what would happen to viewership in the long run if the rules were changed. When the case reached the Supreme Court, the plaintiffs had no data at all (other than the fact, conceded all 'round, that the NCAA's rules reduced the number of contests telecast), and the NCAA had only data concerning the size of the NCAA in relation to all sports (and other entertainment) on TV, and the price per thousand viewers of these shows. Propositions about what the viewership market would look like under alternative rules were easy to state and impossible to test.

Five years after the Court's decision, we still can't test the parties' different perspectives. Once the Court held the NCAA's rules illegal, universities (and conferences) started selling games directly. The number of games shown went up. Many universities also reported that their total income went down—an outcome consistent with the termination of a monopoly price, but *also* consistent with the abolition of an efficient method of competing against movies and other sports for the advertising dollar. Have the total number of viewers of college football gone up or down? No one has gathered the necessary data.

More important, have the total number of (quality-adjusted) viewers of all TV programs on Saturdays in the fall (college football time) gone up or down? A change that diverts viewers from reruns to college football, but reduces the size of the total audience or the homogeneity of viewers and therefore makes them less attractive to advertisers, would imply a reduction in efficiency and consumers' aggregate wealth. The attractiveness of college football depends on some combination of high-quality play and competitive balance (blowouts lose audience quickly); the NCAA justified its system in part on the ground that spreading around TV appearances would facilitate balanced recruiting and competitive games, implying that the "quality" of college football would erode gradually if the system were changed. Has this begun to occur? Surely we could devise some tests, but no one has done so, and the inferences drawn from data showing an erosion in the total audience for (or price per viewer of) college football would be subject to extended debate. Five years after the decision settling the legal question we still lack essential knowledge about the effects of the NCAA's rules.

Third example, a "bottleneck boycott" *Fishman v. Estate of Wirtz*[20] arose out of a fight to buy the Chicago Bulls, a pro basketball team, in 1972. The Bulls played their games in the Chicago Stadium, the largest arena in Chicago. The owners of the stadium wanted to acquire the Bulls, converting a tenancy to a vertically integrated firm. They persuaded the NBA to turn down a bid by a rival group and so grabbed the brass ring. The plaintiffs, the rival bidders, treated this as exclusionary conduct by an "essential facility"—the stadium—which had not played fair and had converted its monopoly of arenas into a double monopoly. One alternative view is that both stadium and team were "natural monopolies"—that Chicago could not support more than one pro basketball team and jumbo stadium—and therefore ought to be merged. Owned separately, each would try to engross the profit in the basketball business, the stadium through monopoly rents and the Bulls through monopoly ticket and TV prices; such "sequential monopolies" injure consumers even more than single-stage monopolies do, and the injury could be alleviated by merger.[21]

How could a court decide between these competing hypotheses? It might accept the logic of one or the other, but if it tried to measure the facts of the case against economic theory it would come up short. The parties had not gathered data about how the merger in 1972 affected ticket prices, gate, TV and radio audience, and other elements of price and output. If they had the data in hand, what could they have done with it to settle the antitrust question? Changes in the quality of the product dominate the effects of a sequential monopoly. A winning team will generate more revenues without any implication of monopoly. Changes in the popularity of basketball compared with other sports (such as hockey or indoor soccer) also would confound attempts to draw inferences from the data. This is not to say it can't be done, but that the inferences drawn from the attempt will be open to debate. Economic study of a single case, even long after the fact (the parties had fourteen years before the final decision), cannot definitively answer questions concerning efficiency and consumers' welfare.

These three examples are not islands of doubt in a sea of knowledge. Ignorance and uncertain inference are the norm in antitrust.[22] They are doomed to remain so, because the monopoly and efficiency explanations so often imply similar traits. Think of vertical restrictions within a dealership network. If these monopolize, the price rises and output falls. If the restraints cause dealers to supply efficient point-of-sale services or otherwise improve the quality of the full package of goods and services delivered to consumers, again price rises, and quantity may fall (although consumers' surplus would rise because they value the higher quality).[23] Courts are starting to use the available data,[24] but eighty years after *Dr. Miles* there are few data to use and no substantial agreement on how to interpret those we possess. After all, the claim of "this industry is different" just might be right.

Exclusionary practices may monopolize by knocking a competitor out, reducing elasticity of supply and allowing remaining firms to increase price. An observer sees the departure of some firms and an increased concentration. Aggressive, competitive conduct also KOs firms, reducing the number of suppliers. An observer sees the departure of some firms and increased concentration. It is very hard to use data to separate exclusionary from beneficial competition.[25]

Questions that occupy the attention of enforcement agencies and courts often call for assessments of the power of potential competition. Airline mergers are much more troublesome if new entry into city-pair markets is hard than if other carriers stand ready to divert their planes into high-price markets to carry off the profits. Domestic mergers are much less troublesome if foreign firms stand ready to divert additional products into the United States than if they are constrained by tariffs, quotas, and political barriers. How do we measure the amount of potential competition in transportation markets? In markets now characterized by some international trade but plagued by the potential for political reaction? No one—not the economics profession, not the enforcement agencies, not the courts—has a good way to measure the elasticity of supply (and thus the power of potential competition) under such circumstances even six months into the future, let alone for the many years that must come within our ken to understand the long-run effects of current transactions.

Sometimes cooperation is an important ingredient of efficiency. Think of standard-setting organizations, through which members of an industry cooperate to set specifications that make products interchangeable and hence useful. Trade groups trying to devise the characteristics of high definition television (HDTV), or the characteristics of a computer's architecture (the microcomputer market pits NuBus vs. Micro Channel vs. Extended Industry Standard Architecture), produce enough common ground that the category of products will be useful.

Only one system of HDTV could work at a time in a country, maybe in the world; multiple small-computer architectures can prosper, but the number seems to be small.

How is antitrust to treat these cooperative efforts? We would like to compare the dynamic gains over the long run against any allocative losses produced in the short run. Yet for reasons already mentioned, enforcers and courts have a dickens of a time identifying, let alone measuring, allocative losses. There is no way at all to assess the future dynamic gains. Courts cope with the activities of trade associations by asking whether they have acted "fairly" or whether they approve "good" products (shades of design-defect tort litigation!), or whether they display vicious intent[26] – none of which has much if anything to do with consumers' welfare or efficient production. You could imagine some simple rules, such as "forbid standard-setting organizations that cover a substantial market share" or "leave standard-setting organizations alone unless they prevent rival sellers from appealing directly to consumers," and you could debate the merits and demerits of such rules, but it is hard even to imagine how a court could engage in coherent case-by-case decisionmaking.

Even the core of antitrust – cartels and large mergers – no longer produces unanimity in the academy. Take for example the structure-conduct-performance paradigm that informs the law of mergers, including the merger guidelines of the Department of Justice and the National Association of Attorneys General. The law of mergers is based on the belief that more concentration makes it easier for firms to raise price by reducing the elasticity of rivals' supply – whether because of express cartels or because every firm tacitly understands that its interest lies in lower output.[27] Logical though this belief may be, the question is empirical: how much concentration produces what effect on price? Concentration may increase as efficient firms grow relative to others or as fusion produces efficient-sized firms. Which effects dominate? This varies from market to market and time to time, bedeviling the implementation of policy.[28] When data are available they give the answer: "Even substantial concentration yields less effect on price than you think." Courts might be able to use this learning to shape a general approach to mergers; they are unlikely to find a use for it in trying to ascertain the effects of a given merger.

As for cartels: at the heart of the per se rule a rumbling is audible. All of us have long known that one cartel may offset the effects of another one, and that the elimination of a particular cartel therefore cannot be an unalloyed blessing – not unless we have the knowledge necessary to reject the possibility that the cartel in question is a second-best solution to other market power.[29] Donald Dewey made the point general in observing that banning cartels reduces the options available in the production of goods and services, and that some of the options surrendered may be valuable.[30]

Lester Telser then introduced palpitations into antitrust theory by contending that the "efficient cartel" is not just a theoretical curiosity but a frequent occurrence – that cartels are *essential* to consumers' welfare when economies of scale and other indivisibilities of production prevent competitive markets from reaching an equilibrium.[31] If efficient-sized auto plants produce 100,000 cars per year with costs declining through most of the range of production, and the market's demand at average total cost is 350,000 cars, then one can demonstrate formally that an agreement allocating production among manufacturers will promote consumers' welfare by allowing them to run plants full blast for a time while accumulating inventory, then shutting down. Anything else leads to the operation of three plants (too few cars and monopoly prices) or full-time production at four, driving price below cost and ejecting someone from the market, producing three plants (and monopoly prices). Telser's approach, based on the corner of game theory known as the "theory of the core," does not justify price-fixing, but it does explain why firms might need to discuss the building of new plants and the use of existing capacity. From courts' perspective, however, these are the same as price-fixing: any change of output affects price, and there is no ready way to separate an agreement designed to solve an empty core from one designed to reach a monopoly price.

Efforts to determine whether a given industry has an empty core are certain to produce errors galore: we will overlook the problem when it exists or think the core empty when it is not. On one path lies inefficient production, and on the other monopoly. On both we will bear steep costs of conducting the inquiry. So it seems best to treat the theory of the core the way we treat the theory of second best: to worry about it occasionally, to wonder whether it should lead to some change in the way we understand practices and shape rules, but to ignore it in any particular case.[32] Systemic knowledge may inform the rules that govern conduct — or may be ignored across the board — but to try to get every case economically right "on its own facts" is to attempt the impossible and to wreak havoc in the process.

III

Do we then abandon antitrust? Hardly! We should instead use more widely the method we apply to cartels: per se rules based on ordinary effects, disdaining the search for the rare counterexamples. Ditch all attempts to domesticate a novel practice through the tools of litigation; redouble efforts to understand the *category* of similar practices of which the case is an example, and to devise a simple rule for adjudicating claims concerning the category. Decide whether the category is allowed or not at the level of rules, not of cases.

In other words, we must jettison the "never" fallacy. Judges and scholars often say that unless a practice is "never" inefficient, "never" costly to consumers, juries must determine whether it was deleterious in the case at hand.[33] Would anyone take such an approach seriously in a cartel case? Should we say that unless cartels are "never" efficient, we must rummage through the facts case by case to determine the consequences of every price-fixing arrangement? Not on your tintype. Courts started applying per se rules to cartels and other practices early in the history of antitrust. These rules are based on probabilities over the run of cases, on the belief that a *category* of practices is so likely to be undesirable that it is not worth the costs (litigation, uncertainty, and error) of sifting through instances to separate beneficent from baleful. Even proof that a practice saves consumers "millions of dollars" every year does not justify case-by-case inquiry, once the practice is located in a group deemed likely to be harmful.[34] If this is the right way to deal with cartels, it is the right way to deal with other practices. Society can't endure an antitrust law in which heads-the-plaintiff-wins-tails-its-a-jury-question.

Per se rules conserve on information and on the costs of litigation. They hold down the sum of excusing conduct that is harmful, condemning conduct that is beneficial, and inducing firms to steer clear of potentially beneficial practices that create risks of condemnation (or costly litigation). We apply per se rules of illegality to cartels and mergers to monopoly. We apply per se rules of legality in fact if not in name to the introduction of new products (although that may destroy desirable substitutes), to the redesign of old products (same potential effects), to price competition (provided price exceeds cost of manufacture), to charging what the traffic will bear (although that may extract monopoly profits), to expanding capacity (even though new plants may discourage entry), to nonprice vertical restraints. All of this we do on a categorical basis, for to examine the practice at hand in any detail is to abandon per se treatment. The coming decades will either see an extension of these two lists or witness the end of antitrust.[35]

Extending the domain of per se rules is not the only information–conservation device in the future of antitrust. Greater use of a market power threshold is another.[36] Courts already say that proof of market power is the first issue in every case under the rule of reason, because unless the defendant has market power the practice cannot inflict antitrust injury on consumers. Courts are beginning to introduce a market power threshold into the domain of per se rules.[37] When firms without market power employ devices that cannot injure consumers *by creating monopoly prices*, their conduct may well be beneficial—and if there are no benefits, the conduct will die out without the need for judicial condemnation. Courts will not be able to see the benefits in many cases, but they will be there just the same. Treating the lack of market power as a trap door out of antitrust law not only saves parties and courts the costs of inquiry but also dramatically reduces the likelihood of mistaken condemnation of beneficial practices.

A firm without market power could of course injure the plaintiff, perhaps in ways we do not want to approve. The McCoys can injure the Hatfields by opening a rival shop next door, wounding their enemies without injuring consumers in the slightest; so too the Hatfields can shoot the McCoys without possessing market power. Lockheed can injure both its rival McDonnell-Douglas and its own investors by building the L-1011, a plane that overlaps existing offerings in the marketplace and ensures that neither manufacturer will be able to obtain the economies of scale necessary to produce efficiently. But injuries of this kind we ignore, just as we ignore the injuries created by murder, because there is nothing distinctive about them. It would be folly to start drawing demand curves to decide whether murder should be unlawful. To say that the lack of market power is a trap door *out of antitrust* is not to say that it is a trap door *out of the legal system*. Dealership terminations that make no sense as antitrust cases (because no market power means no monopoly price) may make perfect sense as breach-of-contract cases.

Antitrust is a complex body of law requiring exceedingly expensive tools, with great potential to injure the economy by misunderstanding and condemning complex practices. Legal problems that would not benefit from the application of these tools should be addressed by bodies of law that are more streamlined, such as contract. If no monopoly overcharge looms, that should be enough of an indicator that some other fount of law is appropriate.[38]

Even cases that look like traditional antitrust problems may reveal a different aspect on examination. Consider briefly the claim that more than a dozen Japanese producers have conspired to sell TV sets for too little, eventually monopolizing the market. The Supreme Court booted the case out of the domain of antitrust (and into the domain of tariff and antidumping law) because it could not conceive how the Japanese producers could make a profit pursuing the strategy attributed to them.[39] But wait!, we are told: "The Japanese aren't like us; they don't maximize profits, and their conduct therefore cannot be assessed according to the standard model of antitrust law." If this is so, however, there is no reason to believe that antitrust penalties—designed on the assumption that the defendants are profit-maximizers—will deter the harmful conduct. More, if the defendants *really* don't maximize profits, then there is no reason to suppose that they would charge a monopoly price if they achieved a large market share. Perhaps they will sell TV sets on the cheap forever. I don't believe for a second that Japanese manufacturers leave money on the table; no one has suggested a strategy that would yield larger profits than those they now enjoy, which suggests that they are indeed maximizers. But if they are maximizers, then there is no antitrust problem (for reasons the Supreme Court gave); and if they aren't maximizers, then antitrust is the wrong instrument to bring to bear. Maybe we should just be thankful for efficient production and low prices.

Another conservation device with great potential is—nothing. That's right. Do nothing, *yet*. Frequently the nub of a case is a prediction. "The practice *will* drive us out of business. Concentration *will* increase. Defendants then *will* raise their prices above the competitive levels." The plaintiff demands that the judge intervene before it is too late. A judicial system that does not believe that it can estimate elasticities of supply and demand[40] is in no position to evaluate claims of this sort. Whether a particular practice such as a "predatory price" or a "price squeeze" will drive a given seller out, increase concentration, and end in monopoly prices depends on the elasticities of supply of actual and potential entrants, and the market elasticity of demand. *Illinois Brick* is dead right in saying that figuring these things out is beyond the judicial system's abilities—and would be too costly (in both process and error costs) if it could be accomplished. The alternative to this costly and imprecise inquiry is: nothing.[41] Wait. See whether the prediction comes true. If it does, collect from the wrongdoer damages so great that the episode is unprofitable.[42] Damages will prevent recurrence (and compensate the truly injured parties, the consumers who pay the eventual overcharge). If the prediction does not come true, the delay will have saved the judicial system much time and the risk of making a big error—for it is easy to confuse hard competition with "exclusionary" conduct, and errors in cases of this sort almost always penalize the conduct that yields the biggest benefits for consumers and the economy. Getting courts out of the business of prophesy could do more than any other change to make antitrust a rational, proconsumer policy.[43]

This list of conservation devices is not exhaustive. The "antitrust injury" rule, the doctrine of *Illinois Brick*, the courts' refusal to award contribution among antitrust offenders, these and more cut down on litigation and error costs. Let me mention just one more that is used in other industrial nations (and in many bodies of our law, such as securities regulation) but rare in antitrust law in the United States: administrative safe harbors.

Information becomes a larger fraction of the cost of production as time passes. The next generations of aircraft, computers, HDTV, and so on, will be made not of steel or silicon or sweat and tears. They will be "assembled" principally from information—from knowledge. No firm has the right incentive to acquire knowledge, because no firm can appropriate all of the benefits of what it knows. To make matters worse, attempts to appropriate the benefits lead to inefficiently little use of products based on the latest knowledge, for the marginal cost of using what is known is zero. Firms can overcome some of the problems by cooperating, sharing both costs and benefits. But as soon as they start cooperating, they expose themselves to treble damages.

Professors Jorde and Teece emphasize in their contribution to this symposium that antitrust law must find a way to accommodate doctrine developed in a world in which production meant riveting steel plates together to the increasing need for cooperation in information–intensive markets (see Chapter 3). This accommodation inevitably will come through safe harbors, similar to those that now apply to research and development joint ventures or to newspaper joint operating agreements. Administrators can formulate rules of nationwide application; a court may speak only for itself.

Antitrust is today a body of common law, always in evolution, subject to different interpretation in thirteen federal circuits and the courts of fifty states. A single practice may be challenged in a dozen forums, by private plaintiffs and state attorneys general, each convinced that litigation advances the nation's welfare. No matter how well-intentioned the plaintiffs, no matter how astute the judges, the process of common law litigation is one of uncertainty. Until the last case is over, no one knows whether the practice can survive—indeed, no one knows whether its practitioners can survive (given the prospect of stupendous damages). Common law antitrust litigation is high-risk litigation, high-delay litigation. By the time the other shoe drops, the moment for this generation of products is past. Some other nation, with a legal system able to give quick and binding answers to tough questions, will take the baton. Antitrust must recognize this and adjust, or a system designed to promote consumers' welfare will inflict the wound of Amfortas.

NOTES

This paper was completed in April 1989 and was revised in only minor ways thereafter, principally by adding a few citations to recent decisions.

1. See, generally, Frank H. Easterbrook, "Workable Antitrust Policy," *Michigan Law Review* 84 (1986): 1696, and "The Limits of Antitrust," *Texas Law Review* 63 (1984): 1.

2. Which is not to say that it has none. See Robert H. Bork, *The Antitrust Paradox* (New York: Basic Books, 1978); Easterbrook, "Limits of Antitrust," *supra* note 1; Douglas H. Ginsburg, "The Appropriate Role of the Antitrust Enforcement Agencies," *Cardozo Law Review* 9 (1988): 1277; William F. Baxter, "Separation of Powers, Prosecutorial Discretion, and the 'Common Law' Nature of Antitrust Law," *Texas Law Review* 60 (1982): 661; Richard A. Posner, "A Program for the Antitrust Division," *University of Chicago Law Review* 38 (1971): 500.

3. To see that this is today's "mainstream" position one need only read Atlantic Richfield Co. v. USA Petroleum Co., 110 S. Ct. 1884 (1990); Business Electronics Corp. v. Sharp Electronics Corp., 485 U.S. 717 (1988); Matsushita Electric Industrial Co. v. Zenith Radio Corp., 475 U.S. 574 (1986); and Phillip Areeda and Donald F. Turner, 1 *Antitrust Law* ¶¶103–13 (Boston: Little, Brown & Co., 1978).

   Louis Kaplow attributes to practitioners of the Chicago approach the belief that judges have taken over wholesale the views of Aaron Director, the father of the Chicago School of antitrust, and proceeds to show that they haven't. "Antitrust, Economics, and the Courts," *Law and Contemporary Problems* 50 (Autumn 1987): 181. I never thought they had, and would not expect lawyers bound by precedent to think or write like economists. It is enough for current purposes that there is wide agreement that the goal of antitrust is economic welfare, and that those who implement and discuss antitrust policy (judges, enforcers, scholars) are engaged in economic analysis and debate. See Easterbrook, "Workable Antitrust Policy," *supra* note 1, at 1705 & n.23.

4. Standard Oil Co. v. United States, 337 U.S. 293, 310 (1949).

5. United States v. Topco Associates, Inc., 405 U.S. 596, 609 (1972).

6. Illinois Brick Co. v. Illinois, 431 U.S. 720, 741–45 (1977).

7. Oliver E. Williamson, "Economies as an Antitrust Defense: The Welfare Tradeoffs," *American Economic Review* 58 (1988): 18, reprinted in Williamson, *Antitrust Economics* (Oxford: Basil Blackwell, 1987), pp. 3–23.

8. Chicago Board of Trade v. United States, 246 U.S. 231, 238 (1918): "To determine [whether a practice is reasonable and therefore lawful] the court must ordinarily consider the facts peculiar to the business to which the restraint is applied; its condition before and after the restraint was imposed; the nature of the restraint and its effect, actual and probable. The history of the restraint, the evil believed to exist, the reason for adopting that particular remedy, the purpose or end to be attained, are all relevant facts. This is not because a good intention will save an otherwise objectionable regulation or the reverse; but because knowledge or intent will help the court to interpret facts and to predict consequences."

9. Richard A. Epstein, *Modern Products Liability Law* (New York: Quantum Press, 1980); Peter W. Huber, *Liability: The Legal Revolution and Its Consequences* (New York: Basic Books, 1988); George L. Priest, "The Current Insurance Crisis and Modern Tort Law," *Yale Law Journal* 96 (1987): 1521. See also Carroll v. Otis Elevator Co., 896 F.2d 210, 215–18 (7th Cir. 1990) (concurring opinion).

10. R. H. Coase, *How Should Economics Choose?* (Chicago: University of Chicago, 1982).

11. Contrast Judge Posner's argument that higher output always vindicates vertical restraints, "The Next Step in the Antitrust Treatment of Vertical Restraints: Per Se Legality," *University of Chicago Law Review* 48 (1981): 6, with Professor Comanor's demonstration that vertical restraints could injure inframarginal buyers more than they aid the marginal buyers responsible for an increase in output, "Vertical Arrangements and Antitrust Analysis," *New York University Law Review* 62 (1987): 1153.

12. Aspen Skiing Corp. v. Aspen Highlands Skiing Corp., 472 U.S. 585 (1985).

13. See generally Frank H. Easterbrook, "On Identifying Exclusionary Conduct," *Notre Dame Law Review* 61 (1986): 972.

14. Thomas M. Jorde and David J. Teece, "Innovation, Cooperation, and Antitrust," Chapter 3 in this volume. A related paper expressing similar concerns is William J. Baumol and Janusz A. Ordover, "Antitrust: Source of Dynamic *and* Static Inefficiencies?", Chapter 4 in this volume.

15. E.g., Morton I. Kamien and Nancy L. Schwartz, *Market Structure and Innovation* (Cambridge: Cambridge University Press, 1982); Douglas H. Ginsburg, "Antitrust, Uncertainty, and Technological Innovation," *Antitrust Bulletin* 24 (1979): 635. The most recent work shows that innovation is negatively related to concentration (the opposite of Schumpeter's claim) but positively related to the degree to which large firms make up the industry, a typically confounding result. Zoltan J. Acs and David B. Audretsch, "Innovation in Large and Small Firms: An Empirical Analysis," *American Economic Review* 78 (1988): 678.

16. What little we do know does not suggest that cases contain nuggets of wisdom that have escaped the attention of the economic profession. E.g., Ward Bowman, *Patent and Antitrust Law* (Chicago: University of Chicago Press, 1973); George Bittlingmayer, "Property Rights, Progress, and the Aircraft Patent Agreement," *Journal of Law & Economics* 31 (1988): 227.

17. 466 U.S. 2 (1984).

18. William J. Lynk and Michael A. Morrisey, "The Economic Basis of *Hyde*: Are Market Power and Hospital Exclusive Contracts Related?", *Journal of Law & Economics* 30 (1987): 399. See also Lynk, "Physician Price Fixing Under the Sherman Act," *Journal of Health Economics* 7 (1988): 95.

19. 468 U.S. 85 (1984).

20. 807 F.2d 520 (7th Cir. 1986).

21. See Roger D. Blair and David L. Kaserman, *Law and Economics of Vertical Integration and Control* (New York: Academic Press, 1983), 31–36; Frederick R. Warren-Boulton, *Vertical Control of Markets* 51–63, 80–82 n.1 (Cambridge, MA: Ballinger Publishing Co., 1978). Contrast the majority opinion in *Fishman*, 807 F.2d at 537 n.15, with the dissent, *id.* at 563–64.

22. See Frank H. Easterbrook, "Allocating Antitrust Decisionmaking Tasks," *Georgetown Law Journal* 76 (1987): 305, 312–20, discussing corners of antitrust law elided here.

23. See Business Electronics Corp. v. Sharp Electronics Corp., 485 U.S. 717, 728–30 (1988).

24. E.g., The Jeanery, Inc. v. James Jeans, Inc., 849 F.2d 1148 (9th Cir. 1988).

25. Easterbrook, "On Identifying Exclusionary Conduct," *supra* note 13.

26. E.g., National Society of Professional Engineers, Inc. v. United States, 435 U.S. 679 (1978); Wilk v. American Medical Association, 719 F.2d 207 (7th Cir. 1983); Moore v. Boating Industry Associations, 819 F.2d 693 (7th Cir. 1987); Hydrolevel Corp. v. American Society of Mechanical Engineers, 635 F.2d 118, 124–27 (2d Cir. 1980), affirmed on other grounds, 456 U.S. 556 (1982); and Indian Head, Inc. v. Allied Tube & Conduit Corp., 817 F.2d 938, 946–47 (2d Cir. 1987), affirmed on other grounds, 486 U.S. 492, 499 n.3 (1988). For criticism of the analysis used in these cases, without the confident offer of an alternative approach, see Schachar v. American Academy of Ophthalmology, 870 F.2d 397 (7th Cir. 1989); Clamp-All Corp. v. Cast Iron Soil Pipe Institute, 851 F.2d 478, 486–89 (1st Cir. 1988); Consolidated Metal Products, Inc. v. American Petroleum Institute, 846 F.2d 284 (5th Cir. 1988). On the older, and easier to analyze, trade association cases, see Richard A. Posner, "Information and Antitrust: Reflections on the Gypsum and Engineers Decisions,"

Georgetown Law Journal 67 (1977): 1187, showing that they aren't so simple to analyze after all, and John Shepard Wiley, Jr., "Reciprocal Altruism As a Felony: Antitrust and the Prisoner's Dilemma," *Michigan Law Review* 86 (1988): 1906, analyzing information-exchange and other trade association problems from the perspective of collective action analysis.

27. See George J. Stigler, "A Theory of Oligopoly," in *The Organization of Industry* (Chicago: University of Chicago Press, 1968), pp. 39–63, and Richard A. Posner, *Antitrust Law: An Economic Perspective* (Chicago: University of Chicago Press, 1976), pp. 39–77, for two theoretical treatments. Empirical work is abundant, and much is collected in Easterbrook, "Workable Antitrust Policy," *supra* note 1, at 1698 n.5. See also Donald M. Brown and Frederick R. Warren-Boulton, "Testing the Structure–Competition Relationship on Cross-Sectional Firm Data," Economic Analysis Group Discussion Paper 88-6 (Department of Justice, May 11, 1988).

28. See Ernest Gellhorn, "The Practical Uses of Economic Analysis: Hope vs. Reality," *Antitrust Law Journal* 56 (1987): 933, 942–44.

29. Compare Richard S. Markovits, "The Allocative Efficiency and Overall Desirability of Oligopolistic Pricing Suits," *Stanford Law Review* 28 (1975): 45 (urging courts to take second-best problems seriously), with Phillip Areeda and Donald F. Turner, 2 *Antitrust Law* ¶411 (Boston: Little, Brown & Co., 1978) (urging courts to ignore the possibility).

30. Donald Dewey, "Information, Entry, and Welfare: The Case for Collusion," *American Economic Review* 69 (1979): 587.

31. Lester G. Telser, *A Theory of Efficient Cooperation and Competition* (Cambridge: Cambridge University Press, 1987), pp. 74–186. Telser sketches the approach with less mathematics in "Cooperation, Competition, and Efficiency," *Journal of Law & Economics* 28 (1985): 271.

32. See John Shepard Wiley, Jr., "Antitrust and Core Theory," *University of Chicago Law Review* 54 (1987): 556; Michael E. DeBow, "What's Wrong With Price Fixing: Responding to the New Critics of Antitrust," *Regulation* 44–50 (1988 No. 2). Unless, of course, we are willing to go whole hog in the other direction, as some have suggested. Dominick T. Armentano, *Antitrust Policy: The Case for Repeal* (Washington, D.C.: Cato Institute, 1986); Richard A. Epstein, "Private Property and the Public Domain: The Case of Antitrust," in *Ethics, Economics, and the Law: NOMOS XXVI*, J. Roland Pennock and John W. Chapman, eds. (New York: New York University Press, 1982); John E. Lopatka, "The Case for Legal Enforcement of Price Fixing Agreements," *Emory Law Journal* 38 (1989): 1. I am not among those who favor turning the other cheek to cartels.

33. E.g., Herbert Hovenkamp, "Fact, Value and Theory in Antitrust Adjudication," *Duke Law Journal* 1987: 897, 901; Eleanor M. Fox and Lawrence A. Sullivan, "Antitrust — Retrospective and Prospective: Where Are We Coming From? Where Are We Going?", *New York University Law Review* 62 (1987): 936.

34. Arizona v. Maricopa County Medical Society, 457 U.S. 332, 342 (1982). See also FTC v. Superior Court Trial Lawyers Ass'n, 110 S. Ct. 768, 780–82 (1990).

35. The alternative is a "trade policy" directed almost exclusively by the executive branch of the national government, the norm in the rest of the world.

36. I do not pursue the question how to define market power, an independent debate. See, e.g., Symposium, "Empirical Approaches to Market Power," *Journal of Law & Economics* 32 (1989): S1; William M. Landes and Richard A. Posner, "Market Power in Antitrust Cases," *Harvard Law Review* 94 (1981): 937; George J. Stigler and Robert A. Sherwin, "The Extent of the Market," *Journal of Law & Economics* 28 (1985): 555. For current purposes I accept the caution of Thomas G. Krattenmaker, Robert

H. Lande, and Steven C. Salop, "Monopoly Power and Market Power in Antitrust Law," *Georgetown Law Journal* 76 (1987): 241, that market power consists in either the ability to cut output in the market (significantly) by reducing one's own output, or the ability to cut market output (significantly) by diminishing one's rivals' output (equivalently, by diminishing rivals' elasticity of supply). The power to diminish *a* rival's production is not market power, though, unless other rivals are unable to fill the gap.

37. *NCAA* asked a market power question in a suit attacking a horizontal agreement. *Hyde* holds that market power is the first question in every tie-in case even though a per se analysis may be used after power has been demonstrated. Northwest Wholesale Stationers, Inc. v. Pacific Stationery & Printing Co., 472 U.S. 284, 296 (1985), adds a market power hurdle to the law of boycotts.

38. After this essay was written, FTC v. Superior Court Trial Lawyers Ass'n, 110 S. Ct. 768, 780–82 (1990), rejected the invitation to search for market power in standard cartel cases. Atlantic Richfield Co. v. USA Petroleum Co., 110 S. Ct. 1884 (1990), then held that even if the defendants' conduct is price-fixing illegal per se, a private plaintiff may recover only if it establishes that it paid higher prices as a result of a monopoly overcharge (or was a victim of predatory pricing); such a demonstration will be impossible in the absence of market power. The net effect is that market power is a threshold requirement in private litigation but not in suits filed by the federal government. (States are treated as "private" antitrust plaintiffs, see California v. American Stores Co., 110 S. Ct. 1853 (1990).)

39. *Matsushita, supra* note 3.

40. See *Illinois Brick, supra* note 6.

41. As in Cargill, Inc. v. Monfort of Colorado, Inc., 479 U.S. 104 (1986), A. A. Poultry Farms, Inc. v. Rose Acre Farms, Inc., 881 F.2d 1396 (7th Cir. 1989), and Indiana Grocery, Inc. v. Super Valu Stores, Inc., 864 F.2d 1409 (7th Cir. 1989) (holding that predatory practices do not violate the antitrust laws unless and until they succeed).

42. On the selection of optimal sanctions, see Frank H. Easterbrook, "Detrebling Antitrust Damages," *Journal of Law & Economics* 28 (1985): 445; William M. Landes, "Optimal Sanctions for Antitrust Violations," *University of Chicago Law Review* 50 (1983): 652. On why sanctions in private litigation should be monetary rather than injunctive, see Frank H. Easterbrook and Daniel R. Fischel, "Antitrust Suits by Targets of Tender Offers," *Michigan Law Review* 80 (1982): 1155, 1159–71.

43. A wait-and-see approach of course creates incentives for strategic conduct. The putative plaintiff may "take a dive" to create a right to sue, or the aggressor may pull its punches. Incentives to do these things already exist, however, and the costs of strategies that conceal the true state of affairs seem to me several orders of magnitude smaller than the costs of intervention on the basis of unverifiable (and therefore also irrefutable) predictions.

Antitrust Lenses and the Uses of Transaction Cost Economics Reasoning

OLIVER E. WILLIAMSON

Ronald Coase once advised that the "applied price theory" approach to industrial organization should be supplanted by a "direct approach to the problem" (1972, p. 73) — not least of all because the former had been responsible for errors of antitrust enforcement and misconceptions of business behavior. Although some of Coase's concerns have been relieved by reshaping applied price theory, a more direct approach to the problem has also been in progress. Both of these developments have had an impact on antitrust economics and antitrust enforcement.

This chapter emphasizes developments of the "direct approach" kind — where, by a (more) direct approach I make reference to transaction cost economics. The section "Alternative Lenses" identifies the main differences between an applied price theory and a transaction cost approach to the study of economic organization. Antitrust enforcement in the 1960s is briefly described in the section "Antitrust Through the Lens of Applied Price Theory" and some of the relief wrought by a reorientation of applied price theory is examined. The very same issues are then re-examined through the lens of transaction cost economics in the section "Transaction Cost Economics." Two antitrust cases in which off-the-shelf solutions — purportedly, forms of "economic analysis" — have been uncritically applied by the courts are the subject of the section "Two Recent Cases." Concluding remarks follow.

ALTERNATIVE LENSES

Milton Friedman has observed that "there is no inconsistency in regarding the firm as a perfect competitor for one problem, and a monopolist for another" (1953, p. 36). I concur and furthermore urge that there is no inconsistency in regarding the firm as a production function (which is the applied price theory concept) for one problem and as a governance structure (the transaction cost economics concept) for another. Economic organization is simply very complex and our understanding of many of the issues is still primitive. Thus different points of view can usefully inform our studies. This is true both in general and with respect to antitrust economics and antitrust enforcement.

What exactly is meant by an applied price theory approach to industrial organization, antitrust economics, and antitrust enforcement has never been made clear. Neither, for that matter, is it entirely clear what is meant by a direct approach to the problem—although certainly the latter is a more microanalytic undertaking (Coase, 1972, p. 73). I attempt here to set out the main features of each approach.

It will be useful for this purpose to ascertain the following: What questions inform each approach? What are the relevant data? How is the firm described? What determines the boundary between firm and market? How are hybrid modes of organization interpreted? What is the "main case" (or rebuttable presumption)?

The Questions

Roy D'Andrade distinguishes between three types of scientists and the questions that they ask. Whereas the physical scientists ask "What's the law here?", the natural scientists ask, less loftily, "What's going on here?", and the semiotic scientists inquire "What does this mean?"[1] Although economics falls in the natural science category, the attractions of a more lawful approach are understandably real and strong.

As between applied price theory and transaction cost economics, the latter is more unabashedly interested in interpreting variety and solving puzzles. Robert Solow's recent characterization of the aspiration of economics lines up closely with the transaction cost economics scheme of things—to wit, "to organize our necessarily incomplete perceptions about the economy, to see connections that the untutored eye would miss, to tell plausible . . . causal stories with the help of a few central principles, and to make rough quantitative judgments about the consequences of economic policy and other exogenous events" (1985, p. 329).

The Data

Albeit a simplification, many users of applied price theory in the 1960s came "close to arguing that prices and quantities are the only relevant data" (Arrow, 1971, p. 180). To be sure, industrial organization had to go beyond that to make provision for differences in industry structure (mainly industry concentration and the condition of entry) and measures of performance (especially profit rates). Details of internal organization, contract, and the related support institutions associated with each, however, were beyond the purview.

Transaction cost economics adopts a comparative contractual approach to the study of economic organization in which the transaction is made the basic unit of analysis and the details of governance structures and human actors are brought under review. Although this focus on microanalytics plainly comes at a cost, the justifications for which are sometimes questioned, discernable movement within economics in the microforces direction has nevertheless been occurring. A rather cautious version of the microforces argument is as follows:

> if one wishes to model the behaviour of organizations such as firms, then study of the firm as an organization ought to be high on one's agenda. This is not strictly speaking, necessary: one can hope to divine the correct "reduced form" for the behaviour of the organization without considering the micro-forces within the organization. But the study of the organization is likely to help in the design of reduced forms that stress the important variables. (Kreps and Spence, 1985, pp. 374–75)

Herbert Simon urges that the lessons of the physical sciences are pertinent.

> In the physical sciences, when errors of measurement and other noise are found to be of the same order of magnitude as the phenomena under study, the response is not to try to squeeze more information out of the data by statistical means; it is instead to find techniques for observing the phenomena at a higher level of resolution. The corresponding strategy for economics is obvious: to secure new kinds of data at the micro level. (1984, p. 40)

Assuming, arguendo, that such a strategy is to be implemented, which microdata are pertinent? Ought the "decision premise" be made the basic unit of analysis (Simon, 1961, p. xxxii)? Why not the "transaction" (Commons, 1924, p. 4; 1934, pp. 4–8)? Why not "the individual" (Jensen, 1983, p. 327)? Plainly, the choice of a basic unit of analysis depends on the questions being asked. If many of the central questions arise as or implicate issues of transaction cost economizing, then it is natural to regard the transaction as the basic unit of analysis.

The Firm

Applied price theory described the business firm as a production function to which a profit maximization objective was ascribed. This is an engineering or technological concept of the business firm in which organizational issues are suppressed. Friedrich Hayek's remarks are pertinent.

> Is it true that, once a plant has been built, the rest is all more or less mechanical, determined by the character of the plant, and leaving little to be changed in adapting to the ever-changing circumstances of the moment? . . . How easy it is for an inefficient manager to dissipate the differentials on which profitability rests, and that it is possible, with the same technical facilities, to produce with a great variety of costs, are among the commonplaces of business experience which do not seem to be equally familiar in the study of the economist. (1945, p. 523)

Transaction cost economics regards the firm not as a technological unit (production function) but as an organizational unit (governance structure). Firms are held to be well suited to govern some transactions and poorly suited for others. The attributes of transactions are of course pertinent in making this assessment. But the details of internal organization also matter. That the "same technical facilities" produce with a "great variety of costs" comes as no surprise if nontrivial cost consequences result when firms are organized and managed differently. More generally, transaction cost economics emphasizes that both organization form and the processes of organization matter, and hence need to be taken systematically into account. Comparative institutional assessments of the efficacy of alternative modes turn crucially on microanalytic features.

Boundaries

A production function concept of the firm leads easily to the view that the natural boundaries of the firm are technologically determined. Accordingly, the allocation of economic activity between firm and market was believed (mainly) to be the unproblematic result of past and current production technologies.

The firm as governance structure concept sees the issues very differently. To be sure, technological economies of scale are sometimes large and need to be respected, but these apply not at the firm level but at individual production stages. Also, technological nonseparabilities explain some decisions to take transactions out of markets and organize them hierarchically (Alchian and Demsetz, 1972). If, however, only a small fraction of the decisions to take transactions out of the market and organize them internally can be explained by reference to economies of scale or technological nonseparabilities, then other factors evidently need to be invoked.

Transaction cost economics maintains that the governance costs of firm and market organization differ systematically with the attributes of transactions and that the boundary of the firm is principally determined by these features. Technology is thus relegated to a secondary role and the principal burden of explaining the boundary of the firm is assigned to transaction cost economizing.

The upshot is that the transaction cost approach regards the boundary of the firm as problematic, being determined only in limited degree by technology. The allocation of activities between firm and market thus needs to be derived rather than taken as given.

Hybrid Forms

Hybrid forms of organization—joint ventures, franchising, reciprocal trading, and the like—are mainly anomalies within the firm as a production function scheme of things and are apt to be regarded as anticompetitive. If an affirmative rationale is to be found, it turns on rather special features—price discrimination being an example.

Transaction cost economics treats firm and market as polar organizational alternatives and recognizes that many transactions are organized by hybrid or intermediate forms. An examination of the powers and limits of markets, hierarchies, *and* hybrid forms is needed in order to unpack the issues. As compared with the applied price theory approach, transaction cost economics displays a deeper curiosity (what is going on here?) about hybrid forms and turns to the microanalytics in seeking answers.

Rather than focus on technology and price-to-cost margins, transaction cost economics focuses on (1) the attributes of transactions (frequency, uncertainty, and asset specificity) and (2) the attributes of governance structures (safeguards, incentive intensity, adaptability), the object being (3) to effect a discriminating alignment between transactions and governance.[2] The purposes of economic organization are thus viewed very differently and a large number of refutable implications obtain.

The new approach is broadly consonant with Vernon Smith's remarks that a new microtheory was needed which "will, and should, deal with the economic foundations of organization and institution, and this will require us to have an economics of information and a more sophisticated treatment of the technology of transacting" (Smith, 1974, p. 321).

Presumptions

Applied price theory mainly ascribed monopolistic purpose to nonstandard or unfamiliar business practices.

> if an economist finds something – a business practice of one sort or another – that he does not understand, he looks for a monopoly explanation. And as in this field we are very ignorant, the number of unununderstandable practices tends to be rather large, and the reliance on a monopoly explanation, frequent. (Coase, 1972, p. 67)

To be sure, there were differences between the Harvard and Chicago schools in this respect. Although both invoked monopoly explanations, Harvard mainly emphasized entry barrier effects while Chicago interpreted the same practices as manifestations of price discrimination (Posner, 1979). Between the two, price discrimination was the more benign interpretation.

Transaction cost economics subscribes to and develops the view that economizing is the main case, to which monopolizing is a qualification. Frank Knight's remarks are apposite.

> men in general, and within limits, wish to behave economically, to make their activities *and their organization* "efficient" rather than wasteful. This fact does deserve the utmost emphasis; and an adequate definition of the science of economics . . . might well make it explicit that the main relevance of the discussion is found in its relation to social policy, assumed to be directed toward the end indicated, of increasing economic efficiency, of reducing waste. (1941, p. 252; emphasis added)

Transaction cost economics regards economizing, of the rudimentary kind described by Knight, as the "main case." To be sure, the main case is not the only case. Other business purposes are sometimes served as well. It nonetheless invites comparison with alternative main case rivals – of which monopolizing is one.[3]

ANTITRUST THROUGH THE LENS OF APPLIED PRICE THEORY

The monopoly presumption was the ruling orientation for antitrust enforcement in the 1960s. This led to some rather extreme interpretations and enforcement excesses, the highlights of which are sketched in "The Ruling Orientation." Ways by which various applied price theory arguments were used to qualify or correct some of these extremes are then discussed in "Applied Price Theory Responses."

The Ruling Orientation

General Mergers

The preoccupation with monopoly is indicated by the Federal Trade Commission's opinion in *Foremost Dairies*, where the Commission ventured the view that necessary proof of violation of Section 7 "consists of types of evidence showing that the acquiring firm possesses significant power in some markets or that its overall organization gives it a decisive advantage in efficiency over its smaller rivals."[4] Although Donald Turner, among others, was quick to label that as bad law and bad economics (1965, p. 1324), in that it protects competitors rather than promoting the welfare benefits of competition, the Supreme Court shortly thereafter declared that "possible economies cannot be used as a defense to illegality."[5]

The low opinion and perverse regard for economies went so far that beleaguered respondents disclaimed efficiency gains. Thus Procter & Gamble insisted that its acquisition of Clorox was unobjectionable because the government was unable definitively to establish that any efficiencies would result.

> [The Government is unable to prove] any advantages in the procurement or price of raw materials or in the acquisition or use of needed manufacturing facilities or in the purchase of bottles or in freight costs. . . . [T]here is no proof of any savings in any aspect of manufacturing. There is no proof that any additional manufacturing facilities would be usable for the production of Clorox. There is no proof that any combination of manufacturing facilities would effect any savings, even if such combination were feasible.[6]

This upside-down assessment of economies was bound to change, and it did — but not before Justice Stewart, in a dissenting opinion in 1966, recorded that the "sole consistency that I can find is that in [merger] litigation under Section 7, the Government always wins."[7]

Vertical Integration

The firm being a production function, a technological point of view was naturally brought to bear. Joe Bain thus emphasized "technical or physical aspects" (such as the thermal economies that would purportedly be realized by bringing blast furnace and rolling mill under common ownership) and held that vertical integration outside of such a context was doubtful (1968, p. 381). The monopoly presumption was expressed as follows: "Where a firm has a fifth or more of an industry's output, its acquisition of more than five or ten percent of the output capacity of industries to which it sells or from which it buys in appreciable quantities shall be presumed to [be monopolistic]" (Stigler, 1955, p. 184). The 1968 Department of Justice *Merger Guidelines* draw the admissible limits on vertical mergers even more narrowly.

Conglomerate Organization

If the firm is a production function, then what explains the conglomerate? Many organizational innovations are regarded with alarm — the leveraged buyout being a recent example. The conglomerate was no exception. Robert Solo characterized the conglomerate as a "truly dangerous phenomenon"—albeit mainly for financial reasons rather than in competitive respects (1972, pp. 47–48). The deep pockets of such firms were held to constitute a "brooding omnipresence," the spectre of which was purportedly troublesome for antitrust.[8] Indeed, conglomerate mergers were alleged to have adverse effects on potential competition "so widespread that [such a merger] might appropriately be described as having an effect upon the economic system as a whole—in every line of commerce in every section of the country" (Blake, 1973, p. 567). Although the 1968 *Merger Guidelines* were more restrained, conglomerate mergers that created a prospect of reciprocity were apt to be challenged because "reciprocal buying . . . is an economically unjustified business practice which confers a competitive advantage on the favored firm unrelated to the merits."

Nonstandard Contracting

Nonstandard forms of contracting likewise operated under a cloud. The monopoly presumption was here expressed as follows: "I approach customer and territorial restrictions not hospitably in the common law tradition, but inhospitably in the tradition of antitrust."[9] The government's arguments in the *Schwinn* case[10] illustrate this inhospitality predisposition. The issue was whether a bicycle manufacturer with 13 percent of the market could lawfully impose nonresale restrictions on franchisees. The Department of Justice held that it could not and advised the Supreme Court to rule against the practices because, among other things:

> Either the Schwinn bicycle is in fact a superior product for which the consumer would willingly pay more, in which event it should be unnecessary to create a quality image by the artificial device of discouraging competition in the price of distributing the product; or it is not of premium quality, and the consumer is being deceived into believing that it is by its high and uniform retail price. In neither event would the manufacturer's private interest in maintaining a high-price image justify the serious impairment on competition that results.[11]

Possible efficiency benefits were disposed of as follows:

> Even if the threat to integrate were not wholly lacking in credibility in the circumstances of this case, we would urge that it was not a proper defense to the restraint of trade charge. In the first place, a rule that treats manufacturers who assume the distribution function themselves more leniently than those who impose restraints on independent distributors merely reflects the fact that, although integration in distribution may sometimes benefit the economy by leading to cost savings, agreements to maintain resale prices or to impose territorial restrictions of unlimited duration or outlet limitations of the type involved here have never been shown to produce comparable economies.[12]

The government's theory in Schwinn thus was premised on two false certitudes: (1) superior products are self-evident and require no supports; and (2) if contractual restrictions are to be imposed, common ownership of the two stages is always superior to the contract.

Applied Price Theory Responses

That these are extreme views is now obvious. Partly this is because a richer theory of economic organization has been taking shape. But applied price theory has also had a bearing. Consider the latter.

General Merger

The implicit assumption of the ruling orientation was that the market power effects of any horizontal merger (or other combination) would surely swamp in economic importance the welfare benefits, such as economies, that might be advanced in support of a merger. As it turns out, this intuition was incorrect.

What was needed was a trade-off model in which varying degrees of economies and market power could be assessed.[13] This is an issue to which the apparatus of partial equilibrium welfare economics can be applied.[14] A naive assessment of the trade-off in question did not confirm the then-prevailing wisdom but disclosed instead that "a merger which yields nontrivial real economies must produce substantial market power and result in relatively large price increases for the net allocative effects to be negative" (Williamson, 1968, p. 23).

To be sure, the basic model was naive and was thereafter subject to a large number of refinements and qualifications. The general proposition that economies needed to be accorded much more respect nevertheless survived. Although the merits of that framework remain open to dispute (Posner, 1976, p. 821), the general approach, if not the framework itself, has since been employed by others.[15]

A common argument against trade-off analysis is that the courts are poorly suited to assess economic evidence and arguments of this kind (Bork, 1978).[16] In fact, however, a simple sensitivity to the merits of economies is sufficient to avoid the inverted reasoning of *Foremost Dairies*. And although errors of the *Schwinn* kind are avoided only upon recognizing that economies can take transaction cost as well as technological forms, the mistakes of the "inhospitality tradition" also become less likely once that step has been taken. The upside-down assessment of economies in the 1960s appears thoroughly to have been vanquished by the economies in antitrust defense literature (Fisher and Lande, 1983).

There are systematic ways, moreover, to introduce economies into antitrust enforcement that come up well short of a *full-blown* presentation of an economies defense in court. For one thing, the *Merger Guidelines* can be relaxed, in part to reflect the benefits of economies — and they have been. Also, economies can be considered in presentations before the antitrust enforcement agencies in deciding whether or not to bring a case — and they have been.[17] And economies arguments can even be introduced into court proceedings without attempting a meticulous assessment of the trade-offs. If the government brings bad cases, as it occasionally does, the respondent needs an opportunity to restore perspectives. Economies arguments can be and have been presented in this connection as well.[18]

Vertical Integration

As Lionel McKenzie (1951) and others have argued, vertical integration can be used as a means by which to check the use of inefficient factor proportions induced by the monopolistic pricing of inputs in a variable proportions production technology. The firm as production function construction is well-suited to the needs of the problem and was appropriately employed for this purpose.[19]

The possibility that vertical integration might be used to support price discrimination was also suggested. As discussed below, however, this rests entirely on transaction cost reasoning.

Conglomerate Organization

Although efficient risk-bearing arguments reach beyond the firm as production function construction, they are broadly in the spirit of applied price theory. Morris Adelman argued that the conglomerate had attractive portfolio diversification properties (1961) and should be more affirmatively regarded for this reason.

Nonstandard Contracting

The main price theoretic justification for nonstandard contracting practices is that these were designed to effect price discrimination, the allocative efficiency effects of which were favorable. A more recent explanation is free riding.

Price Discrimination. Price discrimination is the "utility fielder" on which Chicago relied to deal with tie-ins, block-booking, reciprocal dealing, and the like. If price discrimination led to better resource allocation, which it arguably did, then a more benign interpretation of contractual "irregularities" was warranted.

The older Chicago view, which has since been qualified (Posner, 1979, p. 935), but is nonetheless widely held, has been described by Posner as follows:

> A tie-in makes sense only as a method of price discrimination, based on the fact that the amount of the tied product bought can be used to separate purchasers into more or less elastic demanders of the tying product. There is no need to worry about price discrimination, however, because it does not aggravate the monopoly problem. On the contrary, price discrimination is a device by which the monopolist in effect seeks to serve additional consumers, i.e., those having the more elastic demands, who might be deterred by the single monopoly price that would be charged in the absence of discrimination. Thus, price discrimination brings the monopolist's output closer to that of a competitive market and reduces the misallocative effects of monopoly. (1979, p. 926)

Free Riding. A more recent justification for vertical restraints is that these are needed to check "free riders." The usual concern here is that some distributors (or related group of supply, sales, or service firms) will not pull their weight but will free ride off of the promotional (or other efforts) of others. Thus a firm that incurs the promotional expense to develop a territory will understandably want to prevent other firms from coming in and appropriating the fruits of its efforts. Failure to provide such territorial protection will deter or distort market development efforts.

Although the argument was advanced much earlier (Telser, 1960, pp. 92–93), it was not until the 1970s that it caught the attention of the Supreme Court.[20] In a dramatic reversal of the *Schwinn* decision, the Supreme Court in *GTE Sylvania* declared that vertical market divisions were not per se unlawful but could often serve legitimate business purposes. Robert Bork summarizes the outcome as follows:

> The great virtue of *Sylvania* is not so much that it preserves a method of distribution valuable to consumers, though that is certainly a welcome development, but that it displays a far higher degree of economic sophistication than we have become accustomed to, and introduces an approach that, generally applied, is capable of making antitrust a rational, proconsumer policy once more. Both Justice Powell for the majority and Justice White in concurrence gave weight to business efficiency in framing their respective rules. The majority opinion specified some of the efficiencies involved, including the "free ride" effect. . . . For years the Court has denigrated business efficiencies either as irrelevant to antitrust analysis or a factor weighing on the side of illegality. . . . *Sylvania* may presage a general reformation of a policy gone astray. (1978, p. 287)

Indeed, as discussed below (in "Conglomerate Organization" and "Sharp"), *Sylvania* presaged more. Reference to free riding has become an all-purpose justification for contractual restraints and related business behavior. A good (but limited) argument has been taken to uncritical extremes.

TRANSACTION COST ECONOMICS

A summary of the principal differences between applied price theory and transaction cost economics is shown in Table 7-1. My purpose here is to illustrate how transaction cost economics informs each of the four classes of economic activity—mergers, vertical integration, conglomerate organization, and nonstandard contracting—described above, to which I add a fifth: innovation.

Table 7-1. Stylized Differences Between Applied Price Theory and Transaction Cost Economics

Issue	Alternative Approaches	
	Applied Price Theory	Transaction Cost Economics
Question	What's the law here?	What's going on here?
Data	prices and output	Transactions and governance structures
Firm described as	production function	governance structure
Natural boundary of the firm defined by	technology	contractual dependency
Main purpose served by organizational variety	monopoly	economizing

General Mergers

Transaction cost economics has a bearing on mergers in several respects. First, economies (or diseconomies) of both production and transaction costs need to be factored into the trade-off calculus. Second, the reason why merger has advantages over oligopoly as a means by which to set price and output (and orchestrate other competitive initiatives — product development, promotion, and the like) is because cartel agreements are difficult to reach and enforce. Although this has been evident for a long time (Fellner, 1949; Stigler, 1964; Posner, 1969), the nature of the difficulties becomes especially transparent when the oligopoly issue is posed as a contracting problem (Williamson, 1975, pp. 238-45).

Unified ownership and hierarchical organization have enormous advantages as compared with an interdependent group of autonomous owners joined by contract where the object is to (1) decide on aggregate output, (2) allocate output among the producing parts, (3) adapt to changing circumstances, (4) pool profits and decide on capital investments, and (5) hear and resolve disputes — to say nothing about coordinating R&D, advertising, and the like. Aside from the simplest kinds of interdependencies among small numbers of producers, cartel agreements are apt to be too complex to reach and, even if agreements are reached, are continuously prone to breakdown — especially, as in most cartels, if mechanisms to detect cheating and penalize violators in a discriminating way are weak. The comparison between mergers and cartels as alternative devices to orchestrate collusion is thus preponderantly a transaction cost exercise.

Transaction costs are also pertinent to the following deep puzzle of organization: Why can't a merged firm do everything that a collection of smaller firms do and more? Assuming that the merger realizes economies of coordination in some respects, why not simply advise the merger to replicate the behavior of the (previously) independent entities in other respects? Gain without loss ought thereby to obtain. Transaction cost economics answers this conundrum by explicating the "impossibility of selective intervention" — on which account gain without loss is vitiated.

Another way in which transaction cost considerations can be introduced into the merger calculus is in conjunction with strategic behavior. Efforts to raise the cost of capital to a rival through the strategic use of vertical integration is an illustration and is discussed in the next section.

Vertical Integration

Vertical integration services a variety of purposes. Among other things it is said to (1) afford economies between stages that are joined by "technical or physical aspects," (2) result in the choice of more efficient factor proportions, (3) be a way of effecting price discrimination, (4) be a device by which to evade sales taxes on intermediate products and circumvent quotas and price controls, (5) be a means by which to impede entry by nonintegrated rivals — by increasing the costs of interfirm contracting or increasing the costs of capital should a rival attempt to integrate, (6) encourage investments in transaction specific capital, there being greater confidence that adaptive, sequential decisionmaking will proceed effectively, and (7) facilitate information exchange between stages, thereby to permit investment benefits.

Only the last two of these are ordinarily regarded as transaction cost arguments.[21] Indeed asset specificity is the only wholly "new wrinkle" that transaction cost economics introduces into the vertical integration discussion. This argument, however, is a significant addition — in that a very large fraction of vertically integrated activity is explained by the fact that supplier and buyer are joined in a bilateral dependency condition, by reason of asset specificity, for which unified ownership is (comparatively) the most efficient governance structure.[22]

Note in this connection that an enormous amount of vertical integration is simply taken for granted and is not thought to require an economic rationale. Integration of some degree, however, occurs *within every firm* and even simple forms of integration deserve an economic interpretation. Mundane vertical integration (of the kind that arguably existed between successive [but separable] work stations in Adam Smith's pinmaking factory) is not so unproblematic that it can be ignored.

Ignored, however, it was until Stephen Marglin (1974) argued that the unified ownership and hierarchical organization of successive work stations served no efficiency purposes in pinmaking (or, more generally, among separable work stations in manufacturing) — the reason being that the firm as production function construction, which purportedly exhausted efficiency reasoning, made no provision for hierarchy. Accordingly, Marglin argued that hierarchy had the purpose and effect of conferring power on "bosses."

The disjunction between economics and organization theory explains this condition. Thus although it was obvious to anyone who was familiar with the organization theory literature that the details of organization often had efficiency significance (Barnard, 1938; Simon, 1947; March and Simon, 1958), Marglin made no such connection. Much of antitrust economics, especially the inhospitality tradition, was similarly implicated.

The principal hypothesis out of which transaction cost economics works is that transactions (which differ in their attributes) are aligned with governance structures (which differ in their costs and competencies) in a discriminating (mainly, transaction cost economizing) way. This leads to a different assessment of the purposes served by markets and hierarchies. I submit, moreover, that *all* of the first five conditions of vertical integration listed above rely implicitly on transaction cost reasoning to support it. Accordingly, the relation between transaction cost reasoning and vertical integration is pervasive.

Thus "technical or physical aspects" present problems for autonomous contracting between bilaterally dependent stations *only if* unprogrammed adaptations need to be made. Such would not arise in a regime of complete contracting or in the absence of uncertainty. Bilateral dependency would not, moreover, develop if the stations in question were "on wheels" and could be easily redeployed. Unified ownership thus supplants market procedurement not because of proximity, thermal economies, or other physical or technical conditions per se, but rather because prospective maladaptation problems in bilateral trading are mitigated by internal organization. Governance considerations are therefore ultimately responsible for reconfiguring the contractual relation between successive stages where troublesome "technical or physical aspects" are posed.

Similarly, vertical integration would not be needed if monopolistic input suppliers could stipulate by contract that buyers will use efficient factor proportions when combining the monopolistic input with other inputs. Inasmuch, however, as mere promises without more are not self-enforcing, credible commitment issues arise. The upshot is that the decision to substitute internal for market organization ultimately reflects *differential* incentives and associated auditing and enforcement costs between integrated and nonintegrated (autonomous) contracting stages — rather than that factor proportion distortions "automatically" obtain (for price theoretic reasons) whenever a variable proportions technology procures monopolistically priced inputs from an independent supplier.

Price discrimination is discussed below. Consider, therefore, sale tax, quota, and price control evasion. The differential ease of tracking transactions is the crucial issue for each of these. Market-mediated trades leave a large paper and electronic trail: orders, invoices, accounts receivable and payable, bank records of payment, deposits, and so on. Although some of these records can be suppressed, this is costly and, what is more pertinent, is more costly in trades between firms than in trades within firms.[23] *Differential* transaction costs are thus ultimately responsible for the decision to use vertical integration as a means for (lawful) evasion.[24]

Consider finally the uses of vertical integration as a strategic instrument by which to impede entry or otherwise disadvantage rivals. Interestingly, advocates of applied price theory of both the "diehard Chicagoan" (Bork and Bowman) and of the "reformed Chicagoan" (Posner) kinds deny that vertical integration can be used to deter entry.[25]

Thus Bork contends that "if greater than competitive profits are to be made in an industry, entry should occur whether an entrant has to come in at both levels or not. I know of no theory of imperfections in the capital market which would lead suppliers of capital to avoid areas of higher return to seek areas of lower return" (1969, p. 148). And Posner asserts that the "cost to the monopolist of integrating is prima facie the same as the cost to the new entrant of having to integrate" (1979, p. 936), and expresses concern with vertical integration only in conjunction with the unlikely event that a variable proportions technology leads to an increase in monopoly power.[26]

The Bork and Posner views on cost comparability ignore the possibility that integration can be undertaken for a strategic purpose, the object being to reduce the size of the market for product to which nonintegrated firms can turn for supplies. Thus potential rivals may be forced to choose between purchasing from a noncompetitive fringe at supranormal prices or attempting combined entry at a high cost of capital (the latter assumes that the entrant has demonstrated competence at only one of the two stages). The first of these is an applied price theory qualification. The second turns on transaction cost considerations.[27] To be sure, both are relevant only in the context of pre-existing market power, so the argument applies to a limited set of circumstances. It is nonetheless instructive that a transaction cost economics assessment of vertical integration applies both to the benefits (possible cost savings) as well as to the costs (possible strategic ploys) associated with this form of organization.

Indeed, transaction cost economics is pertinent to still another class of costs that are rarely considered but are truly basic to the matter of vertical integration: "Why is not all production carried on by one big firm?" (Coase, 1952, p. 339). Although this is an ancient puzzle to which applied price theory has offered many explanations, none of the standard explanations withstand comparative institutional scrutiny. Thus the basic comparative test is not whether internal expansion or integration incur costs but rather whether internal organization or integration incur *differential costs*, the magnitude and composition of the activity to be organized being held constant.

Among the applied price theory factors that have been advanced to explain why firm size is limited are (1) diseconomies of plant scale, (2) limited size of the market, (3) increasing factor prices, (4) limited capacities of the peak coordinator, and (5) bureaucratic cost excesses. Some of these factors are plainly wrong. None, without more, passes a comparative institutional test.

Thus diseconomies of plant scale merely limit plant size. No limits to firm size apply if the firm can grow as a multiplant operation. Similarly, size of market limitations can be relieved by diversifying. Although an increase in aggregate demand is commonly responsible for an increase in factor prices, an increase in the size of one firm (say by combining two like firms) does not obviously have such an effect. To assume that two firms, A and B, cannot be joined because the chief executive of the combined enterprise would be overwhelmed assumes a particular hierarchical structure and management style. The top down management can be relieved, however, by divisionalization and selective intervention — the latter being an administrative rule against intrusion unless expected net gains can be projected. And just as relief for top management can be realized in the manner described, so can purported bureaucratic cost excesses in the large firm be relieved by preserving autonomy among the operating parts — the criterion of selective intervention referred to above being the condition that must be satisfied before coordination is attempted.

Wherein then do the comparative limitations reside? As remarked earlier and elaborated elsewhere (Williamson, 1985, Chap. 6; 1988a; 1988b), the answer turns on the impossibility of selective intervention. Thus although integration often facilitates adaptation to a wider range of disturbances (the gain), it is also attended by a reduction of incentive intensity (the cost).[28] Accordingly, only in those transactions for which *the adaptive gains exceed the losses due to diminished incentive intensity* is integration warranted.

The argument, moreover, does not end here. Although the firm or market dichotomy is instructive, it does not exhaust the organizational possibilities. Specifically, hybrid modes of organization — joint ventures, franchising, other forms of constrained long-term contracting — may be able to support intermediate outcomes that are superior to either of the polar alternatives. As I develop elsewhere, these hybrid modes support incentive intensity and adaptability of intermediate degrees (Williamson, 1991). Both economic organization and antitrust enforcement need to come to terms with these ramifications as well (see the section "Nonstandard Contracting" below).

Conglomerate Organization

I have had occasion to discuss the conglomerate form of organization from monopolizing–economizing viewpoints and from applied price theory–transaction cost economics perspectives elsewhere (Williamson, 1974, pp. 1481–93; 1981, pp. 1557–60). The argument, essentially, is this: (1) neither reciprocity nor efficient risk bearing provide an adequate explanation for the conglomerate; (2) anticompetitive objections to conglomerates appeal mainly to a bogey-man economics rationale; and (3) especially in an era of stringent antitrust enforcement against horizontal and vertical mergers, conglomerates can have beneficial effects by supporting the market for corporate control and (provided that the requisite internal organizational and control apparatuses are in place) functioning as miniature capital markets for internal resource allocation purposes. This last point implicates both managerial discretion and organization form issues, both of which have transaction cost origins.

Also, the view expressed by the 1968 *Merger Guidelines* that reciprocity lacks redeeming purposes is mistaken (see the next section). An opposition to those conglomerates that posed a reciprocal trading potential—which was virtually all—was overstated and much too sweeping. Interestingly, the 1984 *Guidelines* no longer express conglomerate reservations by reason of reciprocity.

Nonstandard Contracting

Nonstandard or unfamiliar forms of contracting have long posed antitrust concerns and have been variously interpreted. What I referred to above as the inhospitality tradition held that vertical contractual restraints and the like were presumptively unlawful. A justification that was sometimes offered in support of such restraints was that these were merely devices by which to effect price discrimination, which result was arguably beneficial. A more recent explanation for these restraints is that they are needed as a check on free riding. Both implicate transaction cost issues.

Price Discrimination

There are three points. First, the beneficial allocative efficiency effects of imperfect price discrimination can be disputed. Second, some of the phenomena for which a price discrimination rationale has been advanced are better understood in transaction cost economizing terms. And third, price discrimination makes little or no useful contact with many complex contracting phenomena. Posner has discussed the first of these (1979, p. 935) and I have treated the second elsewhere (Williamson, 1975, pp. 11–13). Consider therefore point three.

Although price discrimination is certainly a leading purpose served by many tie-ins, that appears to be much more problematic of block booking and an even less likely explanation for reciprocity. An alternative explanation for block booking that has been advanced by Roy Kenney and Benjamin Klein (1983) is that this practice can and sometimes does serve as a check on wasteful "over-searching." Similarly, although reciprocity may permit oligopolists to disguise cheating on cartel agreements, reciprocity also permits oligopolists, like others, to infuse "credible commitments" into their contracting relations with buyers and sellers. To be sure, the latter is likewise a limited argument and turns on the presence of asset specificity (Williamson, 1983). It is noteworthy, however, that a great deal of reciprocity occurs outside of the oligopoly context. In the degree to which contractual continuity and related benefits are promoted by reciprocity, a more favorable antitrust assessment of this practice — by conglomerate firms and others — is warranted.

There is still another consideration, moreover. If the object is to induce monopolists to supply the competitive output, why is the initiative to supply on discriminating terms always left to the monopolist? Why don't consumers organize and strike a contract curve bargain with the monopolist? The answer obviously turns on the high costs of organizing a large number of disparately situated groups and individuals, which is to say that there are transaction cost disparities between the two sides of the market (Arrow, 1969, p. 51).

Free Riding

Free riding can take either local or systems forms. The local concern is that the market development (or other demand-enhancing or cost-reducing) efforts of particular firms will not be captured by those who incur the expense but will be partially seized by rivals. Thus if one firm develops a territory (or other customer class) and another supplier comes along and benefits from those market development efforts, the second firm is a free rider. Capturing, as the free rider does, some of the benefits attributable to the efforts of others, the prospect of losing sales to free riders is a deterrent to those who would otherwise be prepared to incur market development expenses. Thus contractual restraints that help to concentrate benefits on those who are responsible for them sometimes arise for this reason. The *GTE-Sylvania* case referred to above posed some of these issues.

A systems concern arises if the success of a product turns partly on providing a uniform quality image and thus requires all members of the system to behave similarly. The *Schwinn* case posed these issues, where the concern was that the Schwinn name would be degraded if the Schwinn bicycle were sold by a discount house that merely delivered a Schwinn "bike in a box" but did not provide assembly and service. The contractual integrity of the Schwinn franchising system could be compromised in the process.[29] Contractual restraints are arguably needed to avoid this outcome.

Albeit relevant to an assessment of vertical restraints, the free rider argument is pertinent to only a small fraction of the cases where nonstandard contracting practices are observed. It is not, therefore, an all-purpose rationale for any contractual irregularity whatsoever. Also, free riding merely describes the effect. The causes reside in transaction cost features. Thus local benefits could not be expropriated if the effects of promotional efforts were fully and costlessly disclosed and property rights attached thereto (which would be feasible in a regime of unbounded rationality) or if customers would self-enforce covenants not to shop and learn from one source and buy from another (the absence of opportunism). The adverse systems effects described above would similarly vanish if spillover costs could be traced to their origins — which the absence of bounded rationality or opportunism would permit.

More generally, free riding is a particular manifestation of an externality problem, of which "market failure is a more general category," which in turn gives way to a still "broader category, that of transaction costs, which in general impede and in particular cases block the formation of markets" (Arrow, 1969, p. 49). If, therefore, we are to attempt systematically to trace nonstandard contracting practices to their origins, an examination of comparative transaction costs is where we inexorably end up.

Innovation

Transaction cost economics has a bearing on product, process, and organizational innovations. Most innovations implicate uniqueness (Marschak, 1968) or deep knowledge (Polanyi, 1962). As compared with applied price theory, transaction cost economics relates easily to both. Thus uniqueness often arises in an intertemporal way, partly as a consequence of learning-by-doing (human asset specificity). And deep or tacit knowledge that cannot be communicated adequately through blueprints, recipes, manuals, and the like is a reflection of the limits of language — which limits are a manifestation of bounded rationality. Also, problems of appropriability are often posed where intellectual property rights are created. What have been referred to as "weak appropriability regimes" (Teece, 1986) invite organizational responses to the hazards of interfirm contracting. Specifically, integration into related stages of production (or distribution) may be a means by which to mitigate the loss or other leakage of proprietary knowledge and supply competence.

Whereas once it was customary to investigate innovation in terms of industry structure, it is now recognized that the organization of innovation is an uncommonly complicated matter. Not only do considerations of uncertainty and incentive intensity confound the analysis of innovative activities, but added systems complications are also posed. Relations between firms are deeply complicated by rivalry, leakage, networks, compatibility, and in duplication respects. Likewise are relations between stages (especially between R&D and commercialization) in terms of the feedback loops that influence the acquisition and sharing of knowledge.

A growing appreciation for these complexities and of the need to work out the microanalytics is now reflected in a more circumspect public policy. Whereas any hint of market power was once sufficient to disallow R&D joint ventures and the like, this thinking has given way to a more affirmative regard for the benefits and an appreciation for the fact that transaction cost–organizational economies matter.

The underlying theme of "General Mergers" through "Innovation" is that the study of economic organization in all of its forms — market, hierarchical, hybrid — is significantly shaped by transaction cost forces. Often these have an economizing purpose and effect. But, in circumstances where market power is present in a nontrivial degree, strategic behavior can also be traced to transaction cost origins.

This is not to say that it is not useful to have broad headings under which different kinds of contracting and organizational practices can be clustered. For example: "This is a variety of the free rider problem." "That has the purpose and effect of price discrimination." "This is designed to safeguard assets of a particular kind." "That reflects a trade-off between incentive intensity and adaptability." And so forth. What is needed, however, to understand the nature and origins of complex forms of organization is an inquiry into the underlying microanalytics.[30] As discussed in "Two Recent Cases" below, such an investigation is vital if the "new learning" is to be applied to antitrust in a discerning way.

Both the anatomy and physiology of complex forms of contracting and organization are thus brought under review. The purposes served by divisionalization are therefore examined and different types of conglomerates are distinguished. If the nature of the assets matters, then these need to be identified and a discriminating approach to contractual safeguards devised. If process matters, then the key processes need to be discovered and their comparative institutional ramifications worked out.[31]

To be sure, the concerted study of the microanalytics of organization from an economizing point of view (where economizing is the main case to which monopolizing is an ancillary factor) pushes economics in a direction that many understandably resist. If, however, more orthodox approaches simply do not engage the issues, there may be no other real choice.[32]

TWO RECENT CASES

The merits of two recent Supreme Court decisions are considered here. In the first (*Matsushita*),[33] the Court eschews microanalytic analysis and places an unduly sanguine competitive interpretation on the events in question. In the second (*Sharp*),[34] the Court appears to be confused and invokes an all-purpose free rider argument that bears no obvious relation to the issues.

Both cases expose the Court to the charge that ideology rather than analysis carries the day. Whether this is correct or not, the remedy in both cases is clear: issues of economic organization need to be engaged "on their own terms." The use of off-the-shelf solutions that finesse or obfuscate the issues is unsatisfactory.

Matsushita[35]

The *Matsushita* case was presented to the Supreme Court as a request by Japanese television manufacturers for a summary judgment against the U.S. firms that had brought suit against them.

The plaintiffs alleged that Japanese firms had engaged in collusion and dumping. The Japanese firms had a protected home market, to which they sold on highly profitable terms, and sold abroad at prices that were held to be predatory. Collusion being a difficult condition to orchestrate and sustain for long periods of time, and with such behavior being crucial to the case, the plaintiffs' argument was naturally regarded as suspect. Summary judgment proceedings nevertheless require that the admissible evidence be construed in the light most favorable to the nonmovant (U.S. firms). Was it plausible to infer conspiracy? What purposes are served by dumping? Are any of these purposes reasonably implicated in this case?

An inference of conspiracy would be difficult to support had this been a case between one group of U.S. firms and another. International competition (with protected home markets) introduces new considerations, however. And there are reasons to believe that coordination among Japanese firms in Japanese markets may differ from that which is characteristic of the United States. Accordingly, a specific showing of comparability is presumably needed if the same threshold tests for conspiracy are to be applied to U.S. and Japanese firms alike.

The purposes served by dumping have been described by Jacob Viner as follows: "Once monopoly control has been achieved in the domestic market, it may pay, if domestic orders do not fully occupy the productive facilities, to bid for orders in other markets at prices lower than those exacted at home" (1923, p. 94). Specifically:

> A producer may engage in export dumping primarily with a view to maintaining full production during a period of depression in the domestic market, but he may at the same time deliberately manage his dumping so that it will inflict as much injury as possible upon his foreign competitors. Moreover, the predatory dumper *may not expect that he will succeed in wholly eliminating* the competitors against whom he is dumping, but he may be content if his dumping so weakens them that they will thereafter refrain from contesting his prices or from extending their activities into his special markets. (Viner, 1923, p. 122)

The Court, however, refused to examine the issues through a lens that was congenial to the plaintiff. Rather, the Court embraced the scenario offered by Frank Easterbrook, which makes no U.S.–Japanese contextual distinctions. Thus Easterbrook argued that

> [t]he plaintiffs maintain that for the last fifteen years or more at least ten Japanese manufacturers have sold TV sets at less than cost in order to drive United States firms out of business. Such conduct cannot possibly produce profits by harming competition, however. If the Japanese firms drive some United States firms out of business, they could not recoup. Fifteen years of losses could be made up only by very high prices for the indefinite future. (The losses are investments, which must be recovered with compound interest.) If the defendants should try to raise prices to such a level, they would attract new competition. There are no barriers into electronics, as the proliferation of computer and audio firms shows. (1984, pp. 20–27)

The strategic model on which Easterbrook relies for his assessment is not expressly stated. He ascribes very severe purposes (drive rivals out) rather than more limited ones (discipline). Recoupment is examined not in *ex ante* respects, but in *ex post* terms. He infers conditions about entry into television manufacturing and marketing from the "proliferation of computer and audio firms." He questions the force of the plaintiffs' case and suggests that "we are left with the more plausible inference that the Japanese firms . . . were just engaged in hard competition" (Easterbrook, 1984, p. 27). The Court was of a like mind. It concluded that a conspiracy was "implausible" because the Japanese firms had "no motive to enter into the alleged conspiracy."[36]

To be sure, *Matsushita* is a complicated case and had already dragged on for a dozen years. Sharing, as I do, many of Easterbrook's reservations about the implausibility of conspiracy and recoupment, the Supreme Court may well be right. But to decide the matter in a proceeding of this kind without a more careful assessment of the underlying microanalytics is cavalier.[37]

Sharp

Business Electronics (the petitioner) had become an exclusive retailer of electronic calculators made by Sharp Electronics (the respondent) in the Houston, Texas area in 1968. In 1972, Gilbert Hartwell was appointed as a second retailer in the Houston area. Business Electronics charged lower prices to which Hartwell objected. The undisputed facts are these.

> [Sharp] published a list of suggested minimum retail prices, but its written dealership agreements with petitioner and Hartwell did not obligate either to observe them, or to charge any other specific price. Petitioner's retail prices were often below respondent's suggested retail prices and generally below Hartwell's retail prices, even though Hartwell too sometimes priced below respondent's suggested retail prices. Hartwell complained to respondent on a number of occasions about petitioner's prices. In June 1973, Hartwell gave respondent the ultimatum that Hartwell would terminate his dealership unless respondent ended its relationship with petitioner within 30 days. Respondent terminated petitioner's dealership in July 1973.[38]

The petitioner then brought suit alleging that respondent and Hartwell had engaged in an unlawful conspiracy that was illegal *per se* under Section 1 of the Sherman Act.

Although it is plain that Business Electronics was a thorn in the side of Hartwell, the strategic basis for a conspiracy between Sharp and Hartwell is not evident. Convoluted antitrust arguments are not, however, uncommon. If antitrust will not hear one kind of complaint—namely, that petitioner was the victim of Hartwell's muscle to which Sharp acceded—but will entertain another—namely, that Hartwell and Sharp conspired to put Business Electronics out of business—then cases are understandably reshaped to fit the law. The courts are too often willing participants in such contrived antitrust games.

The recent *Sharp Electronics* opinion thus purports to continue the antitrust reasoning that informed the Supreme Court's opinion in *GTE-Sylvania*.[39] But whereas the latter was a reasoned opinion that overturned the earlier (mistaken) *Schwinn* decision, the *Sharp* opinion merely parrots "free-riders" and "free-riding" and makes no effort to examine the particulars. Indeed, although it concedes that the evidence about free riding was conflicting, it makes no effort to sort this out. Rather, the Court asserts that a "quite plausible purpose of the restriction [was] to enable Hartwell to provide better services under the sales franchise agreement"[40] and concludes that "our decision [rests] upon the foregoing economic analysis."[41]

This is not the first time that the Supreme Court has invoked economic theory to support its antitrust decisions[42] and it will not be the last. Perverse uses of economic reasoning—in the form of "creative lawyering" and the like[43]—are encouraged, however, by casual application of ready-made arguments. The first question that needs to be asked is "What is going on here?" Failure to ask and answer this rudimentary question invites confusion.

The fact that the larger retailer (Hartwell) was annoyed by the price cutting of the smaller retailer (Business Electronics) and insisted that Sharp choose between them is clear. The fact that Hartwell possessed some bargaining power in the short run, by virtue of its size and established reputation and knowledge of the market, is evidently true. The facts that Sharp acceded to Hartwell's muscle and that Business Electronics objected are both understandable. But it does not follow that this is an antitrust case.

The unconvoluted interpretation is that Hartwell was aggressive and that (mainly in the degree to which it had assets that could not be easily redeployed) Business Electronics was damaged. But there is no indication that the quality of competition in this market is at stake—either in terms of market power (where there is no showing that Hartwell-Sharp bear a strategic relation to the quality of interbrand competition) or in the way in which business is conducted (there being no evident need to impose contractual regularities to support the integrity of the contracting process). If it is merely a matter of muscle, then convoluted antitrust theories (conspiracy by the petitioner; a free-rider defense by the respondent) ought to be dismissed as mindless and opportunistic. The issues ought to be addressed and resolved on their own terms.

To be sure, this effort will often require more self-conscious attention to the microanalytics. But that is the central message of transaction cost economics all along.

CONCLUDING REMARKS

Antitrust enforcement has been substantially and beneficially reformed in the past twenty years. This is true in large measure because efficiency considerations have been prominently and insistently introduced into the antitrust dialogue whereas a monopoly presumption, to include even perverse use of efficiency reasoning, previously carried the day.

Some of the relevant efficiency reasoning involves straightforward applications of or extensions to applied price theory. I have argued, however, that many of the critical efficiency features (and some of the monopoly features) have transaction cost origins. If the true underlying conditions are of a transaction cost kind, they need to be explicated and understood as such. Failure to do so runs the risk of misunderstanding the issues and invites misapplication of antitrust reasoning—of which older incantations of "barriers to entry" and more recent appeals of "free riders" are examples.

Addressing issues of economic organization from a transaction cost economics perspective requires much more detailed knowledge of organizational structure and of contracting practices than is characteristic of applied price theory. If, however, efficiency features are often deeply embedded, then there appears to be no alternative but to engage the issues on their own terms.

The notion that "ideas, not vested interests" drive policy outcomes is understandably attractive to academics. Sometimes, perhaps often, this is wishful thinking. But as Theodore Frech argues, and I agree, "a genuine scientific revolution has occurred . . . [and] has led to a more thoughtful and rational approach to antitrust" (1987, p. 263). Indeed, William Baxter's forcefulness notwithstanding, "it would have been politically impossible for . . . Baxter to have done what he did [as Assistant Attorney General for Antitrust], had there not been an intellectual shift in the underpinnings of antitrust" (Bork, 1985, p. 25).

There are, to be sure, needs to consolidate the gains. A more deliberate use of microanalytic reasoning, to which I refer, should help to accomplish this.

NOTES

1. The discussion of D'Andrade is based on Donald McCloskey's book review of *Metatheory in Social Science* (McCloskey, 1986).
2. See Williamson (1991).
3. Note, however, that strategic anticompetitive purposes can be realized only if the preconditions for monopoly power are satisfied—which is the exception rather than the rule. As discussed elsewhere, the critical preconditions are high concentration coupled with high hurdles to entry (Williamson, 1977, pp. 292–93). Paul Joskow and Alvin Klevorick (1979, pp. 225–31) and Januz Ordover and Robert Willig (1981) concur. Frank Easterbrook (1984) also uses a structural test as his first antitrust "filter." Also see Williamson (1987).
4. In re Foremost Dairies, Inc., 60 F.T.C. 944, 1084 (1962).
5. Federal Trade Commission v. Procter & Gamble Co., 386 U.S. 568, 574 (1967).
6. The disclaimer of efficiencies appeared in Procter & Gamble's brief as Respondent in the Clorox Litigation. See Fisher and Lande (1983, p. 1582, n. 5).
7. United States v. Von's Grocery Co., 384 U.S. 270, 301 (1966) (Stewart, J., dissenting).
8. The phrase was used repeatedly by Walter Adams in his testimony in the Purex v. Procter & Gamble Co. case.
9. The quotation is attributed to Donald Turner by Stanley Robinson, N.Y. State Bar Association, Antitrust Symposium, 1968, p. 29.
10. United States v. Arnold, Schwinn & Co., 388 U.S. 365 (1967).
11. Brief for the United States at 47 (U.S. v. Schwinn, note 32).
12. *Ibid*. at 50.
13. In principal, Arnold Harberger's (1954) analysis of economywide welfare losses of monopoly was pertinent. But this theory operated at a very high level of aggregation and was too removed from firm and market particulars. His later and more general treatment is more germane (Harberger, 1971).
14. On the application of the partial equilibrium welfare economics model to economies as an antitrust defense, see Williamson (1968, 1977) and Fisher and Lande (1983). The latter is much more skeptical.
15. Bain was among the first to acknowledge the merits of an economies defense in assessing mergers (1968, p. 658). Wesley Liebeler (1978), Robert Bork (1978), and Timothy Muris (1979) have all made extensive use of the partial equilibrium trade-off model in their insistence that antitrust enforcement that proceeds heedless of trade-offs is uninformed and contrary to the social interest.

16. See the recent "Symposium on Horizontal Mergers and Antitrust" in the Fall 1987 issue of the *Journal of Economic Perspectives*, where Lawrence White, Franklin Fisher, and Richard Schmalensee also counsel against involving the *courts* in an economies defense.

17. The 1984 *Merger Guidelines* of the Department of Justice expressly declare that "some mergers that the Department otherwise might challenge may be reasonably necessary to achieve significant net efficiencies. If the parties to the merger establish by clear and convincing evidence that a merger will achieve such efficiencies, the Department will consider those efficiencies in deciding to challenge the merger" (U.S. Department of Justice 1984, Sec. 3.5). In effect, firms that are proposing a merger are now invited to present evidence of efficiencies as support for the merger—rather than suppress such evidence (the market power standard) or deny that any efficiencies exist (the perverse condition to which merger enforcement had fallen in the 1960s). Economies of both technological and transaction cost kinds will be entertained (Sec. 3.5 and 4.24).

18. The first indication of a crack was in the decision by the Federal Trade Commission to vacate the administrative judge's order and dismiss the complaint in the *Budd Co.* case (Budd Co. [1973-1976 Transfer Binder] *Trade Reg. Rep.* CCH, ¶ 20,988 (FTC No. 8848, September 18, 1975), a case on which I had served as an expert witness and had managed to introduce efficiency reasoning, to which the Commission made note in its dismissal. For a discussion, see a note in the *Harvard Law Review* 89 (1976): 800, 802, and Williamson (1977, pp. 728-29). The watershed case, however, is when the Supreme Court spoke to the implausibility of a monopoly argument in Continental T.V. Inc. et al. v. GTE Sylvania Inc. 433 U.S. 36 (1977), which reversed the earlier *Schwinn* decision (United States v. Arnold, Schwinn & Co., 388 U.S. 365 [1967]).

19. These and related issues receive extensive treatment in Roger Blair and David Kaserman (1983). A combined efficient factor proportions–monopoly power framework for assessing vertical integration has been successively developed by M. M. Vernon and D. A. Graham (1971), Richard Schmalensee (1973), F. R. Warren-Boulton (1974), and Fred Westfield (1981).

20. Donald Turner and Richard Posner, having been the chief architects of the government's brief in *Schwinn*, were both instrumental in persuading the Supreme Court to reverse itself in *Sylvania*. Both deserve credit for rethinking the issues and reaching a different result.

21. Kenneth Arrow's information–investment argument does not expressly rely on a comparative transaction cost assessment, but it lurks very close to the surface (Arrow, 1975).

22. The arguments and some evidence are set out in Williamson (1985, Chaps. 4-5). It is also noteworthy that the Grossman and Hart treatment of vertical integration assumes an asset specificity condition (1986). The same is true of Riordan (1988). More generally, vertical integration is increasingly viewed as a comparative contracting issue, of which asset specificity is a key feature. See Klein, Crawford, and Alchian (1978).

23. Recall what Arrow observed about bargains: "*It is not the presence of bargaining costs per se but their bias that is relevant*" in determining which bargains with what consequences will be made (Arrow, 1969, p. 51; emphasis in original).

24. Out of awareness of the added difficulties of prosecuting firms for failure to pay sales taxes on internal trades, the government typically exempts intrafirm trades. One easy evasive device to which the firm has access, but the market does not, is to erase a boundary. Rather than have Division A supply intermediate product to Division B, a combined Division AB is created, thereby "eliminating" a transfer payment (but continuing the transaction).

25. The term "diehard Chicagoan" is due to Posner, who defines such a person as one

"who has not accepted any of the suggested refinements of or modifications in Director's original ideas" (Posner, 1979, p. 932).

26. Actually, Posner admits in a footnote the possibility that capital costs could be adversely affected (1979, p. 932, n. 31) and subsequently elevates this to the text (1979, p. 945). But his section on vertical integration maintains that monopolist and entrant experience identical costs. The qualification gets lost in the process.

27. Both are elaborated elsewhere. See Williamson (1975, pp. 111–13, 115–16).

28. The reduction in incentive intensity is deliberately introduced into the relation between integrated stages—so as to mitigate the maladaptation problems that would otherwise arise if integrated stages attempted to operate with unchanged incentive intensity. The issues are elaborated in Williamson (1988a).

29. For an elaboration of the argument, see Williamson (1979, pp. 978–80).

30. There being different levels of microanalytics—in economics and elsewhere—which is the appropriate level for transaction cost economics purposes? A semimicroanalytic level of analysis—located between the Friedmanian view that "prices and output are the only relevant data" (Arrow, 1971, p. 180) and the highly detailed observation that would be needed if the "decision premise" were to be made the basic unit of analysis (Simon, 1957, p. 201)—is what I propose.

31. The transformation, for example, whereby an ex ante large numbers supply condition becomes an ex post bilateral exchange relation—which predictably attends some trades—is a process outcome that has pervasive significance for economic organization. The underlying reasons why one form of organization is able only imperfectly to mimic another, which is responsible for trade-offs in moving from one form of organization to another, also reside in the study of process.

32. Recent empirical work bears out the pervasive influence of transaction cost factors in the organization of economic activity. Much of this work requires that company documents (Williamson, 1985, pp. 197–203), contracts (Joskow, 1988), organizational structures (Armour and Teece, 1978), and the like be examined—although not all of it does. The April 1988 issue of the *Journal of Economic Behavior and Organization* includes three articles that test transaction cost hypotheses, all of which use secondary data sources.

33. Matsushita Electric Industrial Co. v. Zenith Radio Corp., 475 U.S. 571 (1986).

34. Business Electronics Corp. v. Sharp Electronics Corp. 108 S. Ct. 1115 (1988).

35. The argument here closely follows and relies on Williamson (1987, pp. 298–300).

36. Matsushita, 475 U.S. at 595.

37. This is the thrust of the dissenting opinion written by Justice White.

38. Sharp, note 35, at 1518.

39. See note 18 *supra*.

40. Sharp, note 35, at 1522.

41. *Ibid*. at 1523.

42. Recall in this connection that the Warren Court invoked economic theory to support its decision in the *Philadelphia National Bank* case (374 U.S. 321 [1963]). As Donald Baker and William Blumenthal put it, the Court in this case "adopted a structural test of prima facie illegality in horizontal merger cases" (1986, p. 330). The Court proceeded to explain (at 363) that its test

is fully consonant with economy theory. That "competition is likely to be greatest when there are many sellers, none of which has any significant market share," is common ground among most economists.

If all-purpose market structure analysis carried the day then, why not all-purpose free-rider analysis now?

43. Creative lawyering is a euphemism for a contrived case. See the testimony of John Shenefield before the Subcommittee on Antitrust and Monopolies of the Committee on the Judiciary, U.S. Senate, July 18, 1978, p. 65.

REFERENCES

Adelman, M. A. 1961. "The Antimerger Act, 1950–1960," *American Economic Review* 51 (May): 236–44.

Alchian, Armen & Harold Demsetz. 1972. "Production, Information Costs, and Economic Organization," *American Economic Review*, 62: 777.

Armour, H. O., and D. Teece. 1978. "Organizational Structure and Economic Performance," *Bell Journal of Economics* 9: 106–22.

Arrow, Kenneth J. 1969. "The Organization of Economic Activity: Issues Pertinent to the Choice of Market versus Nonmarket Allocation." In *The Analysis and Evaluation of Public Expenditure: The PPB System*, vol. 1. U.S. Joint Economic Committee, 91st Congress, 1st Session. Washington, DC: U.S. Government Printing Office, pp. 49–73.

_____. 1971. *Essays in the Theory of Risk-Bearing*. Chicago: Markham.

_____. 1975. "Vertical Integration and Communication," *Bell Journal of Economics* 6 (Spring): 173–83.

_____. 1987. "Reflections on the Essays." In George Feiwel, ed. *Arrow and the Foundations of the Theory of Economic Policy*. New York: New York University Press, 727–34.

Bain, Joe. 1968. *Industrial Organization*, 2d ed. New York: John Wiley & Sons.

Baker, Donald, and William Blumenthal. 1986. "Ideological Cycles and Unstable Antitrust Rules." *Antitrust Bulletin* 31 (Summer): 323–40.

Barnard, Chester, *The Functions of the Executive*, Harvard Univ. Press, Cambridge, Mass. 1938.

Blair, Roger, and David Kaserman. 1983. *Law and Economics of Vertical Integration and Control*. New York: Academic Press.

Blake, Harlan M. 1973. "Conglomerate Mergers and the Antitrust Laws." *Columbia Law Review* 73 (March): 555–92.

Bork, Robert. 1969. "Vertical Integration and Competitive Processes." In J. Fred Weston and S. Petzman, eds. *Public Policy Towards Mergers*. Pacific Palisades, Calif.: Goodyear Publishing Co., pp. 139–49.

_____. 1978. *The Antitrust Paradox*. New York: Basic Books.

_____. 1985. *California Lawyer* 5 (May): 23–26.

Coase, Ronald H. 1952. "The Nature of the Firm." *Economica N.S.* 4 (1937): 386–405. Reprinted in J. G. Stigler and K. E. Boulding, eds. *Readings in Price Theory*. Homewood, Ill.: Richard D. Irwin.

_____. 1972. "Industrial Organization: A Proposal for Research." In V. R. Fuchs, ed. *Policy Issues and Research Opportunities in Industrial Organization*. New York: National Bureau of Economic Research, pp. 59–73.

_____. 1988. "The Nature of the Firm: Origin," *Journal of Law, Economics, and Organization* 4 (Spring): 3–17.

Commons, John R. 1924. "Law and Economics," *Yale Law Journal*, 34: 371–82.

_____. 1934. *Institutional Economics: Its Place in Political Economy*, New York: Macmillan Co. 1934.

Easterbrook, Frank. 1984. "The Limits of Antitrust," *Texas Law Review* 63 (January): 1–34.

Fellner, William. 1949. *Competition Among the Few*. New York: Alfred A. Knopf.

Fisher, Alan, and Robert Lande. 1983. "Efficiency Considerations in Merger Enforcement." *California Law Review* 71 (December): 1580–1696.

Frech, Theodore. 1987. "Comments on Antitrust Issues." *Health Economics and Health Services Research* 7: 263–283.

Friedman, Milton. 1953. *Essays in Positive Economics*. Chicago: University of Chicago Press.

Grossman, Sanford, and Oliver Hart. 1986. "The Costs and Benefits of Ownership: A Theory of Vertical and Lateral Integration." *Journal of Political Economy* 94 (August): 691–719.

Harberger, Arnold. 1954. "Monopoly and Resource Allocation." *American Economic Review* 44 (May): 77–87.

_____. 1971. "Three Basic Postulates for Applied Welfare Economics: An Interpretive Essay." *Journal of Economic Literature* 2 (September): 785–97.

Hayek, Friedrich. 1945. "The Use of Knowledge in Society." *American Economic Review* 35 (September): 519–30.

Jensen, Michael. 1983. "Organization Theory and Methodology." *Accounting Review* 50 (April): 319–39.

Joskow, Paul L. 1988. "Asset Specificity and the Structure of Vertical Relationships: Empirical Evidence." *Journal of Law, Economics, and Organization* 4 (Spring): 95–118.

_____, and Alvin Klevorick, 1979. "A Framework for Analyzing Predatory Pricing Policy." *Yale Law Journal* 89 (December): 213–70.

Kenney, Roy, and Benjamin Klein. 1983. "Economics of Block-booking." *Journal of Law and Economics* 26 (October): 497–540.

Klein, Benjamin, Robert Crawford, and Armen Alchian. 1978. "Vertical Integration, Appropriable Rents, and the Competitive Contracting Process." *Journal of Law and Economics* 21 (October): 297–326.

Knight, Frank. 1941. "Anthropology and Economics." *Journal of Political Economy* vol. XLIX (April): 247–68.

Kreps, David, and Michael Spence. 1985. "Modelling the Role of History in Industrial Organization and Competition." In George Feiwel, ed. *Issues in Contemporary Microeconomics and Welfare*. London: Macmillan, pp. 340–79.

Liebeler, Wesley C. 1978. "Market Power and Competitive Superiority in Concentrated Industries." *UCLA Law Review* 25 (August): 1231–1300.

McCloskey, Donald. 1986. "The Postmodern Rhetoric of Sociology." *Contemporary Sociology* 15 (November): 815–18.

McKenzie, Lionel. 1951. "Ideal Output and the Interdependence of Firms." *Economic Journal* 61 (December): 785–803.

Marglin, Stephen A. 1974. "What Do Bosses Do? the Origins and Functions of Hierarchy in Capital Production." *Review of Radical Political Economics* 6: 33–60.

Marschak, Jacob. 1968. "Economics of Inquiring, Communicating, Deciding." *American Economic Review* 58 (May): 1–18.

Muris, Timothy. 1979. "The Efficiency Defense Under Section 7 of the Clayton Act." *Case Western Reserve Law Review* 30 (Fall): 381–432.

Ordover, J. A., and R. D. Willig. 1981. "An Economic Definition of Predatory Product Innovation." In S. Salop, ed. *Strategic Views of Predation*. Washington, D.C.: Federal Trade Commission, pp. 301–96.

Polanyi, Michael. 1962. *Personal Knowledge: Towards a Post-Critical Philosophy*. New York: Harper & Row.

Posner, Richard. 1969. "Oligopoly and the Antitrust Laws: A Suggested Approach." *Stanford Law Review* 21 (June): 1562–1606.

Monopoly Conduct, Especially Leveraging Power from One Product or Market to Another

LAWRENCE A. SULLIVAN
AND ANN I. JONES

This chapter, as part of a larger inquiry into innovation and the impact of competition laws on the innovative process, is directed at single-firm conduct. Contrary to the position asserted by other contributors to this volume, it is our contention that there is nothing inherently inconsistent with the antitrust law's prohibitions against monopoly and the protection and encouragement of innovation. We remain to be convinced, by any sound empirical evidence, that there has been a significant diminution or reduction of America's innovative energies in recent years, or, if there has been, that antitrust is responsible for it.[1] Before these two predicates are firmly established, it would be folly, as many business and political leaders are coming to recognize, to amend the antitrust laws to cure an invisible and unproved ill.

Traditional structural theory and the volumes of case law predicated on it, evidence a hostility to monopoly due, in not insignificant part, to the deadening effect that it has on the innovative process. As those materials demonstrate, monopolies threaten allocative, productive, and also dynamic efficiency. The monopolist may produce too little and charge too much; it may produce too little and pay too much for labor, management, or other inputs, thus taking its monopoly returns in the form of the quiet life; and, feeling no competitive spur, it may be inadequately innovative. Indeed, the monopolist may display all three of these characteristics and may, in addition, expend some of its monopoly returns to enhance or protect its power.

Given these baneful consequences, one might expect the law to forbid monopoly except where it is inevitable and then to regulate it. But Section 2 of the Sherman Act has never reached so far. The usual formulations teach only that a monopolist violates Section 2 when it engages in "exclusionary," "restrictive," or "anticompetitive" conduct—that is, when it uses power or position rather than merit to encumber less well-situated rivals and distort the outcomes that the competitive process would yield.

It is, in part, to protect a monopolist's ability to innovate and benefit consumers by building new and better mousetraps that the law leaves unchallenged certain conduct—even when undertaken by a firm dominant in its market. Thus, not only is it settled that Section 2 does not forbid "monopoly in the concrete," it is widely accepted that the law ought not to condemn monopoly innocently obtained.[2] This is common wisdom built up over many decades, the product of experience as well as thought. We do not challenge it. But we do observe that the wisdom undergirding this familiar legal norm may be narrower than is sometimes presupposed and, as a consequence, that the norm itself may sometimes be given a breadth that its own rationale will not support.

Our purpose in this chapter is threefold. First, we restate for emphasis the long-accepted reasons why monopoly itself is not unlawful, focusing particularly on a firm's innovative activities as an area of immunized conduct. We then extrapolate from these reasons in order to explore the general question of what conduct should be forbidden to monopolists. Finally, we apply those general proscriptions to fact situations involving the leveraging of power from one product or market to another and, in particular, to situations that might evoke the essential facilities doctrine. It is this latter doctrine that contains the seeds of the most far-reaching obligations imposed by the law on single-firm innovation. As will be seen, there is nothing in this doctrine that would suppress or otherwise derail innovation. Thus there is little or no justification for tampering with the monopoly prohibitions of Section 2.

THE PROTECTIVE RATIONALE FOR MONOPOLIES

Despite the formidable objections to monopoly, there are three reasons not to condemn a monopoly benignly acquired. First, monopoly is sometimes the most efficient way for a market to be structured. Indeed, monopoly is well-nigh inevitable in thin markets; it would be at once unfair and inefficient to forbid production at an efficient scale when this is so. Second, even in markets capable of supporting several firms, the hope of monopoly (with its supracompetitive returns) is an incentive to the efficient and innovative market performance that the law seeks to encourage. It would be unfair and inefficient to punish a firm that has done what society wants and thus achieved the goal that society sets before it. Supracompetitive pricing, moreover, may help to assure that the monopolist's reward is time-limited; such pricing is better calculated than pricing at cost to encourage from others conduct that may erode a monopoly earned by skill and industry. Third, and perhaps the clincher, to police the level of prices charged by an otherwise benign monopolist would require courts to regulate prices whenever substantial power is present, a role for which courts are ill-equipped.[3] As we go on we shall sometimes refer to these three reasons collectively as "the protective rationale" for the lawful monopoly.

Note the conditional character of these three reasons for tolerating monopoly, both the first two relating to efficiency and the last one relating to administrability. None of them makes a virtue either of power or its exploitive or restrictive use. All are put forth as "second-best" solutions. The ideal would be competitive pricing in all markets, but that goal simply cannot be achieved when a monopolist has gained power in an innocent way, including, *inter alia*, through innovation.

Moreover, the second efficiency rationale has a dynamic quality that requires an intertemporal balancing of interests. It says, in effect, that when the law considers what a monopolist may do, it may not evaluate social consequences solely on the assumption that the monopoly already exists. In that *ex post* posture, the more efficient solution unquestionably would be to insist on prices related to cost. But the law must take account also of the *ex ante* constraint — the social goal of encouraging firms to be dynamic and efficient by tolerating monopolies when attained by such conduct.

In the context of innovation, this constraint acknowledges (following in large measure the policy rationales for patent and other intellectual property protection) that in order to provide a firm with the stimuli needed to ensure the maximum degree of innovative activities, there must be a defined zone of permissible conduct and an opportunity to exploit, with supracompetitive prices and profits, the spoils of a firm's innovative efforts. Thus the generalization that monopolization requires a showing both of monopoly power *and* anticompetitive conduct is a product of one of the law's inescapable compromises. Evil though it may be, monopoly power and even exploitive pricing must be tolerated, so long as the power was innocently gained and is not used in ways yielding even further social harm.

SECTION 2 CONDUCT: A GENERAL APPROACH

The protective rationale for monopoly begins by viewing the dominant firm in isolation, stressing its social benefits without reference to costs. Obviously, however, a monopolist's conduct impacts, in a real and significant fashion, its rivals, its customers and, ultimately, consumers. These effects must influence any Section 2 conduct test.

Conduct that constrains rivals invariably reduces the economic freedom and opportunity that the competitive process provides. In the particular context of innovation, traditional antitrust wisdom has placed greater confidence in nettlesome rivals, small- or middle-sized, even in upstart new entrants, to supply the market with creativity and originality; the well-ensconced dominant firm is not conventionally viewed as a crucial source of innovation. Recall that in *United Shoe*, Judge Wyzanski noted that it was the much smaller competitor, Campo, that first found ways to introduce the cement process after the monopolist had considered and rejected it.

> This experience illustrates the familiar truth that one of the dangers of extraordinary experience is that those who have it may fall into grooves created by their own expertness. They refuse to believe that hurdles which they have learned from experience are insurmountable, can in fact be overcome by fresh, independent minds.[4]

The legislative history and long-standing judicial understanding show that entrepreneurial mobility based on openness to entry and competition based on the merits is the handmaiden of innovation as well as an important antitrust goal.[5]

Although arguably this is reason enough to construe Section 2 banning the monopolist from fettering rivals, the Sherman Act's legislative history and the judicial tradition have never drawn the justification for their conduct rules so narrowly. There is a distinct, although related, social concern expressed; fear that the monopolist will exploit buyers and sellers.[6] Indeed, such exploitive conduct was identified as a primary target of Section 2 as early as the decision in *Standard Oil*.[7] Nothing that has happened since, either legislatively, judicially, or in the realm of social thought, supports a change in that priority.

Nor is the incentive to invent compromised by such a prohibition. The balanced judgment that an innovative monopolist should be allowed to set supracompetitive prices as a reward for its creativity does not imply that it should be free to exploit its customers by other and different techniques which, unlike simple monopoly pricing, are not essential to encourage socially beneficial conduct and are capable of effective judicial remediation.

The Section 2 concept of anticompetitive conduct, then, should be given a meaning reflecting the multiple goals that give competitive processes their value. Conduct that is unduly restrictive of competitors or that exploits buyers or sellers, except when that conduct is shielded by the protective rationale for lawful monopoly, should fail the conduct test. Innovative conduct, nurtured both by the protective rationale and the prohibition against disadvantaging or excluding smaller (and potentially innovative) rivals, is expressly considered and protected by this rule of law.

The Breadth of the Conduct Test During the Formative and the Consensus Years

Over the years the leading cases, certainly in result and often in language, have been consistent with the view that Section 2 forbids as anticompetitive conduct both behavior that unduly restricts rivals and behavior that exploits buyers or sellers in ways not justified by the protective rationale that precludes a challenge to mere monopoly.

In its landmark *Standard Oil* decision, the Supreme Court condemned the oil trust in order to protect both rivals and customers. The opinion demonstrates the vulnerability of every act taken by a monopolist that goes beyond normal methods of industrial development. The basic offense was putting the trust together — an integration creating a monopoly that made "enormous and unreasonable profits."[8] What made the original organization of the trust unlawful was the fact that it created power to exploit buyers and sellers.[9] Among the trust's later acts deemed offensive were obtaining preferential railroad rates and rebates and dismantling properties to reduce production.[10] The railroad rebates both restricted competitors and exploited suppliers. The capacity and output reductions exploited buyers. Yet none of the protective rationale for permitting monopoly was implicated by this conduct. Mergers yielding monopoly, discriminatorily exploitive buying, or the arbitrary withdrawal of efficient and profitability-employed capacity was not necessary to encourage efficient performance, nor did remedying such tactics force the courts into unmanageable roles.

During the period of the structural consensus, from the 1940s through the 1970s, there was broad agreement about the major elements of antitrust policy. Virtually any conduct that might enhance or protect monopoly power or exploit it in ways other than straightforward monopoly pricing was suspect. Familiar examples include expanding capacity beyond need to discourage entry; stockpiling power, patents, ore, or other necessary resources beyond need; refusing to deal with competitors; contracting with suppliers not to supply rivals; marketing in ways that inhibit recycling or reduce the availability of technological information; bundling or otherwise levering power from one product or one market to another; and using discriminatory selling prices.[11]

Throughout this period, however, one area of dominant firm conduct remained presumptively lawful—the spectrum of activities cloaked in the mantle of product innovation. Suggested in *Alcoa*,[12] stated expressly in *United Shoe*,[13] and carefully examined in *Berkey*[14] and *SCM*,[15] Section 2 rarely, if ever, is deemed to constrain research and development efforts or product or process design changes undertaken by a dominant firm.[16] Fearful that the imposition of antitrust sanctions for innovation might result in the very "sluggishness" that the Sherman Act was designed to prevent, *Berkey* and its progeny,[17] for all practical purposes, immunized a wide variety of corporate activities directed at the development and introduction of new products or improvements on existing ones.[18] In so holding, *Berkey* expressly disregarded the efficacy of the invention or product "improvement,"[19] the monopolist's intent in developing its new product, and the detrimental consequences of that new product on the monopolist's rivals.[20]

During these decades, expressly excepting innovation, most of the practices that courts found to violate Section 2 have their primary anticompetitive impact in discouraging entry and restricting rivals.[21] Excess capacity overhanging a market, a payment to a supplier for cutting off rivals, the stockpiling of unneeded resources or technology that might otherwise be accessible, all have that effect. Strategic devices, such as lease-only arrangements that keep control of recycling in the hands of the monopolist, are more subtle ways to achieve similar ends.

The Conduct Test in the Revisionist Era

In recent years some scholars—Chicago School theorists particularly, but not only they—have criticized the conventional conduct test as too broad.[22] Chicagoans are guided by several convictions: (1) they believe that markets work remarkably well; (2) they believe that power tends to be ephemeral; and (3) they believe that efficiency is a residual category into which all market conduct falls, unless on the basis of testable hypothesis about its effects it can convincingly be labeled as output limiting and price enhancing.[23] If you believe these things you are likely to conclude that single-firm conduct should be unconstrained save in extreme situations such as merger to a monopoly or blatant predation by a monopolist. Other commentators, while open to wider concerns, stress that many powerful firms are important to the economy and that overdeterring such firms would have significant efficiency costs.[24] They advise caution in fashioning and applying the conduct test, at least in the areas most difficult to handle, in order to minimize errors of overinclusion.[25]

More consequential is the fact that some courts have moved in the same direction as have revisionist commentators.[26] Not that the courts are in tandem with any group. Chicago theorists, in particular, are well ahead of the courts and race on smartly, while the courts move slowly and test for the stopping point.

It is our own conviction that little, if any, retreat from the traditional conduct test is called for. The recent *Aspen Skiing*[27] opinion, although hardly a blunt rejection of every aspect of Chicago analysis, is more consistent with the traditional conduct test than with revisionist prescriptions. The case shows how fact-intensive conduct issues tend to be. It also shows that courts, in search of justice and fairness as well as efficiency, must sometimes respond by giving weight to influences that never register in an economic model. And, finally, it repudiates those who would place undue burden on a defendant's claim of legitimate business justification.

Simplifying somewhat, the facts amounted to this: at a time when three competitors, Ski, Highlands, and Buttermilk, operated single mountain lifts in Aspen, the three firms acted jointly to offer a three-mountain weekly discount ticket. Later, Ski acquired Buttermilk's facility and also developed another mountain of its own, thus changing the contours of intra-Aspen competition significantly. For awhile, Ski continued to cooperate with Highlands. Together the two firms offered a four-mountain joint ticket and shared revenues on the basis of use. Eventually, however, Ski changed its strategy and refused to cooperate further with Highlands. Its only justification for the change was a series of transparently unconvincing explanations.[28] Highlands sued under Section 2 of the Sherman Act and its treble damage award was upheld by the Tenth Circuit on an essential facility theory[29] and by a unanimous Supreme Court on a broader theory presumably applicable also to other examples of restrictive and exploitive conduct.[30]

The Supreme Court's opinion in *Aspen Skiing* recognizes that a firm that obtains power from its lawful development of a nonunique resource has no general duty to engage in a joint marketing program with a competitor. It holds, however, that in the context here, where the refusal to deal constituted an important change in an established pattern that had originated when the market was competitive, the question put by the district court to the jury was the right one. Did Ski act "'to exclude or restrict competition'" or did its business practices "'reflect[] only a superior product, a well-run business, or luck'" . . . ?[31] The Court did not spell out in detail what particular facts were sufficient to warrant letting the jury choose between those contrasting characterizations. Nevertheless, some things are clear enough and others can be inferred.

First, the Court saw an element of unfairness in Ski's terminating a longstanding relationship. The unfairness was intensified because when the multimountain arrangement was initially put together Ski apparently needed Highlands as surely as Highlands needed Ski. The "free-rider" benefits afforded to Ski during this earlier period by Highlands' participation in the four-mountain pass arguably balanced any "free rider" obligations imposed on them by Highland's continued presence in the marketing program.

Second, the Court reacted negatively to Ski's pseudo-justifications.[32] Ski's historic pattern of cooperation with Highlands and other resorts rendered most of its proffered justifications unconvincing. For example, Ski's claimed difficulty at monitoring usage of a multimountain lift coupon at Highlands was vitiated by evidence that Ski itself participated in interchangeable lift coupon programs with other resorts.[33]

There are two other factors, while not articulated expressly by the Court, that are arguably encompassed within the three-prong analysis of predation laid out in its opinion.[34] The first concerns restricting rivals, the second exploiting consumers. As Areeda and Hovenkamp observed, it would be impermissible for a monopolist blatantly to pay customers not to deal with a competitor. For example, Ski could not grant a discount to customers that agreed not to ski at Highlands.[35] Viewed this way the conduct is certainly restrictive, and the fairness argument is also reinforced.

A second observation is that Ski's conduct also reduced allocative efficiency and, in so doing, exploited consumers. A microtheoretic analysis suggests that Ski's conduct, however profitable to Ski, must have made Aspen marginally less attractive as a destination resort, thereby, reducing aggregate revenues for Aspen as a whole.[36] Considered *ex post*, it is patent that the aggregate of ski industry resources in Aspen were not being deployed most efficiently. Nor is there, under the protective rationale, an adequate *ex ante* justification for it. First, Ski does not have to be permitted to reject joint operation in order to encourage it to develop its own Aspen properties. It actually did develop them while operating under the joint arrangement. Second, remediation is not difficult, at least not the remediation actually sought. Treble damages were calculated and awarded on the basis of conventional instructions.

APPLYING THE CONDUCT TEST IN LEVERAGE SITUATIONS

The term leverage generally refers to a tactic by which a firm with power in one market exploits that power in another.[37] The term also refers to leveraging power from one product to another, as in the tying cases.[38] When leverage occurs the source of power may often be innovation; in this sense, leverage doctrine impacts importantly on innovation concerns. The power to engage in leverage, however, may be attained by some simple expedient like being the first to enter a thin market. Indeed, in *Griffith*, the classic leverage decision, that appears to have been the source of the defendant's power.

Leverage tactics have three characteristics in common: first, all are efforts to maximize monopoly returns (they are "exploitive"); second, all impede the competitive process in ways that straightforward monopoly pricing does not (they are "restrictive"); third, the restrictive impact of the conduct is felt at a point removed from the source of power. Leverage cases have another quality in common. They are a favorite target of Chicago School theorists who regard them as perverse.[39] We do not. We are persuaded that rules about leverage tend, on balance, to reduce the distributional and allocative distortions that can result from power, and do so without discernible injury to dynamic efficiency — perhaps, on balance, by aiding it. Let us explain why.

United States v. *Griffith*[40] will serve as an example. Griffith owned eighty-five theaters, fifty-three located in one-theater towns, thirty-two that faced local competition. Griffith bargained for the chain as a unit, thus obtaining first-run clearance rights in competitive towns that would not have been available but for its monopsony position in other towns. The Court held that leveraging power from closed towns to gain "monopoly rights in towns where [the defendant] had competition" violated Section 2.[41] The Chicago School critique asserts that if Griffith's power were fully exploited in closed towns it would yield deals of a given value for those towns, and that no distributor would both agree to a deal that optimized for Griffith in the closed towns and also conferred advantages on Griffith in open towns that its market position in the latter towns was not alone sufficient to earn. Therefore, Griffith must have taken less than the full fruits of its power in closed towns, trading off a portion of the monopsony returns it might have extracted to gain an advantage in open towns. For a Chicago commentator, these factual inferences justify the conduct. Given that the monopolist cannot increase its power by leveraging (an outcome they believe to be impossible),[42] Chicagoans believe that leveraging as a way to exploit monopoly power ought to be just as lawful as is straightforward monopoly pricing.[43]

Below we will challenge the Chicago assumption that Griffith must have settled for lower monopsony returns in closed towns in order to acquire monopsony-like advantages in open towns. For now let us provisionally accept that claim. We see nothing in that assumption to insulate leveraging conduct from Section 2. Even so viewed, leveraging conduct is both restrictive and exploitive. Looking at the example of *Griffith*, the defendant's conduct restricted the mobility of competing exhibitors in the open towns. But for Griffith's leverage, nonintegrated exhibitors would have had the opportunity to compete on the merits. They might have won first runs and clearances by bidding more than Griffith. In each of the thirty-two open towns, the static and dynamic advantages that such competition might have yielded were lost.

In addition, Griffith's dampening of competition in open towns — towns that structurally could support competition, exploited consumers by denying them choices that competition would have yielded. But for leveraging by Griffith, a more attractive or commodious theater in one of these markets might have obtained first-run rights that, through leverage, went to a less-appealing Griffith theater. Again, Griffith may have obtained longer clearances than, but for leveraging, would have been granted to it; to the extent it did, viewers in open towns had to wait longer than they would have waited in an unleveraged market. It does not seem defensible to assert that harms to consumers in competitive markets such as these were "paid for" by a reduction in the amount by which Griffith exploited distributors (and perhaps, indirectly, consumers) in closed towns. A commitment to competitive process means allowing competitive markets to make such allocations, not making them on the basis either of the monopolist's whim or its judgment about what deployment will best serve its own profits.

Nor was exploitation of consumers in open towns the only harm. Griffith's leverage was probably exploitive of film sellers as well. Unless transaction cost efficiencies could fully explain the deal,[44] Griffith, even though assumed to have given up something in closed towns, must have valued more highly what it gained in open towns. Griffith must have believed that its aggregate monopsony returns would be higher under the leveraged arrangement than they would have been from straight out monopsony pricing in each of the closed towns. There are various factors that might have warranted this conclusion. Perhaps a steady flow of first runs with good clearances in open towns discouraged further entry; perhaps it also discouraged existing rivals, leading to listlessness or even withdrawal. To the inevitable Chicago question — why, then, did distributors agree to the deal if it threatened to enhance Griffith's monopsony power? — the answer may well be — because they did not know the local markets as well as Griffith did and therefore did not realize the extent of the benefit to Griffith in what they had agreed to do.

The Chicagoan might insist that even if Griffith did get a greater return by exploiting in markets other than where the power arose, such leveraged exploitation should be lawful. The claim would be that maximizing returns must be lawful because mere monopoly and monopoly pricing are lawful. But this view ignores the limits of the protective rationale for mere monopoly and monopoly pricing. While the law will not turn on a successful competitor in the market in which its hard-won gains are obtained, there is nothing in this policy to entitle Griffith to lever power to obtain an otherwise unentitled advantage in a second, uncontested-for market. It did not require the right to leverage its power from closed into open towns in order to induce it to operate theaters in closed towns. Special *ex ante* incentives are not needed to encourage investments in these markets.[45] Simple monopoly profits, without special enhancement, are plainly enough and surely a court is competent to remedy this mode of exploitation without falling into an excessively regulatory role. The outcome in *Griffith* itself testifies to this.

We started our discussion of *Griffith* by accepting provisionally the keystone of the Chicago criticism, the inference that Griffith must have taken less than its full monopsony return in closed markets in order to "buy" monopsony-like advantages in open towns. Like much in Chicago analysis, this inference presupposes constricting (although often unstated) assumptions, most notably that all relevant information about all the affected markets is known to both parties, that both parties identify and evaluate a wide range of options, and (at least ideally) that there are not significant differences in the rates at which each of them discounts future benefits.

These assumptions are counterintuitive. Not only that, their validity is challenged by non-Chicago theoretical perspectives. Drawing on alternative perspectives, Kaplow, in a recent article, implies a specific alternative analysis.[46] This alternative analysis, moreover, is spelled out in an unpublished paper by Professor Mark J. Roe, University of Pennsylvania. Drawing on both of those sources, we demonstrate this alternative while staying with the basic *Griffith* facts.

Assume that Griffith knew facts about one or more open towns that lead it to expect future advantage from gaining first-run and clearance positions in those markets. A distributor dealing with Griffith would "charge" for that advantage only if it knew the same facts, thought them through, and realized how Griffith had evaluated them. What is known about how information is deployed and about bounded rationality suggest that this is not likely. Nor are information gaps and bounded rationality the only problems. Picture the first distributor with which Griffith negotiated after deciding that leverage would increase its own return. Even if that distributor were an unboundedly rational and knowledgeable maximizer, it would seek to "charge" Griffith for the advantages Griffith sought only if the distributor, facing a monopsonist, stood ready to put itself at considerable risk. This distributor is not a collective bargaining representative for all distributors. It stands alone. If it bargains for a monopoly offset in closed towns, it must do so without regard to whether or not other distributors with whom Griffith will later deal can be expected to view the matter in the same way and to make the same or similar offset demands. If the distributor had a sense of dependency on Griffith for closed town screens—as no doubt it would have, Griffith being a monopsonist—it would hesitate to stand alone against Griffith, for fear Griffith would, in retaliation, abandon it in favor of other distributors, thus shutting it out of the closed towns. Moreover, even if information gaps, bounded rationality, and caution did not stay its hand, the distributor might well discount the future much more sharply than would the monopsonist. Griffith, being a monopsonist, can indulge in long-term evaluations. But the lone distributor, facing competition, may be focused much more sharply on the here and now. To the extent that Griffith regarded itself as "buying" future benefits in open towns—resulting from the erosion of the strength of rivals in those towns—it may well have been able to buy at a "bargain" price.

This mode of analysis strongly reinforces the conclusion we reached even when the Chicago factual assumptions, even the unstated ones, were fully accepted. When a firm leverages power held in one market into a different market, the initial inference ought to be that unreasonably restrictive and exploitive consequences will result. Competition is being restricted in the second market and the monopolist, by increasing its monopoly return, is in all likelihood exploiting consumers and distorting allocative efficiency to a degree that cannot be justified under the protective rationale for monopoly in the concrete.

A final observation on *Griffith*. Questions are sometimes raised whether leveraging by a monopolist violates Section 2, when the market in which the impact occurs remains structurally competitive despite the fact that power centered in another market was used to distort competitive outcomes here. Nothing in *Griffith* gives support to such a doubt. The open towns remained open and the Court said nothing to suggest that its holding turned on an assumption, far less a finding, that in those towns monopoly was threatened. Nor do we see any justification for holding that monopoly power in one market can be used to distort competitive outcomes in another market, so long as monopoly is not threatened or achieved in the second market. The focus of concern is not the structural position acquired in the adjacent market, but the misuse of the power already held in the first market. By increasing aggregate monopoly returns, leveraging enlarges the exploitive effects of the existing power as well as distorting competitive outcomes in the adjacent market. Like the protective rationale, the factual claim that no leverage actually took place may often come into play in situations where defendants' activities span two markets.[47]

As an example, consider the case where leverage takes the form of a tie. The sponsor, having monopoly power in a product, may wish to discriminate in price by tying an essential complimentary product used with the monopolized product in proportions that vary with intensity of need.[48] It is often argued that this should be legal because discrimination can increase efficiency. Whatever may be the law under the Clayton Act or Sherman Section 1, the logic of Section 2 would condemn tying by a monopolist even when done to discriminate, save in limited situations falling under the protective rationale. Despite its purpose, the tie will have restrictive impacts in the tied product market; other sellers there will be foreclosed from the opportunity to bid for some of the business by competition on the merits and consumer choice will be diminished as a result. Also, on the face of the explanation for its use, the tie will increase the monopolist's returns. It therefore must be classed as exploitive. Finally, the administrative branch of the protective rationale will not shield such a tie. A court need not regulate prices to forbid tying for discrimination; it need merely to forbid the tie.

Returning to the question of interest in this volume, antitrust's hostility to a monopolist's exportation of its power through leveraging is entirely consistent with a policy of maximizing innovative efforts.

Moreover, the prohibition on leveraging protects innovative opportunities in two important ways: it preserves competitive markets for those firms that wish to succeed through innovation and the relative merits of the products or services offered within that market; and it attracts, through the allure of supracompetitive profits in the innovated-product market, a greater spur to further discoveries and improvement that may otherwise by suppressed or deflected by leveraging.

Unless there was some remarkably special and unique relationship between the upstream innovation and the downstream market that negates any incentive to innovate upstream unless permitted to exploit through downstream leverage, there would be no basis for assuming that straight out monopoly returns in the upstream market would not alone be sufficient to bring the innovation on line. Surely, there is no general basis for assuming in a typical situation of integration and leverage that the innovation would not have been forthcoming if the only monopoly returns that could be earned were those coming straight out monopoly pricing.[49] We rely on such returns as the *ex ante* incentive almost universally. At a minimum, then, there should be a strong presumption against assuming that leverage is needed to call forth the innovation.[50]

MONOPOLY CONDUCT AND THE ESSENTIAL FACILITY DOCTRINE

There is a final category of monopolistic conduct that deserves special attention in any article looking at the relationship between antitrust and innovation—the essential facility doctrine. Eschewing the protective rationale for monopoly articulated in this paper's first section, the courts have, in very special circumstances, circumscribed the owner of an essential facility, despite the *ex ante* effects of such marketplace qualifications and regardless of the administrative difficulties inherent in its application. What justification would be sufficiently important to offset the profound costs associated with such judicial interventionism?[51]

The doctrine's principal requirement is that the facility be impractical or uneconomic to duplicate.[52] Clearly, if a rival can reasonably reproduce the facility or otherwise compete using substitutes, the onerous duty for the owner to share access should not be imposed, otherwise free riders would subvert all incentive to innovate. On the other hand, if sharing, because of structural attributes of the particular market, is the only efficient alternative, then the law will not mandate economic waste simply to protect the innovator's right to exclude.[53]

The structural characteristics of markets that may satisfy this element of practical nonreplicability include those in which there are natural limits on available resources;[54] where the thinness of market demand in comparison with efficient levels of production makes more than one supplier impossible;[55] or other special circumstances in which marketplace performance indicates serious structural impediments absent access to the facility.[56] Whatever the definition, to be essential a facility must exhibit some significant advantage not otherwise replicable by the ordinary process of innovation and investment. The paradigm situation is one in which the defendant or defendants have accomplished an innovation so significant that competitive viability is conditional on access to it.

The doctrine arose and is most highly developed in situations where a group of horizontal competitors have together created and then excluded other competitors from a particularly valuable vertically related input or channel of distribution.[57] While all joint ventures need not give access to all competitors that want to participate,[58] access may have to be given if it confers a significant competitive advantage.[59]

The applicable law is thus well-settled where the facility is jointly created. There is little in the case law or literature, however, that articulates its rationale. As we perceive it, the settled doctrine recognizes that if the facility has particular value and requires joint action to achieve, there is little social cost in assuming that the facility would be created even if broader sharing became mandatory. That being so, the question, how should the facility be deployed once it is in existence, can be approached largely, if not entirely, from an *ex post* perspective. And given the joint nature of the undertaking, no insurmountable remedy problems are presented. The terms of access the sponsors use for themselves can be the standard against which access to others is measured.

What changes in the analysis are required when the facility has been created by a single firm, a firm that derives monopoly power from the facility? The issue arises predominantly[60] in situations where the facility innovator also operates in a vertically related market. The monopolist may have motives to use leverage to distort outcomes in the vertically related market. As will be seen, in many respects the essential facility concept tends to merge into other aspects of leverage theory at this point. If one defines the idea of essentiality loosely enough, there seems little need or reason to distinguish the analysis from that in conventional monopoly leverage case law jurisprudence.[61] In fact, however, courts have been reluctant to adopt such an omnibus approach to the analysis. The typical paradigm for two-market essential facilities is a "bottleneck," a narrow opening through which rivals must be allowed to pass lest competition be foreclosed or seriously handicapped as well. Drawn by Neale and reminiscent of the topographic narrows through which St. Louis-bound rail traffic had to travel, the bottleneck theory prohibits the owner of a strategic facility from using it to destroy potential rivals. It differs from leveraging in two important respects: first, the source of the monopolist's power, the facility, is much more carefully scrutinized than is a simple monopoly. Not only do the courts ensure that there is some justification for keeping the primary monopoly intact, they must also satisfy themselves that there is no reasonable way for competition to be accommodated absent equal access. Second, because of the heightened power inquiry, the courts appear to relax the conduct component of antitrust liability. Recall that in *Berkey*, the court required that some "unwarranted" competitive advantage be obtained through the exportation of the power into an otherwise uncompetitive market. Leveraging, therefore, still appears to require some degree of exclusionary, or otherwise unreasonably anticompetitive, conduct that, absent power, would otherwise be unavailable. Thus a defendant's exploitation of the natural benefits of vertical integration will not, in a simple leveraging context, support a claim of monopolization.[62] Conversely, as its name implies, an owner of an essential facility may incur liability based merely on its refusal to cooperate with its rivals, for example, by charging a fee that renders effective access impossible,[63] an otherwise permissible exercise of its business judgment.[64]

In a second significant aspect, the question of remedies, essential facility doctrine departs from its leveraging cousin. Leveraging remedies begin with the identification of the unwarranted advantage in the second market that states the offense; the remedy must be tailored to rectify it. Essential facility doctrine presumes the remedy, reasonable and nondiscriminatory access, without regard to the specific injury incurred by the complaining party in the second market. The latter remedy necessarily requires some type of judicial supervision over the terms of access, although rarely will the task be so unmanageable as to bring the conduct within the protective rationale. If, for example, the facility owner has provided its vertically integrated division access, it may be a fairly simple task to oblige the monopolist to respond in damages sufficient to put its disadvantaged downstream competitor into the same position as if the monopolist had afforded its rivals the same or similar terms. Of course doing this will never be purely a mathematical exercise. There will be contentious factual issues as well as legal issues about offsets and the like. But the task of the plaintiff will be essentially the same as (and not vastly more complex than) the plaintiff's task in any monopoly overcharge case. But even this degree of vagueness, and consequent doubt, can sometimes serve the public interest by creating an atmosphere for a socially wholesome settlement.[65]

In sum, the Section 2 conduct norm must be one that business people can understand, that courts can administer, and that responds adequately to the major antitrust concerns—the avoidance of restrictive and exploitive effects—and that does so without creating undue disincentives to efficiency. Moreover, given both the complexity of economic conduct and context and the limits of judicial procedures, the norm should not be overdetermined. There must be some room for rough approximations as well as precise weighing of competing considerations so that the jury can be given its conventional role.

CONCLUSION

There is little if anything to support the often heard suggestion that the conventional conduct test is too severe. When monopoly power has been established, courts should regard the structure as aberrational. They should then evaluate conduct (or should instruct the jury to do so) to determine whether it operates to restrict rivals or exploit buyers or sellers. If restrictive or exploitive effects are found, the court (or jury) should next apply the protective rationale to determine whether the specific and narrow reasons for not forbidding "mere monopoly" justifies a decision not to punish or enjoin the challenged conduct. If restrictive or exploitive conduct can be convincingly justified under that rationale, it should be lawful. If such conduct is not so justified, it should be forbidden. Applying this analysis, there is no convincing basis for the claim that leverage cases like *Griffith* are wrong. Leverage remains a viable antitrust concept and its use by a monopolist will, as analyzed under traditional conduct formulations, often be found to violate Section 2.

NOTES

1. If one is convinced that American industry does too little innovating, one ought to decide why before setting out to fix the problem. Are savings rates too low? If so, how can savings be encouraged? Does too much of available capital go into current goods, too little into innovation? Then let us shift the incentives by sensible changes in the relevant intellectual property law. Only if antitrust appeared to be even a second or third order constraint on innovation—for example, if there were plausible indications that antitrust fears were inhibiting vertical or conglomerate research collaboration, or horizontal research collaboration among firms lacking significant market shares, or if there were indications that antitrust itself was being utilized by powerful firms as a rent-seeking device similar, for example, to sham patent litigation—would a case for antitrust reform in the interest of encouraging innovation be made out.

2. As Judge Hand eloquently observed in *Alcoa*, "persons may unwittingly find themselves in possession of a monopoly, automatically so to say: that is, without having intended either to put an end to existing competition, or to prevent competition from arising when none had existed; they may become monopolists by force of accident." United States v. Aluminum Co. of America, 148 F.2d 416, 429–30 (2d Cir. 1945). The legislative history supports this limitation. When they proposed the legislation, Senators Hoar and Edmunds considered it as a nationwide codification of the common law's prohibitions on trade constraints, and neither believed it could apply to one, "who merely by superior skill and intelligence got the whole business because nobody could do it as well." 21 Cong. Rec. 3146–52 (1890).

3. When the monopolist is vertically integrated and operates at the same level as its customers, a court can police against discrimination between prices to the firm and to

its other customers, which may make the administrative problems more manageable.

4. United States v. United Shoe Machinery Corp., 110 F. Supp. 295, 346 (D. Mass. 1953), *aff'd per curiam*, 347 U.S. 521 (1954). It is interesting to note the relationship between the Wyzanski insight and the "satisfying" theory soon to be worked out in rich and elaborate detail by Herbert Simon and others. See, e.g., Simon, "A Behavioral Model of Rational Choice," *Q. J. Econ.* 69 (1955): 99. While there is little reason to regard the Simon theory or the Wyzanski insight as vulnerable, courts today are perhaps more cautious about the constraining conduct of dominant firms for fear of inhibiting their efficiency. See Berkey Photo, Inc. v. Eastman Kodak Co., 603 F.2d 263 (2d Cir. 1979), *cert. denied*, 444 U.S. 1093 (1980).

5. 21 Congressional Record, 51st Congress, 1st Session, 2456–62, 2569 (1890) (Senator Sherman). For a complete examination of the legislative history and the intent surrounding passage of the Act, see John J. Flynn, "The Reagan Administration's Antitrust Policy, Original Intent and the Legislative History of the Sherman Act," *Antitrust Bull.* 33 (Summer 1988): 259, 287; see also United States v. American Tobacco Co., 221 U.S. 106, 183 (1911).

6. 21 Congressional Record, 2657 (1890).

7. Standard Oil Co. v. United States, 221 U.S. 1, 76 (1911).

8. *Id.* at 43.

9. *Id.* at 76.

10. *Id.* at 42–43, 76–77.

11. See, e.g., *Alcoa*, 148 F.2d 416; *United Shoe*, 110 F. Supp. 295; Continental Ore Co. v. Union Carbide & Carbon Corp., 370 U.S. 690 (1962); Otter Tail Power Co. v. United States, 410 U.S. 366 (1973); Lorain Journal Co. v. United States, 342 U.S. 143 (1951); Greyhound Computer Corp. v. IBM, 559 F.2d 488 (9th Cir. 1977), *cert. denied*, 434 U.S. 1040 (1978); United States v. Griffith, 334 U.S. 100 (1948); Smith-Kline Corp. v. Eli Lilly & Co., 575 F.2d 1056 (3d Cir.), *cert. denied*, 439 U.S. 838 (1978).

12. Citing to the minority opinion in the *United States Steel* case, Judge Hand rejected an exclusively power-predicated rule for Section 2 liability:

> [T]he [A]ct offers no objection to the mere size of a corporation, nor to the continued exertion of its lawful power, when that size and power have been obtained by lawful means and developed by natural growth, although its resources, capital and strength may give to such a corporation a dominating place in the business and industry with which it is concerned.

Alcoa, 148 F.2d at 430 n.2.

13. *United Shoe*, 110 F. Supp. at 344 ("the process of invention and innovation" is clearly tolerated by the antitrust laws).

14. *Berkey*, 603 F.2d 263.

15. SCM Corp. v. Xerox Corp., 645 F.2d 1195 (2d Cir. 1981), *cert. denied*, 455 U.S. 1016 (1982).

16. In an unpublished opinion, the District Court in the Eastern District of Pennsylvania held that a defendant's intentional suppression of patented innovation for which it had an exclusive licensee to protect its own product from claims of false advertising may state a violation of Section 2. Bloch v. SmithKline Beckman Corp., No. 82–510 (E.D. Pa. Nov. 1, 1988) (LEXIS, Genfed library, Dist. file) (purposeful obstruction of development of potentially competitive product could be found anticompetitive). See also McDonald v. Johnson & Johnson, 537 F. Supp. 1282, 1340 (D. Minn. 1982), *vacated antitrust judgment on other grounds*, 722 F.2d 1370 (8th Cir. 1983), *cert. denied*, 469 U.S. 870 (1984).

17. E.g., In re E.I. Dupont de Nemours & Co., 96 F.T.C. 653 (1980); Foremost Pro Color, Inc. v. Eastman Kodak Co., 703 F.2d 534 (9th Cir. 1983), *cert. denied*, 465 U.S. 1038 (1984); Northeastern Tel. Co. v. AT&T, 651 F.2d 76 (2d Cir. 1981), *cert. denied*, 455 U.S. 943 (1982); Transamerica Computer Co. v. IBM, 698 F.2d 1377 (9th Cir.), *cert. denied*, 464 U.S. 955 (1983).

18. Although the *Berkey* court stopped short of holding that new product innovations were *ipso facto* immune from antitrust scrutiny, it had no difficulty distinguishing every case to find such liability by reference to "some associated conduct" beyond the product introduction itself to supply the gravamen of the violation. *Berkey*, 603 F.2d at 286 n.30.

19. In *Berkey*, the Second Circuit rejected a standard that imposed liability for innovations that were "unnecessary" or that had the effect of lessening the quality of the product. Unwilling to engage in the virtually impossible task of determining *post-hoc* the efficacy of a particular invention or product "improvement," the court rejected Berkey's efforts to characterize the Kodacolor II film as a "disinvention," designed principally to exclude rivals without a corresponding benefit to consumers, despite evidence that the film had a shorter shelf life than its predecessor and its quality was below that expected by the Kodak engineers. *Id.* at 282–83, 286–87 (reading narrowly the *IBM*-peripheral cases to prohibit the use of incompatible technologies only where effect is to coerce purchases in an unrelated market).

20. The Second Circuit specifically rejected the instruction of Judge Frankel that deemed failure to predisclose innovation actionable in those situations where "'[Kodak's] power was so great as to make it impossible for a competitor to compete with Kodak in the camera market unless it could offer products similar to Kodak's.'" *Id.* at 281. Thus, even where essential to the very existence of competition, a monopolist's innovation and full exploitation of that invention did not violate § 2.

21. But all of these devices, although primarily restrictive of rivals, also have exploitive effects. As Kaplow recently stressed, the apparent distinction between what we have called exploitive practices (because they yield higher monopoly returns) and what we have called restrictive practices (because they inhibit rivals) is really a distinction between short-run and long-run strategies. Kaplow, "Extension of Monopoly Power Through Leverage," *Colum. L. Rev.* 85 (1985): 523–25. Some practices increase monopoly returns right now, others (like creating excess capacity) may reduce current returns by increasing costs, but the monopolist uses them because by inhibiting rivals they extend the time over which supracompetitive profits can be earned. Some practices, such as discriminatory pricing and leveraging power into a vertically related market, may have their principal and immediate adverse effect in exploiting buyers and increasing the monopoly return.

22. For a comprehensive contrast between Chicago beliefs and more conventional antitrust attitudes, see Appendix, "Rewriting the Lexicon" to Fox and Sullivan, "Antitrust Retrospective and Prospective: Where Are We Coming From? Where Are We Going?," *N.Y.U. L. Rev.* 62 (1987): 96, 969–88. Footnotes 2 and 3 of that Appendix contain comprehensive citations to the Chicago School and the conventional literature. *Id.* at 969–70 (hereafter "Appendix"); see also Harris and Sullivan, "Horizontal Merger Policy: Promoting Competition and American Competitiveness," *Antitrust Bull.* 31 (1986): 871, 874–85 (hereafter "Merger Policy").

23. See Appendix, *supra* note 22, at 971–74; Merger Policy, *supra* note 22, at 880–82.

24. See Merger Policy, *supra* note 22, at 882–83.

25. Given the tremendous latitude afforded under Section 2 to firms in their research and development efforts, it is difficult to discern how the antitrust law's prohibitions on monopoly could be viewed as chilling innovation or invention. Nevertheless, some

may endorse the position that America's declining stature in technological innovation can be attributed, in part, to the antimonopoly laws in this country. See Jorde and Teece, Chapter 3, in this volume.

26. E.g., Rothery Storage & Van Co. v. Atlas Van Lines, Inc., 792 F.2d 210 (D.C. Cir. 1986) (Bork, J.), *cert. denied*, 479 U.S. 1033 (1987); Will v. Comprehensive Accounting Corp., 776 F.2d 665 (7th Cir. 1985) (Easterbrook, J.), *cert. denied*, 475 U.S. 1129 (1986).

27. Aspen Skiing Co. v. Aspen Highlands Skiing Corp., 472 U.S. 585 (1985).

28. A more realistic explanation is not hard to hypothesize: Ski recognized that a four-mountain joint ticket would enhance Aspen's competitive position vis-à-vis other destination resorts more than would a three-mountain ticket, thus yielding aggregate Aspen revenues marginally higher than would a three-mountain ticket. However, Ski apparently calculated that if it stopped cooperating with Highlands and sold only its own three-mountain ticket, it would increase its own share of aggregate Aspen revenues sufficiently to offset any reduction in that aggregate. This is confirmed by the observation of Ski's president that "the 4-area ticket was siphoning off revenues that could be recaptured by Ski Co., if the ticket were discontinued." *Aspen Skiing*, 472 U.S. at 592. That Ski did not assert this rationale as its "justification" is hardly surprising, instead claiming several logistical and administrative obstacles that neither the jury nor the Court found persuasive.

29. Aspen Highlands Skiing Corp. v. Aspen Skiing Co., 738 F.2d 1509 (10th Cir. 1984), *aff'd*, 472 U.S. 585 (1985).

30. *Id. Aspen Skiing* has been much discussed. For one lively airing of conflicting views, see Wiley, "After Chicago: An Exaggerated Demise?," *Duke L. J.* 1986: 1003; Hovencamp, "Chicago and Its Alternatives," *Duke L. J.* 1986: 1014; and Liebeler, "What Are the Alternatives to Chicago?," *Duke L. J.* 1987: 879, 880–88.

31. 472 U.S. at 595–96 (approving instruction paralleling language in United States v. Grinnell Corp., 384 U.S. 563, 570–71 [1966]).

32. 472 U.S. at 608–9.

33. *Id.* at 609.

34. *Id.* at 605 (it is appropriate to examine the effect of the challenged pattern of conduct on consumers, on Ski's smaller rival, and on Ski itself).

35. P. Areeda and H. Hovenkamp, *Antitrust Law* ¶ 736.1 (1989 Supp.), suggest an analogy between Ski's doing just that and giving a discount on its own three-mountain ticket—a discount which virtually assures that buyers will use Ski's mountains exclusively and Highlands mountain not at all.

36. Ski's action caused some skiers, who would have preferred Aspen to other resorts if a four-mountain ticket were available, to switch. To increase its own monopoly profits, therefore, Ski denied to some consumers the product mix that they would have preferred. Such conduct constitutes monopoly exploitation of a quite conventional kind. See, e.g., Photovest Corp. v. Fotomat Corp., 606 F.2d 704, 720 (7th Cir. 1979), *cert. denied*, 445 U.S. 917 (1980); Aurora Enterprises, Inc. v. National Broadcasting Co., 688 F.2d 689, 695 (9th Cir. 1982).

37. United States v. Griffith, 334 U.S. 100 (1948), is the classic example.

38. At times the term has been used to describe tactics that trade off present monopoly returns to increase future monopoly returns. See, e.g., *United Shoe*, 110 F. Supp. 295 (tactics used by United Shoe to keep used machines off the market said to involve leverage). Because too broad an extension of the concept could obscure the analysis, we apply the term only to tactics leveraging power from one product or market to another.

39. E.g., R. Bork, *The Antitrust Paradox* (1978), 299–309.

40. *Griffith*, 334 U.S. 100.

41. *Id.* at 105.

42. Of course even Chicago theorists—or at least the more thoughtful of them—concede the existence of special situations in which a monopolist will be able to augment its power or profits by leveraging into a complementary market. In Olympia Equip. Leasing Co. v. Western Union Tel. Co., 797 F.2d 370, 374 (7th Cir. 1986), *cert. denied*, 480 U.S. 934 (1987), Judge Posner observed that by entering into the market for telex equipment, and bundling an equipment charge into its telex package, the monopolist could "smuggle into the terminal component of its rates some of the monopoly profits from telex service itself—profits the regulators would otherwise force it to pass on to the ratepayers in the form of lower rates for telex service." In the end, the court found that the monopolist's conduct did not have the effect of discouraging entry or restricting rivals—in short, that no leverage actually occurred. Therefore, no offense could be stated and a directed verdict for the defendant should have been granted.

43. See Bork, *supra* note 39.

44. We leave open the issue of whether the real purpose and effect of the leveraged arrangement in *Griffith* was integration efficiencies—reduced transaction costs through unified bargaining. If so, Griffith might have been able to invoke the protective rationale. No doubt transaction cost reduction may explain why Griffith bargained once for all of its theaters. We do not, however, think it likely that efficiencies can explain the leveraged terms of the deal—the shift of the fruits of monopsony from closed to open towns. In any event, once a leverage transaction with exploitive and restrictive effects is established, a heavy burden of proof should be placed on the party asserting that efficiencies explain and justify it.

45. As to innovation, the court in *Berkey* made this same critical distinction. Asserting that the rewards of innovation could be enjoyed by "charging as high a price for its product as the market will accept," the Second Circuit expressly disapproved a monopolist exporting that power into an otherwise unaffected (and uninnovative) market. Compare *Berkey*, 603 F.2d at 274 n.12 with its discussion of Sargent-Welch Scientific Co. v. Ventron Corp., 567 F.2d 701 (7th Cir. 1977), *cert. denied*, 439 U.S. 822 (1978), 603 F.2d at 286 n.30 (use of power derived from older product to increase demand for new supplies the violation and purges innovation of its presumption of legality).

46. Kaplow, *supra* note 21.

47. Accord *Berkey*, 603 F.2d at 276 n.15 (use of monopoly power to distort competition in second market violates § 2); *Alcoa*, 148 F.2d at 438 (violation for "price squeeze" in aluminum sheet market even though no allegation that Alcoa attempted to monopolize that market); *Sargent-Welch*, 567 F.2d at 711–13 (attempted coercion of customers to buy millibalances in addition to monopolized microbalances constitutes violation even absent an attempt to monopolize millibalance market); Kerasotes Michigan Theatres, Inc. v. National Amusements, Inc., 854 F.2d 135, 137 (6th Cir. 1988) ("To run afoul of the antitrust laws, it is not necessary that the party attempting to leverage . . . possess monopoly power or dominant market position in [the] second market."), *cert. dismissed sub nom.* G.K.C. Michigan Theatres, Inc. v. National Amusements, Inc., 109 S. Ct. 2461 (1989); see also United States v. Western Electric Co., 846 F.2d 1422, 1428 (D.C. Cir. 1988) (construing AT&T consent decree to prohibit BOC from discriminating), *cert. denied sub nom.* Bell Atlantic v. AT&T, 488 U.S. 924 (1988).

48. Kaplow warns that discrimination is often a postlitigation justification for tying, that discrimination may have little to do with why the tie was imposed. Kaplow, *supra* note 21, at 522–23.

49. The monopolist may integrate forward and exclude others in order to reduce transac-

tion costs—because, in the context, hierarchies are more efficient than markets. But it may, instead, be taking these steps for reasons not different in kind from those that led Griffith to leverage from one geographic market to another. There may, in short, be market imperfections rather than potential efficiencies that make it possible for the upstream firm to increase its monopoly returns by integrating and foreclosing. If transaction cost efficiencies are the explanation, the protective rationale comes into play. However, if exploitation of market imperfections is the explanation, it does not.

50. Who should have the burden of persuasion? In instances where leverage is directed to adjacent but not vertically related markets, the cases, including *Griffith*, imply that the defendant would have to justify its conduct by showing some efficiency rationale. We think that would be a sensible rule here as well. It is the defendant that made the decision and knows not only the information on which it acted, but the analysis on which it relied. These could be brought forward by the defendant without undue difficulty.

51. In non-essential facilities cases, courts have indicated a willingness to impose an affirmative duty on the monopolist only where the existence of competition requires it. See Oahu Gas Service, Inc. v. Pacific Resources, Inc., 838 F.2d 360, 368 (9th Cir.), *cert. denied*, 488 U.S. 870 (1988); *Olympia Equip.*, 797 F.2d at 379.

52. Ferguson v. Greater Pocatello Chamber of Commerce, Inc., 848 F.2d 976, 983 (9th Cir. 1988); Fishman v. Estate of Wirtz, 807 F.2d 520, 539–40 (7th Cir. 1986).

53. In part, this accommodation may reflect a shared perception in many opinions that for many essential facilities, the defendant was less an innovator and more the lucky beneficiary of having entered a thin market first. Hecht v. Pro-Football, Inc., 570 F.2d 982, 991 (D.C. Cir. 1977), *cert. denied*, 436 U.S. 956 (1978).

54. In one of the first "essential facility" cases, the natural topography of St. Louis made it accessible from the west by a single narrow valley. Thus all railroads approaching St. Louis from the west were routed through this narrow passage and when the railways were constructed it was impracticable for all of them to have their own separate terminal facilities. Therefore, in 1889, several railroads joined in constructing terminal facilities and set up a jointly owned company, the Terminal Railroad Association of St. Louis, to run them. Although in an ordinary market the joining together of a large number of railroads into a single-joint terminus would not be unlawful, the inability of other companies to replicate this facility because of the physical limitations in St. Louis required that autonomy give way to competition and that they be required to afford nonproprietary companies reasonable and nondiscriminatory access to the facility. A. Neale, *The Antitrust Laws of the U.S.A.* (2d ed. 1970), 127; United States v. Terminal R.R. Ass'n, 224 U.S. 383 (1912).

55. *Hecht*, 570 F.2d at 990 (one such situation is where demand is so limited that it is impossible to produce at all and meet the cost of production except by a plant large enough to supply the whole demand).

56. This formulation can be found in Comment, "Refusals to Deal by Vertically Integrated Monopolists," *Harv. L. Rev.* 87 (1974): 1720, 1752. To be essential, a facility need not be nonduplicable, it is enough that replication of the facility would be inefficient or economically impracticable, or, with existing technology, it is impossible for firms to eliminate their dependence on the facility. *Hecht*, 570 F.2d at 992; MCI Communications Corp. v. AT&T, 708 F.2d 1081, 1132 (7th Cir.) (competitor inability to duplicate practically or reasonably), *cert. denied*, 464 U.S. 891 (1983).

57. *Terminal R.R.*, 224 U.S. 383; Associated Press v. United States, 326 U.S. 1 (1945); Silver v. New York Stock Exchange, 373 U.S. 341 (1963); Gamco, Inc. v. Providence Fruit & Produce Bldg., Inc., 194 F.2d 484 (1st Cir.), *cert. denied*, 344 U.S. 817 (1952). Recent commentary includes James R. Ratner, "Should There Be an Essential Facility Doctrine," *U.C. Davis L. Rev.* 21 (1988): 327, and Note, "Rethinking the

Monopolist's Duty to Deal: A Legal and Economic Critique of the Doctrine of Essential Facilities," *Va. L. Rev.* 74 (1988): 1069.

58. Northwest Wholesale Stationers, Inc. v. Pacific Stationery & Printing Co., 472 U.S. 284 (1985) (where venturers lacking marketing power refuse participation to a competitor, calling their conduct a "boycott" does not render it illegal).

59. *Terminal R.R.*, 224 U.S. at 409–11; *Associated Press*, 326 U.S. at 17, 21; *Gamco*, 194 F.2d at 489.

60. Cf. Official Airline Guides, Inc. v. FTC, 630 F.2d 920 (2d Cir. 1980) (so long as an owner of an essential facility does not itself have a position in a vertically related market, little or no antitrust problem), *cert. denied*, 450 U.S. 917 (1981). One is hard pressed to identify a case involving a nonintegrated essential facility monopolist, much less ascertain whether access is required and on what terms. Arguably, *Hecht* could be read to imply that RFK Stadium, as well as the Redskins, could have been obligated to offer its field to other teams, provided that the facility could be shared practicably. So too, *Aspen Skiing*, viewed as an essential facility of mountains uniquely suitable for skiing, implied an obligation on the part of a horizontal competitor to share access equally with its smaller rival.

61. Like its nonessential cousin, an "essential facility" monopolist, in at least three different situations, can increase its monopoly profits by integrating vertically and cutting off competitors at the second level: when entry barriers are thus increased; when integration facilitates price discrimination; and when integration aids cross subsidization in avoidance of price regulation. It also seems clear that competitive injury can result if the monopolist uses its power over the facility to raise the costs incurred by its rivals in a vertically adjacent market, relative to its own. Examples can be found in the literature and we shall not restate them. If any of these situations prevail, the denial of access serves to increase monopoly returns and is exploitive. It is also restrictive; it changes the outcomes that competitive processes would yield in the foreclosed market, reduces consumer choice, and undercuts the mobility of all affected firms save the monopolist. Any one of these situations could prevail in the essential facility context.

62. E.g., Catlin v. Washington Energy Co., 791 F.2d 1343, 1346 (9th Cir. 1986).

63. *Western Electric*, 846 F.2d at 1428.

64. The paradigm "bottleneck" case is the Supreme Court decision in Otter Tail Power Co. v. United States. In *Otter Tail*, a private power company used its control of the transmission lines that delivered bulk power to wholesale customers to foreclose franchise competition in the downstream market for electricity by refusing to wheel bulk power to smaller municipal utilities with which it competed for customers. Lacking any engineering or operational rationale for refusal to deal, Otter Tail was held to have violated Section 2 [410 U.S. 366, 378 (1973)].

65. The settlement of the Mead Data monopolization suit against West Publishing Co. may exemplify that. Relying on the essential facility doctrine, Mead took the position that it could freely enter the West national reporter system, sans headnotes and key numbers, into the LEXIS database. Essentiality was claimed because lawyers using LEXIS could not communicate with lawyers using West and Westlaw, without access to West internal citations since, over the years, those had become an industry standard. Relying on its copyrights and business tort theories, West asserted otherwise. It thought lawyers wishing to use West internal cites ought to be put to the trouble of looking up the page numbers in a West volume. The dispute has been settled on the basis of royalty commitments by Mead that presumably compensate West adequately for its contribution. One of the authors served as a consultant to the attorneys for West in respect of this litigation.

Market Structure and Technical Advance: The Role of Patent Scope Decisions

ROBERT P. MERGES
AND RICHARD R. NELSON

Many of the papers in this volume are concerned with the effect of antitrust law on technical advance in industry. Some—the Jorde-Teece paper (see Chapter 3), for example—argue that in its present form, U.S. antitrust law forecloses certain combinations of firms that, if implemented, would facilitate technical progress.

This is a long way from arguing that highly concentrated market structures are the best setting for technical advance, and Jorde and Teece do not make that case. However, since the time Joseph Schumpeter wrote *Capitalism, Socialism, and Democracy*, the issue of whether a highly concentrated industry or a structurally more competitive one is the best basis for technical change has been a prime topic for research and controversy among economists. While Schumpeter's name has been associated with the former position, he should not be implicated in it. He did point out that while perfect competition of the textbook variety was not the setting we had in our technically progressive industries, he did stress the importance of large firms capable of supporting significant R&D efforts, and he did argue that innovation was worthwhile for firms only if they could get some temporary monopoly on the technology they created. But the hallmark of Schumpeter's description of "capitalism as an engine of progress" is rivalry among firms in innovation.

It is not useful to review here the by now vast and inconclusive research on the question. Among other reasons Wesley Cohen and Richard Levin just recently reviewed this literature.[1] Suffice it to say that there is no evidence supporting the proposition that a highly concentrated industry is a necessary or optimal setting for technical advance. Contrary to rumors, Schumpeter never said that it was. Moreover, as Cohen and Levin point out, it long has been apparent to many analysts that, misreading of what Schumpeter actually argued aside, the whole debate has been unduly narrow. Much more than simply the "structure" of an industry matters in determining the rate and direction of innovation. The maturity of the technology matters, and the nature of the customers. The presence or absence of strong ancillary organizations like universities and professional societies matter. And the nature and strength of the mechanisms available to firms to appropriate returns to innovation is important, and interacts with the relationships between structure and innovation.[2]

This paper is about this latter topic or, rather, an important piece of it. But before getting into it, it is important to review a general theoretical argument.

While Schumpeter never made it, a theoretical case can in fact be made that monopoly is a more efficient structure for technical advance than a rivalrous setting. Under various models of technical advance that we will discuss later, competition in innovation is wasteful and inefficient. In principle, technical advance can proceed more efficiently if it is under the control of a single organization. While this theoretical proposition has not carried much standing in the debate about antitrust law, it has found its way into a number of aspects of patent law, in particular the analysis of appropriate patent scope. That debate and this issue is the subject of this paper.

Edmund Kitch is the writer most clearly associated with the proposition that, in view of the waste and inefficiency associated with rivalrous development of technology, our patent system is designed to allow the inventor of a technology that has the potential for significant improvement and variegation to control the development of the broad "prospect."[3] This concept of the patent system would argue for granting an initial patent of broad scope to enable the pioneering inventor or firm to plan, undertake, or orchestrate future developments.

The Kitch argument raises two important questions. First, what in fact has been the position of the Patent Office and the courts regarding patent scope? Kitch has suggested that they have in general been generous. Beck has argued that generally they have not.[4] Second, what should be the policy on patent scope? It is clear that, within the law, both the Patent Office and the courts often have considerable room for discretion on these matters. Where should they come out? Kitch argues that granting broad claims leads to good social results. We are not sure.

This essay is basically about the role of patent scope in creating and fostering an environment for technical advance. We begin by considering the legal doctrines that define patent scope, identifying the room for discretion that often exists, and pointing out areas of consistency and inconsistency in current practice.

Next, we develop an economic analysis that illuminates the central issue at stake in varying allowed patent scope. Unlike certain recent models by economists, we as Kitch see the important question as how patent scope decisions influence the level and efficiency of inventive work in a field as invention proceeds over a relatively long period of time. However, while Kitch's prospect theory argues for a general policy of broad patents, we consider the matter open.

While most analyses of the effects of patents assume that invention is the same in all technologies, we argue that there are important interindustry differences that need to be taken into account. Thus we develop several models of technical advance in an industry that differ in terms of how various inventions are related to each other. A broad or narrow patent scope decision will determine whether an original inventor has, or does not have, control over subsequent related inventions that may be made. Thus the influence of a patent scope decision is largely determined by the nature and strength of these interconnections.

We aim to lay out the broad issues theoretically. However, theoretical argument alone cannot resolve the question of whether technical advance proceeds more vigorously and effectively under competition or under a regime where one person or organization has a considerable amount of control over development. Therefore we follow our theoretical analysis with an empirical–historical examination of the course of technical advance in several industries, guided by the various models we have developed. In each industry, critical rulings regarding the scope of important early patents significantly influenced the subsequent path of the technology and who was involved in advancing it. Our focus will be on these critical decisions and their consequences.

Based on our analysis, we come out with a judgment regarding what is appropriate patent scope that differs significantly from that put forth by Kitch. Our position is that, by and large, while there surely are wastes, technical change proceeds much more vigorously and creatively under a regime where there are many rivalrous sources of invention than in a setting where one or a few organizations control developments. This position, we suggest, argues against granting patents of unduly wide scope, at least at the margin, and signals that the courts should be wary about protecting wide monopoly prospects in litigation.

PATENT LAW DOCTRINES

In this section we describe and raise some questions concerning various patent law doctrines bearing on patent scope. To assist in making our discussion orderly, the threshold issues of patentability, disclosure doctrine, and infringement doctrine will be discussed separately.

Patent Prosecution: Threshold Issues

During prosecution, a Patent Office examiner reviews an application to determine what is patentable. To be patentable an invention must meet all the statutory requirements for patentability — novelty, utility, and nonobviousness. Let us assume that the invention satisfies these statutory requirements. The issue of patent scope largely concerns how the invention is described and claimed in the patent.

A patent application has two main parts. The first is a specification of the invention, which is written like a brief science or engineering article describing the problem the inventor faced and the steps she took to solve it. It also provides a precise characterization of the "best mode" of solving the problem, in accordance with the first paragraph of section 112 of the patent statute, which reads:

> The specification shall contain a written description of the invention, and of the manner and process of making and using it, in such full, clear, concise, and exact terms as to enable any person skilled in the art to which it pertains . . . to make and use the same, and shall set forth the best mode contemplated by the inventor of carrying out his invention.

The second part of the patent application is a set of claims, which usually encompass much more than the example(s) described in the specification. The second paragraph of section 112 of the patent statute reads: "The specification shall conclude with one or more claims particularly pointing out and distinctly claiming the subject matter which the applicant regards as his invention." Claims define what the inventor considers to be the scope of the invention, the technological territory she claims is hers to control by suing for infringement.

Note that the specification and claims serve different functions. The specification is used by the Patent Office to determine whether the inventor has made a patentable invention, and to bring the invention into the public domain by enabling others to recreate it. This fundamental principle—that legal protection is premised on an adequate disclosure by the inventor—is built deep into the history of patent law.[5]

The patent claims serve a different function. Analogous to the metes and bounds of a real property deed, they distinguish the inventor's intellectual property from the surrounding terrain. The issue being addressed in this essay is how broad allowed claims ought to be.

The Patent Office and the courts have been inconsistent on this question. However, one can discern two bodies of doctrine that have been applied frequently. One of these ties allowed claims to what the patent disclosure enables. The other body of doctrine ties infringement rulings to a notion of equivalents. We consider each in turn.

Doctrines of Disclosure and Enablement

One important issue in patent law is how broad the knowledge communicated by the disclosure should be. Under section 112, the disclosure must be sufficient to enable someone skilled in the art to make and use the invention claimed in the patent. But this requirement is applied rather loosely; a specification that contains detail on the "central core" of an invention but that supplies little guidance on the subject matter at the fringes of a patent's claims is usually sufficient. Shouldn't the disclosure provide illumination to someone skilled in the art about the full range of variants implicitly encompassed within the claims? If not, what evidence is there that the inventor actually invented all that she claims? If one follows out the logic of this question, one is drawn to the conclusion that claims ought to be bounded to a significant degree by what the disclosure enables, over and beyond prior art.

As we shall see, the courts often but not always have been attracted to this principle. Thus many cases have turned on the answer to the question "Was the patentee's disclosure sufficient to support the claims?" In some of these cases, the alleged infringer argued noninfringement successfully by showing that extensive experimentation was required to make the allegedly infringing embodiment.[6] We now turn to some revealing cases where this principle has been applied and to some where it has apparently been ignored.

In 1904, King Gillette received a patent for the first disposable blade safety razor.[7] One of the problems Gillette faced was how to keep a very thin, detachable blade rigid during shaving. His solution, as described in his specification, was to "secure [the] blade to a holder . . . [so that] it receives a degree of rigidity sufficient to make it practically operative."[8] Claim two of the Gillette patent reads "[I claim as] a new article of manufacture a detachable razor blade of such thinness and flexibility as to require external support to give rigidity to its cutting edge."[9]

Gillette's success drew imitators, including the Clarke Blade and Razor Company. When Gillette sued for patent infringement, Clarke claimed that Gillette's patent did not sufficiently describe all the possible embodiments of the blade and that in particular its design fell outside the range of what Gillette's patent had described. The Third Circuit rejected this argument, quoting broad language from the Supreme Court:

> We must reject [defendant's argument that claim 2 is invalid because it does not describe an operative device,] for, if such were the law, patentability must have been denied to Elias Howe for "the grooved and eye-pointed needle" which constituted his seventh claim . . . , and of which it was said [by the Supreme Court] in Deering v. Winona . . . :
>
>> "The invention of a needle with the eye near the point is the basis of all the sewing machines used, but the methods of operating such a needle are many; and, if Howe had been obliged to make his own method a part of every claim in which the needle was an element, his patent would have been practically worthless."[10]

Therefore, the law would not require King Gillette to make "his own particular method" of holding the blade "part of every claim in which [the blade] was an element." The claims would not be restricted, that is, to the *particular* embodiment of the invention Gillette had disclosed in his specification. The court found, however, that the Clarke design followed the principle illuminated by the Gillette patent. The variation from the particular specification was inconsequential.

The *Gillette* case illustrates the notion that a patent's specification need not point out precisely how to make every device[11] that would fall within its claims. Disclosure of an inventive *principle*, whose precise contours are defined by the claims, is enough.[12] At some point an accused infringer who makes a device only roughly analogous to the patentee's must be able to escape from infringement. But at what point will a court draw the line between infringement on the one hand, and, on the other, noninfringement due to differences between the invention and the accused infringer's device? The ruling in a case involving Thomas Edison is illustrative of how the courts have often dealt with this question.

In 1895, Edison brought a Supreme Court challenge to a very broad patent held by Sawyer and Mann for materials used in light bulb filaments.[13] The patentees had found that carbonized paper worked as an effective light-emitting conductor in light bulbs. Based on this invention, they filed a patent claiming the right to use all carbonized fibrous or textile material as an incandescing conductor.[14] Edison challenged Sawyer and Mann contending that the claim was too broad: it did not indicate which of the thousands of "fibrous or textile materials" would work as conductors in light bulbs, since most do not. Nor did it describe any method for finding out. In effect Edison argued that all Sawyer and Mann had invented was a carbonized paper conductor for use in a light bulb, not a broad class of materials. Edison pointed to his own painstaking experimentation with a wide variety of materials, arguing that his discovery that a particular part of a variety of bamboo plant performed well as a filament was not made any easier by Sawyer and Mann's disclosure. The Supreme Court agreed, stating that "if the description be so vague and uncertain that no one can tell, except by independent experiments, how to construct the patented device, the patent is void."[15] The patent would have been upheld, the Court suggested, if it had claimed only what Sawyer and Mann had actually invented (carbonized paper incandescence); it was invalid, however, since it would take a good deal of additional experimentation to determine whether incandescing conductors could be made out of the many materials they claimed.

In an earlier case, *O'Reilly v. Morse*[16], the Supreme Court considered a similar issue. The case involved a challenge to the scope of a claim in Samuel Morse's famous telegraphy patent. Morse claimed "the use of the motive power of the electric or galvanic current, which I call electromagnetism, however developed, for making or printing intelligible characters at any distance."[17] In essence, Morse declared ownership of all methods of communicating at a distance using electromagnetic waves. But since he had not actually disclosed "all methods" in his specification, much less even imagined them, the Court ruled the claim invalid.[18] As with the light bulb case, the patentee's disclosure was found to be nonenabling.

The infamous Selden patent episode, which will be discussed at some length later, shows that courts can be much less careful in these matters. The Selden patent on an automobile design had as its key claim the use of a light gasoline-powered internal combustion engine.[19] The claim was quite general; it failed to specify many important details about the engine. The Patent Office allowed that claim, and the courts upheld it twice,[20] despite arguments that the broad idea was obvious, that the engine referred to was of a particular kind, and that Selden himself was never able to build a working vehicle based on that engine. Eventually, the Second Circuit drastically narrowed the claim, stating that it covered only the particular kind of a gasoline engine used by Selden.[21]

In light of the Edison and Selden cases, consider a recent patent granted to Doctors Phillip Leder and Timothy Stewart of the Harvard Medical School for their successful work involving transgenic mice. They isolated a gene that is associated with cancer in mammals (including humans) and then injected the gene into a fertilized mouse egg, which yielded transgenic mice that are extremely sensitive to carcinogens.[22] This makes the mice excellent animal "models" for studying cancer drugs. Leder and Stewart claimed not only the technique they had used, or the particular transgenic mice variety they had created, but rather all "non-human transgenic animals" produced by their technique. It may well turn out that their admittedly important discovery was indeed this broad.[23] On the other hand, significant work may be required to obtain similar results in higher-order mammals. If one reflects on the Edison case, one wonders whether arguments by an accused infringer that she had to do considerable experimenting and problem-solving prior to producing a transgenic dog, or that she created a transgenic cat using a substantially different technique, would be sufficient to take her invention outside the Leder and Stuart claims.[24]

One can raise similar questions about the patent recently given to Genentech, whose broad claims cover a basic genetic engineering technique — the insertion of a gene into a host (usually a bacterium) and the subsequent expression of the protein for which that gene codes.[25] Their contribution was to refine existing gene-expression techniques to achieve the first successful expression of a human protein in a bacterium.[26]

In their specification, the inventors describe one particular technique for expressing and recovering proteins, and apply this technique to the production of two polypeptides.[27]

The "principle" disclosed by the patent no doubt legitimately covers many more specific embodiments than those expressly disclosed. But how broadly should the claims based on this principle be allowed to reach? Of special concern is the situation where broad claims cover embodiments that can only be made by supplementing what the patentee knew. The Genentech patent, for example, broadly claims microbial expression techniques for producing proteins. What if newer and better expression techniques are developed in the future? Will these be found infringing under the Genentech patent?

It is difficult to answer questions like these when a patent is filed; the future developments are only speculative. Thus there is an argument for granting a broad set of claims for pioneering inventions.[28] Since the inventor may have enabled a broad new range of applications, courts reason, it is unfair to limit the patentee to the precise embodiment through which she discovered the broader principle claimed. As one opinion put it,

> To restrict [a patentee] . . . to the . . . form disclosed . . . would be a poor way to stimulate invention, and particularly its early disclosure. To demand such restriction is merely to state a policy against broad protection for pioneer inventions, a policy both shortsighted and unsound from the standpoint of promoting progress in the useful arts, the constitutional purpose of the patent laws.[29]

But surely one can go too far. Although as a general rule a patentee should be able to claim beyond precise disclosure, current practice seems to permit a range of claims that may stretch beyond the spirit of the enablement doctrine.[30] If the patent examiner can point to a reasonable indication in the prior art that some embodiments of the claimed invention will be impossible to make without much more information than the inventor (or anyone else) knows, the claims will be narrowed.[31] But if the examiner cannot point to such information in the prior art, even very broad claims may be allowed.[32] This means that claims to pioneer inventions often are allowed to cover ground that examiners *believe*, but cannot prove, is well beyond the area actually explored and disclosed by the inventor.[33] The rule puts the burden of *disproving* enablement on the examiner. If this burden cannot be carried, the claims are allowed — even if the inventor cannot prove that she has enabled all the way to the borders of her claims. The rationale is that any other rule would leave claim scope too much in the hands of individual examiners and their technological forecasting abilities.[34] Narrowing is left to the courts in particular infringement suits.

But perhaps this puts too much burden on the courts and causes undue uncertainties. It might be better and more consistent with enablement doctrine for examiners to allow claims where there is at least some indication that the patentee has substantially enabled the full range of embodiments. In these cases it could be left to the courts to sort out close questions of enablement. But we believe it more consistent with enablement doctrine that, at the Patent Office, mainly the burden should be reversed; the patentee should prove affirmatively that she has enabled all that she claims. Otherwise there is nothing to stop her from expanding her claims far beyond the perimeter of her actual invention. As we explore in detail below, overbroad claiming deters subsequent firms from developing improvements, which entails significant costs at the level of both firms and society. The courts can and have narrowed the claims, but the process is expensive, and the uncertainties have deterred inventors. We discuss infringement in the following section.[35]

We turn now to a more specialized scope issue, indirectly raised by the Genentech patent discussed above. In many cases biotechnology companies are using techniques described in Genentech's patent to induce bacteria and other expression "vehicles" to produce purified versions of naturally occurring proteins.[36] These patents typically cover a class of products, as opposed to protecting a process or technique that can be used to produce the product. These products already exist in nature, although they would be difficult, if not impossible, to isolate in comparable purity. It can be argued that it is stretching the concept of invention greatly to say that the patentee really invented the products, as contrasted with invented a way of producing those products in a desirable form. This issue of product versus process patents arises often in chemical patents. It is relevant to our discussion of scope doctrines because a claim on a particular product is clearly a much broader claim than one simply on a particular way of making that product.[37] Thus the product versus process patent issue in chemical and biological technologies is an interesting variation on the patent scope issue.

We also note that, if patent scope were more effectively circumscribed by enablement doctrine, in many cases process patents would be granted rather than product patents. Consider the situation where an inventor comes up with a significantly better process for making a chemical product, but the inventor of the earlier process holds a product patent. One might think that an Edison-like argument that the disclosure of the early product patent was no help whatsoever toward the discovery of the new process might carry weight, but in the case of chemical patents it often has not. This doctrine is now taking root in the related field of biotechnology patents, where a product produced by Genentech using recombinant DNA technology was recently found to infringe a patent covering the old product, even though the recombinant version of the product was much simpler and cheaper to prepare.[38]

A related question concerns what is patentable when an important new use is discovered for a known, patented product, an event relatively common in chemical products. In *Dawson Chemical Co. v. Rohm & Haas Co. v. Roberts Chemical Co.*[39] the Fourth Circuit upheld a patent for a new application of a well-known chemical. The patentee claimed a process for using the known chemical as a fungicide, a use that had not been known previously.[40] The case thus illustrates how process patents can be used to protect a newly discovered use for a known compound. It encourages patent applicants to draft claims in the form "the process of applying Old Product X to New Application Y," and thereby protect their discovery—a new application—in spite of the fact that their application exploits a well-known compound which is not itself patentable.

We conclude that, outside the field of chemical patents, the courts have been drawn toward a doctrine that patent claims should be curbed to reflect what the disclosure enables in light of the prior art. This does not mean that allowed claims have not included variants that the inventor had not brought to practice, or even variants whose perfection would entail considerable additional work. But it does mean that, for the most part, claims have not been allowed to extend far beyond the area where the inventor has made an enlightening contribution. However, there have been glaring exceptions.

Infringement Doctrines and the Interpretation of Equivalents

Doctrines relating to enablement have provided a way of determining the appropriate scope of claims. But claims inevitably leave room for interpretation. Even when a claim is not disputed, it is not always clear on its face whether an allegedly infringing device falls within the claim. Further, in many cases an allegedly infringing device may lie outside the literal scope of the claims, yet a court will find that it falls so close to this scope as to be justly included as an equivalent.

Courts analyze infringement in two steps. First, they ask whether the challenger's product falls squarely within the boundaries of the patentee's claims— that is, whether there is "literal infringement" of the patent. If the court determines that there is no literal infringement, it moves on to the second question: whether the challenger infringes under the "doctrine of equivalents." The doctrine of equivalents developed because of the frequency of cases where, even though the accused product or process does not literally infringe a claim, it may be considered essentially the same device as was patented. Of the many articulations of the doctrine of equivalents, Judge Learned Hand's captures it the best:

> [A]fter all aids to interpretation have been exhausted, and the scope of the claims has been enlarged as far as the words can be stretched, on proper occasions Courts make them cover more than their meaning will bear.[41]

What is such a "proper occasion"? The Supreme Court wrote in 1950, quoting from an earlier case:

> [I]f two devices do the same work in substantially the same way, and accomplish substantially the same result, they are the same, even though they differ in name, form, or shape.[42]

A good application of the doctrine of equivalents is *International Nickel Company, Inc. v. Ford Motor Company*.[43] International Nickel obtained a patent which "covers a cast ferrous alloy"[44] called "nodular iron."[45] The patent taught the addition to molten iron of a "small but effective" quantity of magnesium,"[46] fixed by the patent as "about 0.04%" as a minimum.[47] The magnesium caused "the graphite [i.e., crystallized form of carbon] to occur in spheroidal rather than flake form thereby producing a product with vastly improved physical properties."[48] International Nickel accused Ford Motor Company of infringement when Ford began making a nodular iron. Even though Ford's iron contained under .02% magnesium — less than half the minimum required in International Nickel's patent — it was judged to be an equivalent substance, and thus to infringe the patent.[49]

Courts have determined how broadly they see "equivalents" based on the degree of advance over the art the original patent represents. When the patent is on a "mere improvement," the Courts tend not to consider as "equivalent" a product or process that is even a modest distance beyond the literal terms of the claims. On the other hand, a patent representing a "pioneer invention" (which the Supreme Court has defined as "a patent concerning a function never before performed, a wholly novel device, or one of such novelty and importance as to make a distinct step in the progress in the art"[50]) is "entitled to a broad range of equivalents."[51] That is, when a pioneer patent is involved, a court will stretch to find infringement even by a product whose characteristics lie considerably outside the boundaries of the literal claims. (The patent in the *International Nickel* case was in this category.)[52]

Of course the question of infringement also turns on the precise characteristics of the allegedly infringing device. Following the test laid down by the Supreme Court in *Graver Tank*, courts confronted with a device accused of infringing inquire whether it performs the same function and achieves the same result as the invention in the claims, and whether it does so in the same way. Where the accused device shows only minor variations in one of these elements — such as the small movement of one part or a minor change in structure — infringement will be found even if the patentee's invention is a "mere improvement".[53] And even a pioneer patent is not infringed by a device that achieves a broadly different result in a different way.[54]

One important set of cases under this doctrine has grappled with the question of whether new technologies, unforeseen at the time the patent was issued, can constitute equivalents. This issue arises when a subsequent device that uses new technology is accused of infringing the original patent. The early cases were split, but the prevailing view now is that new technology can be equivalent.[55] Thus a device performing the same function and achieving the same result in the same way as a patented invention can be found to infringe even if it uses technology developed after the patent was issued. This is subject to two caveats: (1) new technologies can constitute equivalents only so long as they do not perform a different function[56] or cause the device to operate in a substantially different way;[57] and (2) a truly meritorious improvement can escape even *literal* infringement under the "reverse" doctrine of equivalents discussed below.

That these distinctions may not always be easy to make is demonstrated by the case of *Hughes Aircraft Co. v. United States*.[58] Hughes Aircraft had a patent, developed by employee Williams, on a means of controlling the attitude of a communications satellite. The claims called for receiving and directly executing control signals from a ground station on earth. After the patent was issued, advances in semiconductor technologies permitted satellites to use on-board microprocessors to process and execute control signals without communicating with the ground. "Advanced computers and digital communications techniques developed since [the] Williams [patent]," said the Federal Circuit, "permit doing on-board a *part* of what Williams taught as done on the ground." The court concluded: "[P]artial variation in technique, an embellishment made possible by post-Williams technology, does not allow the accused spacecraft to escape the 'web of infringement.'"[59] Another case found a patented method for laying pipe, calling for a beam of light to align pipe segments, infringed by the use of later-developed laser beam technology.[60]

One should note that these decisions, while we discuss them here under equivalents doctrine, come into conflict with the enablement principles discussed earlier.[61] If one adheres to the doctrine that limits claims to what is enabled by the disclosure, one would think that the doctrine of equivalents would distinguish between allegedly infringing devices that used "new technologies" basically to get around the claims from those that used the technologies to do something significantly better. In some cases, *Hughes* for example, this distinction does not seem to have been made.

A recent case involving Texas Instruments' pioneering patent on the hand held calculator shows the court applying the doctrine of equivalents in a way more consistent with the principles of enablement.[62] The Federal Circuit held that major improvements in all the essential elements of hand held calculators rendered the improved devices noninfringing.[63] The court concluded "that the total of the technological changes beyond what the inventors disclosed transcends . . . equitable limits . . . and propels the accused devices beyond a just scope for the [Texas Instrument] patent."[64] This opinion is instructive for its focus on the merits of the accused device. As we note in the "Conclusions" section, it should serve as a model for applying the doctrine of equivalents.[65]

Blocking Patents and Reverse Equivalents

The doctrine of equivalents helps the patentee by expanding the scope of her claims beyond its literal boundaries. In a roughly symmetrical way, two similar devices are available to the accused infringer: blocking patents and the reverse doctrine of equivalents.

Two patents are said to block each other when one patentee has a broad patent on an invention and another has a narrower patent on some improved feature of that invention. The broad patent is said to "dominate" the narrower one. In such a situation, the holder of the narrower ("subservient") patent cannot practice her invention without a license from the holder of the dominant patent. At the same time, the holder of the dominant patent cannot practice the particular improved feature claimed in the narrower patent without a license.[66]

It is of course preferable for an inventor to have her own patent free and clear of anyone else's claims. An inventor will therefore not often voluntarily characterize the invention as subservient.[67] But a court may do so in the course of litigation. Where the court upholds the validity of an accused infringer's patent on some enhanced feature, but nevertheless finds that the accused product infringes a prior, broad patent, it is in effect making the accused infringer's patent subservient to the broad patent.[68]

Even where a court finds a patent subservient to another—hence creating blocking patents—the holder of the subservient patent is still better off than if she had never filed a patent at all, for two reasons. First, the patentee can exclude the holder of the broad patent from practicing the improvement. Second, because of this, she may be able to reduce the "lost profits" component of the dominant patentee's damages in an infringement action; the dominant patentee would not have replaced all the infringer's sales, presumably, because the infringer's sales were based in part at least on the improved feature.[69]

As a consequence, an inventor who obtains a subservient patent might reduce the impact of a broad patent. This is the key point: although the improver may literally infringe the broad patent, she may gain some bargaining leverage by obtaining the subservient patent. The improver can, in a sense, mitigate the effects of the literal infringement of the broad, dominant patent by obtaining a patent on the improved feature.

We turn now to a doctrine that can much more effectively mitigate the impact of literal infringement — the "reverse" doctrine of equivalents. Courts have long recognized that "[c]arried to an extreme, the doctrine of equivalents could undermine the entire patent system."[70] Scope could be enlarged so far beyond the literal language of claims that patents would take on unlimited power. To check the potentially destructive impact of this doctrine, and to preserve symmetry in the rules on infringement,[71] the Supreme Court long ago ruled that while

> a charge of infringement is sometimes made out, though the letter of the claims be avoided. . . . The converse is equally true. The patentee may bring the defendant within the letter of his claims, but if the latter has so far changed the principle of the device that the claims of the patent, literally construed, have ceased to represent his actual invention, he is as little subject to be adjudged an infringer as one who has violated the letter of a statute has to be convicted, when he has done nothing in conflict with its spirit and intent.[72]

An example, drawn from the case just quoted, may help to illuminate the "reverse" doctrine. In 1869 George Westinghouse invented a train brake that used a central reservoir of compressed air for stopping power. Further advances in his design, primarily the addition of an air reservoir in each brake cylinder, resulted in a brake that was patented in 1887. An improvement on this 1887 brake, invented by George Boyden, added an ingenious mechanism for pushing compressed air into the brake piston from both the central reservoir *and* a local reservoir in each brake cylinder. (Westinghouse's brake required a complicated series of passageways to supply air from the two sources.)[73] With the added stopping power of the Boyden brake, engineers could safely operate the increasingly long trains of the late nineteenth century.

The Westinghouse patent included a claim for "the combination of a main air-pipe, an auxiliary reservoir, a brake-cylinder, a triple-valve [the device that coordinated the airflows from the main reservoir and the individual brake reservoir] and an auxiliary-valve device, actuated by the piston of the triple-valve . . . for admitting air in the application of the brake."[74] The Court noted that the literal wording of the Westinghouse patent could be read to cover Boyden's brake, since it included what could be described as a "triple valve."[75] But it refused to find infringement, on the ground that Boyden's was a significant contribution that took the invention outside the equitable bounds of the patent:

We are induced to look with more favor upon this device, not only because it is a novel one and a manifest departure from the principle of the Westinghouse patent, but because it solved at once in the simplest manner the problem of quick [braking] action, whereas the Westinghouse patent did not prove to be a success until certain additional members had been incorporated in it.[76]

The *Westinghouse* decision has influenced a number of cases.[77] In *SRI International v. Matsushita Electric Corporation of America* (1985), the Federal Circuit reaffirmed the availability of the "reverse" doctrine of equivalents as a defense to literal infringement. The case involved a patent on a filter used to encode color information in a color television camera. The patent claimed a filter with two sets of parallel stripes of equal width "relatively angularly superimposed" over one another.[78] The image to be televised is placed behind the filter. When a scanning beam passes over the image the stripes on the filter encode three distinct output signals corresponding to the three-primary-color content of the image.[79] The stripes must be at different angles with respect to the vertical for the filter to work. The accused device used a similar design to achieve the same result, but the stripes in its filters must be at forty-five-degree angles to one another. The resulting pattern of overlapping stripes causes a different type of signal to be encoded by the scanning beam. By using a different device to decode these signals, defendant's camera filter ultimately achieves the same output signal as the patentee's.[80]

The court unanimously recognized the validity of a reverse equivalents defense:

The law . . . acknowledges that one may only appear to have appropriated the patented contribution, when a product precisely described in a patent claim is in *fact* "so *far* changed in principle" that it performs in a "*substantially different* way" and is not therefore an appropriation (reverse doctrine of equivalents).[81]

But the court divided sharply on the issue of whether the defendant's camera filter was "so far changed in principle" that it was excused from infringement without more factual proof.[82] It remanded the case with explicit instructions for the trial court to consider the accused infringer's reverse equivalents defense.

These cases demonstrate the use of the reverse equivalents doctrine by the courts to limit the reach of a patentee's claims in the face of substantial technological improvements. However, use of the doctrine is fairly rare.[83] We think it should be used much more often.

To see why, consider the problem we touched on earlier in the section on enablement — broad claims encompassing embodiments that can be made only after significant additional research is performed. The *Westinghouse* case is an example; Boyden's brake involved a triple valve, and was therefore within the boundaries of the Westinghouse patent. The Supreme Court nevertheless refused to find infringement, since Boyden's invention was "a manifest departure from the principle of the Westinghouse patent."[84]

The two biotechnology patents we used earlier to illustrate enablement principles may someday give rise to a similar situation. Our concern with the breadth of these patents would be triggered if subsequently developed technology falling within their claims requires very substantial additional research. If, for instance, a latter-day Boyden comes along with a substantially improved technique for expressing proteins in microbes, a court should find that technique noninfringing.[85]

A similar practice, although one not traditionally remediable through equivalents doctrine, is the granting of a product patent to the first inventor to make a new product, where the achievement of the inventor is really in the process. This raises serious questions when subsequent inventors discover superior processes for making the product. We noted earlier that this problem is highlighted by a recent biotechnology case, where a product produced through recombinant DNA technology was found to infringe a patent covering the original product, even though the recombinant version of the product was much simpler and cheaper to prepare. If the Patent Office persists in granting product patents in cases where the real invention is a process, a far-sighted court might extend the reverse equivalents rationale and hold products produced by subsequently invented superior processes noninfringing. To do otherwise would perpetuate the wrong that reverse equivalents was designed to remedy — permitting patentees to control subsequent accomplishments which were not enabled by their research.

THE ECONOMICS OF THE PATENT SYSTEM REVISITED

The Social Benefits and Costs of the Patent System

As noted earlier, in most analyses of the different aspects of the patent system, concern has centered on a simple trade-off. The analysis has concentrated on how changing patent coverage affects the balance between incentives to the inventor and use of the invention due to patent monopolies. Thus Nordhaus's analysis of optimum patent life is concerned with the trade-off between increased inventive effort resulting from longer anticipated patent life, and greater dead weight costs associated with longer monopoly. Kaplow uses these two variables to analyze the effects of allowing the patent holder greater freedom regarding licensing agreements. Gilbert and Shapiro's recent work on optimal patent breadth as well as length builds on the trade-off model, and so too does Klemperer's.

However, other analyses of the effects of the patent system open up a much more complex set of issues. These studies recognize that at any time many actors may be in the invention game, and that the game may have many rounds. This broader orientation brings into view the question of how the lure or presence of a strong patent can influence the multiactor portfolio of inventive efforts. It also alerts the analyst to the possible effects of patents on the ability or desire of different parties to stay in the inventing competition over time, and on the efficiency of the inventive effort over the long run.

We believe that analysis of the effects on inventing varying patent scope needs to recognize this long-run multiactor context. Our problem with the analysis of Gilbert and Shapiro and Klemperer is that this is not done. Both papers treat greater scope as roughly similar to greater duration in terms of their incentive effects on initial invention. We have no real trouble with that. Both treat the social costs of greater patent scope as those associated with the blocking of a wider range of substitutes. However, they treat these substitutes as if they were already in existence or could be made so trivially. It is here that we find their analysis inadequate. Wide patent scope that exceeds the enablement of the disclosure makes anyone who attempts to invent in that area beholden to the patent owner. Since some of these efforts could produce something not simply slightly different but significantly better than what the patent holder has achieved, such broad patents discourage others from participating in efforts to advance technology in the area covered by the patent.

Economists' models that do try to encompass multiactor dynamics are quite stylized. In some, invention is seen like fishing from a common pool. There are many competitive inventors, and the first to make an invention gets the patent on it. Each knows that as others catch (invent) there is less in the pool for them. The result is "overfishing": too many people seeking inventions at once. Other economists have modeled technical advance in terms of a multifirm "race to patent," in which many would-be inventors identify a particular goal, and the first to achieve that goal gets the patent. A good deal of variation has been introduced into these models, with different assumptions being made about such variables, the strength of patents and the costs and benefits of innovating versus imitating. Many of the implications of these models are sensitive to particular assumptions but some are robust. In particular, under a wide range of assumptions, rivalrous inventive efforts generate a lot of inefficiency.

While all of the models are quite stylized, the authors of this paper regard the latter basic conclusion as persuasive. Proprietary control of technology not only tends to cause "dead weight" costs due to restrictions on use. (We presume here that, in general, it is not possible to write licensing agreements to completely offset this problem, a matter to which we shall return shortly.) Where invention is rivalrous, inventive efforts themselves are inefficient. We pay both kinds of costs in exchange for the benefits of technical advance induced by the incentives yielded by the prospect of proprietary gain.

Recognition of the costs of rivalrous inventive efforts leads one to speculate, however, about how these costs might be mitigated. This is the source of Edmund Kitch's prospect theory.

The Prospect Theory and Its Problems

Edmund Kitch, in formulating his "prospect theory" of patent rights, moved beyond that static trade-off model mentioned earlier, and incorporated into his analysis some of the insights of the common pool models. Kitch analogized patents to mining claims. Like an exclusive claim to the minerals that may be produced from a plot of land, Kitch emphasized that patents are granted *after* invention but *before* commercialization. According to Kitch, this has two advantages: (1) it allows "breathing room" for the inventor to invest in development without fear that another firm will preempt her or steal her work; and (2) it allows the inventor to coordinate activities with those of potential imitators to reduce inefficient duplication of inventive effort. This amounts to granting rights over an unexplored pool, with the rightholder being permitted to charge for access to various parts of the pool. Thus the inefficiencies associated with rivalrous uncoordinated invention, as in the fishing or race models, can be avoided.

Kitch goes further in suggesting that the prospect theory "may clarify the process and conditions under which a monopolistic industry will be more efficient than a competitive one." He states that this enhanced efficiency "turns not upon the size of the firm, but its dominance over a fruitful technological prospect."

Reacting to the inefficiencies highlighted by the fishing models, Kitch clearly has a preference for single-firm domination of a technological prospect. He notes that a firm can develop the prospect by itself. Alternatively, it may engage in carefully controlled licensing of others to develop different parts of the prospect. In either case, the advantage seen by Kitch is that development is under the control of a single entity. Rivalry is avoided. Planning is possible.

We have trouble with the view that coordinated development is better than rivalrous. In principle it could be. Our argument is that in practice it generally is not. Much of our case is empirical; we consider the record. But there are also sound theoretical reasons for doubting the advantages of centralization.

For one thing, under rivalrous competition in invention and innovation there is a stick as well as a carrot. Block rivalry and one blocks or greatly diminishes the threatened costs of inaction. Kitch has in his head a model of individual or firm behavior where if an action is profitable it will be taken, regardless of whether inaction would yield a comfortable or uncomfortable position. Different models of behavior, Simon's satisficing hypothesis is one example, predict otherwise. As we shall see, there are many instances that, when a firm had control over a broad technology, it rested on its laurels, until jogged into action by an outside threat. Interestingly, the mining law used by Kitch as an analogy has safeguards to prevent inaction. The law requires a claimant who has identified a mineral deposit to actively work the claim before property rights will vest. This safeguard does not exist in U.S. patent law.

More generally, the model of behavior Kitch is employing explicitly or implicitly repressed the limits on cognitive capacity and the tendency to focus on what one knows that are characteristics of other models (see, e.g., Nelson and Winter 1982) and of organizational behavior as we know it. Once a firm develops and becomes competent in one part of a "prospect," it may be very hard for it to give much attention to other parts, even though in the eyes of others, there may be great promise there. Again, our empirical explorations show many examples of this. Here is a major reason why one might expect a context where there are many independent inventors to generate a much wider and diverse set of exploration than when the development is under the control of one mind or organization.

This flags still another limitation of the "pool" or "mining" models. In these models the "fish" or the "minerals" are out there and known (with perhaps some uncertainty) to all parties. The characteristic of "prospects" for technological development, and perhaps even real life mineral prospects, is that no one knows for sure what is out there, and it generally is not even possible to list the possibilities, much less assign probabilities to them on which all knowledgeable people will agree. Indeed different parties are almost certain to see these prospects differently. The only way to find out what works and what does not is to let a variety of minds try.

Of course, Kitch's notions about how a broad patent prospect can be worked out by the patent holder do not preclude involving many minds. However, we regard as fanciful the notion that wider talent can be brought in without real competition through selective licensing practices. Substantial literature documents the steep transaction costs of technology licensing, and there is indirect evidence that these costs increase when major innovations are transferred. Moreover, various studies have indicated that transaction costs tend to be very high if licenses are tailored to particular licensees. It is much simpler to grant roughly identical licenses to all who will pay a standard rate. In our own research we have not found a single case where the holder of a broad patent used it effectively through tailored licensing to coordinate the R&D of others.

Rivalry no doubt causes waste. Yet we have little faith in the imagination and willingness of "prospect" holders to develop their prospect as energetically or creatively unless engaged in competition. We are also skeptical about their ability to orchestrate development. Given the way humans and organizations think and behave, we believe we are much better off with considerable rivalry in invention than with too little.

Can we prove it? We can present empirical evidence that the granting of broad patents in many cases has stifled technical advance and that where technical advance has been rapid there almost always has been considerable rivalry. However, we grant that it is possible to see our evidence as not completely persuasive in this regard, or to posit that we have only looked at a few cases and these might not be representative.

And even if our case is accepted that, up to a point at least, rivalry facilitates technical advance and unified control dampens it, one can respond by saying "Yes, but what about the costs and the wastes?" We can rejoin that, in our cases at least, it is not evident that the presence of a broad patent or a set of them made progress any more efficient. Indeed a hallmark of some of the cases we present where there was a broad patent is very considerable waste.

In the social sciences, there are "proofs" only in models. We think we have a persuasive case, but the readers will have to judge.

Differences in Industrial Patterns of Technical Advance

Of course the issue under examination here is not single organizational control versus rivalry per se, but rather the effects of granting broader or narrower patent scope. We want to argue that the effect differs from industry to industry, depending on the way in which technological advance proceeds. This pattern also varies significantly from field to field. One of the authors, Nelson, has proposed that at least four different generic models are needed. The first describes discrete invention. A second concerns "cumulative" technologies. Chemical technologies have special characteristics of their own. Finally, there are "science-based" technologies where technical advance is driven by developments in science outside the industry. In each of these models patent scope issues take on a special form. In any industry one or another of these models may be applicable at any given time, or appropriate characterization may require a mix. But the mix differs from industry to industry, and so too, therefore, the salient issues involving patent scope.

What we call the discrete invention model corresponds to much of the standard writing about invention. It assumes that an invention is discrete and well-defined, created through the inventor's insight and hard work. In the standard discussions it may be recognized that the original invention can be improved, or even that improvement or complementary advances may need to be made if the invention is to be of much use. The basic invention may be amenable to tailoring for different uses or customers. But it is implicit that the invention does not point the way to wide-ranging subsequent technical advances. It does not define any broad prospect. There are many inventions that fit this model, and these may be of considerable economic and social value. Two examples are King Gillette's safety razor, discussed above, and the ballpoint pen. New pharmaceuticals like AZT may fit this model. In some industries technical advance appears largely to proceed through inventions of this kind. The power hand tool industry is an example. For inventions and industries like these, while tight and broad control of a particular invention may enable a firm to profit handsomely, possession by that firm of a proprietary lock on the invention is not a serious hindrance to inventive work by other firms in any broadly defined field.

However, in a number of technologies the characterization above is quite inappropriate. In industries like those producing automobiles, aircraft, electric light systems, semiconductors, and computers, technical advance is cumulative, in the sense that today's efforts to advance the technology start from and aim to improve the prevailing technology.[86] This by no means implies that technical advance is slow or inconsequential. Over time dramatic advance occurs in these technologies from improving one aspect or another, or by adding this new feature or that. In many cases the technology in question defines a complex system with many components, subcomponents, and parts, and technical advance may proceed on a number of different fronts at once.

There is much more at stake regarding allowed patent scope in these cumulative technologies than in those where inventions are discrete and stand separate. Particularly when the technology is in its early stages, the grant of a broad-gauged pioneer patent to one party may preclude other inventors from making use of their inventions without infringing the original patent. In a sense, the broad patent grants exclusive fishing rights in a pool, where the inventions in the pool are all improvements on a given basic system. Recall the Selden patent, which was used to control the development of automobiles, and Edison's successful attack on the blockage in light bulb technology. Thus a broader pioneer patent may give one party legal control over a large area. Alternatively, in multicomponent products, broad patents on different components held by several inventors may lead to a situation where no one can or will advance the technology in the absence of a license from someone else. As we shall see, these are not just theoretical possibilities; they describe the development of several important technologies.

Despite the nature of technical advance in cumulative technology industries, improvement patents (discussed earlier) are no more common in these industries than in others. This is because an improvement patent in the patent law sense — also known as a dominant-subservient or blocking-patents situation — is undesirable, and because patent lawyers can usually just as easily claim a new or improved component or subcomponent as a distinct product. Accordingly it is important not to confuse the patent law concept of an improvement patent with the commercial reality that in some industries technical advance proceeds cumulatively, that is, via a series of improvements.

Technical advance in the chemical industries has some attributes that fit the discrete invention model, some that fit the cumulative technologies model, and some particular characteristics of its own. A new chemical product is in most cases a discrete entity, or it may encompass a particular class of products, like penicillin. But particular chemical product innovations are seldom the keystones to broad areas of product development. Further, in almost all cases there are reasonable substitutes. On the other hand, the processes that are used to make chemical products tend to be improved along the lines of the cumulative technology model. What makes invention unique in the chemical fields is first, the striking uncertainty involved in product R&D, and second, the many uses of a new chemical product cannot be predicted when the product's structure is first developed. These special features of the chemical industries mean that scope decisions affect these industries differently than others.

An invention in any of the three regimes described above may be assisted by recent developments in science. But technologies whose development is largely driven by recent scientific advances — we shall call them science-based — while rare, warrant special recognition. In these technologies, of which modern biotechnology is a prominent example, R&D efforts attempt to exploit recent scientific developments. These scientific developments tend to narrow and focus perceived technological opportunities in the industry, and concentrate the attention of inventors on the same things.

Such science-based technologies warrant analytic distinction for several reasons. In the first place, this area is a context that engenders inventive races of the sort described earlier, particularly if it is anticipated that the first to apply a scientific finding will get a patent of considerable scope. Many are rushing toward the same objective that all see as feasible, and several will get there, but only the first receives a patent. Such races are wasteful, and patent practice should not encourage them. Second, this context poses complications for a theory that sees a patent as a "just reward." New scientific and technological developments "in the air" open the possibility of a major advance over prior practice, and the contribution made by the individual or firm who first makes these possibilities operational may be relatively small. The invention may diverge drastically from "prior art," in the sense of actual technological accomplishments, and sweep the market, yet still be a successful application of possibilities that are only obvious to the scientifically sophisticated.

Third, and this is where our focus will be, there is a real danger that allowing patent scope to be overbroad may enable the individual or firm who first came up with a particular practical application to control a broad array of other potential applications.

Rivalry versus Control in the Market for Inventions

In the last three models above, we saw how a broad-based patent can give control over not just a particular product or process, but over important future inventions. Compared with the costs of allowing monopolization of a particular discrete invention, the potential costs of ceding to one firm control of a sizeable arena of future technological developments are of much greater concern.

We have made it apparent that we take a different stance than Kitch regarding the costs and benefits of rivalry versus coordination in advancing a technology. Kitch has noted the inefficiencies involved in rivalry and argued that in principle one would do better by coordinating developments. Indeed he has proposed that a primary function of a patent is to enable an inventor to develop the "prospect" that the invention initially defined. Under this view, control can be exercised several ways. The inventor can develop the field herself, coordinate licensing of others, or arrange some combination of the two.

We do not deny that, in principle, a "prospect" patent permits less wasteful development. But we are concerned that if a single organization controls future developments in a field, one loses the energy that active competition generates. One also loses the variety of approaches provided by competition among many minds and talents. For the reasons stressed by Williamson and Teece, among other, we regard as fanciful the notion that wider talent can be brought in without real competition through selective licensing of ideas. Various studies have indicated that transaction costs tend to be very high if licenses are tailored to particular licensees. It is much simpler to grant roughly identical licenses to all who will pay a standard rate.[87] In our own research we have not found a single case where the holder of a broad patent used it effectively through tailored licensing to coordinate the R&D of others.

Rivalry no doubt causes waste. Yet we have little faith in the imagination and willingness of a "prospect" holder to develop that prospect as energetically or creatively unless engaged in competition. We are also skeptical about her ability to orchestrate development. Given the way humans and organizations think and behave, we believe we are much better off with considerable rivalry in invention than with too little.[88]

There is no system of logic that can resolve these arguments. In order to come to some judgment one must look at various histories. So we now turn to a more detailed discussion of these models of technical advance, with an eye toward what they can teach us about the effects of patent scope.

EFFECTS OF PATENT SCOPE IN VARIOUS INDUSTRIES

Since we are concerned with the effects of patent scope decisions on the subsequent development of technology, we are not interested in the cases of discrete invention. We shall now deal with what we have called cumulative technologies, chemical industries, and science-based industries, in that order.

Cumulative Technologies

We have asked two questions about the effects of broad patents on cumulative technologies. One concerns the consequences of "pioneer" patents. We wish to test the validity of Kitch's hypothesis that the granting of broad patents is likely to make subsequent invention and development more orderly and productive. The second question is how the presence of broad patents on components of a cumulative technology affects subsequent development.

We begin by considering two infamous cases regarding pioneer patents: the Selden patent in the development of automobile technology,[89] and the Wright patent's influence on the growth of aircraft technology in the United States. As we have seen, the Selden patent claimed a basic automobile configuration, one using a lightweight internal combustion engine as the power source. The Wright patent was based on a broadly defined airplane stabilization and steering system. In both of these cases, the holders of the pioneer patent engaged in extensive litigation against companies that did not recognize the patent and refused to license it. Our question is how the presence of these patents affected the evolution of the technologies.

One can argue that the broad Selden patent should not have been granted in the first place. His critics argued that Selden never built or operated the automobile that was pictured and described in the specification, and that in any event his claims exceeded what the specifications enabled. And the claim that gave his patent force—his understanding that a viable automobile required a light, powerful engine—was scarcely news to many others working in the field.

In any case it is evident that Selden viewed his patent merely as a way of collecting royalties; he had little intention of becoming a serious participant in the automobile production business. The patent certainly was not used by Selden to orchestrate the efficient improvement of automobile technology. He stood willing, at least initially, to license anyone who would acknowledge the validity of his patent and pay his fees. Later, the Association of Licensed Automobile Manufacturers was formed to control licensing of the patent; this group did try to regulate who was in the automobile design and production business.[90] The Association's purpose was thus to control competition in the industry, rather than to facilitate orderly technological development.

Did the presence of the Selden patent hinder technological progress in the industry? Law suits based on it surely did absorb considerable time and attention of people like Henry Ford, whose production methods revolutionized the industry.[91] The Selden patent did not stop Mr. Ford, but it did slow him down.

An interesting result of this experience with patent litigation was that, even before the Selden patent was pruned back in 1911,[92] the automobile industry, through the Association, developed a procedure for automatic cross-licensing of patents. While formal agreements to cross license all new patents no longer exist, the practice of relatively automatic cross-licensing has endured to the present.

The Wright brothers' patent is somewhat different in a number of regards. First, the achievement described in the patent — an efficient stabilizing and steering system — was in fact a major one, and it did enable a multiplicity of future flying machines.[93] Second, the Wright brothers were very interested in producing aircraft and in improving their design, and they did so actively. However, there were other important people and companies, who wanted to enter the aircraft design and manufacture business. They had their own ideas about how to advance the design of aircraft, and they strongly resisted being blocked by the Wright patent. In this case, and others, it turned out to be extremely difficult to work out a license agreement that satisfied both the holder of the broad patent and an aggressive potential competitor who believed that there was a lot of his own work in his design. The early attempts by the Wright brothers and Glen Curtiss, who was the most prominent potential competitor, came to naught. Litigation followed.[94]

There is good reason to believe that the Wright patent significantly held back the pace of aircraft development in the United States by absorbing the energies and diverting the efforts of people like Curtiss. The aircraft patent case is similar to that of automobiles in that the problems caused by the initial pioneer patent were compounded as improvements and complementary patents, owned by different companies, came into existence. The situation was so serious that at the insistence of the Secretary of the Navy, during World War I, an arrangement was worked out to enable automatic cross-licensing.[95] This arrangement, like the licensing of automobile patents, turned out to be a durable institution. By the end of World War I, there were so many patents on different aircraft features that a company had to negotiate a large number of licenses to produce a state-of-the-art plane. The cross-licensing system greatly reduced transaction costs, but these costs would not have existed without the broad patents on the various components.

We call attention now to two other cases, also marked by broad pioneer patents, where a different solution prevailed. One involves Edison's lighting technology which, after the initial stages, was developed by General Electric. The other is Bell's telephone, which later became the monopoly of AT&T. In these cases, unlike those above, an initial broad patent, or collection of patents, was used as the basis for the establishment of a large company that controlled the subsequent development of the related technology, and did so energetically and effectively. If these examples support Kitch, the tally is two for and two against his theory. But even these cases are ambiguous. Many of the important advances in electric lighting and telephone technologies were prompted by competition to the dominant companies. Thus work on metalized lamp filaments was much more actively pursued in Europe than by GE, and GE's active entry in the field was largely stimulated by fears that it was behind. Competition in electricity-generating systems from Westinghouse forced a reluctant GE to recognize the superiority of AC transmission over DC. The triode, which turned out to be of critical importance in the radio and telephone, was the invention of neither GE nor AT&T, but of Lee DeForrest, a private inventor.[96]

The case of radio in the United States warrants at least a brief recounting, for it is an excellent example of what happens when several companies each hold patents of broad scope. Three large American companies, with their main production bases in different fields, became interested in radio because it overlapped with their main businesses. General Electric entered radio as a natural extension of its expertise in light bulbs (hence vacuum tubes) and electricity-generating systems. Westinghouse entered because of its interest in electrical generation and machinery. AT&T became concerned that radio could become a possible competitor to its long-distance telephone line technology. Still another company, American Marconi, held American rights to the basic British Marconi patents on radio. The situation soon became similar to that described above in aircraft, where different companies could block each other from using key components. It turned out to be virtually impossible to work out licensing case by case, and no one could produce state-of-the-art radio without being threatened by litigation. As was the case with aircraft, during World War I the armed services stepped in and essentially decreed that companies could design and produce radio technology immune from law suits. After World War I the practice of pooling radio patents was continued.

Radio is a canonical instance where the presence of a number of broad patents, which were held by different parties and difficult to invent around, interfered with the development of the technology.[97] The resolution required a general cross-licensing agreement, and eventually a consolidated company.[98] Does this support the position that development would have been more efficient had control been in the hands of one party from the beginning? No. First, the scope of an initial pioneer patent on radio would have to have been extremely broad to cover all aspects of the system, many of which came to be recognized only in the 1920s. Second, even if such a stretched pioneer patent were granted to a single company, it would not have prevented other companies with expertise in overlapping fields from inventing better components than described in the original patent. These components would, at least, have been granted the protection of improvement patents. Thus the requirement for licensing or cross-licensing could not have been evaded. Third, the presence of such a broad pioneer patent might have provided strong disincentives to participate for a number of individual inventors and small firms, who played a large role in the evolution of radio.

In cumulative technologies, some arrangements need to be made so that the many players in the invention game do not block each other from further improving the technology. We conclude this section by describing post-World War II examples of important complex technologies, which have advanced rapidly, because no one held a pioneer patent that could be used to restrict access.

The first involve semiconductors. There are two instances in the history of this technology where a broad-gauged patent could have given its holder control over a large "prospect" but in fact did not. One was on the initial transistor patents held by AT&T. Because of an antitrust consent decree, AT&T was foreclosed from the commercial transistor business. Some have argued that AT&T would not have gone into the merchant transistor business even without a consent decree. In any case, since it was not going to do so, AT&T had every incentive to encourage other companies to advance transistor technology, because of the value of better transistors to the phone system. AT&T quicly entered into a large number of license agreements at low royalty rates. Thus many companies ultimately contributed to the advance of transistor technology, because the pioneer patents were freely licensed instead of being used to block access.

The second instance involved the parallel inventions of the integrated circuit (by Texas Instruments) and the Planar process for producing them cheaply (by Fairchild Instruments). Both of these companies obtained patents on their own inventions, which meant that each had to get a license from the other in order to effectively produce integrated circuits. Further, the Department of Defense, which for some time had provided the lion's share of the market for semiconductors, traditionally has avoided being at the mercy of a firm or a small number of firms with key patents. Through a variety of maneuvers it encouraged general cross-licensing, which set the tone for deliberations to resolve the problem created by the two patents. Faced with an impasse regarding integrated circuit technology, general cross-licensing was continued. It is hard to argue that this has slowed down the development of integrated circuits.

The third recent cumulative technology developed without strong, broad patents is electronic computers. Although original computer inventors Eckert and Mauchley did file for and receive a patent on their basic ENIAC design, the patent was ruled invalid because of a judgment that the prior art included much of what they claimed.[99] But even during the period before the Eckert-Mauchley patent was invalidated, a number of other computer inventors received patents on their own contributions. As in the semiconductor case, the armed services were the principal purchasers of the technology, and were ill-disposed toward being held up by a dominant patent. As a result, cross-licensing became the norm in this industry as well, and again the pace of technical change has been rapid.

The cases we have discussed certainly are not a random sample, nor do they tell a uniform story. In automobiles and aircraft, a strong pioneer patent probably interfered with the evolution of technology. In the cases of electric lighting and the telephone, companies used a pioneer patent or patents to monopolize the field. While these firms advanced the technologies in an effective and relatively orderly fashion, much of the inventing was done by others, and on some occasions only the threat of competition forced the dominant firms to go in the right direction. The cases of radio, aircraft, and automobiles after 1910 share the phenomena of different patent holders blocking each other, and resolution through some kind of institutional cross-licensing scheme. In semiconductors and aircraft, no one held and enforced strong intellectual property rights, yet technology progressed very rapidly in a competitive setting.

While others may read the evidence differently, we believe that the granting and enforcing of broad pioneer patents is a dangerous social policy. It can, and has, hurt in a number of ways. It has made entry of creative and energetic newcomers difficult. In "systems" technologies, interference has proved to be especially problematic. Resolution has required some sort of institutionalized cross-licensing system. And there are many cases where technical advance has been very rapid under a regime where intellectual property rights were weak or not stringently enforced. We think the latter regime is the better social bet.

Chemical Industries

The chemical products industries produce an incredibly diverse range of products, from bulk chemicals like sulfuric acid, to synthetic materials like plastics, to pharmaceuticals.[100] Despite the diversity of products, however, invention in the chemical industries shares several key attributes. To a large extent chemical product invention tends to fit the "discrete invention" model described earlier. Thus product patents tend to define a well-delineated class of substances.[101] Sulfuric acid is sulfuric acid and, while subject to some variation, valium is valium. However, R&D on new chemical products is subject to an unusual degree of uncertainty and costly experimentation, both because it is difficult to predict the precise chemical structure needed to achieve a given end, and because the effects of using a new chemical substance in a particular way can be startling.[102] Further, once a new product or use is discovered, it is easy for a competitor to replicate. Thus patent protection on products or novel ways of applying them is vital if the inventor is to reap returns.[103]

In contrast with product technology, most chemical production processes evolve cumulatively in the sense discussed earlier. the first versions of new chemical processes tend to be amenable to a wide range of improvements. Thus one might expect to see the same kinds of problems regarding chemical process patents as we have seen in our examination of other cumulative technologies in the previous section.

To analyze the importance of process and product inventions in the chemical industries, it is helpful to disaggregate those industries into three groups: bulk chemicals, synthetics, and pharmaceuticals.

Bulk chemicals consist of products like sulfuric acid, ammonia, ethylene, and other substances that have been known and widely used for some time. Many are natural substances. In any case there are no effective product patents on bulk chemicals.[104]

As a consequence, most R&D is concerned with creating new or improved processes. The development of chemical process technology tends, as noted, to be cumulative; at any time there tends to be one process that is the dominant mode of production. From time to time a dominant process is superseded by a new one. And the early patent or patents on that new process have the characteristics of "pioneer" patents. However, these patents have not generally been used to control subsequent development, which by and large has proceeded with multiple sources of initiative. This growth is due primarily to the inherently limited power of control conferred by patents in the chemical field. Pervasive cross-licensing in chemical industries confirms this.

Thus until 1861 the Leblanc process dominated the production of alkalis.[105] This process was widely licensed, and a number of different companies contributed to its improvement.[106] When, in 1861, the Solvay process was developed and patented, the original patent holder also had a chance to control future development of the process.[107] However, here too the policy of the original patent holder was one of reasonably wide licensing of the basic patent. A number of different companies made improvements; these were also cross-licensed.[108]

Of course there are patent suits and short-term holdups in the field of bulk chemical process technology, but these problems are usually settled and licensing is a general practice.[109]

The recent development of new processes for making acrylamide is a good example. Acrylamide is an organic chemical commonly used to make polymers for water treatment, pulp and paper processing, textiles treatment, food preparation, and other applications.[110] Until the 1960s, it was made in a two-step process using sulfuric acid and ammonia.[111] In the mid-1960s, researchers at several different companies all began investigating ways to improve the traditional process.[112] Both Standard Oil and American Cyanamid came up with processes using copper as the catalytic agent. Dow Chemical also made several patentable inventions in this field.[113]

Lawsuits were filed. Standard Oil sued American Cyanamid arguing that its process infringed Standard Oil's patent. The court ruled against Standard Oil in this case.[114] On the other hand, Dow successfully sued American Cyanamid for infringing its patents.[115] However, after this round of legal scuffling, the companies cross-licensed each other. No single company tried to hold exclusively the right to use the new technology, or control its future development.[116]

In short, the pattern of development in bulk chemical process technology is similar to several of the cases of cumulative technologies considered earlier. It is sometimes possible to obtain a fairly broad patent, when a new technology is invented, that can give its holder a measure of control over subsequent development. However, by and large, the chemical companies have not used their patents that way, partly under the pressure of competing inventions. These firms choose instead to license or cross-license. Thus several companies tend to be involved in the subsequent development of the technology.

In contrast with the case of bulk chemicals, product patents are very important in the field of synthetic materials. Sometimes process patents are important. And the two can be related: research on a new process for making an established product may yield a distinct and patentable version of the product.[117] Also, as in bulk chemicals, reasonably liberal licensing is common in the synthetic chemical industry.[118]

When Dupont wanted to enter the business of producing Rayon it took out licenses on the product and the key processes from the French firm that held them.[119] Dupont similarly took out a license on cellophane technology.[120] Subsequent R&D at Dupont on both of these products significantly improved them.[121] In turn, Dupont licensed Nylon[122] to both Imperial Chemical Industries of Great Britain and IG Farben of Germany.[123] Both of these companies later came up with variants on the original Nylon.

The fact that product patent claims are narrowly bounded keeps the advance of synthetic material technology a competitive business. Thus Dupont's Nylon provided a superior alternative in many uses to the earlier Rayon.[124] And newer fibers like Dacron and Orlon subsequently replaced some of Nylon's market.[125]

Another good example of the interdependence of product and process technology in synthetic materials is the effort to develop an improved process for the manufacture of polyethylene. Research teams at several firms worked on this project simultaneously. In the 1950s, researchers at the Max Planck Institute, led by a chemist named Karl Zeigler, invented a superior process, based on a new understanding of catalytic compounds.[126] Not only was the new process patentable, but due to the relatively restrictive claims on the older polyethylene patent, the product it produced was outside the scope of Imperial Chemical's basic patents.[127]

In turn, work by an Italian chemist, Giulio Natta, led to significant improvements in the Zeigler process. Natta's group also discovered a way to produce polypropylene, another important polymer.[128] Groups at other companies and research institutes were following the same trail. At least five different companies filed product patents on a version of polypropylene between 1953 and 1955.[129]

Needless to say, the customary round of law suits resulted; these dragged on for some time.[130] However, the result was not that a single company controlled the basic technology and its subsequent development, but rather a series of cross-licensing agreements that kept the technology open to a number of firms.[131]

We turn now to the two matters regarding the scope of chemical patents that are especially important: what to do when someone discovers a new use for an established product, and how to treat a process invention that yields a much purer form of a natural substance than was available earlier.

Earlier we observed that chemical products have a surprising range of uses. Often some of these cannot be foreseen when a product is invented and patented. In a number of cases, researchers looking for a way to meet a new need will discover that an old product can do the job. In other cases, the discovery of a new use may be accidental—a by-product of looking for something else. In either case, this is important inventive work that ought to be encouraged and rewarded. But how to do this? The Patent Office and the courts have been struggling with this issue for some time.

One solution has been to award a process patent to the discoverer of a novel use for a pre-existing product. We cited an example earlier, the case of *Rohm & Haas* v. *Roberts Chemical Company*.[132] In this case the defendant's patent on use of a well-known product for use as a fungicide was upheld, because this use was not anticipated or claimed in the original patent.[133] This process patent would not enable the patent holder to produce the product in question, but rather only to control its new use. If the use is an important one, the process patent can handsomely reward the patent holder.

There are problems with this solution, however, It may be difficult to monitor whether the compound is being used for the new (patented) application or for its old, well-established use. Consider the case of Urbaine Thuau, who filed a patent application containing product claims over a compound he had found useful in the treatment of cervical diseases. However, the compound itself was not new. It had long been used in the leather tanning industry. The Patent Office rejected the patent application, and the court later affirmed.

> That appellant has made a valuable discovery in the new use of the composition here involved we have no doubt, and it is unfortunate for him if he can not make claims adequate to protect such discovery, but to hold that every new use of an old composition may be the subject of a patent upon the composition would lead to endless confusion and go far to destroy the benefits of our patent laws.[134]

The court expressed particular concern with the "confusion" that might result if purchasers of the product for its newly discovered use bought it from the traditional suppliers. Although these suppliers might have no way of knowing what use the purchaser had in mind, if the new patent were granted, they would be liable nonetheless for patent infringement. While the patent statute includes a detailed provision to deal with this problem,[135] enforcing the rule may be quite difficult.[136]

The Patent Office has been more comfortable about giving a patent for a new use of an old substance when the patent applicant has modified the substance.[137] There has been recognition, however, that this practice provides incentive for trivial or obvious modifications of an old compound, and results in the granting of a new product patent rather than a new use (or process) patent.[138] In a ruling denying a new use product patent on an obvious variant of an old compound, the court proposed that the solution might be to eliminate patents on obvious variants of old compounds altogether, instead rewarding inventors with process patents on the applications they have discovered.

> It is basic to the grant of a patent that the scope of a patent should not exceed the scope of the invention. If what makes a structurally obvious chemical substance patentable is the new and unobvious properties or uses discovered by the first person to compound the substance, the discoverer should have protection on what he discovered, i.e. the new properties of the substance, but should not be entitled to a seventeen year monopoly on the substance itself. . . . We think that the purposes of the patent law will be adequately served if patents on compounds which are structurally obvious from the prior art are limited to method (i.e. process) patents directed to the new and useful characteristic or property which is the essence of the discovery or invention.[139]

This suggestion has so far been ignored, however. In general, courts have yet to solve the problem of how to reward and thus give incentives to the discovery of new uses. While the problem is not confined to the realm of chemical substances, it crops up mostly here. For reasons which should be clear, we strongly endorse the notion of granting process patents on new uses. We recognize, however, that in some cases enforcement problems may be formidable.[140]

Another special problem that crops up in the chemical patent field involves the invention of a way of making available a substance found in humans or animals. Typically the discovery involves enhancing purity or lowering cost. Today this issue arises mainly in the field of biotechnology, but the problem has existed for some time. Thus in 1911 Learned Hand upheld a product patent on purified human adrenalin made via a new process.[141] The patent was not simply on the process, but also on the purified natural substance.

The problem with this practice is that it grants patents of unncessarily wide scope. The adrenalin patent would be infringed by the use of a radically different, and better, process for making the same natural product unless the characteristics of the product were judged substantially different. Yet the argument is not convincing that what the original inventor invented was the product, in addition to the particular process for making it.

The recent case involving Genentech, which we mentioned earlier, raises the same concerns. Genentech had invented a recombinant DNA method for producing the human blood clotting protein factor VIII:C.[142] This process had major advantages over an earlier, patented technique of purifying the substance drawn from natural blood. Genentech's process was not only better; it was completely different. Yet in the first part of the case, the court upheld the earlier patent, held by the Scripps Institute, on the ground that it was a legitimate product patent, and thus Genentech's new method of producing it was an infringement.[143]

In a later ruling, the court invalidated the Scripps patent, saying that it did not adequately disclose the purification method that Scripps itself judged best.[144] But the court did not retract its earlier judgment that a product patent was quite legitimate in this case. We think this is unfortunate social policy. Unless changed, it is likely to inhibit technical advance in biotechnology, where invention involves improving ways to produce purified natural products. If the initial patent is granted on the product, rather than on the process for making it, subsequent process research by others will be discouraged. While licensing by firms can mitigate this problem, there is no guarantee this will take place in such a highly competitive industry.

The doctrine of reverse equivalents might be employed to limit the blocking power of product patents in appropriate cases. Under this doctrine a court could rule that an important process invention yielding a more purified form of the product escapes infringement. Although compulsory licensing might be another option, our law does not for the most part permit judicially mandated licensing.[145] Thus a court is faced with a difficult choice: find the far-improved product an infringement, or find no infringement at all under reverse equivalents.

Science-Based Industries

By a *science-based technology* we mean one in which the direction of inventive effort at any time is strongly influenced by recent scientific or other developments coming from outside the industry, usually from university research. These developments help to illuminate problems or provide solutions to achieving results that previously had seemed impossible. Many technologies draw on science, but the hallmark of what we call science-based technology is that recent science focuses on today's inventive efforts.

Perhaps the most dramatic contemporary example is the biotechnology industry. Scientific advances, especially in molecular biology and biochemistry, created this industry, and continue to feed it ideas, theories, discoveries, and techniques.[146] Other examples include the chemistry of catalysis and semiconductors during the 1950s,[147] and the burgeoning new field of superconductivity. Because science-based industries rely so heavily on scientific discoveries, one relevant patent issue is the appropriate scope of patents in the face of the (usually published) science that makes invention in these industries possible.

The modern biotechnology industry is built around two different sets of technologies.[148] Both of these are based on prior, more general advances in molecular biology and both were initially discovered and employed by scientists concerned with pure research. One of these technologies was originally developed in 1975 by Kohler and Milstein, who discovered that individual immune system cells, which generate antibodies to a specific antigen, could be fused with immortal cancer cells to create a small "factory" to produce antibodies. They did not take out a patent on their creation. They were awarded a Nobel prize.

The pathbreaking Kohler-Milstein research almost immediately was recognized as opening up a myriad of commercial possibilities. Hybritech was an early entry into the race to develop applications. It was the first to use monoclonal antibodies in diagnostic kits sold to doctors and hospitals to identify the presence of diseases (e.g., AIDS) or heightened hormone levels (e.g., pregnancy tests). And it received a patent covering this whole family of diagnostic kits.

Other companies saw exactly the same opportunity, if not so quickly. Monoclonal Antibodies Inc. was one of these, and it created a similar technique only after Hybritech. Monoclonal Antibodies made and sold these kits, and Hybritech sued. Monoclonal defended by claiming the Hybritech patent invalid, at least in its broad scope, because given the work of Kohler and Milstein the generic technique was obvious. The trial court recognized the argument and acknowledged:

> [T]he major advance was the invention of Kohler and Milstein in the making of monoclonal antibodies. . . . Once the scientific community had the monoclonal antibody it was obvious and logical to those expert in the field to use them in known assays as substitutes for . . . polyclonal antibodies . . . of inferior quality.[149]

However, it ruled the patent valid. Granted, the call was not an easy one. Hybritech clearly invented something. The question was, given that it was building on public science, what was the limit of its contribution? The Patent Office allowed Hybritech a broad prospect and the court concurred. We think that was a mistake.

While a case has not yet come to court, the Patent Office also allowed Genentech a very broad prospect on the second major advance in the new biotechnology industry. The basic genetic technique was developed earlier by two scientists, Cohen and Boyer. The two scientists involved saw their basic technique — the insertion of a specific gene into a host cell and subsequent expression of the protein product the gene codes for — primarily as a contribution to ongoing public science. Their universities urged them to take out a patent, which they did, but the patent is licensed to all comers.

Genentech clearly contributed to expression techniques. But it also can be argued that they simply were the first to practice techniques that persons "skilled in the art" knew could be made to work. It is difficult to tell yet whether the breadth implicit in this patent will hold up, but it has created a good deal of trepidation in the industry.[150]

But, given the fact that the patent was issued, the courts will ultimately have to resolve the scope problems it raises. And quite a bit may turn on these issues. According to the head of a rival biotechnology firm, "If interpreted most narrowly, there are certain bacterial [production] systems that wouldn't even be covered. If interpreted most broadly, it could cover all production systems in bacteria, yeast and cells."[151]

Fortunately for the industry, an even broader patent on gene expression was rejected on obviousness grounds because several of the inventors published results prior to the invention.[152] The investigators had discovered that a gene for a nonoperational protein taken from a frog could be inserted into a bacterium and expressed there.[153] On the basis of that research they filed a patent claiming a process for producing proteins comprising "linking [a] natural or synthetic heterologous gene [i.e., one from a foreign source] . . . to an indigenous [bacterium] gene portion."[154] It is worth noting that there is no indication that these claims would have been rejected because of their *breadth*. Thus if the prior publication had not been judged to render the claimed invention obvious, it might have received a patent. Judging from the quoted claim language, this would have been very broad indeed.

The holder of a patent on a broad prospect opened by advances in science need not attempt to control the development of that prospect in any detail. Instead, she could license widely and collect royalties. This practice has been the case with the Cohen-Boyer patent. We prefer licensing to a situation where the patent holder restricts entry. But if used this way, the grant of a broad prospect cannot be justified on the grounds laid out by Kitch. Holders of broad patents would be operating as tollkeepers, not coordinators, and the subsequent development of prospects would proceed in spite of, or at least in indifference to, the broad patent. Nevertheless, if a broad prospect patent is granted and upheld, we would much rather see the patent holder widely granting licenses than trying to develop the prospect herself.

Biotechnology is not the only industry where today scientific breakthroughs spark a scramble to obtain broad patents. The current rush to obtain patents over superconductors demonstrates that patent positioning often is important at the birth of science-based industries.

As a new science-based technology matures, the issues relating to patent scope change largely because particular technologies get established. Thus the early work on catalysis was science-based. But as catalytics were developed, further innovation became more cumulative than science-based. Step-by-step process improvements now dominate the field, succeeding the early advances that came quickly on the heels of the Zeigler and Natta research. As a result, the issues involved in setting appropriate patent scope have changed.

CONCLUSIONS

Our general conclusion is that multiple and competitive sources of invention are socially preferable to a structure where there is only one or a few sources. Public policy, including patent law, ought to encourage inventive rivalry and not hinder it. By this we most emphatically do not mean to imply more competitors are always better than fewer. We recognize, with Schumpeter, that in most modern industries technological advance requires firms large enough to support an efficient-sized R&D laboratory. We also recognize that after a point more rivalry is likely to be wasteful. Rather, our argument is that there are major social dangers of letting the advance of a technology be under the control of one or a few organizations. While there are exceptions, when this was the case, technical advance was sluggish. The company with the inside track has often failed to move aggressively; the Selden automobile patent is perhaps the best example. At the same time, the history of many industries — beginning with the steam engine — show that outsiders with promising approaches have been held back.[155] Further, in what we have called cumulative technologies, particularly when the product in question was a multicomponent system, broad patents on components led to blockages. These were resolved, in effect, by the development of more or less automatic (if elaborate) cross-licensing schemes. These should not be understood as mechanisms to achieve orderly development of the "prospect" but rather as mechanisms to cancel out the blocking effects of broad patents. While sometimes these have come about privately, in other cases patent logjams have been broken only with the powerful force of government intervention. These episodes testify to the blocking power of broad patents as well as the social creativity in working around them; they do not argue for the social efficacy of broad patents.

The problem of product patents on artificially produced substances also deserves special notice. As we have seen, product patents are often granted on purified forms of compounds that occur naturally. Subsequent recombinant versions of the compounds are therefore blocked from effective protection, as in the case of *Scripps* v. *Genentech*.[156] While there is reason to believe that the instances of this kind have multiplied in recent years, we have noted that the tradition of granting a product patent rather than a process one goes back as far as *Mulford* v. *Parke-Davis*,[157] when Learned Hand upheld a product patent on purified human insulin. In such cases protection consistent with the actual achievement of the inventor would have been provided if the initial patent had been for a *process*, or at most a "product-by-process," rather than for a product. And inventive efforts to come up with a significantly better process to make the product would not be blocked.

Also, awarding these more limited patents would be much more consistent with the enablement doctrine; the principle there is to allow the inventor only what she has actually invented as described in the principle spelled out in the specification. This practice would thus bring the principles applied in determining patent scope in chemicals in line with practice elsewhere.

We also want to flag attention to the problem of granting broad patents in the science-based industries. In our discussion we emphasized the dangers of awarding overly broad patents early in the history of an industry founded on recent scientific advances. Hybritech's broad patent on diagnostic assays using monoclonal antibodies provided a useful example. Its breadth seems to exceed the actual contributions of the company's researchers; it includes a good deal of what was previously accomplished by scientists working in the area. As the experience of a number of industries (aircraft, automobiles, radio) has proven, broad early patents can bog down an industry in its formative stage. Scope limitations based on close adherence to the inventor's disclosure provide the surest way around this danger.

It is a good bet that more and more inventions will be science-based, in the sense that the invention is an application of recent public science. It is not equitable, our argument being that it hinders subsequent technical advance, to grant such an inventor a broad prospect simply because she was the first to find a way to apply science, that many knew was achievable and were seeking.

Now just as we do not want to be understood as advocating that more competitors are always better than fewer, we do not want to be said as arguing that narrower patent scope is always better than wider. Our proposal is that claims should be bounded on the one side by prior art, including what science illuminates, and that an applicant should not be granted control over what another party enabled. On the other side, claims should be bounded by what the disclosure enables, and not include broad uncharted prospects. Allowed claims should not be larger than defined, nor any smaller.

We have argued above that such a principle would call for the pruning back of allowed claims in some cases. While it may seem at first blush that this inevitably will reduce the incentives to invent, we do not think so.

In the first place, we do not advocate that others be free to use an inventor's contribution. In no event will our suggested limitations on scope diminish the patentee's property below the level of the actual contribution. Our case is that claims not be allowed to extend significantly beyond what the inventor's work has enabled.

Second, economists have come to understand that patents are regarded by firms in only a very few industries as important in allowing them to profit from inventive and innovative work. The most recent and complete study of the means for capturing returns from research shows that in most industries advantages associated with a head start, including establishment of production and distribution facilities, and moving rapidly down a learning curve, were judged significantly more effective than patents in enabling a firm to reap returns from innovation. In industries like computers and semiconductors, where these mechanisms are primary, patents do play a supporting role. But to repeat, we are not proposing to eliminate that support, only that patents not be allowed to enable an inventor to control a much larger area than she has in fact invented.

In some important industries—pharmaceuticals, chemicals more generally, and scientific instruments are salient examples—patents do play an essential role in appropriating returns from invention. However, these are fields where inventions are reasonably well-defined and bounded, in contrast with opening up broad prospects the boundaries of which are difficult to define. Thus our proposal does not threaten the profitability of the particular inventions actually made in these fields. It only strikes at those cases where allowed patent scope extends far beyond what the inventor has actually invented and plausible equivalents.

And one must bear in mind that every potential inventor is also a potential accused infringer. Thus a "strengthening" of property rights will not always increase incentives to invent; it may also greatly increase an inventor's chances of becoming enmeshed in litigation. Indeed this is at the very heart of our case. Granting a very broad patent today, or at least the expectation on the part of the potential inventors that they will be granted a broad patent, may at the start induce more inventive effort than were the expectation for a patent more closely trimmed to actual achievements. But when that patent is won and granted, its scope diminishes incentives for others to stay in the invention game, compared again with a patent whose claims are trimmed to what the accomplishment enables. This diminution would not be desirable if the evidence indicated that control of subsequent developments by one party made possible more effective subsequent inventive effort. But the evidence, we think, is the other way.

While this is a book about antitrust, not about patent law and policy, the topics are not unrelated. In the first place, patent law and policy, in particular scope decisions, can profoundly influence what kind of a market structure evolves in an industry. Since market power based on patents and their legitimate use is not easily attacked under antitrust law, patent scope decisions influence how concentrated or rivalrous an industry is likely to be in a given regime of antitrust law and enforcement. One view of our argument is that patent decisions should not unnecessarily hinder antitrust law in its goal in keeping industries competitive.

At the same time, our case that by and large technical change proceeds more vigorously when there are multiple sources of invention than when there is monopoly or near monopoly, applies to what we consider under antitrust as well as under patent law. Thus one question to ask about proposals for reform of antitrust law is whether they would tend to unduly contract the number of capable and motivated rivalrous sources of invention. Note that this would require more than a conventional market share analysis; a change that would enable several weak firms to cooperate and achieve together an effort of critical mass could increase rather than decrease the number of potential sources of invention. Whether it does or not depends on a number of variables: the cost of the activities in question, the resources the firms can marshall on their own, and the savings from coordinated efforts. But our general message is to be wary of arguments that say it is not important to preserve, or if need be create, real rivalry in invention and innovation.

In sum, the arguments and evidence presented in this chapter strongly support the case economists have made that society benefits when there is vigorous competition and puts itself at jeopardy when one or a very few firms control an industry or technology. The reasons developed here why competition is valuable and monopoly is dangerous differ in essential respects from similar arguments in the standard textbooks on static economic theory. The argument is Schumpeterian, rather than neoclassical.

The world is drastically different now than it was when the Sherman Act was signed. The nature and scope of competition are different, and in many industries and technologies competition must be understood as global. With the changing of conditions, the precise policies to usefully further the goal of vigorous competition change as well. But the goal continues to be a sound one.

ACKNOWLEDGMENTS

The authors are grateful for financial support from the Julius Silver Program in Law, Sciences, and Technology at Columbia University, and to the Sloan Foundation through its funding of the Consortium on Competition and Cooperation. We would like to acknowledge the helpful comments and suggestions received from Harold Edgar, Donald Chisum, Joe Brodley, and participants in faculty workshops at Boston University and Columbia Law Schools. They contributed only helpful advice, not any of the shortcomings that may remain.

NOTES

1. W. Cohen, and R. Levin, "Empirical Studies of Innovation and Market Structure" in R. Schmalensee and R. Willig, eds., *Handbook of Industrial Organization* (Amsterdam: North-Holland, 1989).
2. See R. Nelson, "Capitalism as an Engine of Progress," *Research Policy*, forthcoming.
3. E. Kitch, "The Nature and Function of the Patent System," *J.L. and Economics 20* (1977): 266–283.
4. R. Beck, "The Prospect Theory of the Patent System and Unproductive Competition," *Res. in L. and Economics 5* (1983).
5. See, e.g., Grant v. Raymond, 31 U.S. (6 Pet.) 218 (1832). ("An enabling disclosure is necessary in order to give the public, after the privilege shall expire, the advantage for which the privilege is allowed, and is the foundation of the power to issue the patent.")
6. See, e.g., The Incandescent Lamp Patent, 159 U.S. 465 (1895).
7. U.S. Patent 775, 134, issued Nov. 4, 1904. See Gillette Safety Razor Co. v. Clarke Blade & Razor Co., 187 F. 149, 149 (C.C.D.N.J. 1911), *aff'd* 194 F. 421 (3d Cir. 1912).
8. 187 F. 149 at 156.
9. *Id*. at 149.
10. Clarke Blade & Razor Co. v. Gillette Safety Razor Co., 194 F. 421, 423 (3d Cir. 1912), quoting from Deering v. Winona, 155 U.S. 286, 302 (1894). Note that current practice is to say that a specification, not a claim, is inoperative. However, perhaps owing to the similarity in language between specification and claim, both quoted in the text, the court analyzed the enablement defense in light of the claim.
11. As we use the term in this article, *device* means a product, process, or compound.
12. It is important to distinguish our use of the term "principle" here from its use in other contexts. We mean principle in the narrow sense of an underlying characteristic that supplies a family of devices with an identifiable quality. We do not mean a scientific or natural principle, i.e., a broadly applicable law, such as gravity or magnetism, which cannot be patented.
13. The Incandescent Lamp Patent, 159 U.S. 465 (1895).
14. *Id*. at 468.
15. *Id*. at 474.
16. 56 U.S. (15 How.) 62 (1854).
17. *Id*. at 114.
18. *Id*. at 119–120:

> If the eighth claim of the patentee can be maintained, there was no necessity for any specification, further than to say that he had discovered that, by using the motive power of electro-magnetism, he could print intelligible characters at any distance. . . . [T]his claim can derive no aid from the specification filed. It is outside of [the specification], and the patentee claims beyond it.

19. See Columbia Motor Car Co. v. A.C. Duerr & Co., 184 F. 893 (2d Cir. 1911).
20. See Electric Vehicle Co. v. Winton Motor-Carriage Co., 104 F. 814 (C.C.S.D.N.Y. 1900); Electric Vehicle Co. v. C.A. Duerr & Co., 172 F. 923 (C.C.S.D.N.Y. 1909),

rev'd sub nom Columbia Motor Car Co. v. C.A. Duerr & Co., 184 F. 893 (2d Cir. 1911).

21. Columbia Motor Car Co. v. C.A. Duerr & Co., 184 F. 893 (2d Cir. 1911).

22. See U.S. Patent No. 4,736,866, issued April 12, 1988.

23. See K. Bozicevic, "The 'Reverse Doctrine of Equivalents' in the World of Reverse Transcriptase," *J. Pat. & Trademark Off. Soc'y* 71 (1989): 353, 358 [hereinafter Bozicevic, "Reverse Equivalents"] ("[The Leder and Stewart] patent is a pioneering patent for a number of reasons. . . . [T]he inventors . . . are world renowned for their work in this quickly developing area of technology.") (footnote omitted).

24. Under current law, these arguments would be less likely to succeed for a number of reasons. See notes 28–42, 74–90 *infra* and accompanying text. It has been suggested that the broad claims of the Leder and Stewart patent should be subject to the reverse doctrine of equivalents, and therefore held not to cover some subject matter literally within its claims, if a subsequent inventor uses a substantially different technique to create transgenic animals. Bozicevic, "Reverse Equivalents," at 362–371, 371 (illustrating several techniques for introducing foreign genes into a mammal's fertilized egg which are not described in the Leder and Stewart specification; therefore, "a court might hold that any transgenic mammals produced by the[se] methods . . . would not infringe the claims of the . . . patent.").

25. See U.S. Patent No. 4,704,362, Issued Nov. 3, 1987, Filed Nov. 5, 1979, entitled "Recombinant Cloning Vehicle Microbial Polypeptide Expression."

26. S. Hall, *Invisible Frontiers: The Race to Synthesize a Human Gene* (1987), 152–153 (no one had successfully cloned and expressed a human protein before Genentech.).

27. U.S. Patent No. 4,704,362, columns 10–23.

28. See, e.g., *In re* Hogan, 559 F.2d 595, 606 194 U.S.P.Q. 527 (C.C.P.A. 1977; *In re* Goffe, 542 F.2d 564 191 U.S.P.Q. 429.

29. *In re* Hogan, 559 F.2d 595, 606 194 U.S.P.Q. 527 (C.C.P.A. 1977).

30. This explains the broad scope of pioneer claims. By definition there is little prior art in these cases. See Patent and Trademark Office, *Manual of Patent Examining Procedures* §706.03(d), at 700–12 (5th ed. 1983, rev. 1986) ("The fact that a claim is broad does not necessarily justify a rejection on the ground that the claim is vague and indefinite or incomplete. In non-chemical cases, a claim may, in general, be drawn as broadly as permitted in the prior art."). The need for a slightly more restrictive rule in chemical cases is justified on the grounds that the chemical arts are more unpredictable; the average *mechanic*, it is said, can easily predict which substitute components will work in a given situation, while chemists cannot. Because of this, mechanical patents are permitted broad scope over the objection that they do not enable those in the art to make a broad range of embodiments of the inventive idea. Chemical patents are not. See *id.*, at §§706.03(a), 706.03(2); Samuel S. Levin, "Broader than the Disclosure in Chemical Cases," *J. Pat. Off. Soc'y* 31 (1949): 5, 7. See also Ellen P. Winner, "Enablement in Rapidly Developing Arts—Biotechnology," *J. Pat. Off. Soc'y* 70 (1988): 608, 609 (pointing out that biotechnology is often lumped with chemistry and is therefore considered an unpredictable art).

31. This is the rationale behind the distinction introduced earlier between predictable and unpredictable arts. See *supra* note 30.

32. Enablement must be established only as of the date the inventor filed for a patent. Thus new technological developments which require information not in the inventor's specification and which occur after the filing date cannot be used to prove the inventor's disclosure was not enabling. This is true even if these new developments fall within the scope of the inventor's claims. The somewhat counterintuitive result is this: an inventor can properly claim subject matter that later turns out to be

beyond her actual research, so long as her research enables one skilled in the art to make and use her claimed invention *as that invention was understood as of the filing date*. For an example, consider an inventor who claims "crystalline polypropylene," and provides an enabling disclosure to make what everyone in the art would agree was "crystalline polypropylene" as of the filing date. After the filing date, it is discovered that with substantial modifications of the inventor's technique one can make polypropylene of high molecular weight and intrinsic viscosity — two properties that make the fiber commercially useful. It has been held that the inventor's original disclosure is sufficient to sustain a patent since it was enabling as of the filing date. The result: the inventor's claims cover the later-developed, commercially useful form of the fiber. Phillips Petroleum Co. v. United States Steel Corp., 673 F.Supp. 1278, 6 U.S.P.Q.2d 1065, 1068, 1074 (D.Del. 1987), *aff'd sub nom* United States Steel Corp. v. Phillips Petroleum Co., 865 F.2d 1247, 9 U.S.P.Q.2d (BNA) 1461, 1466 n.9 (Fed. Cir. 1989).

33. See In re Armbruster, 512 F.2d 676, 680, 185 U.S.P.Q. (BNA) 152 (C.C.P.A. 1952) (reversing rejection of patent application, since there was nothing in the specification to justify the examiner's doubts about enablement); In re Geerdes, 491 F.2d 1260, 1265, 180 U.S.P.Q. (BNA) 789 (C.C.P.A. 1974) ("[I]t is possible to *argue* that process claims encompass inoperative embodiments on the premise of unrealistic or vague assumptions, but that is not a valid basis for rejection.").

34. See Winner, "Enablement in Rapidly Developing Arts," at 608, 619–623. The author of this article summarizes the somewhat conflicting cases on the topic, and concludes that "[t]o reject claims for lack of enablement of embodiments that were only imagined by the examiner does not seem fair." *Id.* at 623.

35. See notes 74–90 and accompanying text, *infra*. It may be worth noting that at least some aspects of the Genentech patent were called into question by a recent decision striking down a related patent, where the court recognized, in a footnote, that the Genentech inventors may have been assisted by previous work done elsewhere. In re O'Farrell, 853 F.2d 894, 7 U.S.P.Q.2d (BNA) 1673 (Fed. Cir. 1988). Also, a recent British case invalidating a Genentech patent on TPA emphasizes that recombinant techniques were being used by a significant number of researchers after the pathbreaking work of Stanley Cohen and Herb Boyer in the late 1970s. Note, however, that TPA was cloned and expressed some time after the research leading up to the "expression" patent. See Genentech, Inc. v. Wellcome Foundation, [1989] R.P.C. See also Mellor, "Patents and Genetic Engineering — Is It a New Problem?," *Eur. Intellectual Prop. L. Rev.* 6 (1988): 135 (describing British TPA litigation).

36. The TPA protein at issue in the British patent case discussed earlier is an example. Further examples include erythropoietin (EPO), see Amgen, Inc. v. Chugai Pharmaceutical Co., 706 F. Supp. 94, 9 U.S.P.Q.2d 1833 (D.Mass. 1989), *rev'd on other grounds*, 18 U.S.P.Q. 1016 (Fed. Cir. 1991), and Factor VIII, see *infra* notes 142–144 and accompanying text.

37. This is not to imply that product is always broader than process. A process that is useful in producing only product A will have the same scope as a patent on product A. A patent on a process that produces products A through E, on the other hand, is broader in scope than a patent on any one of those products.

38. Scripps Clinic and Res. Found. v. Genentech, Inc., 666 F.Supp. 1379, 3 U.S.P.Q.2d 1481, 1488 (N.D.Cal. 1987), *patent invalidated in* Scripps Clinic and Res. Found. v. Genentech, Inc., 724 F.Supp. 690 (N.D.Cal. 1989).

39. 245 F.2d 693, 113 U.S.P.Q. (BNA) 423 (4th Cir. 1957).

40. *Id.* Cf. D. Chisum, 1 *Patents* § 1.03[8][c] (1978, rev. 1988) (new use must be nonobvious).

41. Royal Typewriter Co. v. Remington Rand, Inc., 168 F.2d 691, 691, 77 U.S.P.Q. (BNA) 517 (2d Cir.) *cert. denied* 335 U.S. 825 (1948).
42. Graver Tank & Mfg. Co., Inc. v. Linde Air Prods, Co., 339 U.S. 605, 608 (1950).
43. 166 F. Supp. 551, 119 U.S.P.Q. (BNA) 72 (S.D. N.Y. 1958).
44. *Id*. at 552.
45. *Id*. at 563.
46. *Id*. at 555.
47. *Id*. at 555.
48. *Id*. at 554.
49. On the other hand, Ford might have been able to obtain a patent on its improvement of the basic International Nickel invention. If Ford could establish that its nodular iron composition met the requirements of patentability — i.e., utility, novelty, and nonobviousness — it would then have the right to control this improvement. International Nickel would have had to take a license from Ford to use this improvement, even though it held the basic or dominant nodular iron patent. And of course Ford could not use its improvement without a license from International Nickel. This is an example of so-called blocking patents, a situation often resolved by a cross-licensing agreement.
50. Boyden Power-Brake Co. v. Westinghouse, 170 U.S. 537, 569 (1898). Another test of pioneer status is whether the patent led to a new branch of industry. See, e.g., Ludlum Steel Co. v. Terry, 37 F.2d 153 (N.D.N.Y. 1928).
51. D. Chisum, 4 *Patents* § 18.04[2] (1978, rev. 1988). Inventions falling somewhere between the two extremes are given an intermediate range of equivalents. See Price v. Lake Sales Supply R.M., Inc., 510 F.2d 388, 183 U.S.P.Q. (BNA) 519 (10th Cir. 1974).
52. 166 F. Supp. at 564.
53. See, e.g., Tigrett Indus., Inc. v. Standard Indus., Inc., 162 U.S.P.Q. (BNA) 32, 36 (W.D.Tenn. 1967), *aff'd*, 411 F.2d 1218, 162 U.S.P.Q. (BNA) 13 (6th Cir. 1969), *aff'd by an equally divided court*, 397 U.S. 586 (1970) (claim for playpen calling for "a pair of spaced openings" for two converging drawstrings to adjust side webbing infringed by device with one hole for drawstrings); Weidman Metal Masters Co. v. Glass Masters Corp., 623 F.2d 1024, 1030, 207 U.S.P.Q. (BNA) 101 (5th Cir. 1980) ("even the minimum equivalency due to any patent normally forbids the mere reversal of a function of two parts and the small movement of one part to avoid literal infringement by accepting a less efficient job").
54. See, e.g., Mead Digital Sys., Inc. v. A.B. Dick Co., 723 F.2d 455, 464, 221 U.S.P.Q. (BNA) 1035 (6th Cir. 1983) (finding noninfringement even though ink-jet printer patent was "quantum leap" in the art).
55. Compare Graver Tank & Mfg. Co. v. Linde Air Prods. Co., 339 U.S. 605, 608 (1950) ("An important factor [in determining equivalency] is whether persons reasonably skilled in the art would have known of the interchangeability of an ingredient not contained in the patent with one that was.") and Gould v. Rees, 82 U.S. (15 Wall.) 187, 194 (1872) (no infringement where accused infringer "substitutes another [ingredient] in the place of the one omitted, which was new or performs a substantially different function, or [which] . . . is old, but was not known at the date of the plaintiff's invention as a proper substitute . . . ") with Texas Instruments, Inc. v. United States Int's Trade Comm'n, 805 F.2d 1558, 1563, 231 U.S.P.Q. (BNA) 833, 835 (Fed. Cir. 1986) ("It is not required that those skilled in the art knew, at the time the patent application was filed, of the asserted equivalent means of performing the claimed functions; that equivalent is determined as of the time infringement takes place.") and Pennwalt Corp. v. Durand-Wayland, Inc., 833 F.2d 931, 4 U.S.P.Q.2d 1737, 1745 n.4 (Fed. Cir. 1987) ("It is clear that an equivalent can be found in

technology known at the time of the invention, as well as in subsequently developed technology.") (Bennett, J., dissenting).

56. See Pennwalt Corp. v. Durand-Wayland, Inc., 833 F.2d 931, 938, 4 U.S.P.Q.2d (BNA) 1737, 1742–1743 (Fed. Cir. 1987) ("[T]he facts here do not involve later-developed computer technology which should be deemed within the scope of the claims to avoid the pirating of an invention . . . [T]he memory components of the [accused] sorter were not programmed to perform the same or an equivalent function of physically tracking the items to be sorted . . . as required by the claims.").

57. Cf. Mead Digital Sys., Inc. v. A.B. Dick Co., 723 F.2d 455, 464, 221 U.S.P.Q. (BNA) 1035 (6th Cir. 1983) (finding noninfringement under doctrine of equivalents because accused ink-jet printer operated on different principle).

58. 717 F.2d 1351, 219 U.S.P.Q. 473 (Fed. Cir. 1983).

59. Id. at 1365 (emphasis in original) (citation omitted). See also William D. Noonan, "Understanding Patent Scope," Or. L. Rev. 65 (1986): 717, 733 (criticizing the opinion by Judge Markey in Hughes, stating that it was "a curious inversion of the patentee's burden of proving infringement . . . [to say] that the burden was on the infringer to explain why his structure was not an equivalent of the claimed satellite system," and concluding that "the Hughes approach would create an unfortunate aura of uncertainty around the scope of claims issued by the [Patent Office]").

60. Laser Alignment, Inc. v. Woodruff & Sons, Inc., 491 F.2d 866, 180 U.S.P.Q. (BNA) 609 (7th Cir. 1974). See also D. Chisum, 4 Patents § 18.04[3] (1978, rev. 1988). One older case with a similar holding is Edison Elec. Light Co. v. Boston Incandescent Lamp Co., 62 F. 397, 398 (C.C.D.Mass. 1894). Here the court found that since Edison's patent was a pioneering invention, it was entitled to a broad construction, which included finding that after-developed technology was equivalent to that specified in the claims.

61. See Martin J. Adelman and Gary L. Francione, "The Doctrine of Equivalents in Patent Law: Questions Pennwalt Did Not Answer," U. Pa. L. Rev. 137 (1989): 673 (criticizing equivalents doctrine's broad reach in light of availability of reissue proceedings, and suggesting that the doctrine should only be available when a new technology is used to supply an equivalent component of a patented device).

62. Texas Instruments, Inc. v. United States Int'l Trade Comm'n, 805 F.2d 1558, 231 U.S.P.Q. (BNA) 833 (Fed. Cir. 1986).

63. 805 F.2d at 1570, 231 U.S.P.Q. (BNA) at 840:

It is not appropriate in this case, where all of the claimed functions are performed in the accused devices by subsequently developed or improved means, to view each such change as if it were the only change from the disclosed embodiment of the invention. It is the entirety of the technology embodied in the accused devices that must be compared with the patent disclosure.

This "invention as a whole" standard was repudiated by an en banc decision of the same court the next year calling for an "element-by-element" comparison. Pennwalt Corp. v. Durand-Wayland, Inc., 833 F.2d 931, 936, 4 U.S.P.Q.2d (BNA) 1737, 1741 (Fed. Cir. 1987). ("[I]f . . . even a single function required by a claim or an equivalent function is not performed by [an accused device], . . . [a] finding of no infringement must be upheld."). Judge Pauline Newman, who wrote the Texas Instruments opinion, dissented along with five of 12 judges, and wrote separately: "One-to-one correspondence between every element of a claim and an accused device is the standard formula for inquiry into literal infringement. But this formula is an incorrect application of the doctrine of equivalents. . . . The doctrine can not, by its nature, be reduced to rigid rules." Perhaps this sunk in; in a later opinion, the

Federal Circuit seemed to soften its definition of "element" to allow more flexibility. See Corning Glass Works v. Sumitomo Elec. U.S.A., Inc., 868 F.2d 1251, 9 U.S.P.Q.2d (BNA) 1962 (Fed. Cir. 1989) ("In the All Elements rule, 'element' is used in the sense of a *limitation* of a claim. . . . [Defendant's] analysis is faulty in that it would require equivalency in components. . . . However, the determination of equivalency is not subject to such a rigid formula.").

64. 805 F.2d at 1571. Some contend the "as a whole" test yields unpredictable results and thus creates a great deal of uncertainty. Bretschneider, "How to Craft and Interpret Means Plus Function Claims in Light of the *Pennwalt* and *Texas Instruments* Cases," *Am. Intellectual Prop. L. Ass'n. Sel. Legal Papers* 6 (1988): 68, 73 ("the degree of uncertainty created by this 'invention as a whole' test is nearly intolerable"). Cf. N. Linck, "The Doctrine of Equivalents: A Two-Tier Analytical Approach," in *Am. Intellectual Prop. L. Ass'n. Sel. Legal Papers* 6 (1988): 19 (asserting that a synthesis of the "as a whole" and "all elements" approaches can be made to work).

65. There are two more limitations on the doctrine of equivalents that should be mentioned: first, just as an applicant cannot claim anything in the prior art when applying for a patent, so are the courts limited by the prior art when "stretching" claim language under the doctrine of equivalents. Loctite Corp. v. Ultraseal Ltd., 781 F.2d 861, 228 U.S.P.Q. (BNA) 90 (Fed. Cir. 1985). See also *Wilson Sporting Goods*, 14 U.S.P.Q.2d 1942 (Fed. Cir. 1990). And second, the doctrine of "prosecution history estoppel" prevents the patentee from recapturing through equivalents claimed subject matter given up during prosecution. Thus a court recently dismissed an infringement action where the patentee, a biotechnology company, originally claimed a recombinant process for making erythropoietin, a polypeptide that stimulates red cell production. During prosecution of the patent the examiner rejected certain claims as obvious in light of the prior art; in response, the patentee surrendered all process claims. The patentee at trial nevertheless urged the court to interpret its claims to include the rejected material to find infringement by defendant's process for producing the polypeptide. The court declined; it would not adopt an "interpretation [that] would 'resurrect subject matter surrendered during prosecution.'" Amgen, Inc. v. Chugai Pharmaceutical Co., No. Civ. A. 87-2617-Y, D. Mass., Jan. 31, 1989, *quoting* Thomas & Betts Corp. v. Litton Systems, Inc., 720 F.2d 1572, 1579 220 U.S.P.Q. (Fed. Cir. 1983). Note that there is some dispute whether claims rejected on the basis of claim indefiniteness or lack of disclosure—rather than inclusion of prior art—may serve as the foundation for a defense of prosecution history estoppel. See S.C. Johnson & Son v. Carter-Wallace, Inc., 614 F.Supp. 1278, 1306–1308, 225 U.S.P.Q. (BNA) 1022 (S.D.N.Y. 1985) (refusing to apply prosecution history estoppel to claims rejected for indefiniteness or inadequate disclosure); R. Harmon, *Patents and the Federal Circuit* § 6.3(b) (1988) (summarizing Federal Circuit cases). The better view, however, is that claims rejected for *any* reason should give rise to prosecution history estoppel. See D. Chisum, 4 *Patents* § 18.05[2] (1990, rev. 1988), at 18–134-35 ("statements that [prosecution history] estoppel is 'limited to changes made to overcome rejections . . . [that] the claim was anticipated by the prior art' are not supportable." (citation omitted)). See, e.g., Sargent v. Hall Safe Co., 144 U.S. 63 (1885); Mannesman Demag Corp. v. Engineered Metal Products Co., 793 F. 2d 1279, 230 U.S.P.Q. 45 (Fed. Cir. 1986). The Federal Circuit has provided a useful definition of prosecution history:

The prosecution history . . . of the patent consists of the entire record of proceedings in the Patent and Trademark Office. This included all express representations made by or on behalf of the applicant to the examiner to induce a patent grant. . . . Such representations include amendments to the claims and arguments made to convince the examiner that the claimed invention meets the statutory requirements of novelty, utility, and nonobviousness.

Standard Oil Co. v. American Cyanamid Co., 774 F. 2d. 448, 452, 227 U.S.P.Q. (BNA) 293 (Fed. Cir. 1985). The question of how broadly to define prosecution history is distinct from another question that has engaged the attention of the courts: whether there can be *any* equivalents left when the prosecution history reveals a rejection. *See* Note, "Patent Claims and Prosecution History Estoppel in the Federal Circuit," *Mo. L. Rev.* 53 (1988): 497.

66. Two aspects of this situation may seem counterintuitive: that the narrower (subservient) patent could ever be issued by the Patent Office, given the existence of the broad patent in the prior art; and that once the subservient patent were issued the holder of the dominant patent would be prevented from practicing an invention that clearly falls within the scope of her claims. Subservient patents may be issued, however, when they disclose an improved feature that meets the statutory tests of novelty and nonobviousness. See, e.g., Atlas Powder Co. v. E.I. du Pont & Co., 750 F.2d 1569, 224 U.S.P.Q. 409 (Fed. Cir. 1984). (The fact that the subservient patentee has invented a nonobvious variant of a device covered by a broad patent does not mean that the broad patent is invalid for lack of enabling disclosure under 35 U.S.C. § 112. See, e.g., B.G. Corp. v. Walter Kidde & Co., 79 F.2d 20, 22 (2d Cir. 1935) (L. Hand, J.) ("It is true that [the inventor of the spark plug] did not foresee the particular adaptability of his plug to the airplane. . . . Nevertheless, he did not shoot in the dark; he laid down with perfect certainty what he wished to accomplish and how. . . . He is not charged with a prophetic understanding of the entire field of its usefulness."); Amerace Corp. v. Ferro Corp., 532 F.Supp. 1188, 1202, 213 U.S.P.Q. 1099, 1202 (D. Tex. 1982)). And a subservient patent can prevent a dominant patent holder from practicing the particular improved feature claimed in the subservient patent. This stems from the fact that the patent grant is a right to *exclude*, not an affirmative right to practice an invention. See 35 U.S.C. § 154. Thus the dominant patentee can exclude the subservient patentee from practicing her invention at all; and the subservient patentee can exclude the dominant patentee from practicing her specific improved feature. See Atlas Powder, *supra*; Ziegler v. Phillips Petroleum Co., 483 F.2d 858, 177 U.S.P.Q. 481 (5th Cir. 1973), *cert. denied* 414 U.S. 1079. Cf. Cochrane v. Deener, 94 U. S. 780, 787 (1856); Cantrell v. Wallick, 117 U. S. 689, 694 (1886).

67. One example of patents that are so characterized is an improvement patent whose claims are drafted in a special format called "Jepson claims." See, e.g., Pentec, Inc. v. Graphic Controls Corp., 776 F.2d 309, 227 U.S.P.Q. 766 (Fed. Cir. 1985). See generally R. Ellis, *Patent Claims* § 197 (1949).

68. See Ziegler v. Phillips Petroleum Co., 483 F.2d 858, 177 U.S.P.Q. 481 (5th Cir. 1973); Bryan v. Richardson, 254 F.2d 191 (5th Cir. 1958).

69. See Water Technologies Corp. v. Calco, Ltd., 850 F.2d 660, 7 U.S.P.Q.2d 1097 (Fed. Cir. 1988). Cf. Oil Well Improvements Co. v. Acme Foundry & Mach. Co., 31 F.2d 898, 901 (8th Cir. 1929) ("Obviously, there could be no recovery of such lost profits on account of sales to those who bought because of supposed superiority of the infringing device.") Note that the subservient patentee would, however, be liable for damages as measured by the value of royalties to the patentee under a license agreement. See D. Chisum, 5 *Patents* § 20.03[3] (1989), at 20–135 through 20–136 ("In a case of blocking industrial property rights, the reasonable royalty would have

to reflect an appropriate apportionment of the expected economic benefits. On the other hand, the patent owner's valid claim may have stood as a sole but complete legal obstacle to the manufacture of the product by the infringer.")

70. Borg-Warner Corp. v. Paragon Bear Works, Inc. 355 F.2d 400, 404, 147 U.S.P.Q. (BNA) 1 (1st Cir. 1965).

71. The limitation on the doctrine of equivalents discussed in the text—the "reverse doctrine of equivalents"—is not the only check on this sweeping principle. The Patent Office and the courts also restrict claim scope by prohibiting patentees from arguing that an accused device is infringing if that device embodies features from the prior art which the patentee explicitly argued to a patent examiner were *not* contained in her invention when she was prosecuting her patent. That is, a patentee may not argue that her patent application should be allowed because it describes an invention different from the prior art, and later, during litigation involving that patent, make the inconsistent argument that an accused device which has the very features described in that prior art nevertheless falls inside the scope of the patentee's claims. See, e.g., Mannesman Demag Corp. v. Engineered Metal Prods. Co., 793 F.2d 1279, 230 U.S.P.Q. (BNA) 45 (Fed. Cir. 1986) (describing doctrine of "prosecution history estoppel"). This doctrine applies only when a patentee is arguing that there is infringement under the doctrine of equivalents. R. Harmon, *Patents and the Federal Circuit* (1988), 131.

72. Westinghouse v. Boyden Power-Brake Co., 170 U.S. 537, 562 (1898).

73. *Id.*

74. *Id.* at 561.

75. *Id.* at 568. See also Charles F. Piggott, Jr., "Equivalents in Reverse," *J. Pat. Off. Soc'y* 48 (1966): 291, 295 (noting that in *Westinghouse*, "the claims literally read upon the accused structure.").

76. 170 U.S. 537 at 572. On the application of this standard to specific cases, see Jacoby-Bender, Inc. v. Foster Metal Products, Inc., 152 F.Supp. 289, 114 U.S.P.Q. (BNA) 534 (D.Mass. 1957), *aff'd* 255 F.2d 869, 117 U.S.P.Q. (BNA) 373 (1st Cir. 1958) ("I am disposed to regard [the accused] device as . . . an equivalent unless what it accomplished was a marked improvement. . . . In such event it would be appropriate to judge equivalency by the extent of the improvement—the significance of the departure in relation to the remaining basic concept."); Piggott, "Equivalents in Reverse," at 291, 295–299.

77. See, e.g., Leesona Corp. v. United States, 530 F.2d 896, 905–906, 192 U.S.P.Q. (BNA) 672 (Ct. Cl. 1976). See also Piggott, "Equivalents in Reverse," at 291.

78. 775 F.2d at 1111.

79. SRI Int'l v. Matsushita Elec. Corp. of America, 591 F.Supp. 464, 465–469, 224 U.S.P.Q. 70 (N.D.Cal. 1984), *rev'd in part and remanded*, 775 F.2d 1107, 227 U.S.P.Q. (BNA) 577 (Fed. Cir. 1985).

80. *Id.*

81. 775 F.2d at 1123, 227 U.S.P.Q. (BNA) 577 at 580 (emphasis in original) (lead opinion, five judges joining); *Id.*, at 1132 (Davis, J., concurring); *Id.* at 1132, 1133 (Kashiwa, J., dissenting, five judges joining). See D. Chisum, 4 *Patents* § 18.03[1] (1978, rev. 1988).

82. Compare 775 F.2d at 1125 (genuine issues of material fact still unresolved) (lead opinion, five judges joining); *with Id.*, at 1132 (reverse equivalents is always a matter of fact, not law) (Davis, J., concurring) *and Id.* at 1132, 1133 (no genuine factual issues left to resolve; one of two alternative legal findings is that reverse equivalents defense is valid here as a matter of law) (Kashiwa, J., dissenting, five judges joining). See Chisum, 4 *Patents* § 18.03[1].

83. But see United States Steel Corp. v. Phillips Petroleum Co., 865 F.2d 1247, 9 U.S.P.Q.2d (BNA) 1461, 1466 n.9 (Fed. Cir. 1989) (approving of trial court's treatment of reverse equivalents as question of whether "the 'principle' of the contribution made by the inventor [is] . . . unchanged in the accused product").

84. Westinghouse, *supra*, 170 U.S. 537, 572. Judge Newman of the Federal Circuit has acknowledged that the reverse equivalents doctrine "is involved when claims are written more broadly than the disclosure warrants." Texas Instruments, Inc. v. United States Int'l Trade Comm'n, 846 F.2d 1369, 1372 (Fed. Cir. 1986), *denying rehearing of* 805 F.2d 1558, 231 U.S.P.Q. (BNA) 833, 835 (Fed. Cir. 1986).

85. See Bozicevic, "Reverse Equivalents," *supra* note 23, at 360–369 (arguing that the Leder and Stewart patent ought to be narrowed under reverse equivalents if, for example, a subsequent inventor discloses a "substantially different" method of introducing foreign genetic material into a mammal's genome).

86. R. Nelson and S. Winter, *An Evolutionary Theory of Economic Change* (1982), 329–351; D. Sahal, *Patterns of Technological Innovation* (1982); Giovanni Dosi, "Technological Paradigms and Technological Trajectories: A Suggested Interpretation of the Determinants and Directions of Technical Change," *Res. Pol'y* 11 (1982): 147.

87. See O. Williamson, *Markets and Hierarchies* (1975) and D. Teece, "Profiting from Technological Innovation," *Research Policy* (Dec. 1986) for a general discussion. For a more specific one, see Caves, Crookell, and Killing, "The Imperfect Market for Technology Licenses," *Oxford Bull. Econ. & Stats.* 45 (1983): 249, 260–262. A group led by Edwin Mansfield of the University of Pennsylvania reached the same general conclusion after conducting a similar empirical study. See E. Mansfield, A. Romeo, D. Teece, S. Wagner, and P. Brach, *Technology Transfer, Productivity, and Economic Policy* (1982).

88. For a general discussion, see R. Nelson, "Capitalism as an Engine of Progress," *Res. Pol'y* (forthcoming).

89. George Selden received a very broad patent in 1895 on the basic elements of the early automobile — "carriage," drive mechanism (transmission), and engine — which quickly gave him a commanding position in the burgeoning automotive field. See U.S. Patent No. 549,160, issued Nov. 5, 1895; Columbia Motor Car Co. v. A.C. Duerr & Co., 184 F. 893 (2d Cir. 1911).

90. In 1903, after the Selden patent survived its first challenge, Electric Vehicle Co. v. Winton Motor-Carriage Co., 104 F. 814 (C.C.S.D.N.Y. 1900), the Association of Licensed Automobile Manufacturers (A.L.A.M.) was formed. Until it was dissolved in 1911, following the first case finding that the Selden patent had not been infringed, A.L.A.M. controlled the automobile industry through its power to deny licenses to new companies. Consequently the improvements of new competitors were suppressed for a time.

91. One historian of the industry states:

    That consumers were in some cases actually intimidated from buying the products of perfectly "good and reliable" but unlicensed manufacturers is . . . quite probable; certainly the advertisements of the A.L.A.M. attempted to accomplish this result. In response to the association's repeated warning "Do Not Buy a Lawsuit with Your Automobile," the Ford Motor Company offered to give each purchaser a bond protecting him against any damages that might arise from this quarter.

    R. C. Epstein, *The Automobile Industry* (1928), 233.

92. See Columbia Motor Car Co. v. A.C. Duerr & Co., 184 F. 893 (2d Cir. 1911).

93. See Wright Co. v. Paulhan, 177 F. 261, 271 (S.D.N.Y. 1910) (Hard, J.). Cf. Zollman, "Patent Rights in Aircraft," *Marquette L. Rev.* 11 (1927): 216, 218–219.

94. See Wright Co. v. Herring-Curtiss Co., 204 F. 597 (W.D.N.Y. 1913) (finding that defendants' admittedly different design infringed plaintiff's broad pioneer patent on airplane stabilization), *aff'd*, 211 F. 654 (2d Cir. 1914).

95. See G. Bittlingmayer, "Property Rights, Progress, and the Aircraft Patent Agreement," *J. L. & Econ.* 31 (1988): 227, 232.

96. L. Reich, *The Making of American Industrial Research: Science and Business at GE and Bell, 1876–1926* (1986).

97. Cf. S. G. Sturmey, *The Economic Development of Radio* (1958), 275 (broad patents retarded growth of British radio industry).

98. RCA was formed, primarily at the insistence of the navy, to overcome the tangled web of conflicting patents in the radio field:

> The Navy, in a patent investigation in 1919, had "found that there was not a single company among those making radio sets for the Navy which possessed basic patents sufficient to enable them to supply, without infringement, . . . a complete transmitter or receiver."

W. R. MacLaurin, *Invention and Innovation in the Radio Industry* (1949), 103.

99. See N. Stern, *From ENIAC to UNIVAC: An Appraisal of the Eckert–Mauchly Computers* (1981), 2–4, citing Honeywell, Inc. v. Sperry-Rand Corp., No. 4-67 Civ. 138 (Minn. Oct. 19, 1973) (unpublished opinion) (finding that Eckert and Mauchly's patent was invalid under 35 U.S.C. § 102(g) since the two inventors derived their invention from a professor at the University of Illinois).

100. David Landes, the noted historian of technology, has called the business of chemical manufacture "the most miscellaneous of industries." D. Landes, *The Unbound Prometheus* (1969), 269.

101. Most chemical claims cover a single compound only in the sense that Gillette's claim covered a single *type* of razor. That is, chemical claims routinely embrace minor variations on the basic structure the inventor discovered. For example, a patentee might claim a compound of structure "Atom 1 – Atom 2 – Sidegroup," where "Sidegroup" is defined in the claim as including *either* "N-O-O-H" or "N-H2." See Ex parte Markush, 1925 Dec. Comm'r Pats. 126, 340 Off. Gazz. Pat. Off. 839 (Comm'r Pat. 1924); D. Chisum, 2 *Patents* § 8.06[2] (1978, rev. 1988). The "family" of variations must share a common principle to be patented using a so-called Markush claim; as stated in re Schechter, 205 F.2d 185, 189, 98 U.S.P.Q. (BNA) 144 (C.C.P.A. 1953), such a claim will be allowed "where the substances grouped have a community of chemical and physical characteristics which justify their inclusion in a common group, and such inclusion is not repugnant to the principles of scientific classification."

102. See, e.g., Studiengesellschaft Kohle mbH v. Eastman Kodak Co., 616 F.2d 1315, 1341, 206 U.S.P.Q. 577 (5th Cir. 1980):

> [I]n catalytic chemistry, minor changes in components, their ratio, or the external condition of the reaction may produce major changes in the reaction itself. A catalyst which works well at one temperature and pressure, for example, may be totally ineffective at another. Similarly, a small change in the oxidation state of one element of a compound may produce an entirely new catalytic process. Each component of the process – the precise compounds, the ration of their combination, the external condition of the reaction – may be critical.

A practice guide for chemical patent lawyers suggests the same applies to product patents in the polymer field: "Given that [the] basic formula of the polymer is already known, it is still possible to obtain new and patentable polymers by various kinds of modification, provided they give useful and nonobvious results." P. Grubb, *Patents for Chemists* (1982), 155.

103. See C. Taylor and Z. Silberston, *The Economic Impact of the Patent System* (1973), 396. See also E. von Hippel, *The Sources of Innovation* (1988), 53, 66 (describing unusual strength of patents in pharmaceutical and chemical industries relative to other industries).

104. Taylor and Silberston, *id.* at 268.

> The range of [bulk] products has not widened very much over half a century, although naturally their relative importance has greatly changed. Most research efforts are directed towards the reduction of unit costs and improvements in the purity and consistency of standard products. There is relatively little work on new products.

105. See *infra* note 109, C. Freeman at 28–29; Landes, *Unbound Prometheus*, 111.

106. *Id.*

107. J. Jewkes, D. Sawers, and R. Stillerman, *The Sources of Invention* (2d ed. 1969), 50.

108. On the improvement patent of 1873, see *id.* at 50; Solvay Process Co. v. Michigan Alkali Co., 90 F. 818 (6th Cir. 1898). On the American licensee, see D. Noble, *America by Design* (1977), 14.

109. Christopher Freeman has described how the pattern of rather liberal cross-licensing in chemical industries led to the development of a separate industry of chemical plant construction firms:

> Technological progress in established basic industrial chemicals is so rapid and so internationalized that more is generally to be gained for both the firm and the country if each national process innovation is exploited by licensing the contracting industry and selling know-how.

C. Freeman, "Chemical Process Plant: Innovation and the World Market," *Nat'l Inst. Econ. Rev.* 1968 (No. 45): 29, 50.

110. See Standard Oil Co. v. American Cyanamid Co., 774 F.2d 448, 450 227 U.S.P.Q. 293 (Fed. Cir. 1985).

111. *Id.*

112. *Id.*

113. *Id.* at 450 (Standard Oil patent) and 451 (American Cyanamid patent); Dow Chemical Co. v. American Cyanamid Co., 816 F.2d 617, 2 U.S.P.Q.2d (BNA) 1350 (Fed. Cir. 1987).

114. 774 F.2d at 453.

115. 816 F.2d at 617.

116. None of the patents at issue in the various suits appear broad enough to serve the "prospect" function. Under the cases, for example, the Standard Oil process does not appear to infringe Dow's patents. Thus an independent route to the acrylamide-producing process is left open.

117. In the early 1950s, researchers at DuPont and at the Max Planck Institute in Germany began exploring alternative methods of producing polyethylene. Their research into new metal catalysts made it possible to produce a polymer of higher density at lower pressures and temperatures. See Jewkes, Sawers, and Stillerman, *supra* note 107, at 280. Because the original patent contained limitations relating to temperature, pressure, and oxygen concentration, both the new process and the product it yielded were outside the scope of basic patents held by Imperial Chemical Industries of Great Britain. In fact, one historian of the industry suggests that the search for high-density polyethylene may have been motivated in part by a desire to skirt the Imperial patents. J. Allen, *Studies in Innovation in the Steel and Chemical Industries* (1967), 47: "Many of the early would-be Zeigler licensees . . . were, however, probably seeking a route free from the I.C.I. patents, either because they wished to be

free, or could not get the know-how as well as the patents." But these researchers invented more than an improved process for making polyethylene. They discovered catalytic principles that made it possible to cheaply produce another important polymer: polypropylene. See Standard Oil Co. v. Montedison, 494 F.Supp. 370, 374–375 (D.Del 1980). Polypropylene has emerged as a substitute for polyethylene in several key applications. See *Modern Plastics* (February 1988), at 98–100 (discussing strong market for "polyolefin foam," including both polyethylene and polypropylene, in applications relating to packaging); *Textile World* (May 1987), at 12 (describing interchangeability of polyethylene and polypropylene in uses such as specialty papers, films, and disposables, all in the general category of nonwoven polymers).

118. See, e.g., Standard Oil Co. v. American Cyanamid Co., 774 F.2d 498 at 450, 227 U.S.P.Q. 293 (Fed. Cir. 1985) (listing licensees of acrylamide production process patent); *Id*. at 451 ("[Standard Oil] offered Cyanamid a license . . . in 1974, [but] Cyanamid took the position that it did not need a license.").

119. W. Mueller, "The Origins of the Basic Inventions Underlying DuPont's Major Product and Process Inventions," in *The Rate and Direction of Inventive Activity: Economic and Social Factors*, R. Nelson, ed. (1962), 323, 326 (hereinafter Mueller, "Origins of Dupont Inventions").

120. *Id*. at 328.

121. See C. Freeman, *The Economics of Industrial Innovation* (2d ed. 1982), 61. See also S. Hollander, *The Sources of Increased Efficiency: A Study of DuPont Rayon Plants* (1965) (detailed study of major and minor process improvements at various DuPont rayon plants.

122. DuPont researchers first synthesized nylon in the late 1930s. The company obtained a series of broad product patents, culminating with the "Nylon 66" patent covering a commercially valuable form of the fiber. See O'Brien, "Patent Protection and Competition in Polyamide and Polyester Fibre Manufacture," *J. Ind. Econ.* 12 (1964): 224, 229; Taylor and Silberston, *supra* note 103 at 342.

123. W. J. Reader, 2 *Imperial Chemical Industries: A History* (1975), 52–53.

124. See D. Hounshell and J. Smith, *Science and Corporate Strategy: DuPont R&D, 1902–1980* (1988), 384–386.

125. *Id*. at 420–422.

126. See Jewkes, Sawers, and Stillerman, *supra* note 107 at 280.

127. The original patent contained limitations relating to temperature, pressure, and oxygen concentration. In fact, one historian of the industry suggests that the search for high-density polyethylene may have been motivated in part by a desire to skirt the Imperial patents. Allen, *see supra* note 117; at 47. *See supra* note 117; see also Standard Oil Co. v. Montedison, 494 F.Supp. 370, 374–375 206 U.S.P.Q. 676 (D.Del. 1980).

128. Freeman, *supra* note 109 at 67.

129. See Standard Oil Co. v. Montedison, 494 F.Supp. 370, 374, 206 U.S.P.Q. 676 (D.Del. 1980) (patent interference between four firms).

130. The interference just mentioned, for example, was declared in 1958 and resolved by the District Court only in 1980. See also United States Steel Co. v. Phillips Petroleum Co., 856 F.2d 1247, 9 U.S.P.Q. 2d (BNA) 1461 (Fed. Cir. 1989) (upholding Phillips' polypropylene product patent).

131. Recall from our earlier discussion that the polypropylene patent is a good example of the need for a reverse doctrine of equivalents. This is because the enablement doctrine is poorly equipped to deal with the situation where significant improvements are made to an invention by another firm after a patent is filed. Recall that in such a situation, the firm making the improvement will be unable to invalidate the original

inventor's claims for lack of enablement; enablement is measured as of the filing date. See Phillips Petroleum Co. v. United States Steel Corp., 673 F.Supp. 1278, 6 U.S.P.Q.2d 1065, 1068, 1074 (D.Del. 1987), *aff'd sub nom* United States Steel Corp. v. Phillips Petroleum Co., 865 F.2d 1297, 9 U.S.P.Q.2d (BNA) 1461, 1466 n.9 (Fed. Cir. 1989). This is precisely the reason why the reverse doctrine of equivalents is important. *See* notes 74–90, *supra*, and accompanying text.

132. 245 F.2d 693, 113 U.S.P.Q. (BNA) 423 (4th Cir. 1957).

133. *Id*.

134. In re Thuau, 135 F.2d 344, 347, 30 C.C.P.A. 979 (1943).

135. See 271 U.S.C. § 271(c) (1988).

136. See in re Thuau, 135 F.2d at 347.

137. See, e.g., Eli Lilly & Co. v. Generix Drug Sales, Inc., 460 F.2d 1096 174 U.S.P.Q. 65 (5th Cir. 1972) (patent for Darvon upheld despite close similarity to prior art structures).

138. See John Hoxie, "A Patent Attorney's View." in *Seminar on Chemical Invention, J. Pat. Off. Soc'y* 47 (1965): 630, 638 ("This . . . has led to inequitable results in that of two discoveries of equal value and 'inventiveness,' one may be patentable and the other not depending on whether or not the 'gimmick' novelty [i.e., minor structural variation] can be supplied.")

139. Monsanto Co. v. Rohm & Haas Co., 312 F.Supp. 778, 790–791, 164 U.S.P.Q. 556 (E.D.Pa. 1970), *aff'd*, 956 F. 2d. 592, 172 U.S.P.Q. 323, (1972). *Cert, denied* 907 U.S. 934 (1972). See also Comment, "Uses, New Uses and Chemical Patents – A Proposal," *Wis. L. Rev.* 1968: 901, 915 (proposing abolition of product patents on compounds in favor of patents on methods of production and methods of using – two species of process patents).

140. Enforcement may be somewhat more tractable in light of recent legislation making it legal to tie an unpatented product (e.g., the fungicide in *Rohm and Haas*) to the sale of a patented item (e.g., the right to practice the process patent), so long as the patentee does not have market power in the market for the tying (patented) item. See Patent and Trademark Authorization Act, approved Nov. 19, 1988, Pub. L. No. 100–703, § 201, (codified at 35 U.S.C. § 271(d)(4) & (5)). See also R. Merges, "Reflections on Recent Legislation Concerning Patent Misuse," *J. Pat. & Trademark Off. Soc'y* 70 (1988): 793.

141. Hand held that the purified adrenalin, although it existed in the human body, was transformed by the inventor's purification process into a useful drug, and therefore constituted "for every practical purpose a new thing commercially and therapeuti-cally," Parke-Davis & Co. v. H.K. Mulford & Co., 189 F. 95 (C.C.S.D.N.Y. 1911), *aff'd* 196 F. 496 (2d Cir. 1912).

142. Scripps Clinic and Res. Found. v. Genentech, Inc., 666 F.Supp. 1379, 3 U.S.P.Q.2d 1481, 1488 (N.D.Cal. 1987), *patent invalidated in* Scripps Clinic and Res. Found. v. Genentech, Inc., 724 F.Supp. 690, 694 (N.D.Cal. 1989).

143. *Id*. at 694: "Scripps is entitled to claim purified Factor VIII:C having the characteris-tics of human Factor VIII:C, whether derived through its disclosed process or any other process achieving the same result."

144. Scripps Clinic and Res. Found. v. Genentech, Inc., 724 F.Supp. 690, at 694 Cal., Feb. 24, 1989 (Slip Op.), at 4–10, 10 (patentee failed to disclose best mode known to it of carrying out its invention).

145. *See* note 12, *supra*, and accompanying text.

146. *See* M. Kenney, *Biotechnology: The University-Industrial Complex* (1986); M. Ken-ney, "Schumpeterian Innovation and Entrepreneurs in Capitalism: A Case Study in the U.S. Biotechnology Industry," *Res. Pol'y* 15 (1986): 21. Cf. Koenig, "A Biblio-

metric Analysis of Pharmaceutical Research," *Res. Pol'y* 12 (1983): 15 (reviewing data on the number of industrial patents that cite basic scientific research articles in various pharmaceutical industry sectors, including biotechnology–derived pharmaceuticals).

147. AT least in its earliest stages. See R. Nelson, "The Link Between Science and Invention: The Case of the Transistor," in *Rate and Direction of Inventive Activity*, 549; Shockley, "The Path to the Conception of the Junction Transistor," *IEEE Trans. on Electron Devices* 23 (1976): 597.

148. This discussion is taken from a longer account of the case in R. Merges, "Commercial Success and Patent Standards: Economic Perspectives on Innovation," *Cal. L. Rev.* 76 (1988): 803.

149. Hybritech, Inc. v. Monoclonal Antibodies, Inc., 623 F.Supp. 1344, 227 U.S.P.Q. (BNA) 215, 221 (N.D.Cal. 1985), *rev'd* 802 F.2d 1367, 231 U.S.P.Q. (BNA) 81 (Fed. Cir. 1986).

150. See, e.g., note 166 *infra*.

151. George B. Rathman, Chairman and Chief Executive Officer of Amgen, Inc., quoted in M. Chase, "Genentech Receives Broad Patent for Basic Gene-Splicing Techniques," *Wall St. J.* (Nov. 4, 1987), 8, cols. 1–2. There are some indications that Genentech is pursuing a strategy of construing the patent claims broadly, but charging a fairly low royalty so as not to create an incentive to challenge the patent. See "G-tech to Push for Royalties," *BioEngineering News* (Nov. 12, 1987), 1, cols. 1–2 ("Genentech . . . apparently intends to lay claim to royalties on all polypeptide expressed in microorganisms").

152. In re O'Farrell, 853 F.2d 894, 7 U.S.P.Q.2d (BNA) 1673 (Fed. Cir. 1988).

153. *Id.* at 1677–1678. The frog protein was not truly nonoperational; it formed part of the structure of ribosomes, the cell components where proteins are made. This relatively rare type of ribosomal protein is to be contrasted with the much more common proteins coded for in a cell's DNA—everything from hormones to collagen to antibodies. *See Id.* at 1676.

154. *Id.* at 1674.

155. F. M. Scherer, in his study of the Watt-Boulton enterprise, concluded that "Watt & Boulton's refusal to issue licenses allowing other engine makers to employ the separate–condenser principle clearly retarded the development and introduction of improvements." F. M. Scherer, "Invention and Innovation in the Watt-Boulton Steam Engine Venture," in *Innovation and Growth: Schumpeterian Perspectives* (1984), 25.

156. See notes 142–144, *supra*. See also Mellor, "Patents and Genetic Engineering—Is It a New Problem?," *Eur. Intellectual Prop. L. Rev.* 1988: 135 (describing British TPA litigation raising the same set of issues).

157. 189 F. 95 (C.C.S.D.N.Y. 1911), *aff'd* 196 F. 496 (2d Cir. 1912) (patent on purified form of adrenalin).

10

Conclusion

THOMAS M. JORDE
AND DAVID J. TEECE

The authors in this volume have demonstrated concern about technological innovation and competitiveness. Unfortunately, the linkage between these issues and antitrust is not well recognized by most antitrust scholars and courts. The reason for this, we contend, is not because scholars and courts consider such issues to be unimportant. Rather, it is because, as Oliver Williamson suggests (Chapter 7), the lens that is used to explore complex business practices—applied price theory—is highly limited. Baumol and Ordover suggest that contestability theory has a larger role to play in antitrust analysis; Williamson indicates how transaction cost approaches can complement the standard applied price theory. Jorde and Teece suggest that all approaches need to recognize the role of innovation in stimulating competition, and how the analytics could be different if innovation was incorporated into antitrust economics. A neo-Schumpeterian view of competition, which recognizes that competition is driven by innovation and takes place largely outside the price-output domain of standard microeconomics, would lead to concerns about certain mainstream views. Because all of this has not been fully worked through—the main efforts here being concentrated on the issues of market definition and on interfirm agreements in the context of innovation—one cannot accurately calibrate the social cost of an antitrust regime that proceeds with a highly stylized, static, and inaccurate view of the nature of competition.

The editors wish they could share the comfortable views of those who maintain that the current system is about right. We believe that the analytic lenses still commonly employed today in antitrust analysis were more suitable in a world where competition was less global, where innovation was less a multinational phenomenon, where time to market was less critical, and where the successes of the pioneers and the followers were clearly separated. Changes in the global economy mean that some of "modern" antitrust is anachronistic, at least in a setting of rapid technological change.

These concerns magnify the procedural issues addressed by Easterbrook. Generating more sophisticated rules of reason does not make life easier for judges, and especially for juries. However, "safe harbors," which provide de facto exemptions in instances where substantial market power does not exist, provide clear benefits and may be a good first step. Indeed, none of the authors in the book appear to have concerns about business practices where market power is not present, and we know of no evidence suggesting that competition is harmed by the cooperative activities of firms having small to moderate combined market shares.

Antitrust policy in the 1990s, it seems to us, will be shaped more by concerns about innovation and competitiveness than in any other period in recent history. In this new environment, the Chicago approach (applied price theory) may be up against its natural limits. Pre-Chicago traditions are already substantially weakened. An emerging set of theories and evidence about the nature of competition, technological change, and the nature of the business enterprise will eventually need to be recognized and developed further. We hope this book is viewed as part of that needed effort and will spur others to enter the dialogue. With careful scholarship and a little luck, antitrust policy and future generations of Americans will be among the beneficiaries.

Index